Computer Accounting with QuickBooks® 2002

Fourth Edition

Donna Ulmer, MBA, Ph.D.
St. Louis Community College

**QuickBooks 2002, QuickBooks Pro 2002, QuickBooks Premier 2002
QuickBooks Premier 2002: Accountant Edition**

Boston   Burr Ridge, IL   Dubuque, IA   Madison, WI   New York   San Francisco   St. Louis
Bangkok   Bogotá   Caracas   Kuala Lumpur   Lisbon   London   Madrid   Mexico City
Milan   Montreal   New Delhi   Santiago   Seoul   Singapore   Sydney   Taipei   Toronto

Publisher: *Brent Gordon*
Sponsoring editor*: Melody Marcus*
Developmental editor: *Jackie Scruggs*
Marketing manager: *Richard Kolasa*
Production supervisor: *Gina Hangos*
Supplement producer: *Susan Lombardi*
Cover Image: ©*Digital Vision*

McGraw-Hill Higher Education

*A Division of The **McGraw-Hill** Companies*

COMPUTER ACCOUNTING WITH QUICKBOOKS® 2002
QuickBooks 2002, QuickBooks Pro 2002, QuickBooks Premier 2002,
QuickBooks Premier 2002: Accountant Edition
Donna Ulmer

1 2 3 4 5 6 7 8 9 0 QPD/QPD 0 9 8 7 6 5 4 3 2

ISBN 0-07-253020-0

About the Author

Donna Ulmer is a member of the accounting faculty at St. Louis Community College. She has provided computer software training to college students, faculty, businesses, and non-profit organizations.

Listed in Who's Who Among America's Teachers, she is the recipient of the first St. Louis Community College Faculty Service Learning Award for her use of service learning with computer accounting applications. She earned her B.S. from Southern Illinois University at Edwardsville where she also earned an MBA with an emphasis in accounting and information systems. She obtained her Ph.D. from Saint Louis University where she conducted doctoral research on the effectiveness of instructional techniques for the computer classroom.

Donna is a member of the American Institute of Certified Public Accountants, Missouri Society of CPAs, Missouri Association of Accounting Educators, and Teachers of Accounting at Two-Year Colleges. She has served on the American Accounting Association's Committee to Promote Interaction Between Two-Year College Faculty and Faculty at Other Institutions, AAA Benchmarking Listserv, and the AAA Committee to Develop a Faculty Competency Model for College Accounting Professors.

Preface

Welcome!

Computer Accounting with QuickBooks® 2002 *makes learning QuickBooks software easy. What distinguishes this book is quite simple: while software training materials usually focus on the software, this text focuses on the learner—incorporating sound pedagogy and instructional techniques that make learning software as effortless as possible.*

Using a hands-on approach, the text integrates understanding accounting with mastery of the software. Each chapter builds on the previous chapter as you progress from entering simple transactions to using the QuickBooks advanced features. The text provides both the "big picture" overview ("Where am I going?") and step-by-step instructions ("Where do I click?").

Designed for flexibility in meeting the learner's needs, the text can be used either in a QuickBooks course or by an individual who wants to learn QuickBooks at his or her own pace. The text can be used to learn QuickBooks® 2002, QuickBooks Pro® 2002, QuickBooks Premier® 2002, or QuickBooks Premier® 2002: Accountant Editon. Features available with only QuickBooks Pro 2002 software (such as time tracking, estimates, and progress billing) or QuickBooks Premier 2002 (such as remote access) are noted in the text.

The text begins with a vignette describing the realistic travails of a software user. Subsequent chapters continue the case that runs throughout the text. The case approach requires the learner to apply both software skills and problem-solving skills. End-of-chapter activities and virtual company projects offer additional practice using the software.

*Internet assignments in each chapter provide web sites with useful information for small business accounting. (**Note:** The web sites are subject to change due to web page updates.)*

FYI: Visit the QuickBooks web site (www.quickbooks.com**) to obtain a free trial version of QuickBooks Pro 2002 software while available.**

Have fun learning QuickBooks!

Text Overview

A virtual company case runs throughout the text, enabling students to better understand how various transactions and activities are interrelated.

Part I of the text, Exploring QuickBooks with Rock Castle Construction, focuses on learning the basics of entering transactions and generating reports. Part II, Small Business Accounting with QuickBooks 2002, covers the entire accounting cycle including setting up a new company as well as using advanced features of QuickBooks software.

Part I includes:

- *Chapter 1: Guided Tour of QuickBooks 2002. This chapter provides a guided tour of the software using QuickBooks Navigators and the QuickBooks sample company, Rock Castle Construction. Other topics include how to backup and restore company data.*

- *Chapter 2: Chart of Accounts. This chapter introduces the chart of accounts and how to customize the chart of accounts to suit specific business needs. Other topics include creating passwords and using the Reminders List.*

- *Chapter 3: Banking. This chapter focuses on the checking account and check register for a small business. Topics include making deposits, writing checks, and reconciling a bank statement.*

- *Chapter 4: Customers and Sales. Chapter 4 demonstrates how to record customer transactions. Topics include how to create invoices, record sales, record customer payments, and print customer reports.*

- *Chapter 5: Vendors, Purchases, and Inventory. This chapter focuses on recording vendor transactions, including creating purchase orders, paying bills, and printing vendor reports.*

- *Chapter 6: Employees and Payroll. Chapter 6 covers how to use the time tracking feature, how to transfer tracked time to* customer invoices, and how to process payroll using QuickBooks.

- ◆ ***Chapter 7: Reports and Graphs.*** *In this chapter, you will complete the accounting cycle by creating a trial balance and entering adjusting entries. In addition, you will learn how to create a number of different reports and graphs using QuickBooks, including how to export reports to Microsoft® Excel® software.*

After mastering the basics in Part I, you will learn how to set up a new company in Part II. Fearless Painting Service, a case that runs throughout the second part, starts out as a sole proprietorship service business, then expands to become a merchandising corporation. Using a building block approach, the text gradually introduces advanced features while maintaining continuity and interest. Part II includes:

- ◆ ***Chapter 8: Creating a Service Company in QuickBooks.*** *Chapter 8 covers how to use the EasyStep Interview feature to set up a new company in QuickBooks. You also learn how to create customer, vendor, and item lists.*

- ◆ ***Chapter 9: Accounting for a Service Company.*** *Chapter 9 records transactions for an entire year using the company created in Chapter 8. Project 9.1 and Project 9.2 provide an opportunity to integrate all the QuickBooks skills covered. Project 9.2 can be used by individual students or by student teams.*

- ◆ ***Chapter 10: Merchandising Corporation: Sales, Purchases, and Inventory.*** *After learning how to set up a merchandising corporation with inventory, you record transactions for the first month of operations. Project 10.1 and Project 10.2 are comprehensive cases. Again, Project 10.2 can be used by individual students or by student teams.*

- ◆ ***Chapter 11: Merchandising Corporation: Payroll.*** *Chapter 11 covers how to set up payroll for a company and how to record payroll and create paychecks using QuickBooks. Project 11.1 and Project 11.2 are continuations of Project 10.1 and Project 10.2.*

+ *Chapter 12: Advanced Topics. This chapter covers the advanced features of QuickBooks software including budgets, estimates, progress billing, credit card sales, accounting for bad debts, memorized reports, and the audit trail. Using the advanced features of QuickBooks, Project 12.1 and Project 12.2 are continuations of Project 9.1 and Project 9.2.*

Pedagogy: The Art and Science of Teaching

This text is based on sound pedagogy for learning software effectively. The pedagogy's strengths include:

+ *Constructivist Instructional Approach*

+ *Virtual Company Cases*

+ *Real World QuickBooks Project*

+ *Page Referenced Learning Objectives*

+ *Unique Annotated Screen Captures*

+ *Instructor's Resource Manual, including Instructional Techniques for the Computerized Classroom*

Constructivist Instructional Design

Constructivist instructional methodology is increasingly recognized as an effective approach to computer software training. Based on theories of educator John Dewey, the constructivist approach is student-directed using realistic, practical applications to aid learners in constructing a deeper understanding with improved retention.[1]

Utilizing a constructivist instructional design, the training materials presented here use a two-step approach:

+ *Each chapter is a hands-on guided instructional tutorial that familiarizes the student with software tasks. The guided instruction portion of the chapter may be used by students individually or the instructor can demonstrate the tasks with students completing the tasks at individual workstations. Realistic company cases are used in the guided instruction sessions.*

---

[1] R.Cwiklik, "Dewey Wins!: If the "New" Teaching Methods Pushed by High-Tech Gurus Sound Familiar, It Isn't Surprising," *The Wall Street Journal*, (November 17, 1997), R19.

◆ *End-of-chapter assignments provide practical applications to gain mastery. The assignments use a problem-solving case approach and consist of both activities and projects. Each activity contains multiple tasks that ask students to apply what they learned in the guided instruction session. Comprehensive projects review and integrate the various topics.*

Virtual Company Cases

Each section of the text uses a virtual company case that runs throughout the section. Part I focuses on Rock Castle Construction, while Part II sets up Fearless Painting Service that grows from a sole proprietorship service company into a merchandising corporation. The use of Rock Castle and Fearless Paint provide a real world context to enhance understanding of how various tasks are related.

Real World QuickBooks Project

The Real World QuickBooks Project (Appendix A) guides you through the development of a real world QuickBooks application. Integrating and applying the skills learned in the course, real applications provide learners with the most effective software training.

The Real World QuickBooks Project can be used in several different ways. The project can be assigned as a capstone project for the course. The project can also be used as a service learning project where students learn while providing community service using their computer accounting skills. Finally, the small business user who is creating a QuickBooks accounting system can use the Real World QuickBooks Project as a development tool.

Page-Referenced Learning Objectives

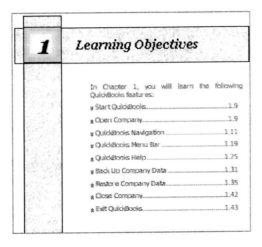

Learning objectives at the beginning of each chapter are page-referenced. The page references allow the instructor and students to easily focus on areas of interest. In addition, the page-referenced learning objectives are an efficient way for students to locate information needed to complete end-of chapter activities and projects.

Annotated Screen Capture System

Screen captures are an essential tool for helping learners bridge the gap between printed page and computer screen. The text provides concise, easy-to-follow instructions. The Annotated Screen Capture System uses arrows to connect the text instructions with the related screen capture.

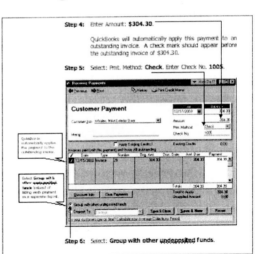

Instructor's Resource Manual

The Instructor's Resource Manual is a valuable resource for faculty. In addition to providing complete solutions for all assignment material in the text, the Instructor's Resource Manual offers successful teaching strategies for computer accounting with QuickBooks, including instructional techniques for the computerized classroom.

Acknowledgments

I would like to express my appreciation to the McGraw-Hill/Irwin team who made this text possible: Melody Marcus for her vision and guidance, Jackie Scruggs for her follow-through, Melissa Larmon for her marketing ideas, and Sue Lombardi for her thoroughness. A special thanks to Beth Woods for her careful accuracy checking and to Angie for her enthusiasm and sense of humor. My sincere gratitude to Audrey, Alex, Claire, Diane, and Michael for their support and encouragement and to my students, who continue to teach me how to be a better educator.

Floppy Disks Required to Complete Assignments

You will need formatted blank floppy disks to complete the text's 12 chapters and 8 projects. Label one disk for each chapter (Chapters 1-12). Label the project disks as follows:

- *Project 9.1 & 12.1*
- *Project 9.2 & 12.2*
- *Project 10.1 & 11.1*
- *Project 10.2 & 11.2*

> **Note:** For information about using QuickBooks with a network, see QuickBooks Help. Also, see Appendix D for information about using QuickBooks in Multi-User Mode.

Installing QuickBooks 2002 Software:

> **Note:** If you are using a networked computer classroom, install the QuickBooks software to the local hard drives (C:).

To install QuickBooks software:

1. *Insert the QuickBooks CD-ROM in the computer's CD-ROM drive.*

2. *If the installation program starts automatically, a CD Install window appears. Click **Install QuickBooks**, then follow the onscreen instructions.*

3. *If the installation program does not start automatically, complete the following steps to install QuickBooks:*
   - *Click **Start** on the Windows® taskbar.*
   - *Select **Settings**.*
   - *Select **Control Panel**.*
   - *Double-click **Add/Remove Programs**.*
   - *Click **Install**.*
   - *Follow the onscreen instructions to install QuickBooks software.*

Contents

Part I: Exploring QuickBooks with Rock Castle Construction

Part II:
Small Business Accounting with QuickBooks 2002

Part

I

Exploring QuickBooks
with
Rock Castle Construction

Chapter 1:
Quick Tour of
QuickBooks 2002

Chapter 2:
Chart of Accounts

Chapter 3:
Banking

Chapter 4:
Customers and Sales

Chapter 5:
Vendors, Purchases,
and Inventory

Chapter 6:
Employees and Payroll

Chapter 7:
Reports and Graphs

Quick Tour
of
QuickBooks 2002

Scenario

Mr. Rock Castle, owner of Rock Castle Construction, called to hire you as his accountant. His former accountant unexpectedly accepted a job offer in Hawaii and Rock Castle needs someone immediately to maintain its accounting records. Mr. Castle indicates that they use QuickBooks to maintain the company's accounting records. When you tell him that you are not familiar with QuickBooks software, Mr. Castle reassures you, *"No problem! QuickBooks is easy to learn. Stop by my office this afternoon."*

When you arrive at Rock Castle Construction, Mr. Castle leads you to a cubicle as he rapidly explains Rock Castle's accounting.

"Rock Castle needs to keep records of transactions with customers, vendors, and employees. We must keep a record of our customers and the sales and services we provide to those customers. Also, it is crucial for the company to be able to bill customers promptly and keep a record of cash collected from them. If we don't know who owes Rock Castle money, we can't collect it.

"Rock Castle also needs to keep track of the supplies, materials, and inventory we purchase from vendors. We need to track all purchase orders, the items received, the invoices or bills received from vendors, and the payments made to vendors. If we don't track bills, we can't pay our vendors on time. And if Rock Castle doesn't pay its bills on time, the vendors don't like to sell to us.

"Also, we like to keep our employees happy. One way to do that is to pay them the right amount at the right time. So Rock Castle must keep track of the time worked by its employees, the amounts owed to the employees, and the wages and salaries paid to them.

"QuickBooks permits Rock Castle to keep a record of all of these transactions. Also, we need records so we can prepare tax returns, financial reports for bank loans, and reports to evaluate the company's performance and make business decisions.

"Your first assignment is to learn more about QuickBooks." Mr. Castle tosses you a QuickBooks training manual as he rushes off to answer a phone call.

Slightly overwhelmed by Mr. Castle's rapid-fire delivery, you sink into a chair. As you look around your cubicle, you notice for the first time the leaning tower of papers stacked beside the computer, waiting to be processed. No wonder Mr. Castle wanted you to start right way. Opening the QuickBooks training manual, you find the following.

1 *Learning Objectives*

In Chapter 1, you will learn the following QuickBooks features:

Accounting Information Systems

Accounting is the language of business. Learning accounting is similar to learning a foreign language. As you use this text, you will learn terms and definitions that are unique to accounting.

QuickBooks is accounting software that provides an easy and efficient way to collect and summarize accounting information. In addition, QuickBooks creates many different reports that are useful when managing a business.

The objective of an accounting system is to collect, summarize, and communicate information to decision makers. Accounting information is used to:

♦ Prepare tax returns to send to the IRS and state tax agencies.

♦ Prepare financial statements for banks and investors.

♦ Prepare reports for managers and owners to use when making decisions about the business. Such decisions include: Are our customers paying their bills on time? Which of our products are the most profitable? Will we have enough cash to pay our bills next month?

Transactions

An accounting system collects information about *transactions*. As a company conducts business, it enters into transactions (or exchanges) with other parties such as customers, vendors, and employees. For example, when a business sells a product to a customer, there are two parts to the transaction:

1. The business *gives* a product or service to the customer.
2. In exchange, the business *receives* cash (or a promise to pay later) from the customer.

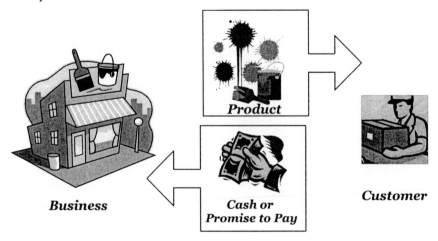

Business   *Product*

Cash or Promise to Pay   **Customer**

Double-entry accounting

Double-entry accounting is used to record the two parts to a transaction: (1) the amount received is a debit, and (2) the amount given is a credit. Each entry must balance; debits must equal credits.

Double-entry accounting has been used for more than 500 years. In Italy in the year 1494, Luca Pacioli, a Franciscan monk, and Leonardo da Vinci collaborated on a mathematics book that described double-entry accounting. The double-entry system was used by the merchants of Venice to record what was given and received when trading.

In a manual accounting system, accountants make debit and credit entries in a journal using paper and pencil. When using QuickBooks for your accounting system, you can enter accounting information in two different ways: (1) onscreen journal, and (2) onscreen forms.

1. Onscreen Journal. You can make debit and credit entries in an onscreen journal shown below. Instead of using the onscreen journal, you can use onscreen forms to enter information in QuickBooks.

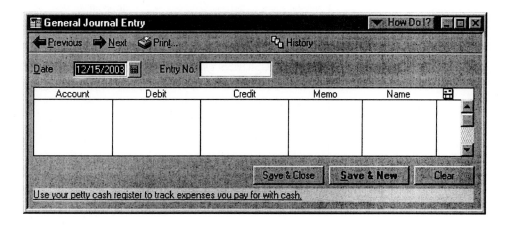

2. Onscreen forms. You can enter information about transactions using *onscreen forms* such as those shown below.

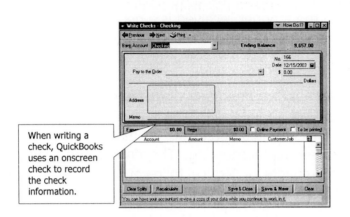

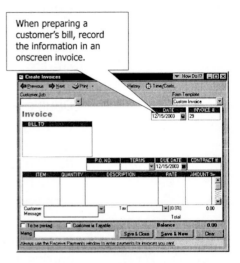

When preparing a customer's bill, record the information in an onscreen invoice.

When writing a check, QuickBooks uses an onscreen check to record the check information.

QuickBooks automatically converts information entered in onscreen forms into double-entry accounting entries with debits and credits. QuickBooks maintains a list of journal entries for all the transactions entered—whether entered using the onscreen journal or onscreen forms.

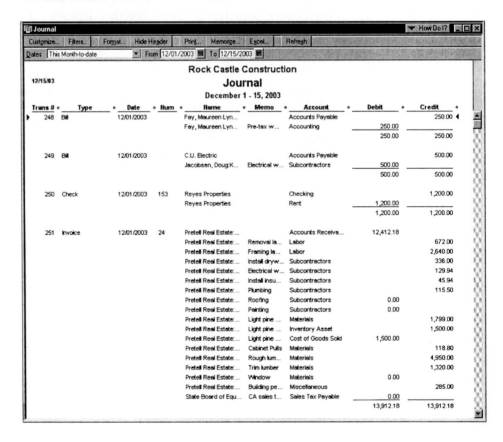

Creating an Accounting System in QuickBooks

Steps to create an accounting system using QuickBooks are:

Step 1: **Set up a new company data file.** QuickBooks uses an EasyStep Interview that asks you questions about your business. QuickBooks then automatically creates a company data file for your business. In Part I of this text, Exploring QuickBooks, you will use a sample company data file that has already been created for you. In Part II, you will set up a new company using the EasyStep Interview.

Step 2: **Create a Chart of Accounts.** A chart of accounts is a list of all the accounts for a company. Accounts are used to sort and track accounting information. For example, a business needs one account for Cash, another account to track amounts customers owe (Accounts Receivable), and yet another account to track inventory. QuickBooks automatically creates a chart of accounts in the EasyStep Interview. QuickBooks permits you to modify the chart of accounts later, after completing the EasyStep Interview.

Step 3: **Create Lists.** QuickBooks uses lists to record and organize information about:

- **Customers**
- **Vendors**
- **Items** (items sold and items purchased, such as inventory)
- **Employees**
- **Other** (such as owners)

Step 4: **Enter transactions.** Enter information about transactions into QuickBooks using the onscreen journal or onscreen forms (such as onscreen invoices and onscreen checks).

Input Information → **QuickBooks** *Onscreen forms* *Onscreen journal* → **Output—Reports**

Step 5: **Prepare reports.** Reports summarize and communicate information about a company's financial position and business operations. Financial statements are standardized financial reports given to external users (bankers and investors). Financial statements summarize information about past transactions. The primary financial statements for a business are:

♦ **Balance sheet**: summarizes what a company owns and owes on a particular date.

♦ **Profit and loss statement** (or **income statement**): summarizes what a company has earned and the expenses incurred to earn the income.

♦ **Statement of cash flows**: summarizes cash inflows and cash outflows for operating, investing, and financing activities of a business.

Other financial reports are created for internal users (managers) to assist in making decisions. An example of such a report is a cash budget that projects amounts of cash that will be collected and spent in the future.

In Part I: Exploring QuickBooks, you will learn about Step 2: creating a chart of accounts; Step 3: creating lists; Step 4: entering transactions; and Step 5: preparing reports. In Part II: Small Business Accounting, you will learn how to set up a new company in QuickBooks as well as review Steps 2 through 5.

Start QuickBooks

To start QuickBooks software, click the **QuickBooks** icon on your desktop. If a QuickBooks icon does not appear on your desktop, in Microsoft® Windows®, click the **Start** button, **Programs**, **QuickBooks Premier** (or QuickBooks Pro), **QuickBooks Premier** (or QuickBooks Pro).

Open Company

Another way to open a company file is:
1. Select **File** (menu).
2. Select **Open Company.**

After starting QuickBooks software, the next step is to open a company data file. To open the sample company data file, Rock Castle Construction, complete the following steps:

Step 1: Select **Open a sample file**.

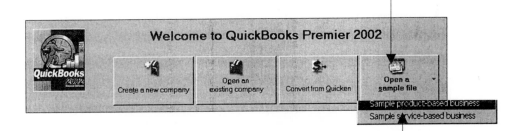

Step 2: Select **Sample_product-based business**.

Step 3: The following message will appear about the sample company. Click **OK** to close the window.

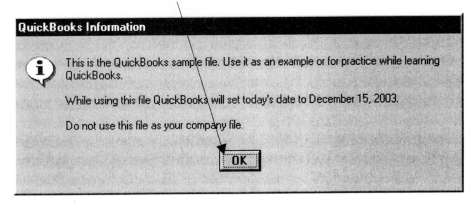

QuickBooks Navigation

QuickBooks offers four different ways to navigate QuickBooks 2002 software:

*   Navigators

*   Icon Bar

*   Shortcut List

*   Menu Bar

Icon Bar: Click on icons to display frequently used windows, such as customer invoices.

Menus: Click on the menu to reveal a drop-down menu for each area.

Navigators: Click on Navigator to display flowcharts of customer, vendor, and employee transactions.

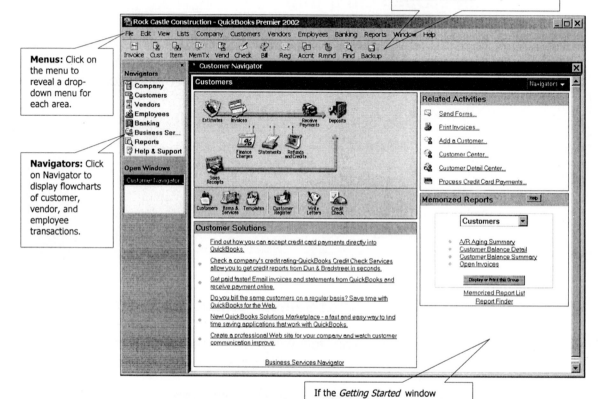

If the *Getting Started* window appears on your screen, click ⊠ in the upper right corner of that window to close it.

QuickBooks Navigators

There is a Navigator for each of the four main categories of transactions:
1. Customer or sales transactions
2. Vendor or purchase transactions
3. Employee or payroll transactions
4. Banking transactions

Step 1: To open the Customers Navigator, click **Customers** in the *Navigators* window.

Click the Navigators button to view a different Navigator.

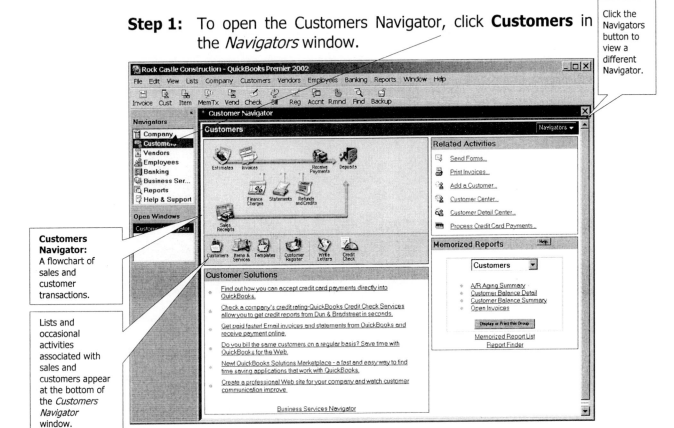

Customers Navigator: A flowchart of sales and customer transactions.

Lists and occasional activities associated with sales and customers appear at the bottom of the *Customers Navigator* window.

The Customers Navigator is a flowchart of the main activities associated with sales and customers. From the Customers Navigator, you can:

◆ Create estimates.

◆ Create invoices to bill customers.

◆ Calculate finance charges on unpaid customer bills.

◆ Create billing statements.

◆ Record refunds and credits for merchandise returned by customers.

◆ Record payments received from customers (cash, check, and credit card payments).

◆ Record bank deposits.

The Customers List and the Items List appear in the lower section of the *Customers Navigator* window.

Step 2: Click **Vendors** in the *Navigators* window to open the Vendors Navigator.

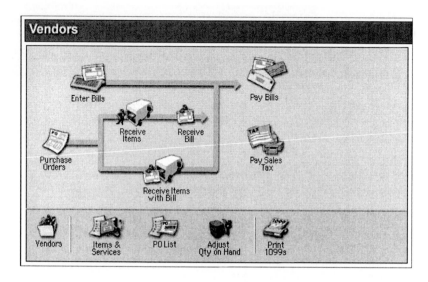

From the *Vendors Navigator* window, you can record:

- ◆ Purchase orders (orders placed to purchase items).
- ◆ Items received (such as inventory).
- ◆ Bills received.
- ◆ Bills paid.
- ◆ Sales tax paid.

At the bottom of the *Vendors Navigator* window, you can access the Vendors List and the Items List.

Step 3: Click **Employees** in the *Navigators* window to open the following Employees Navigator.

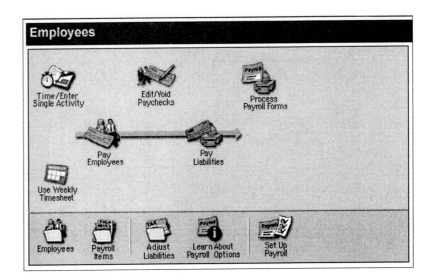

From the *Employees Navigator* window, you can:

- ◆ Track time worked.

- ◆ Pay employees.

- ◆ Pay payroll tax liabilities.

- ◆ Process payroll forms.

- ◆ Process W-2s. (Tax forms sent to employees each year reporting total wages and withholdings.)

The Employees List is accessed from the bottom of the *Employees Navigator* window.

Step 4: Click **Banking** in the *Navigators* window to view the Banking Navigator shown below.

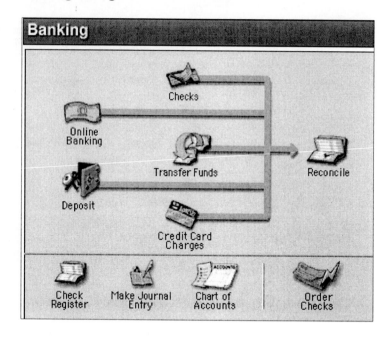

From the Banking Navigator, you can:

+ Record deposits.

+ Write checks.

+ Transfer funds from one checking account to another.

+ Record credit card transactions.

+ Conduct online banking.

+ Reconcile your bank statement.

You can also access your Check Register, make journal entries and access the chart of accounts from the Banking Navigator.

Step 5: Click **Company** in the *Navigators* window to view the Company Navigator shown below.

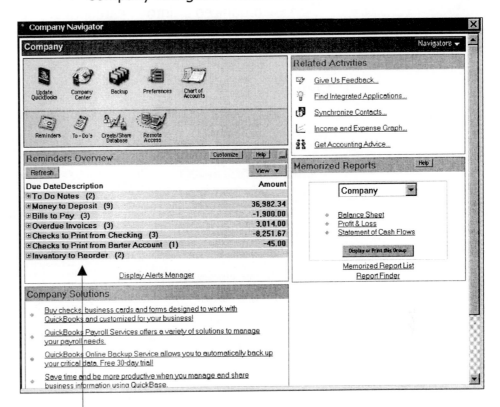

From the Company Navigator, you can access:

◆ **Chart of Accounts**: a list of accounts a company uses to track accounting information.

◆ **To Do List**: a list of tasks to do.

◆ **Reminders**: a reminder list appears on screen to remind you to perform tasks, such as pay bills. Tasks on the To Do List are automatically transferred to the Reminders List when the task is scheduled to be performed.

◆ **Company Center**: a center that summarizes important information about a company and its operations.

◆ **Remote Access**: access QuickBooks company files from a remote location using the Internet.

Step 6: Click **Business Services** in the *Navigators* window. The Business Services offered through QuickBooks are organized into categories: Leverage Technology Solutions, Use Financial Management Tools, Manage Your Employees, and Streamline Administrative Tasks.

Step 7: Click **Reports** in the *Navigators* window to view the Report Finder.

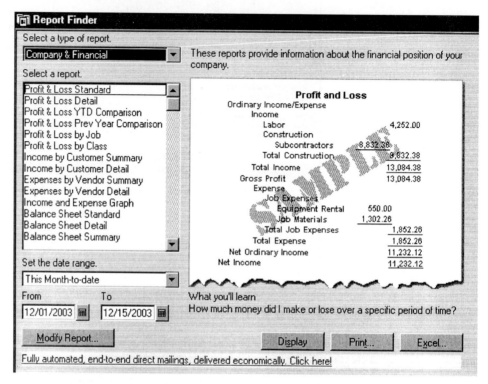

To prepare a report:

◆ Select the desired report.

◆ Select the date range.

◆ Select Display to view the report onscreen.

◆ Select Print to print out the report.

◆ Select Excel to export the report to Microsoft Excel.

To close the *Report Finder* window, click the ⊠ in the upper right corner of the window.

Step 8: Click the **Help and Support** Navigator. The *Help and Support* window provides information about the following QuickBooks features:

- QuickBooks Help

- QuickBooks Support

- Business Resources

- Product Updates

To close the *Help and Support* window, click the ⊠ in the upper right corner of the window.

QuickBooks Iconbar

The QuickBooks Iconbar is a toolbar that appears beneath the Menu Bar and contains buttons for frequently used activities. The Iconbar can be used in addition to the Menu Bar and Navigators.

To display the iconbar if it does not appear on your screen:

Step 1: Click **View** on the Menu Bar.

Step 2: Select **Icon Bar**.

The Iconbar can be customized to display the tasks that you use most frequently. To customize the Iconbar:

Step 1: Click **View** on the Menu Bar.

Step 2: Select **Customize Icon Bar**.

Step 3: Select the tasks and order in which you would like them to appear on the Icon Bar, then click the **Close** button.

QuickBooks Shortcut List

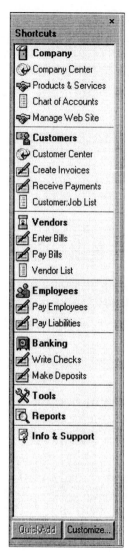

If you were a QuickBooks 2000 user, the Navigation Bar in QuickBooks 2000 is now called the Shortcut List in QuickBooks 2001 and QuickBooks 2002. To access the Shortcut List in the newer versions:

Step 1: Click **View** (Menu Bar).

Step 2: Select **Shortcut List**.

The Shortcut List (called the Navigation Bar in QuickBooks 2000) appears on the left side of the screen. Notice that from the Shortcut List, you can access all of the Navigators and in addition can directly access frequently used tasks, such as Create Invoices and Write Checks.

To hide the Shortcut List, click **View** (menu), then click **Shortcut List** to remove the checkmark and deselect the Shortcut List.

QuickBooks Menus

In addition to using Navigators, you can also use the Menu Bar across the top of the QuickBooks window to access tasks.

Step 1: Click **File** on the menu bar and the following drop-down menu will appear.

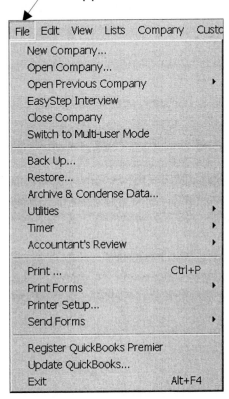

From the File drop-down menu, you can perform tasks including the following:

◆ Create a new company file.

◆ Open an existing company file.

◆ Set up a new company using EasyStep Interview.

◆ Close a company file.

◆ Switch to Multi-user mode when QuickBooks is used on a network.

◆ Back up your company file.

◆ Restore a company backup file.

Print tasks include:

- Print Forms which permits you to print forms such as invoices, sales receipts, and tax forms.

- Printer Setup which permits you to select a printer as well as fonts and margins.

- Send Forms which permits you to e-mail or fax various QuickBooks forms, such as sending invoices to customers.

To remove the File drop-down menu from the screen, click anywhere outside the drop-down menu or press the **Esc** (Escape) key.

Step 2: Click **Edit** on the menu bar and the following drop-down menu appears:

Tip: See **Appendix B: Correcting Errors** for more information about correcting mistakes.

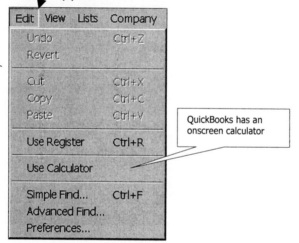

QuickBooks has an onscreen calculator

From the Edit drop-down menu, you can undo, cut, copy, paste, and edit information entered in QuickBooks.

The Edit menu changes based upon which windows are open. For example:

- Click **Vendors** to display the Vendor Navigator, then click the **Purchase Orders** icon on the Vendor Navigator to display the Purchase Order form.

◆ Click **Edit** (menu). Now the Edit menu will appear as follows:

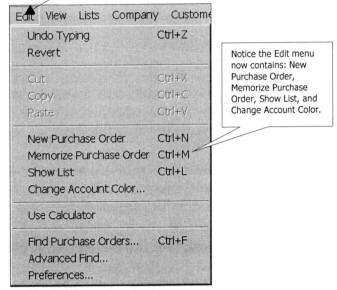

Notice the Edit menu now contains: New Purchase Order, Memorize Purchase Order, Show List, and Change Account Color.

Step 3: Click **Lists** on the menu bar to display the following drop-down menu.

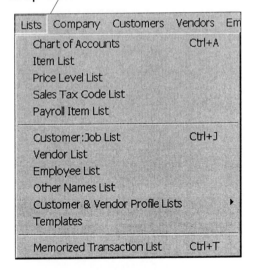

From the List drop-down menu, you can access various lists of information.

◆ **Chart of Accounts**: a list of accounts used to record transactions.

◆ **Item List**: a list of inventory items that you buy and sell or a list of services provided to customers.

◆ **Payroll Item List**: a list of items related to payroll checks and company payroll expense such as salary, hourly wages, federal and state withholding, unemployment taxes, Medicare, and Social Security.

* **Customer: Job List**: a list that identifies each customer and customer job.

* **Vendor List**: a list of vendors or suppliers from whom your company purchases.

* **Employee List**: a list of employee names, social security numbers, addresses, and phone numbers.

* **Templates**: a list of templates for business forms, such as invoices and purchase orders.

* **Memorized Transaction List**: a list of recurring transactions that are memorized or saved. For example, if your company pays $900 in rent each month, then the rent payment transaction can be memorized to eliminate the need to reenter it each month.

Step 4: Click **Company** on the menu bar to display the drop-down menu.

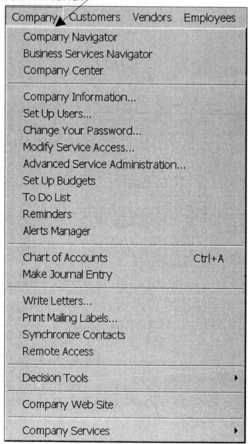

From this menu, you can:

- Set up users and restrict access to certain parts of QuickBooks.
- Change your password.
- Set up budgets.
- Create To Do and Reminder Lists.
- Access the Chart of Accounts and onscreen journal.

Step 5: The next four items on the menu bar display drop-down menus listing various activities related to the four major types of transactions for a company:

- Customer
- Vendor
- Employee
- Banking

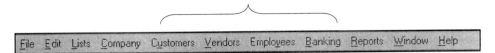

File Edit Lists Company Customers Vendors Employees Banking Reports Window Help

The activities on these drop-down menus can also be accessed from the Navigators.

Step 6: Click **Reports** on the menu bar to display the list of reports that QuickBooks can create for your company. These reports can also be accessed from the Report Finder in the *Navigators* window.

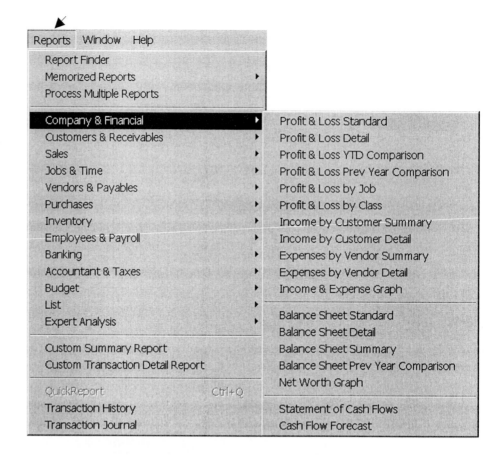

QuickBooks Help

QuickBooks has several Help features to assist you when using QuickBooks software. Click **Help** on the menu bar to display the drop-down menu of Help features.

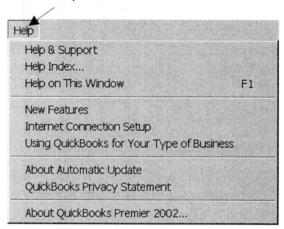

The Help features that QuickBooks provides include:

- **Help & Support** (Help & Support Navigator)
- **Help Index** (Help Menu)
- **Help on This Window** (Help Menu)
- **Using QuickBooks for your Type of Business** (Help Menu)
- **How Do I?** (Upper corner of the displayed window)

Help & Support Center

The Help & Support Center is accessed by clicking **Help & Support** in the *Navigators* window. From the Help & Support Center, you can search QuickBooks Help and the Support Database to find answers by typing in your question.

Help Index

The Help Index permits you to search for information about specific topics. Next, you will use the Help Index to search for information about contact management. QuickBooks has a contact synchronization feature that permits you to transfer information from your contact management software (Symantec ACT! or Microsoft Outlook) to update your customer and vendor lists in QuickBooks 2002. This feature permits you to enter the contact information only once.

To learn more about using contact management with QuickBooks:

Step 1: Click **Help Index** on the drop-down menu and the window shown below should appear.

Step 2: Click the **Index** tab.

Step 3: Type **contact** in the *Type the first few letters of the word you're looking for* field.

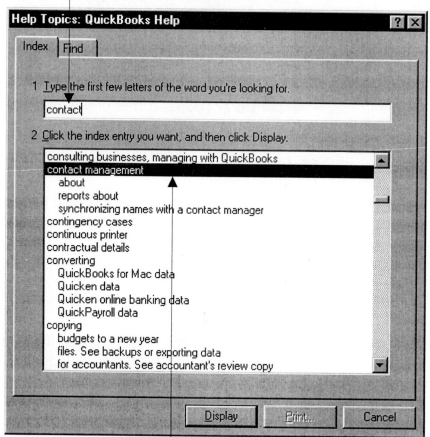

Notice that after typing only a few letters, contact management appears in the index entry window.

Step 4: Double-click **contact management** to learn more.

Step 5: Read the *Help* window about contact management. To print the Help information, click the **Options** button, then click **Print Topics**. Click **OK** to print.

Step 6: Close the *QuickBooks Help* window.

Help on This Window

Another QuickBooks Help feature is **Help on This Window**. Use this feature to obtain help about an open window.

Step 1: Open the Banking Navigator, then open the *Write Checks* window by clicking the **Checks** icon on the Banking Navigator. The *Write Checks* window is an onscreen form that looks like a check.

Step 2: With the *Write Checks* window still open, click **Help** on the menu bar.

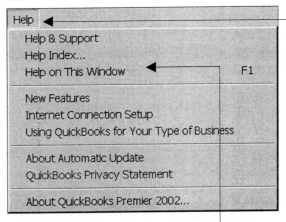

Step 3: Select **Help on This Window**. The following *Help* window containing *What's Important about the Write Checks window* should appear.

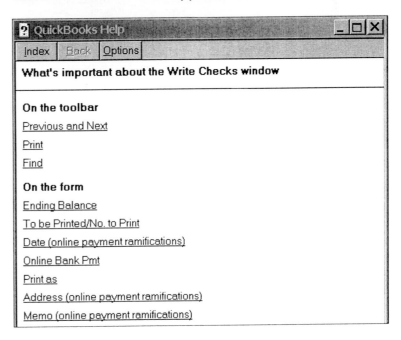

Step 4: The *Help on This Window* screens provide general information about the window with hyperlinks to additional information about specific features of the window.

Step 5: Close the *QuickBooks Help* window by clicking the ⊠ in the upper right corner of the *QuickBooks Help* window. Leave the *Write Checks* window open to use in the next activity.

How Do I?

QuickBooks also provides onscreen assistance with the *How Do I?* feature. The *How Do I?* button appears in the upper right corner in many QuickBooks windows.

Step 1: Click on the **How Do I?** button in the upper right corner of the *Write Checks* window.

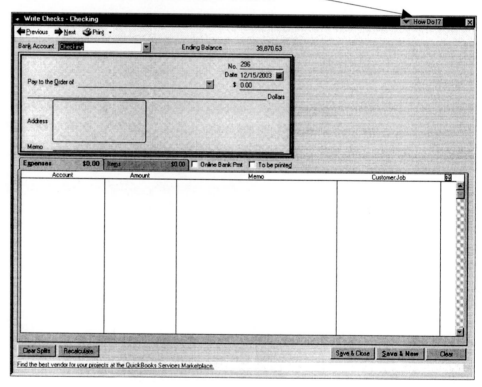

Step 2: The following drop-down menu identifying various tasks associated with this window appears. If an arrow [▸] appears to the right of the task, this indicates there is yet another pull-down menu.

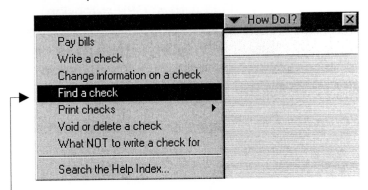

Click **Find a check**. A *QuickBooks Help* window appears listing the steps to find a check recorded in QuickBooks. Read the information about how to find a check.

Step 3: Print the **Find a check** instructions.

Step 4: Close the *QuickBooks Help* window by clicking the ⊠ in the upper right corner of the *Help* window.

Step 5: Close the *Write Checks* window.

Back Up Company Data

QuickBooks automatically saves your company data to the hard drive (C:). QuickBooks permits you to back up your company data file to:

Tip: For a business, a good backup system is to have a set of backup disks for each business day (Monday Backup, Tuesday Backup, Wednesday Backup, etc.). In addition, keep at least one backup copy at an offsite location other than your business premises.

- ◆ Floppy disk (A:)
- ◆ Hard drive (C:)
- ◆ Network drive

If necessary, the backup company data file can be restored and used. Therefore, it is important that the backup copy be as up to date as possible in case you must use it to replace lost company data.

When using this training manual, after each session you will back up your company data file to a floppy disk in drive A. The company working file (identified with a .QBW file extension such as Rock Castle Construction.QBW) is on the C drive. The backup file (identified with a .QBB extension) compresses the working file so it can fit on a floppy disk. If necessary, you can restore the backup file with a .QBB extension to the C drive with a .QBW extension.

When creating a backup for the Rock Castle Construction data for this chapter, you will change the file name. This permits you to enter changes in the new file without overwriting the original sample company data.

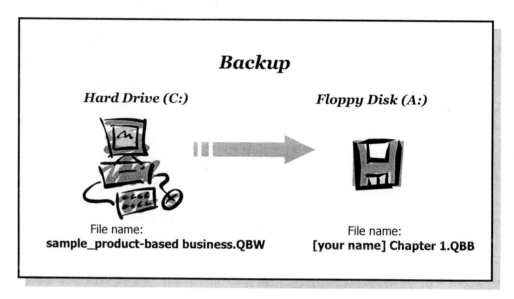

To back up the sample company data file to your floppy disk and rename the file:

Step 1: Insert a **_formatted_** 3.5 floppy disk in Drive (A:).

> **_Note:_** Format a 3.5 floppy disk using full format (not Quick Format) of Microsoft Windows as follows:
> 1. Right-click on the Start button at the bottom of the Windows screen.
> 2. Click Explore.
> 3. Right-click on 3 ½ Floppy (A:).
> 4. Click Format.
> 5. Click Full.
> 6. Click Start.
> 7. When formatting is finished, click Close.

Step 2: Click **File** on the menu bar.

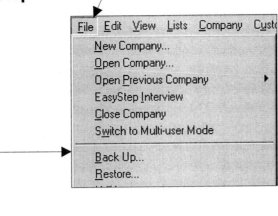

Step 3: Click **Back Up**.

Step 4: When the following window appears:

◆ Change the Filename to your **first initial**, **last name**, **Chapter 1** as shown below.

◆ Change Location to **A:**.

This is the company file (.QBW) that is the working file on the C drive.

This is the compressed backup file (.QBB) that is saved on the A drive.

Backup files have a **.QBB** extension. Your Windows settings determine whether the .QBB displays automatically.

Or click **Online** to save your files offsite.

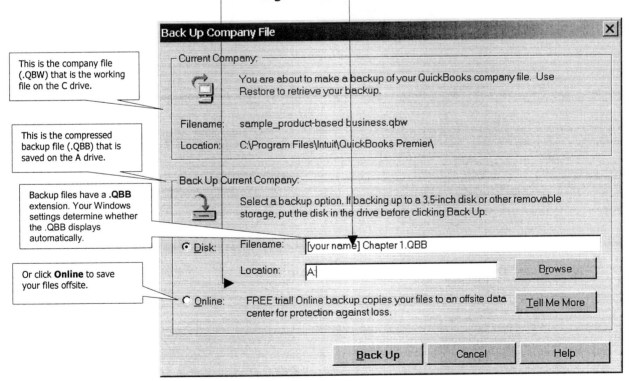

Step 5: Click the **Back Up** button to backup your company file to a floppy disk. QuickBooks makes a compressed copy of the company file on your floppy disk. If the backup is too large to fit on one 3.5 floppy disk, QuickBooks will prompt you to insert additional disks.

Step 6: When the message appears that the backup is complete, click **OK**.

Step 7: Close the company file on your C drive by clicking **File** (menu), **Close Company**.

Step 8: ✎ Label the backup disk with your name, course name, and **Chapter 1**.

Restore Company Data

The Restore command retrieves your compressed QuickBooks backup file and restores the file to the C drive.

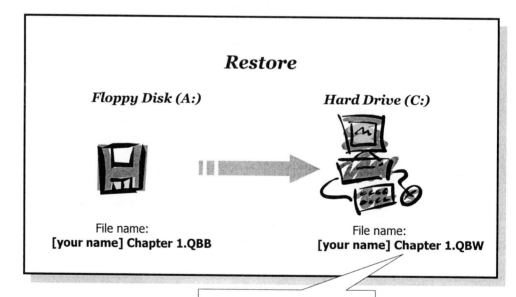

Restore

Floppy Disk (A:)

Hard Drive (C:)

File name:
[your name] Chapter 1.QBB

File name:
[your name] Chapter 1.QBW

Note: When you restore to the hard drive (C:), if you use the same file name as a company file already residing on the hard drive, QuickBooks will overwrite the existing file on the hard drive. To avoid overwriting an existing file, use a new QBW file name different from existing files on the hard drive.

When you restore your Chapter 1 backup file, to avoid overwriting the sample company file, you will name the restored file on the C drive: [your name] Chapter 1. QuickBooks will then create a QuickBooks company on the C drive of your computer with the file name: [your name] Chapter1 instead of overwriting the existing sample company file.

To restore your Chapter 1 company data file from the backup floppy disk (drive A) to drive C.

Also you can restore a backup file by clicking **File** (menu), **Restore**.

Step 1:   ▦ Insert your **Chapter 1** backup disk in the floppy disk drive (A:).

Step 2:   Click **Restore a backup file.**

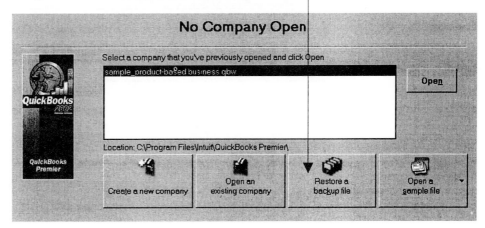

If there is another file open, QuickBooks will ask if you want to close the current company. Click **OK**.

Step 3:   Identify the backup file:

♦ Filename: **[your name] Chapter 1.QBB**.

♦ Location: **A**.

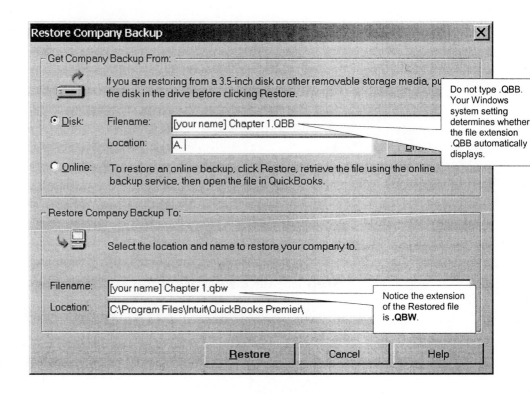

Step 4: Identify the restored file:

- Filename: **[your name] Chapter 1.QBW**.

- Location: **C:\Program Files\Intuit\QuickBooks Premier** (or QuickBooks Pro).

Step 5: Click **Restore.** Your Chapter 1 backup file has now been restored to the C: drive. Click **OK**.

Note: Since you used a Chapter 1 file name, the existing sample company file on the C drive was not overwritten or modified.

Change the Company Name

In order to identify your assignment printouts, add your initials to the company name and checking account. When you print out reports, your initials will then appear on the printouts.

To change a company name in QuickBooks, complete the following steps:

Step 1: Click **Company** on the Menu Bar, then select **Company Information**.

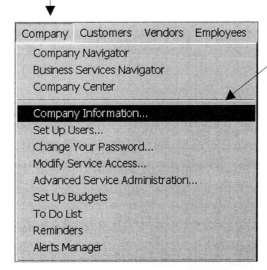

Step 2: When the following *Company Information* window appears, enter **your initials** and **Chapter 1** in the *Company Name* field before Rock Castle Construction.

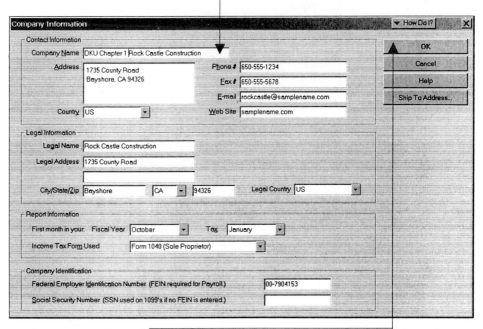

Step 3: Click **OK** to save the changes and close the *Company Information* window.

To add your initials to the company Checking account, complete the following:

Step 1: Click the **Chart of Accounts** icon in the Company Navigator.

Step 2: When the following *Chart of Accounts* window appears, select **Checking**.

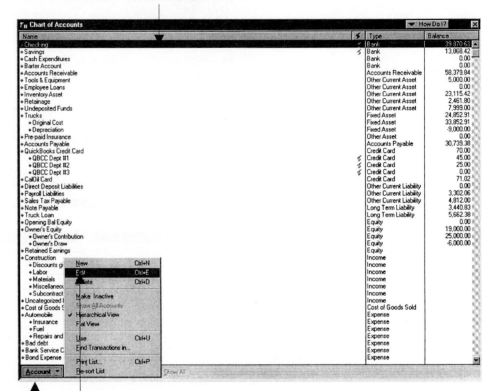

Step 3: Click the **Account** button.

Step 4: Click **Edit**.

Step 5: When the following *Edit Account* window appears, enter **your initials** in the *Name* field before the word Checking.

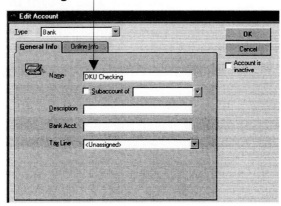

Step 6: Click **OK** to save the changes and close the *Edit Account* window.

Step 7: Close the *Chart of Accounts* window by clicking the ⊠ in the upper right corner of the *Chart of Accounts* window.

Back Up Company File

To save the company name changes on your backup file, back up your Chapter 1 file to your floppy disk.

Step 1: Insert your backup disk labeled Chapter 1 in drive A.

Step 2: Click **File** (menu), **Back Up**.

Step 3: When the following window appears:

> ◆ Change Name to your **first initial**, **last name**, **Chapter 1** as shown below.
>
> ◆ Change Location to **A:**.

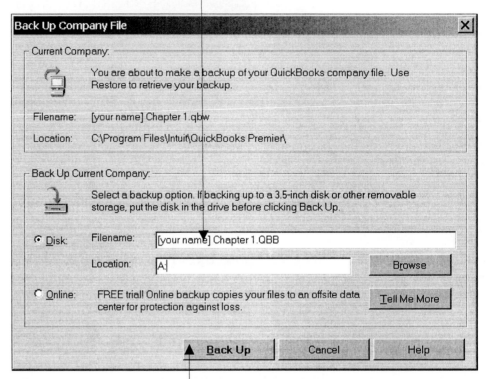

Step 4: Click the **Back Up** button to create a backup file.

Step 5: Click **Yes** to replace your previous backup file.

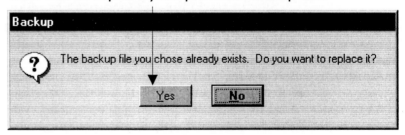

Step 6: Click **OK** when the message appears that your data has been backed up successfully.

If you are quitting your computer session now, follow the directions below to (1) close the company file and (2) exit QuickBooks.

If you are continuing your computer session, close the company file then proceed to Activity 1.1.

Close Company

To close a QuickBooks company file:

Step 1: Click **File** on the menu bar.

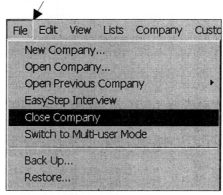

Step 2: Click **Close Company**.

Note: If the company file is left open when you exit QuickBooks, the next time anyone uses the QuickBooks software, the company file may still be open, permitting access to your company accounting records.

Exit QuickBooks

If you are completing the end-of-chapter activities at this time, do *not* exit QuickBooks until after completing the activities.

To exit QuickBooks:

1. Click the ⊠ in the upper right corner of the *QuickBooks* window, *or*

2. Click the **File** menu, then **Exit**.

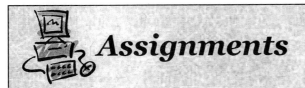

Assignments

Activity 1.1: Printing Financial Statements

Scenario

While working at your computer, you notice Mr. Castle heading toward you. Adding another stack of papers to your overflowing inbox, he says, *"I need a profit and loss statement and a balance sheet for November as soon as possible. I haven't seen any financial statements since our former accountant left."*

As he walks away, Mr. Castle calls over his shoulder, *"From now on I'd like a P&L and balance sheet on my desk by the first of each month."*

Task 1: Restore Company File

The first task is to retrieve your backup for Chapter 1 from the A drive to the C drive, changing the file name to Activity 1.1. Changing the file name enables you to enter the information for this activity without overwriting the Chapter 1 file.

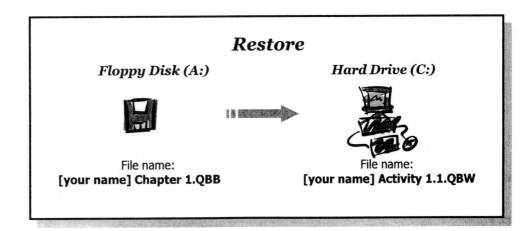

Restore the backup file from the floppy disk to the C drive as follows. (Restore instructions also appear on page1.33.)

Step 1: 💾 Insert the **Chapter 1** backup disk into drive A.

Step 2: Click **Restore a backup file** (or click **File, Restore** from the menu).

Step 3: Identify the backup file as shown below.

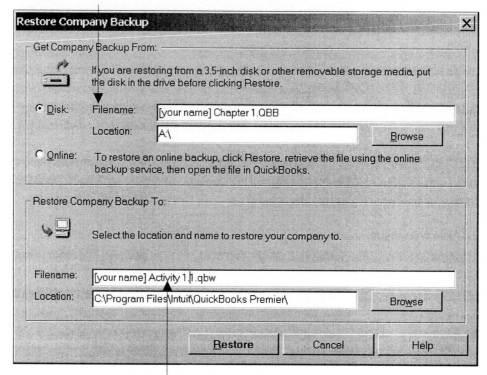

Step 4: Identify the restored file:

- Filename: **[your name] Activity 1.1.QBW**.
- Location: **C:\Program Files\Intuit\QuickBooks Premier** (or QuickBooks Pro).

Step 5: Click **Restore.** Your backup file will be restored to the C drive. Note that since you changed the file name to Activity 1.1, you should now have two working files (.QBW) on the C drive: (1) Chapter 1, and (2) Activity 1.1.

Step 6: Change the company name to:
[your name] Activity 1.1 Rock Castle Construction.
(To change the company name, select Company (menu),
Company Information.)

Task 2: Print Profit and Loss Statement

The profit and loss statement (also called the income statement) lists income earned and expenses incurred to generate income. Summarizing the amount of profit or loss a company has earned, the profit and loss statement is one of the primary financial statements given to bankers and investors.

Print the profit and loss statement for Rock Castle Construction by completing the following steps:

Step 1: Click **Reports Navigator** to open the *Report Finder* window.

Step 2: Select type of report: **Company & Financial**.

Step 3: Select report: **Profit & Loss Standard**.

Step 4: Select the date range: **Last Month**. The *From* field should now be: 11/01/2003. The *To* field should be: 11/30/2003.

Step 5: Click the **Display** button to view the profit and loss statement. Your screen should appear as shown on the following page.

Step 6: Next, add **your name** and **Activity 1.1** to the report footer as follows:

◆ Click the **Modify Report** button.

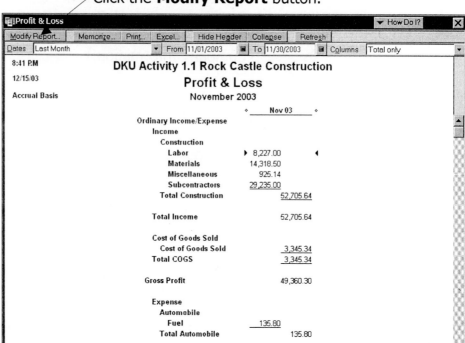

◆ From the *Modify Report* window, you can change the display, filters, header/footer, and fonts for the report. To modify the header and footer information for the report, click the **Header/Footer** tab on the *Modify Report* window.

- Check **Print header on pages after first page**.

- Check **Extra Footer Line**. Then enter **your name** and **Activity 1.1** in the *Extra Footer Line* field.

- Click **OK** to save your changes and close the *Modify Report* window.

Step 7: Click the **Print** button at the top of the *Profit and Loss* window.

- Select the appropriate printer.

- Select **Portrait** orientation.

- Select **Fit report to 1 page(s) wide**.

- Click **Print** to print the profit and loss statement for November.

Step 8: Close the *Profit and Loss* window.

✓ ***Net income is $252.25.***

Step 9: ✎ Circle the single largest income item appearing on the profit and loss statement for the month of November.

Step 10: ✎ Circle the single largest expense item appearing on the profit and loss statement for the month of November.

Task 3: Print Balance Sheet

The balance sheet is the financial statement that summarizes the financial position of a business. Listing assets, liabilities, and equity, the balance sheet reveals what a company owns and what it owes.

To print the balance sheet for Rock Castle Construction at November 30, 2003, complete the following steps:

Step 1: From the *Report Finder* window, select type of report: **Company & Financial**.

Step 2: Select report: **Balance Sheet Standard**.

Step 3: Select date range: **Last Month**.

Step 4: Click the **Display** button to view the onscreen balance sheet.

Step 5: Insert **your name** and **Activity 1.1** in the report footer.

Step 6: Print the balance sheet.

Step 7: Close the *Balance Sheet* window.

✓ **Total Assets equal $173,485.96.**

Step 8: ✎ Circle the single largest asset listed on Rock Castle Construction's November 2003 balance sheet.

Step 9: Close the *Report Finder* window.

Task 4: Back Up Activity 1.1 File

Back up the Activity 1.1 working file to a floppy disk.

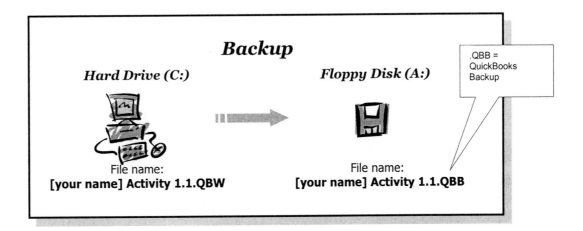

Step 1: 🖫 Insert the **Chapter 1** backup disk in drive A.

Step 2: Click **File**, **Back Up**.

Step 3: Enter the backup file name: **[your name] Activity 1.1**.
To save the backup file to **drive A**, click **Back Up**.

Step 4: Click **OK** after the backup is complete.

Step 5: Close the company file by clicking **File** (menu), **Close Company**.

Activity 1.2: QuickBooks Help

In this activity, you will use QuickBooks Help to obtain additional information about using QuickBooks.

Task 1: Backup and Restore Help

Use the QuickBooks Help Index to locate information about the Backup and Restore Features of QuickBooks. Print out the information you find. ✎ Circle or highlight the information on the printout that you find the most helpful.

Task 2: Your Choice

Use the QuickBooks Help Index to learn more about a QuickBooks feature of your choice. Print out the information. ✎ Circle or highlight the information on the printout that you find the most useful.

Activity 1.3: WebQuest

QuickBooks provides business services to assist the small business owner and operator.

Step 1: Go to the www.QuickBooks.com web page.

Step 2: Locate information about the various QuickBooks products on the QuickBooks web page.

Step 3: Print out information about comparison of QuickBooks Basic, QuickBooks Pro, QuickBooks Premier, and QuickBooks Accountant Premier versions.

Step 4: ✎ On your printout, circle or highlight the factors that you find to be the most important in making a software selection decision.

Computer Accounting with QuickBooks 2002
Chapter 1 Printout Checklist
Name:_____ Date:_____

Instructions:
1. **Check off the printouts you have completed.**
2. **Staple this page to your printouts.**

☑	*Printout Checklist – Chapter 1*
☐	Contact Management Printout
☐	Find a Check Instructions Printout
☑	*Printout Checklist – Activity 1.1*
☐	Task 2: Profit and Loss Statement
☐	Task 3: Balance Sheet
☑	*Printout Checklist – Activity 1.2*
☐	Task 1: Backing Up Your Data—Help Topic Printout
☐	Task 1: Restoring Your Data—Help Topic Printout
☐	Task 2: Your Choice Help Topic Printout
☑	*Printout Checklist – Activity 1.3*
☐	QuickBooks Product Comparison

Notes:

2 Chart of Accounts

Scenario

The next morning when you arrive at work, Mr. Castle is waiting for you, pacing in the aisle outside your cubicle.

He looks at you over the top of his glasses, his voice tense when he asks, *"Do you have the P&L and balance sheet ready?"*

"Yes sir!" you reply, handing him the financial statements.

The creases in his brow disappear as his eyes run down the statements, murmuring to himself as he walks away, *"The banker waiting in my office should like this...."*

As he rounds the corner, he calls back to you, *"See your inbox for account changes we need to make. And password protect that QuickBooks file so every Tom, Dick and Harry can't get into our accounting records!"*

2

Learning Objectives

In Chapter 2, you will learn the following QuickBooks features:

Introduction

To begin Chapter 2, start QuickBooks software and then restore your backup file.

Start QuickBooks software by clicking on the **QuickBooks** desktop icon or click **Start**, **Programs**, **QuickBooks Premier** (or QuickBooks Pro) , **QuickBooks Premier** (or QuickBooks Pro).

Retrieve the backup named Activity 1.1 from the A drive to the C drive, naming the restored working file Chapter 2.

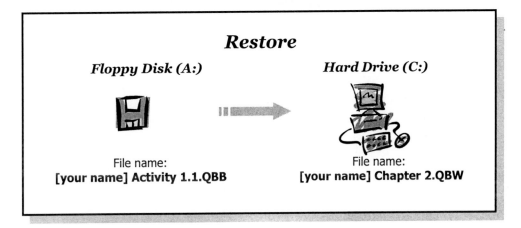

Restore

Floppy Disk (A:)   *Hard Drive (C:)*

File name: File name:
[your name] Activity 1.1.QBB   **[your name] Chapter 2.QBW**

Step 1: 🖫 Insert the **Chapter 1** backup disk into drive A.

Step 2: Click **Restore a backup file** (or click **File**, **Restore**).

Step 3: Identify the backup file:

   ◆ Filename: **[your name] Activity 1.1.QBB**.

   ◆ Location: **A:**.

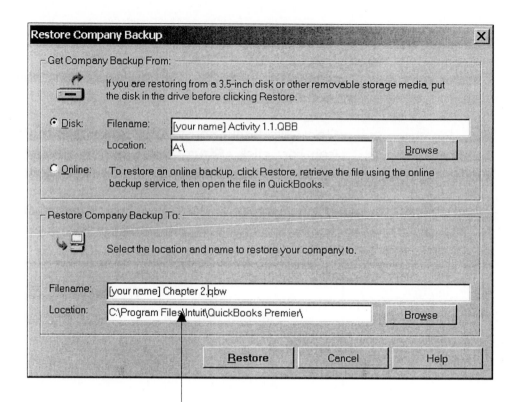

Step 4: Identify where QuickBooks should place the restored company file:

- Name: **[your name] Chapter 2.QBB**.

- Location: **C:\Program Files\Intuit\QuickBooks Premier** (or QuickBooks Pro).

Step 5: Click **Restore**. Your backup file will be restored to the C drive as a new working file with the name, Chapter 2.

Step 6: Change the company name to: **[your name] Chapter 2 Rock Castle Construction**.

(To change the company name, click Company (menu), Company Information.)

Note: in this text you are changing the filename for each chapter and activity so that you can restore from any point in the text. However, for a typical business application, you would open the company file (File, Open Company) and then create a backup with the same filename. The backup would normally only be restored if the company data file was damaged or destroyed.

Password Protection

QuickBooks is an accounting information system that permits a company to conveniently collect accounting information and store it in a single file. Much of the accounting information stored in QuickBooks is confidential, however, and a company often wants to limit employee access.

Password protection can be used to limit access to company data.

Two ways to restrict access to accounting information stored in a QuickBooks company data file are:

1. The company data file can be password protected so that individuals must enter a user ID and password in order to open the company data file. Once the company file is open, then the user has access to all accounting information stored in QuickBooks.

2. Access is limited to selected areas of the company's accounting data. For example, a user may access accounts receivable to view customer balances but not be able to access payroll or check writing.

Only the QuickBooks Administrator can add users with passwords and limit user access to selected areas of QuickBooks. The QuickBooks Administrator is an individual who will have access to all areas of QuickBooks.

In addition, it is also possible to password protect the Internet connection to online QuickBooks services (click Company, Modify Service Access).

To add a new user and password protection to a company file:

Step 1:   Click **Company**, then click **Set Up Users**.

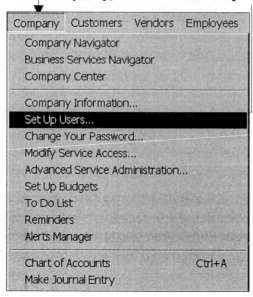

Step 2:   First, set up a QuickBooks Administrator who has access to all areas of QuickBooks. Then the Administrator can add new users.

You will enter Mr. Rock Castle as the Administrator. Then you will add your name to the User List.

♦   Enter **Rock Castle** in the *Administrator's Name* field.

♦   Enter and then confirm a password of your choice. Click **OK**.

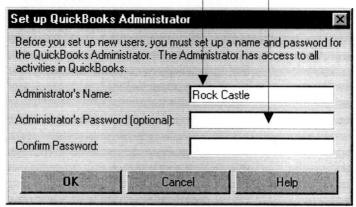

Step 3: After the QuickBooks Administrator logs on, he or she can add new users. Click **Add User**.

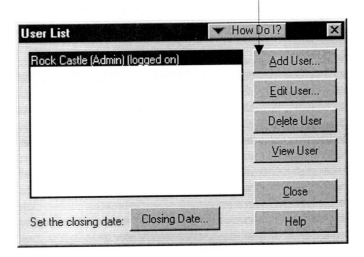

Step 4: In the following *Set up user password and access* window:

- Enter **your name** in the *User Name* field.

- At this point, if you were adding another employee as a user, you would ask the employee to enter and confirm his or her password. In this instance, simply enter and confirm a **password** of your choice.

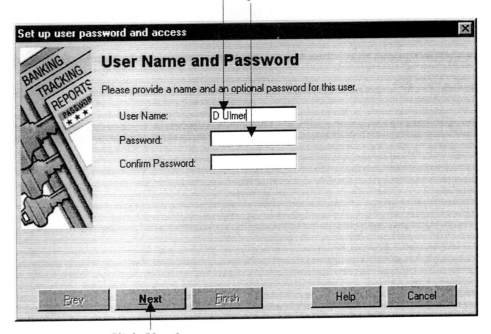

- Click **Next**.

Step 5: In the following window, you can restrict user access to selected areas of QuickBooks or give the user access to all areas of QuickBooks. Select: **All areas of QuickBooks**, then click **Next**.

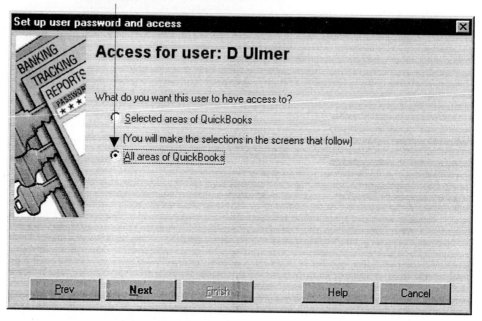

Step 6: Select **Yes** to confirm that you want to give access to all areas of QuickBooks, including payroll, check writing, and other sensitive information.

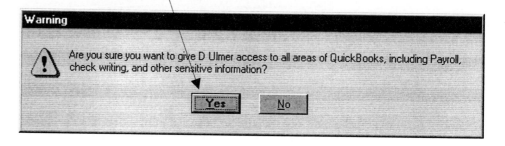

Step 7: The next window summarizes the user's access for each QuickBooks area, indicating access to create documents, print, and view reports. Click **Finish**.

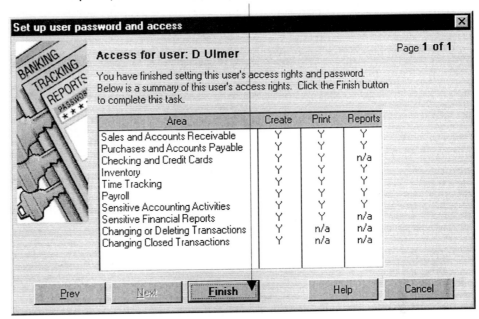

Step 8: Now two names (Rock Castle as Administrator and your name) should appear on the User List.

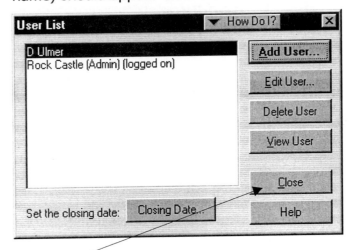

Warning!
You will not be able to access your company file without your password.

Step 9: Click **Close** to close the *User List* window.

Now whenever you open the company file for Rock Castle Construction, you will be asked to enter your user name and password.

Chart of Accounts

The chart of accounts is a list of accounts and account numbers. A company uses accounts to record transactions in the accounting system. Accounts (such as the cash account or inventory account) are a way to sort and track information.

QuickBooks will automatically create a chart of accounts when you set up a new company. Then you may edit the chart of accounts, adding and deleting accounts as necessary to suit your company's specific needs. QuickBooks also permits you to use subaccounts (subcategories) of accounts.

Accounts can be categorized into the following groups:

Balance Sheet Accounts

Assets

Liabilities

Equity

Profit & Loss Accounts

Income (Revenue)

Cost of Goods Sold

Expenses

Non-Posting Accounts
Purchase Orders
Estimates

Balance Sheet Accounts

The balance sheet is a financial statement that summarizes what a company owns and what it owes. Balance sheet accounts are accounts that appear on the company's balance sheet.

Review the balance sheet you printed in Activity 1.1 for Rock Castle Construction. Three types of accounts appear on the balance sheet:

1. Assets
2. Liabilities
3. Owners' (or Stockholders') Equity

Tip: If unsure whether an account is an asset account, ask the question: *Does this item have future benefit?* If the answer is yes, the item is probably an asset.

> *Assets = Liabilities + Owners' Equity*

1. **Assets** are resources that a company owns. These resources are expected to have future benefit.

   Asset accounts include:

   - Cash.

   - Accounts receivable (amounts to be *received* from customers in the future).

   - Inventory.

   - Other current assets (assets likely to be converted to cash or consumed within one year).

   - Fixed assets (property used in the operations of the business such as equipment, buildings, and land).

   - Intangible assets (such as copyrights, patents, trademarks, and franchises).

Tip: If unsure whether an account is a liability account, ask the question: *Is the company obligated to do something, such as pay a bill or provide a service?* If the answer is yes, the item is probably a liability.

2. **Liabilities** are amounts a company owes to others. Liabilities are *obligations*. For example, if a company borrows $10,000 from the bank, the company has an obligation to repay the $10,000 to the bank. Thus, the $10,000 obligation is shown as a liability on the company's balance sheet.

   Liability accounts include:

   - Accounts payable (amounts that are owed and will be *paid* to suppliers in the future).

   - Sales taxes payable (sales tax owed and to be *paid* in the future).

Note: The difference between a note payable and a mortgage payable is that a mortgage payable has real estate as collateral.

- Interest payable (interest owed and to be *paid* in the future).
- Other current liabilities (liabilities due within one year).
- Loan payable (also called notes payable).
- Mortgage payable.
- Other long-term liabilities (liabilities due after one year).

Owners' Equity =

Assets - Liabilities

3. **Owners' equity** accounts (stockholders' equity for a corporation) represents the net worth of a company. Equity is calculated as assets (resources owned) minus liabilities (amounts owed).

   Three different types of business ownership are:

   - Sole proprietorship (an unincorporated business with one owner).
   - Partnership (an unincorporated business with more than one owner).
   - Corporation (an incorporated business with one or more owners).

   Owners' equity is increased by:

   - Investments by owners. For a corporation, owners invest by buying stock.
   - Net profits retained in the business rather than distributed to owners.

   Owners' equity is decreased by:

   - Amounts paid to owners as a return for their investment. For a sole proprietorship, this is called withdrawals. For a corporation, it is called dividends.
   - Losses incurred by the business.

   Balance sheet accounts are referred to as *permanent accounts*. Balances in permanent accounts are carried forward from year to year. Thus, for a balance sheet account, such as cash, the balance at December 31 is carried forward and becomes the opening balance on January 1 of the next year.

Income Statement (Profit & Loss) Accounts

The income statement (also called the profit and loss statement or P&L statement) reports the results of a company's operations, listing income and expenses for a period of time. Income statement accounts are accounts that appear on a company's income statement.

Review the income statement you printed in Activity 1.1 for Rock Castle Construction. QuickBooks uses three different income statement accounts:
1. Income accounts
2. Cost of Goods Sold
3. Expense accounts

1. **Income** accounts record sales to customers and other revenues earned by the company. Revenues are the prices charged customers for goods and services provided.

   Examples of income accounts include:
   ◆ Sales or revenues
   ◆ Fees earned
   ◆ Interest income
   ◆ Rental income
   ◆ Gains on sale of assets

2. **Cost of goods sold** accounts are accounts used to track the cost of items sold to customers.

3. **Expense** accounts record costs that have expired or been consumed in the process of generating income. Expenses are the costs of providing goods and services to customers.

   Examples of expense accounts include:
   ◆ Salaries expense
   ◆ Insurance expense
   ◆ Rent expense
   ◆ Interest expense

Net income is calculated as income (or revenue) less cost of goods sold and other expenses. Net income is an attempt to match or measure efforts (expenses) against accomplishments (revenues).

> *Income (or Revenue)*
>
> - *Cost of Goods Sold*
>
> - *Expenses*
>
> = *Net Income*

Income statement accounts are called *temporary* accounts because they are used for only one year. At the end of each year, temporary accounts are closed (the balance reduced to zero). For example, if an income statement account, such as Advertising Expense, had a $5,000 balance at December 31, the $5,000 balance would be closed or transferred to owner's equity at year-end. The opening balance on January 1 for the Advertising Expense account would be $0.00.

Non-Posting Accounts

Non-posting accounts are accounts that do not appear on the balance sheet or income statement. However, these accounts are needed to track information necessary for the accounting system.

Examples of non-posting accounts include:

- Purchase orders: documents that track items that have been ordered from suppliers.

- Estimates: bids or proposals submitted to customers.

Lists

QuickBooks uses lists to provide additional supporting detail for selected accounts.

In addition to the Customer List, Vendor List, and Employee List, other QuickBooks lists include:

1. **Item List:** provides information about the items or services sold to customers, such as hours worked and types of items.

2. **Payroll Item List:** tracks detailed information about payroll such as payroll taxes and payroll deductions. The Payroll Item list permits the use of a single or limited number of payroll accounts while more detailed information is tracked using the Item List for payroll.

Tip: Obtain a copy of the tax return form for your business at www.irs.gov. Then modify your chart of accounts to track the information needed for your tax return.

3. **Class List:** permits income to be tracked according to the specific source of the income. An example of a class might be a department, store location, business segment, or product line.

When you set up a new company, QuickBooks automatically creates a chart of accounts. Then you can modify the chart of accounts to suit your specific needs. Next, you will learn how to display the chart of accounts, then add, delete, and edit accounts.

Display Chart of Accounts

To view the chart of accounts for Rock Castle Construction, complete the following steps:

Step 1: Click **Company** in the *Navigators* window to open the Company Navigator.

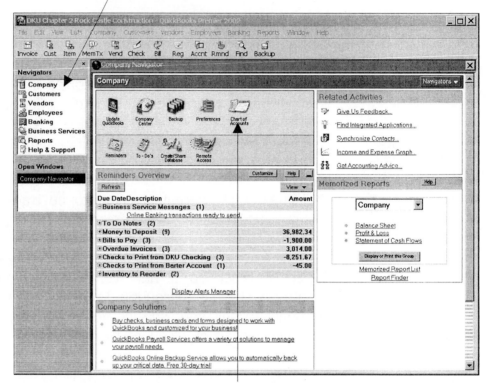

Step 2: Click the **Chart of Accounts** icon in the Company Navigator to display the following *Chart of Accounts* window.

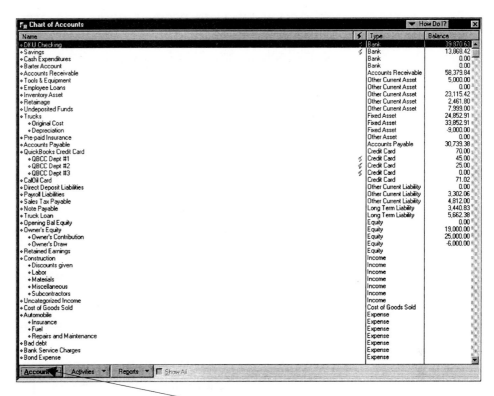

For each account, the account name, type of account, and the balance of the account is listed. The Account button at the bottom of the window displays a drop-down menu for adding, editing, and deleting accounts.

Display Account Numbers

Account numbers are used to identify accounts. Usually the account number also identifies the *account type*. For example, a typical numbering system for accounts might be as follows.

> Account Type determines whether the account appears on the balance sheet or income statement.

Account Type	Account No.
Asset accounts	1000 – 1999
Liability accounts	2000 – 2999
Equity accounts	3000 – 3999
Revenue (income) accounts	4000 – 4999
Expense accounts	5000 – 5999

To display both the account name and account number for Rock Castle Construction's chart of accounts, you must select a QuickBooks preference for viewing the account numbers.

To display account numbers:

Step 1: From the Company Navigator, click the **Preferences** icon.

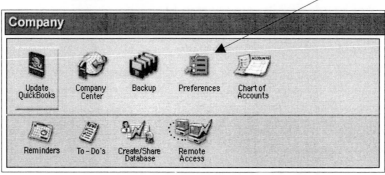

Step 2: When the *Preferences* window appears, the left scrollbar lists the different types of preferences. Click the **Accounting** icon in the left scrollbar. Then select the **Company Preferences** tab.

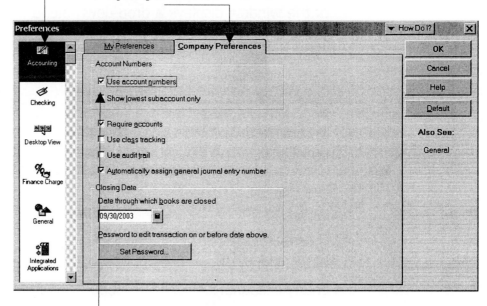

Step 3: Select **Use account numbers** to display the account numbers in the chart of accounts. Then click **OK**.

Step 4: To view the chart of accounts, click **Chart of Accounts** listed in the Open Windows section on the left of the screen.

The chart of accounts should now list account numbers preceding the account name.

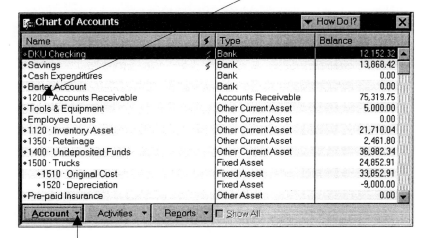

Add New Accounts

You can modify the chart of accounts to add new accounts, delete accounts, or edit accounts as needed to suit your company's specific and changing needs.

Rock Castle Construction has decided to begin advertising and would like to add an Advertising Expense account to the chart of accounts.

To add a new account to the chart of accounts:

Step 1: Display the *Chart of Accounts* window.

Step 2: Click the **Account** button at the bottom of the *Chart of Accounts* window to display a drop-down menu. Then click **New**.

Step 3: Enter information in the *New Account* window.

      • Select Account Type from the drop-down list: **Expense**.

      • Enter the new Account Number: **6040**.

      • Enter the Account Name: **Advertising Expense**.

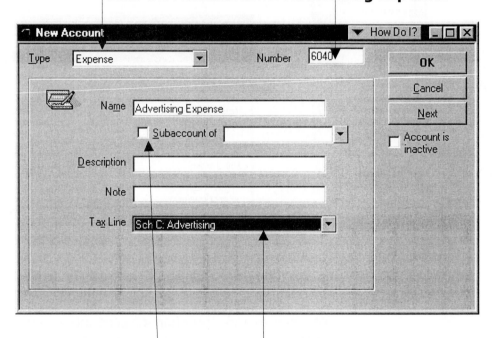

      • Leave subaccount unchecked. Subaccounts are subcategories of an account. For example, Rock Castle Construction has an Automobile Expense account (Account No. 6000) and two Automobile Expense subaccounts: Repairs and Maintenance (Account No. 6010) and Fuel (Account No. 6020).

> **Important!**
> Selecting the appropriate Tax Line will ensure that your accounting records provide the information needed to complete your tax return.

      • Select Tax Line: **Sch C: Advertising**. This indicates the Advertising Expense account balance will appear on Schedule C of Rock Castle Construction's tax return.

Step 4: Click **OK** to save the changes and close the *New Account* window.

Notice that Account 6040 Advertising Expense now appears on the chart of accounts.

If the new account had been a balance sheet account (an asset, liability, or equity account), QuickBooks would ask you for the opening account balance as of your QuickBooks start date. Since Advertising Expense is an expense account that appears on the income statement and not a balance sheet account, QuickBooks did not ask for the opening balance.

Delete Accounts

Occasionally you may want to delete unused accounts from the chart of accounts. You can delete only accounts that are not being used. For example, if an account has been used to record a transaction and has a balance, it cannot be deleted. If an account has subaccounts associated with it, that account cannot be deleted.

Rock Castle Construction would like to delete an account it does not plan to use: the Printing and Reproduction Expense account.

To delete an account:

Step 1: Display the *Chart of Accounts* window.

Step 2: Select the account you want to delete. In this case, click **6900: Printing and Reproduction**.

Step 3: Click the **Account** button at the bottom of *the Chart of Accounts* window.

Step 4: Click **Delete**.

Step 5: Click **OK** to confirm that you want to delete the account.

Edit Accounts

Rock Castle Construction would like to change the name of the Advertising Expense account to: Advertising & Promotion.

To make changes to an existing account, complete the following steps:

Step 1: Display the *Chart of Accounts* window.

Step 2: Select the account to edit: click on account **6040 Advertising Expense**.

Step 3: Click the **Account** button in the lower left corner of the *Chart of Accounts* window.

Step 4: Click **Edit** to open the *Edit Account* window.

Step 5: Make changes to the account information. In this case, change the account name to: **Advertising & Promotion**.

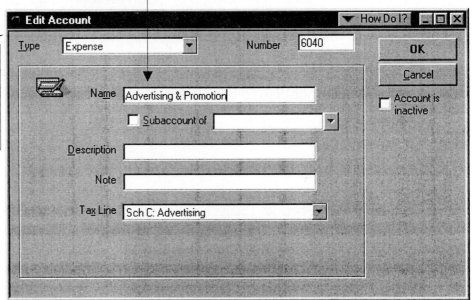

Note: You cannot change the type of account if there are subaccounts associated with the account.

Step 6: Click **OK** to save the changes. Advertising Expense should now appear as Advertising & Promotion in the *Chart of Accounts* window.

QuickBooks permits you to rearrange the order in which the accounts appear in the chart of accounts. A chart of accounts is often arranged in numerical order by account number.

To demonstrate how to move accounts in the chart of accounts, you will move the account you just added, Advertising & Promotion, to a new location in Rock Castle Construction's chart of accounts.

To move an account within the chart of accounts:

Step 1: In the *Chart of Accounts* window, move the mouse pointer over the diamond that appears to the left of the Advertising & Promotion account.

Tip: To change a subaccount to an account, drag the subaccount to the left.

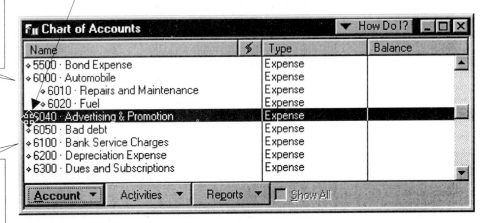

Tip: To change an account to a subaccount, simply drag the account to the right.

Step 2: Hold down the left mouse button and drag the **Advertising and Promotion** account to the desired location above the Bad Debt Account (Account No. 6050), then release the mouse button.

Print Chart of Accounts

QuickBooks calls the Chart of Accounts printout an Account Listing report.

To print the chart of accounts:

Step 1: Display the *Chart of Accounts* window.

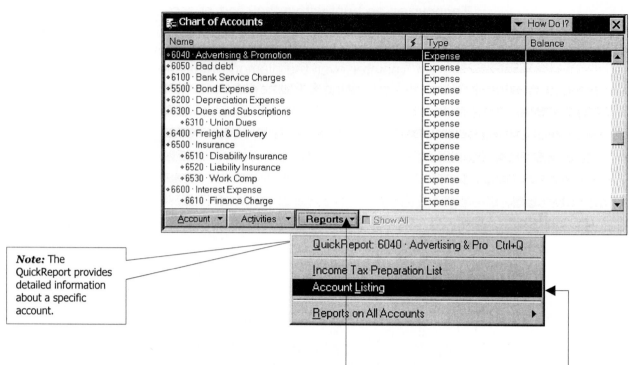

Note: The QuickReport provides detailed information about a specific account.

Step 2:   Next, display the Accounting Listing report on your screen. Click the **Reports** button at the bottom of the *Chart of Accounts* window, then click **Account Listing** on the drop-down menu.

Step 3:   The following Account Listing report should appear. Insert your name and Chapter 2 in the report footer as follows:

*   Click the **Modify Report** button at the top of the *Accounting Listing* window.

*   When the *Modify Report: Accounting Listing* window appears, click the **Header/Footer** tab.

*   Check the **Extra Footer Line** checkbox, then enter **your name** and **Chapter 2** in the *Extra Footer Line* field.

*   Click **OK** to save your changes and close the *Modify Report* window.

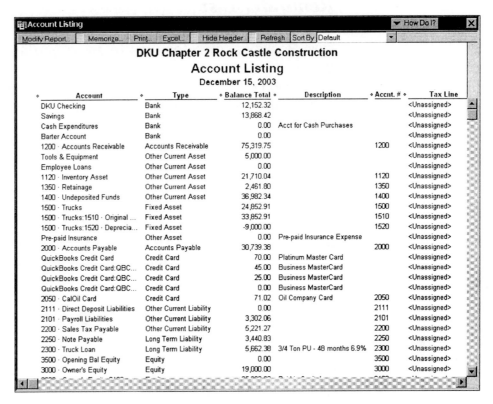

Step 4: To print the Accounting Listing report:

 • Click the **Print** button at the top of the *Account Listing* window.

 • Select orientation: **Portrait**.

 • Select **Fit report to 1 page(s) wide** that appears in the lower left of the window.

 • Click the **Print** button.

Step 5: Close the *Account Listing* window, then close the *Chart of Accounts* window.

Reminder List

QuickBooks has two features to assist you in tracking tasks to be done:

1. To Do List: The To Do List tracks all tasks to be completed. You can add items to the To Do List, mark items complete, and print the list.
2. Reminders List: This list shows only those tasks that are currently due.

To display the Reminders List:

Step 1: Click **Company** to display the Company Navigator. The **Reminders Overview** will automatically appear in the Company Navigator.

You can also click the **Reminders** icon to display the *Reminders List* window.

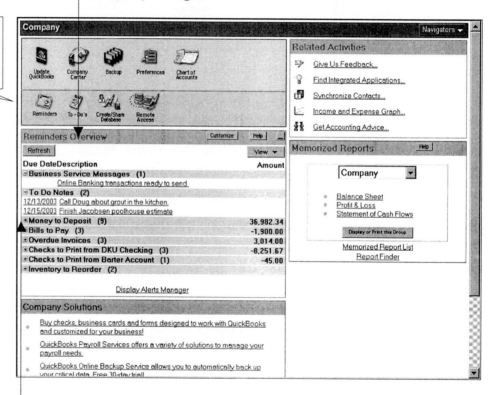

Step 2: To display the detail for the To Do Notes, click the **+** sign beside To Do Notes.

Back Up Chapter 2

Back up your Chapter 2 file to a floppy disk. Use the file name: [your name] Chapter 2. For more information about backing up company files, see backup instructions in Chapter 1.

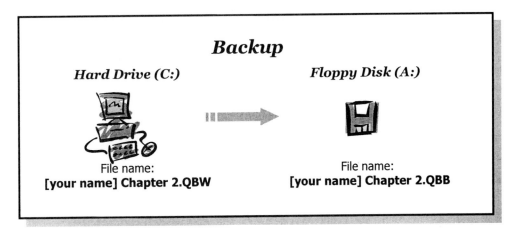

Step 1: 🖫 Insert the **Chapter 2** backup disk in drive A.

Step 2: Click **File, Back Up**.

Step 3: Enter the file name: **[your name] Chapter 2.QBB**.
Enter location: **A:**.

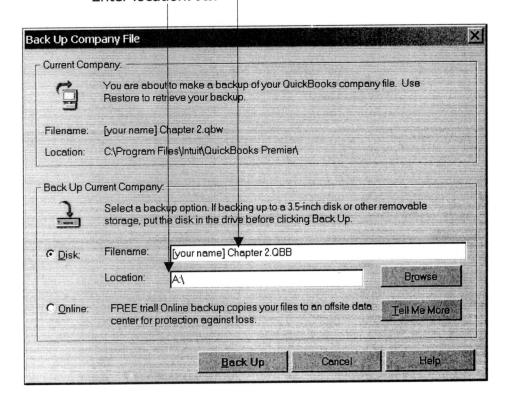

Step 4:   Click **Back Up**.

You have now backed up the Chapter 2 company file to your Chapter 2 floppy disk.

If you are continuing your computer session, close the company file, then proceed to Activity 2.1.

If you are quitting your computer session now (1) close the company file and (2) exit QuickBooks.

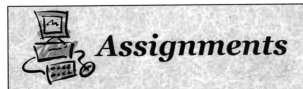

Assignments

Activity 2.1: To Do List

Scenario

When you return to your cubicle after lunch, you find the following note stuck to your computer screen.

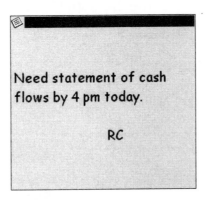

Need statement of cash flows by 4 pm today.

RC

In addition to printing out the statement of cash flows, you decide to add a task to your QuickBooks To Do List to remind you to print out the financial statements for Rock Castle each month.

Task 1: Restore Company File

The first task is to retrieve your Chapter 2 backup from the A drive to the C drive, changing the file name to Activity 2.1. Changing the file name enables you to enter the information for this activity without overwriting the Chapter 2 file.

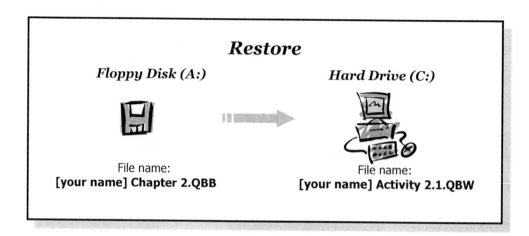

Restore the backup file from the floppy disk to the C drive as follows. (Additional Restore instructions appear in Chapter 1.)

Step 1: ⊟ Insert your **Chapter 2** backup floppy disk into drive A.

Step 2: Click **Restore a backup file** (or click **File**, **Restore**).

Step 3: Identify the backup file as shown below.

 ◆ Filename: **[your name] Activity 2.1.QBB**.

 ◆ Location: **A:**.

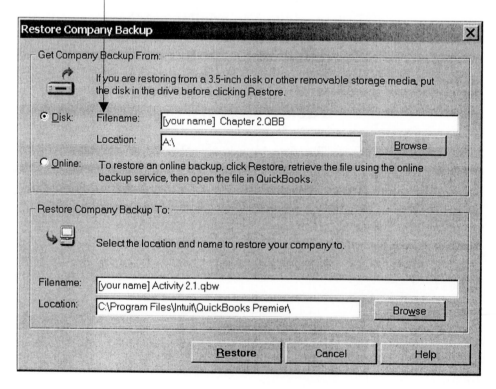

Step 4: Identify the restored file:

- Filename: **[your name] Activity 2.1.QBW**.

- Location: **C:\Program Files\Intuit\QuickBooks Premier**.

Step 5: Click **Restore.** Your backup file will be restored to the C drive. If prompted, enter your User ID and Password.

Note: Since you changed the file name to Activity 2.1, on your C drive, you should now have a Chapter 2.QBW file and an Activity 2.1.QBW file.

Step 6: Change the company name to:
[your name] Activity 2.1 Rock Castle Construction. (To change the company name, select Company (menu), Company Information.)

Task 2: Add a Task to the To Do List

Add a task to your To Do List to prepare financial statements for Mr. Castle each month. You will add the task for December and January.

To add a task to the To Do List, complete the following steps:

Step 1: Open the Company Navigator. (Click **Company** in the *Navigators* Window.)

Step 2: Click the **To-Do's** icon.

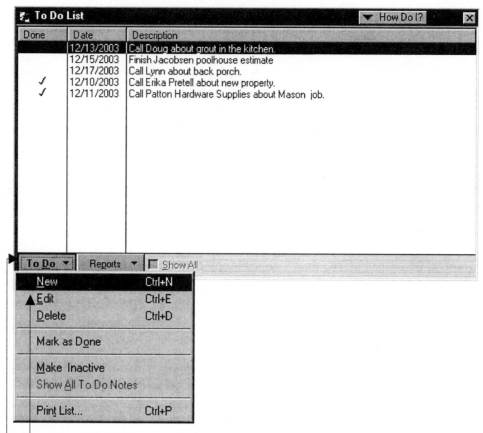

Step 3:   Click the **To Do** button in the lower left corner of the *To Do List* window.

Step 4:   Click **New**.

Step 5:   Enter the December task: **Print financial statements for Mr. Castle**. Remind me on: **12/12/2003**.

Step 6:   Click the **Next** button to add another task.

Step 7:   Enter the January task: **Print financial statements for Mr. Castle**. Remind me on: **01/01/2004**.

Step 8:   Click **OK** to save the task and close the window.

Task 3: Print Statement of Cash Flows

The Statement of Cash Flows summarizes a company's cash inflows and cash outflows. The cash flows are grouped by activity:

- Cash flows from operating activities: Cash flows related to the operations of the business—providing goods and services to customers.

- Cash flows from investing activities: Cash flows that result from investing (buying and selling) long-term assets, such as investments and property.

- Cash flows from financing activities: Cash flows that result from borrowing or repaying principal on debt or from transactions with owners.

Print the Statement of Cash Flows for Rock Castle Construction by completing the following steps:

Step 1: Click **Reports** in the Navigator window to open the *Report Finder* window.

Step 2: Select type of report: **Company & Financial**.

Step 3: Select report: **Statement of Cash Flows**.

Step 4: Select the date range: **Last Month**. The *From* field should now be: 11/01/2003. The *To* field should be: 11/30/2003.

Step 5: Click the **Display** button to view the Statement of Cash Flows on your screen.

Step 6: Next, insert your name and Activity 2.1 to the report footer to identify your printout:

- Click the **Modify Report** button.

- Click the **Header/Footer** tab in the *Modify Report* window.

- Check **Extra Footer Line**. Then enter **your name** and **Activity 2.1** in the *Extra Footer Line* field.

> • Click **OK** to save your changes and close the *Modify Report* window.

Step 7: Print the Statement of Cash Flows. Click the **Print** button at the top of the *Statement of Cash Flows* window. Select the appropriate printer. Select **Portrait** orientation. Select **Fit to 1 page(s) wide**. Then click **Print** to print the Statement of Cash Flows.

Step 8: Close the *Statement of Cash Flows* window. Then close the *Report Finder* window.

> ✓ *Net cash provided by operating activities is $22,260.83.*

Step 9: ✐ Circle the net change in cash for the period on the Statement of Cash Flows printout.

Task 4: Mark Task Complete

Mark the task to print November financial statements as completed.

To mark a task complete:

Step 1: Open the *To Do* window.

Step 2: Select the To Do task: **12/12/2003 Print financial statements for Mr. Castle**.

Step 3: With the mouse pointer on the selected task, right-click. When the onscreen menu appears, select **Mark as Done**.

A ✓ should now appear in front of the task and the task drops to the bottom of the To Do List.

Step 4: Print the To Do List as follows:

- Click the **Reports** button (at the bottom of the *To Do* window).

- Click **Detail List**.

- Insert **your name** and **Activity 2.1** in the report footer. (Click Modify Report button.)

- Click **Print**. Select Print to: **Printer**. Click **Print**.

- Close the *To Do* windows.

Task 5: Back Up Activity 2.1 File

Back up the Activity 2.1 file to a floppy disk.

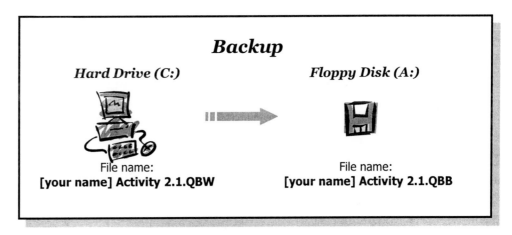

Step 1: 🖫 Insert your **Chapter 2** backup disk in drive A.

Step 2: Click **File**, **Back Up**.

Step 3: Specify the backup file name: **[your name] Activity 2.1.QBB**. Specify location: **A:**.

Step 4: Click **Back Up** to backup Activity 2.1 to your backup floppy disk. Close the company file. (From the File menu, select Close Company.)

You have now backed up Activity 2.1 file to your floppy disk.

Activity 2.2: Edit Chart of Accounts

Scenario

When you return to your cubicle after your afternoon break, another note is stuck to your computer screen.

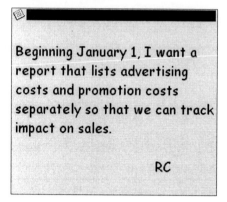

Beginning January 1, I want a report that lists advertising costs and promotion costs separately so that we can track impact on sales.

RC

In order to track advertising costs separately from promotion costs, you decide to make the following changes to the chart of accounts.

1. Rename Account 6040 Advertising & Promotion account to: Selling Expense.

2. Add two subaccounts: 6041 Advertising Expense and 6042 Promotion Expense.

After these changes, the chart of accounts should list the following accounts:

> Account 6040: Selling Expense
> Subaccount 6041: Advertising Expense
> Subaccount 6042: Promotion Expense

Task 1: Restore Company File

Restore your Activity 2.1 backup to the hard drive, changing the file name to Activity 2.2. Changing the file name enables you to enter the information for this activity without overwriting the Activity 2.1 file.

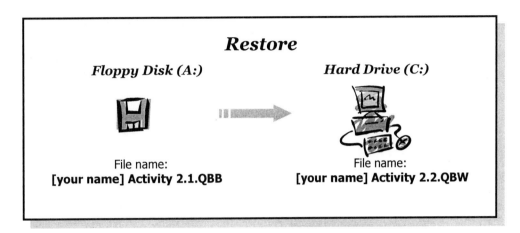

Restore

Floppy Disk (A:)   *Hard Drive (C:)*

File name: File name:
[your name] Activity 2.1.QBB   **[your name] Activity 2.2.QBW**

Restore the backup file from the floppy disk to the C drive as follows:

Step 1: Insert the **Chapter 2** backup floppy disk into drive A.

Step 2: Click **Restore a backup file** (or click **File, Restore**).

Step 3: Identify the backup filename and location:

- Filename: **[your name] Activity 2.1.QBB**.
- Location: **A:**.

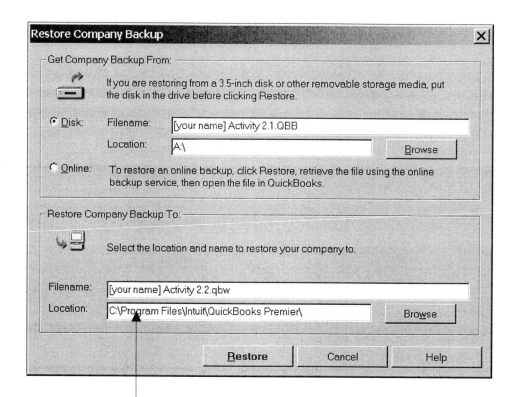

Step 4: Identify the restored file:

+ Filename: **[your name] Activity 2.2.QBW**.

+ Location: **C:\Program Files\Intuit\QuickBooks Premier**.

Step 5: Click **Restore.** Your backup file will be restored to the C drive. If prompted, enter your User ID and Password. *Note:* Since you changed the file name to Activity 2.2, on your C drive, you should now have a Chapter 2.QBW file, an Activity 2.1.QBW file, and an Activity 2.2.QBW file.

Step 6: Change the company name to: **[your name] Activity 2.2 Rock Castle Construction**. (To change the company name, select Company (menu), Company Information.)

Task 2: Edit Account

Edit the chart of accounts to change the name of Account 6040 from Advertising & Promotion to Selling Expense.

Step 1: Open the *Chart of Accounts* window. (Open the Company Navigator, then click the Chart of Accounts icon.)

Step 2: Select account: **6040 Advertising & Promotion**.

Step 3: Click the **Account** button at the bottom of the *Chart of Accounts* window, then select **Edit** from the drop-down menu.

Step 4: Change the account name from Advertising & Promotion to: **Selling Expense**.

Step 5: Click **OK** to save the changes.

Task 3: Add Subaccounts

Add two subaccounts to the Selling Expense account:
(1) Advertising Expense and (2) Promotion Expense.

Step 1: Click the **Account** button at the bottom of the *Chart of Accounts* window, then select **New** to open the *New Account* window.

Step 2: Select Account Type: **Expense**.

Step 3: Enter Account Number: **6041**

Step 4: Enter Account Name: **Advertising Expense**.

Step 5: Check the checkbox in front of the *Subaccount of* field.

Step 6: From the drop-down list, select subaccount of: **6040 Selling Expense**.

Step 7: From the drop-down list for Tax Line, select **SchC: Advertising**.

Step 8:   Click **Next**. Using the instructions above, add the next subaccount: **6042 Promotion Expense**.

Step 9:   Print the revised chart of accounts. (Hint: From the *Chart of Accounts* window, click the **Reports** button, then click **Account Listing**. Remember to include your name and Activity 2.2 in the report footer and use Portrait orientation and Fit to 1 page(s) wide.)

Task 4: Back Up Activity 2.2 File

Back up the Activity 2.2 file to a floppy disk.

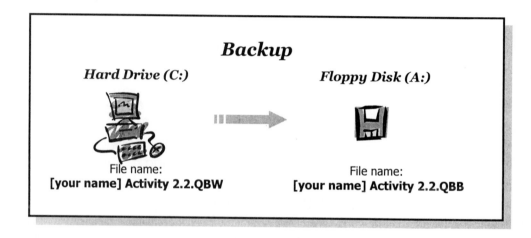

Step 1:   🖫 Insert the **Chapter 2** backup disk in drive A.

Step 2:   Click **File**, **Back Up**.

Step 3:   Save to the backup filename: **[your name] Activity 2.2.QBB**. Specify location: **A:**.

Step 4: Click **Back Up** to backup Activity 2.2 to your backup floppy disk. Insert additional floppy disks when prompted if necessary. Close the company file. (From the File menu, select Close Company.)

You have now backed up the Activity 2.2 file to your floppy disk.

Activity 2.3: Web Quest

When setting up a chart of accounts for a business, it is often helpful to review the tax form that the business will use. Then accounts can be used to track information needed for the business tax return.

In this activity, you will download tax forms from the Internal Revenue Service web site.

Step 1: Select two of the following types of business organization in which you are most interested.

Type of Organization	Tax Form
Sole Proprietorship	Schedule C (Form 1040)
Partnership	Form 1165 & Form K-1
Corporation	Form 1120
S Corporation	Form 1120S

Step 2: Go to the Internal Revenue Service web page: www.irs.gov

Step 3: Download and print the tax forms for two types of organizations that you selected above.

Computer Accounting with QuickBooks 2002
Chapter 2 Printout Checklist
Name:_____ **Date:**_____

Instructions:
1. **Check off the printouts you have completed.**
2. **Staple this page to your printouts.**

☑	***Printout Checklist – Chapter 2***
☐	Chart of Accounts (Accounting Listing)
☐	To Do List
☑	***Printout Checklist – Activity 2.1***
☐	Task 3: Statement of Cash Flows
☐	Task 4: To Do List
☑	***Printout Checklist – Activity 2.2***
☐	Task 3: Revised Chart of Accounts (Account Listing)
☑	***Printout Checklist – Activity 2.3***
☐	Two tax return forms

3

Banking

Scenario

The next morning as you pass the open door of Mr. Castle's office, you notice he is looking at the financial statements you prepared. You try to slip past his door unnoticed, but you take only a few steps when you hear him curtly call your name.

You turn to see Mr. Castle charging toward you with documents in hand.

"I need you to keep an eye on the bank accounts. Cash is the lifeblood of a business. A business can't survive if it doesn't have enough cash flowing through its veins to pays its bills. So it's very important that someone keep an eye on the cash in our bank accounts—the cash inflows into the accounts and the cash outflows from the accounts. That is your job now."

Handing you more documents, Mr. Castle continues, *"We fell behind on our bank reconciliations. Here is last month's bank statement that needs to be reconciled."*

3

Learning Objectives

In Chapter 3, you will perform the following QuickBooks activities:

Introduction

To begin Chapter 3, start QuickBooks software and then restore your backup file.

Start QuickBooks software by clicking on the QuickBooks desktop icon or click **Start**, **Programs**, **QuickBooks Premier**, **QuickBooks Premier**.

Restore your Activity 2.2 backup file from your floppy disk to the C drive, renaming the file Chapter 3.

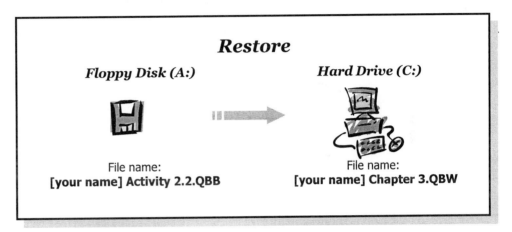

Restore

Floppy Disk (A:) ⟹ *Hard Drive (C:)*

File name:
[your name] Activity 2.2.QBB

File name:
[your name] Chapter 3.QBW

Step 1:   ⊞ Insert the **Chapter 2** backup disk into drive A.

Step 2:   Click **Restore a backup file** (or click **File, Restore**).

Step 3:   Identify the backup file:

- Filename: **[your name] Chapter 3.QBB**.
- Location: **A:**.

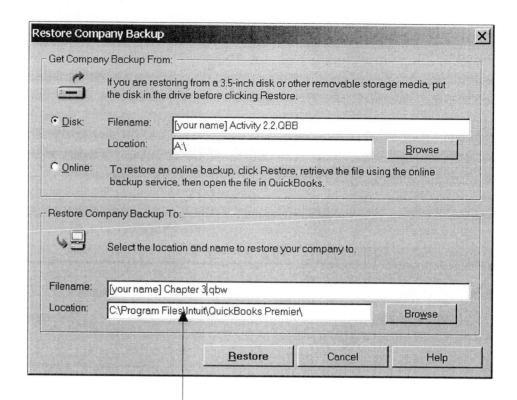

Step 4: Identify the restored file:

- Filename: **[your name] Chapter 3.QBW**.

- Location: **C:\Program Files\Intuit\QuickBooks Premier**.

Step 5: Click **Restore**. Your backup file will be restored to the C drive with a new filename, Chapter 3.QBW.

Step 6: Change the company name to:
[your name] Chapter 3 Rock Castle Construction.

(To change the company name, click Company (menu), Company Information.)

After restoring your backup file for Rock Castle Construction, click **Banking** in the *Navigators* window to open the Banking Navigator shown below.

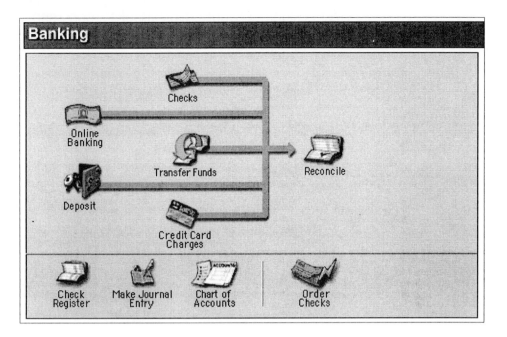

From the Banking Navigator, you can record:

* Deposits (cash flowing into the Checking account).
* Checks (cash going out of the Checking account).
* Transfers between bank accounts.
* Credit card transactions.
* Online banking.

A business should establish a *business* checking account completely separate from the owner's *personal* checking account. The company's checking account should be used *only* for business transactions, such as business insurance and mortgage payments for the company's office building. Owners should maintain a completely separate checking account for personal transactions, such as mortgage payments for the owner's home.

View and Print Check Register

The check register is a record of all transactions affecting the Checking account. QuickBooks' onscreen check register looks similar to a checkbook register used to manually record deposits and checks.

To view the QuickBooks check register:

Step 1: From the Banking Navigator, click the **Check Register** icon in the lower left.

Step 2: The following window will appear asking you to specify a bank account. Select **Checking**, then click **OK**.

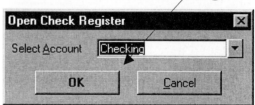

Step 3: The following *Check Register* window should appear on your screen. Notice there are separate columns for:

- ◆ Payments (checks)
- ◆ Deposits
- ◆ Balance of the checking account

> **Note:**
> Split indicates that a payment is split between two or more accounts.

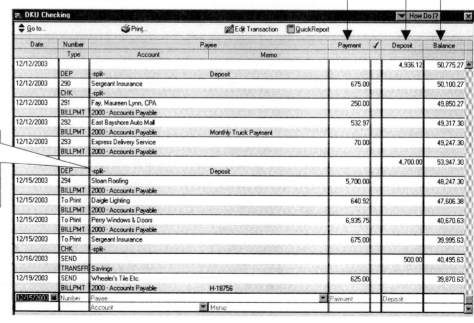

Date	Number	Payee		Payment	✓	Deposit	Balance
	Type	Account	Memo				
12/12/2003						4,936.12	50,775.27
	DEP	-split-	Deposit				
12/12/2003	290	Sergeant Insurance		675.00			50,100.27
	CHK	-split-					
12/12/2003	291	Fay, Maureen Lynn, CPA		250.00			49,850.27
	BILLPMT	2000 · Accounts Payable					
12/12/2003	292	East Bayshore Auto Mall		532.97			49,317.30
	BILLPMT	2000 · Accounts Payable	Monthly Truck Payment				
12/12/2003	293	Express Delivery Service		70.00			49,247.30
	BILLPMT	2000 · Accounts Payable					
						4,700.00	53,947.30
	DEP	-split-	Deposit				
12/15/2003	294	Sloan Roofing		5,700.00			48,247.30
	BILLPMT	2000 · Accounts Payable					
12/15/2003	To Print	Daigle Lighting		640.92			47,606.38
	BILLPMT	2000 · Accounts Payable					
12/15/2003	To Print	Perry Windows & Doors		6,935.75			40,670.63
	BILLPMT	2000 · Accounts Payable					
12/15/2003	To Print	Sergeant Insurance		675.00			39,995.63
	CHK	-split-					
12/16/2003	SEND					500.00	40,495.63
	TRANSFR	Savings					
12/19/2003	SEND	Wheeler's Tile Etc.		625.00			39,870.63
	BILLPMT	2000 · Accounts Payable	H-18756				
12/15/2003	Number	Payee		Payment		Deposit	
		Account	Memo				

If necessary, scroll down to locate the Sergeant Insurance entry.

Step 4: To view the source documents for the transaction with Sergeant Insurance, double-click on the **Sergeant Insurance** entry on 12-12-2003 in the check register.

Notice that the $675 payment is split between 3 different expense accounts.

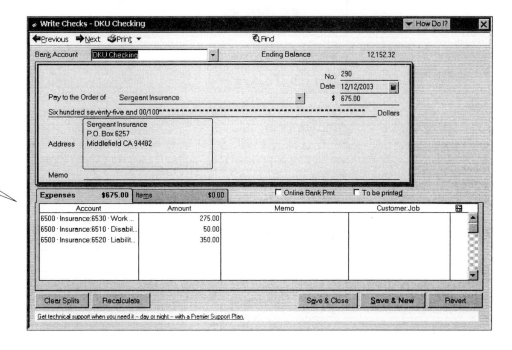

Step 5: Close the *Write Checks* window by clicking on the ⊠ in the upper right corner of the window.

To print the Check Register:

Step 1: Display the check register, then click **File** (menu), **Print Register**.

Step 2: Enter the Date Range: From: **01/01/2003** Through: **12/15/2003**. Click **OK**.

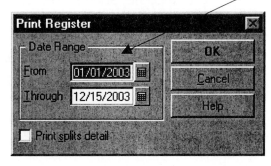

Step 3: Select the appropriate print options, then click **Print**.

✓ ***The check register printout for Rock Castle should list a deposit on 12/14/2003 for $4,700.00 and the Checking Account balance on 12/14/2003 is $5,035.32.***

Step 4: Close the *Check Register* window by clicking the ⊠ in the upper right corner of the *Check Register* window.

You can either record deposits and checks directly in the check register or use the *Make Deposits* window and the *Write Checks* window.

Make Deposits

Deposits are additions to the Checking account. Any cash coming into a business should be recorded as a deposit to one of the company's accounts.

QuickBooks classifies deposits into two types:

1. Payments from customers.

2. Nonsales receipts (deposits other than customer payments) such as:

  ◆ Cash received from loans.

  ◆ Investments from owners.

  ◆ Interest earned.

  ◆ Other income, such as rental income.

Payments from customers are entered using the Customer Navigator. For more information about recording payments from customers, see Chapter 4: Customers and Sales.

Deposits other than customer payments are recorded using the Banking Navigator.

Mr. Castle wants to invest an additional $3,000 in the business by depositing his $3,000 check in Rock Castle Construction's Checking account.

To record nonsales receipts (a deposit other than a customer payment):

Step 1: From the Banking Navigator, click the **Deposits** icon. The *Payments to Deposit* window will appear.

Payments to Deposit						How Do I?	✕

Select the payments you want to deposit, and then click OK.

✓	Date	Type	No.	Pmt Meth	Name	Amount
	12/15/2003	LIAB ADJ			Great Statewide Bank	124.00
	12/15/2003	PMT		Cash	Roche, Diarmuid:Gare	440.00
	04/11/2003	PMT	3402	Check	Fisher, Jennifer	5,164.00
	09/10/2003	PMT	5668	Check	Luke, Noelani:Kitchen	2,481.80
	09/23/2003	PMT	2957	Check	Dunn, Eric C.W.:Utility	2,400.00
	09/26/2003	PMT	1556	Check	Johnson, Gordon:Utilit	2,400.00
	10/30/2003	PMT	41022	Check	Memeo, Jeanette	16,537.54
	11/25/2003	PMT	15785	Check	Pretell Real Estate:15	5,435.00
	12/14/2003	PMT	986	Check	Jacobsen, Doug:Kitch	2,000.00

Buttons: OK, Cancel, Help, Select All, Select None

Step 2: QuickBooks uses a two-step process to record customer payments:
(1) Record the customer's payment received but not yet deposited (undeposited funds) and
(2) Record the deposit.

> If you wanted to deposit the above payments, you would select the payments to deposit and then click OK.

The payments listed above are undeposited funds that have been recorded as received but not yet deposited in the bank.

Since you will not deposit the payments shown above at this time, just click **OK**.

Step 3: When the following *Make Deposits* window appears, record Mr. Castle's $3,000 deposit as follows:

♦ Select Deposit To: **Checking.**

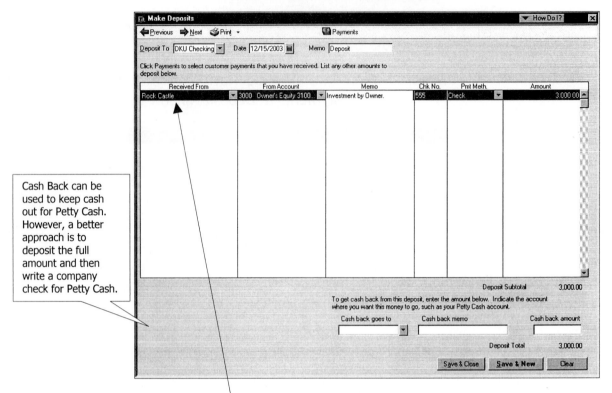

Cash Back can be used to keep cash out for Petty Cash. However, a better approach is to deposit the full amount and then write a company check for Petty Cash.

♦ Click in the Received From column, then type **Rock Castle**. Press the **Tab** key. When prompted, select **Quick Add** to add the name to the Name List.

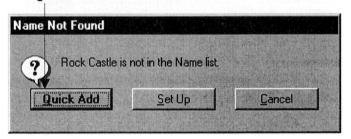

♦ Select Name Type: **Other**, then click **OK**.

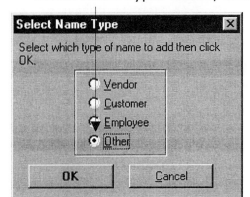

Select the account from the drop-down list or type 3100 and QuickBooks automatically completes the account title.

♦ Click in the *From Account* column. From the drop-down list of accounts, select **3100 Owner's Contribution Equity**. Press **Tab**.

♦ Enter Memo: **Investment by owner**.

♦ Enter Check No. **555** (the number of Mr. Castle's check).

♦ From the Payment Method drop-down list, select **Check**.

♦ Enter Amount: **3000**. (QuickBooks will automatically enter the comma in the amount.)

Step 4: Next, you will print a deposit summary. QuickBooks permits you to print a deposit slip (you must use a QuickBooks preprinted form) and a deposit summary.

To print a summary of the deposit you just recorded:

♦ Click the **Print** button at the top of the *Make Deposits* window.

♦ Select **Deposit summary only**. Then click **OK**.

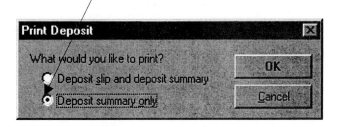

♦ Select the appropriate printer, then click **Print**. The deposit summary should list the $3,000 check from Mr. Castle.

Mr. Castle's $3,000 investment in the company has now been recorded as a deposit in Rock Castle Construction's Checking account.

To verify, print the Deposit Detail report:

Step 1: With the mouse pointer over the *Make Deposits* window, *right*-click to display a pop-up menu.

> **QuickZoom:** Drill down by double-clicking on a transaction to display the source document.

Step 2: Select **Deposit Detail**.

Step 3: When the following Deposit Detail report appears, select **This Month-to-date**.

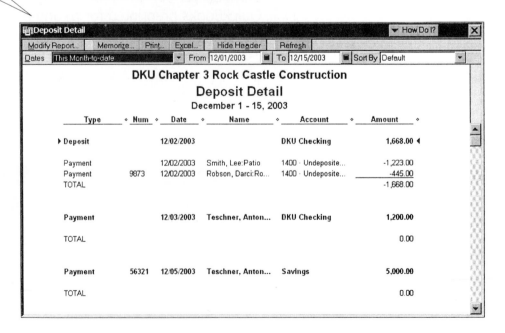

Step 4: Insert **your name** and **Chapter 3** in the report footer.

Step 5: Click **Print**. Select appropriate printer settings, then click **Print**.

Step 6: ✎ On the printout, circle the $3,000 deposit that you just recorded.

Step 7: Close the *Deposit Detail* window and then close the *Make Deposits* window by clicking **Save & Close**.

Write Checks

A business needs to track all cash paid out of the company's checking account. Examples of payments include purchases of inventory, office supplies, employee salaries, rent payments, insurance payments, and more.

Supporting documents (source documents) for payments include canceled checks, receipts, and paid invoices. These source documents provide proof that the transaction occurred; therefore, source documents should be kept on file for tax purposes.

QuickBooks provides two ways to pay bills:

One-step approach to bill paying:

❶ Record and pay the bill at the same time. When using this approach, the bill is paid when it is received.

Two-step approach to bill paying:

❶ Record the bill when it is received.

❷ Pay the bill later when it is due.

One-Step Approach to Bill Paying

> Covered in
> Chapter 3: Banking.

❶ *Pay Bills When Received:* Record bill and print check to pay

Write Checks window
(Banking Navigator)

> QuickBooks:
> 1. Reduces the Checking account (credit).
> 2. Records the Expense (debit).

Two-Step Approach to Bill Paying

> Covered in
> Chapter 5: Vendors.

❶ *Record Bill When Received:* Record bill to pay later.

Enter Bills window
(Vendor Navigator)

> QuickBooks records:
> 1. An Expense (debit).
> 2. An obligation (liability) to pay later (credit).

❷ *Pay Bills:* Select bills to pay, then print checks.

Pay Bills window
(Vendor Navigator)

> When the bill is paid and the obligation fulfilled, QuickBooks:
> 1. Reduces the liability account (debit).
> 2. Reduces cash (credit).

The *Write Checks* window (One-Step Approach) should **not** be used to pay:

1. Paychecks to pay employees' wages and salaries. (Use the Employee Navigator, *Pay Employees* window instead).

2. Payroll taxes and liabilities (Use the Employee Navigator, *Pay Liabilities* window instead).

3. Sales taxes (Use the Vendor Navigator, *Pay Sales Taxes* window).

4. Bills already entered in the *Enter Bills* window (Use the Vendor Navigator, *Pay Bills* window instead).

The *Write Checks* window (One-Step Approach) can be used to pay:

1. Expenses, such as rent, utilities, and insurance.

2. Non-inventory items, such as office supplies.

3. Services, such as accounting or legal services.

> You can also open the *Write Checks* window by clicking **Write Checks** on the Iconbar or the Shortcut List.

In this chapter, you will use the *Write Checks* window (One-Step Approach) to pay a computer repair service bill for Rock Castle Construction.

To use the *Write Checks* window to pay bills:

Step 1: Open the Banking Navigator if it is not already open by clicking **Banking** in the *Navigators* window.

Step 2: Click the **Checks** icon and the following onscreen check will appear.

QuickBooks automatically completes the address using address information from the Vendor list.

Write Checks – DKU Checking

▼ How Do I?   ✕

⬅Previous ➡Next 🖶Print ▼   🔍Find

Bank Account DKU Checking ▼   Ending Balance   15,152.32

No. To Print
Date 12/15/2003 🔲
Pay to the Order of Kershaw Computer Services ▼ $ 300.00

Three hundred and 00/100************************************** Dollars

Kershaw Computer Services
101 Main St
Bayshore CA 94326
Address

Memo

Expenses **$300.00** Items $0.00   ☐ Online Bank Pmt ☑ To be printed

Account	Amount	Memo	Customer:
7200 · Repairs:7220 · Com... ▼	300.00		

Clear Splits   Recalculate   Save & Close   Save & New

You won't have to worry about payroll taxes with QuickBooks Payroll Services.

Leave *To be printed* unchecked if you handwrite a check and just need to record the check in QuickBooks, but not print the check.

Step 3: Enter the check information:

♦ Select Bank Account: **Checking**.

♦ Select Date: **12/15/2003**.

Tip: If you use hand-written *and* computer-printed checks, to keep check numbers in sequence, set up 2 subaccounts for the Checking account:
1. Computer-printed checks subaccount.
2. Hand-written checks subaccount.

♦ For the *Pay to the Order of* field, select: **Kershaw Computer Services**. (Select Kershaw from the drop-down list or type the first few letters of the name.)

♦ Enter the check amount: **300**.

Tip: If you use more than one Checking account, change the Checking account color:
1. Edit menu.
2. Change Account Color.

♦ Click the checkbox preceding **To be printed** so that a check mark appears. This tells QuickBooks to both record and print the check. The Check No. field will now display: *To Print*. QuickBooks will automatically print the appropriate check number on the check.

Step 4: Next, record the payment in the correct account using the lower portion of the *Write Checks* window:

Use the Items tab to record an inventory item.

♦ Click the **Expenses** tab.

♦ Select Account: **7220 Repairs: Computer Repairs**. The $300 should automatically appear in the expense Amount column.

> Instead of printing one check at a time, you can record all your checks and then print them all at once:
> 1. **File**
> 2. **Print Forms**
> 3. **Checks**

- ◆ Notice that if the payment was related to a specific customer or job, you could enter that information now.

Step 5: Print the check:

- ◆ Click the **Print** button located at the top of the *Write Checks* window.

- ◆ Enter Check No.: **295**, then click **OK**.

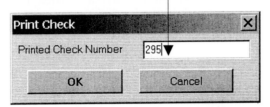

- ◆ If you are using the preprinted check forms, insert check forms in the printer now.

- ◆ Select Check Style: **Standard**.

- ◆ Select: **Print company name and address**.

- ◆ Select the appropriate printer.

- ◆ Click **Print**.

- ◆ Click **OK** if your check printed correctly. If not, enter the first incorrectly printed check.

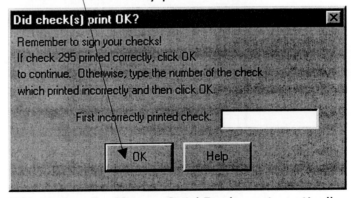

Step 6: Click **Save & Close**. QuickBooks automatically records the check in the Check Register.

Print Journal

QuickBooks uses two different ways to enter information:
1. Onscreen forms, such as the onscreen check you just completed.
2. An onscreen journal that uses debits and credits.

When you enter information into an onscreen form, QuickBooks automatically converts that information into a journal entry with debits and credits. If you will not be using the journal, you may skip this section.

To view the journal entry for the check that you just recorded:

Step 1: Click **Reports** in the *Navigators* window to open the *Report Finder* window.

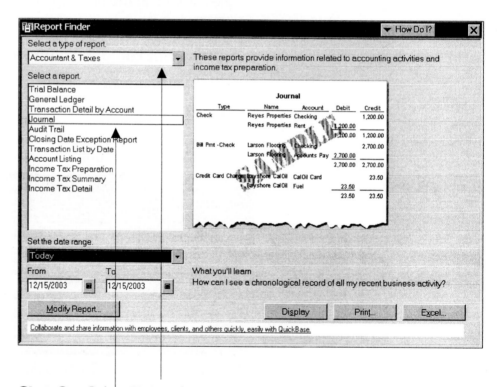

Step 2: Select Type of Report: **Accountant & Taxes**.

Step 3: Select Report: **Journal**.

Step 4: Set the Date Range: **Today**. From: **12/15/2003** To: **12/15/2003**.

Step 5: Click **Display** to display the journal report onscreen. Your *Journal* window should appear as shown below.

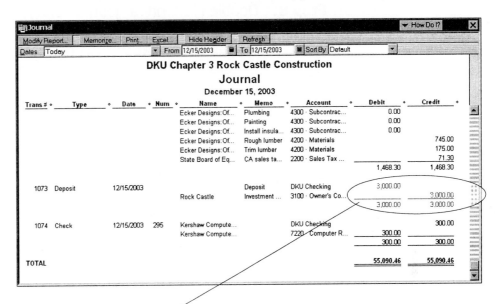

Step 6: The journal entry to record the deposit of Mr. Castle's $3,000 check includes a debit to the Checking account and a credit to Account 3100 Owner's Contributions.

Account	Account Type[a]	Debit/ Credit	Effect on Balance[b]
Checking	Asset	Debit	Increase
Owner's Contributions	Equity	Credit	Increase

[a]Listed below are the five different types of accounts.
[b]Listed below are the effects that debits and credits have on the different types of accounts.

Account Type[a]	Debit/ Credit	Effect on Balance[b]
Asset	Debit	Increase
Liability	Credit	Increase
Owner's Equity	Credit	Increase
Revenues (Income)	Credit	Increase
Expenses	Debit	Increase

Step 7: Notice the entry on 12/15/2003 to record the check written for computer repair services. This entry debits (increases) the Computer Repair Expense balance and credits (decreases) the Checking account balance.

Step 8: Double-click on a journal entry, to *drill down* to the related source document. If you double-click on the journal entry that records the computer repair, the *Write Checks* window appears, displaying the onscreen check that you just prepared. Close the *Write Checks* window.

Step 9: Enter **your name** and **Chapter 3** in the report footer. (Click Modify Report, Header/Footer.)

Step 10: Print the Journal report.

Step 11: ✐ Circle the journal entry on your printout that corresponds to the check written to Kershaw Computer Services.

Step 12: Close the *Journal* window and the *Report Finder* window.

Reconcile Bank Statements

Typically once a month, the bank sends a checking account bank statement to you. The bank statement lists each deposit and withdrawal from the account during the month.

A bank reconciliation is the process of comparing, or reconciling, the bank statement with your accounting records for the Checking account. The bank reconciliation has two objectives: (1) to detect errors and (2) to update your accounting records for unrecorded items listed on the bank statement (such as service charges).

Differences between the balance the bank reports on the bank statement and the balance the company shows in its accounting records usually arise for two reasons:

1. **Errors** (either the bank's errors or the company's errors) or

2. **Timing differences.** This occurs when the company records an amount before the bank does or the bank records an amount before the company does. For example, the company may record a deposit in its accounting records, but the bank does not record the deposit before the company's bank statement is prepared and mailed.

Timing differences include:

Items the bank has not recorded yet, such as:

*   **Deposits in transit:** deposits the company has recorded but the bank has not.

*   **Outstanding checks:** checks the company has written and recorded but the bank has not recorded yet.

Items the company has not recorded yet, such as:

*   **Unrecorded charges:** charges that the bank has recorded on the bank statement but the company has not recorded in its accounting records yet. Unrecorded charges include service charges, loan payments, automatic withdrawals, and ATM withdrawals.

*   **Interest earned on the account:** interest the bank has recorded as earned but the company has not recorded yet.

The following bank statement lists the deposits and checks for Rock Castle Construction according to the bank's records as of November 20, 2003.

BANK STATEMENT

Rock Castle Construction Company		11-20-03
1735 County Road		Checking
Bayshore, CA 94326		

Previous Balance	10-20-03	$24,457.79
+ Deposits	3	5,210.00
- Checks	6	6,958.90
- Service Charge		10.00
+ Interest Paid		0.00
Ending Balance	11-20-03	$22,698.89

Deposits

Date	Amount
11-05-03	5,000.00
11-20-03	210.00

Checks Paid

Date	No.	Amount
11-13-03	239	1,297.75
11-14-03	242	3,200.00
11-14-03	243	850.00
11-15-03	245	675.00
11-15-03	246	711.15
11-19-03	249	225.00

Thank you for banking with us!

To reconcile this bank statement with Rock Castle's QuickBooks records, complete the following steps:

Step 1: From the Banking Navigator, click the **Reconcile** icon to display the *Begin Reconciliation* window shown below.

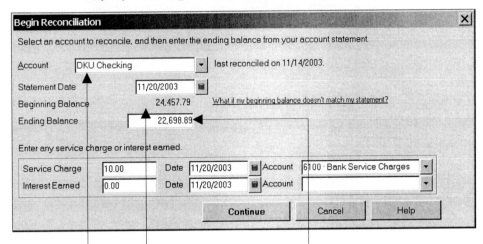

Step 2: Select *Account* to Reconcile: **Checking**.

Step 3: Compare the amount shown in the *Beginning Balance* field with the beginning (previous) balance of **$24457.79** on the bank statement.

Step 4: In the *Ending Balance* field, enter the ending balance shown on the bank statement: **$22,698.89**.

Step 5: In *Service Charge* field enter the bank's service charge: **$10.00**. Then change the date to **11/20/03** and select the Account: **Bank Service Charges**.

Step 6: Click **Continue**.

Scroll down to view more checks.

If you use Online Banking, click the **Matched** button to reconcile online transactions and mark online transactions as cleared.

Previous Reports prints a list of all uncleared checks and deposits as of the last bank statement.

Warning! After you click **Reconcile Now**, you cannot return to this Bank Reconciliation. If you plan to return later, click **Leave**. To change the status of a cleared item:
1. Display the Checking Register.
2. Click the Cleared Status (✓) column until the appropriate status (cleared or uncleared) appears.

Click on deposits and checks that have cleared the bank and are listed on the bank statement.

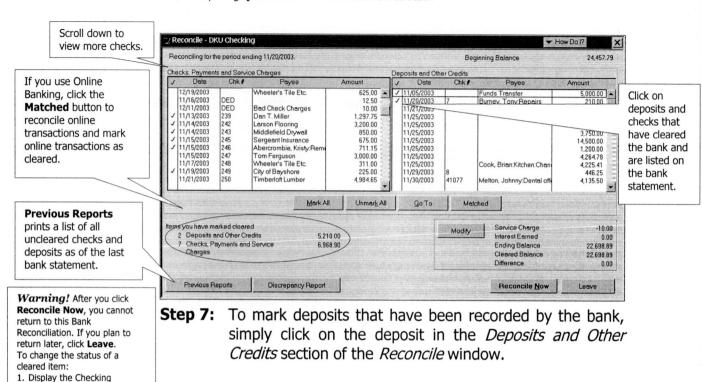

Step 7: To mark deposits that have been recorded by the bank, simply click on the deposit in the *Deposits and Other Credits* section of the *Reconcile* window.

Step 8: To mark checks and payments that have cleared the bank, simply click on the check in the *Checks and Payments* section of the *Reconcile* window.

Step 9: After marking all deposits and checks that appear on the bank statement, compare the Ending Balance and the Cleared Balance at the bottom of the *Reconcile* window. If the difference is $0.00, click **Reconcile Now**.

If there is a difference between the Ending balance and the Cleared balance, then you can try to locate the error or have QuickBooks make a balance adjustment.

Step 10: When the *Select Reconciliation Report* window appears, select type of Reconciliation Report: **Detail**. Click **Print**.

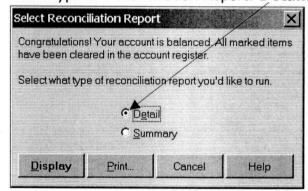

You have now completed the November bank reconciliation for Rock Castle Construction.

✔ Online Banking

QuickBooks offers an Online Banking feature so that you can conduct banking transactions online using the Internet. To use Online Banking with QuickBooks, you must complete the following steps to set up Online Banking:

Step 1: Obtain Internet access through an Internet Service Provider (ISP) or Local Area Network (LAN).

Step 2: Have an account with a financial institution that offers online banking services. (Note: Your financial institution may charge a fee for online banking services.)

To view a list of financial institutions providing online banking services, from the *Banking* menu select **Set Up Online Financial Services**, **Online Financial Institutions List**.

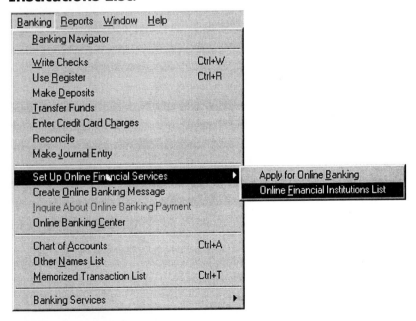

Step 3: Obtain a PIN/password from your financial institution for online banking.

Step 4: Enable accounts using QuickBooks Online Banking Setup Interview:

- From the *Banking* menu, select **Set Up Online Financial Services**, **Apply for Online Banking**.

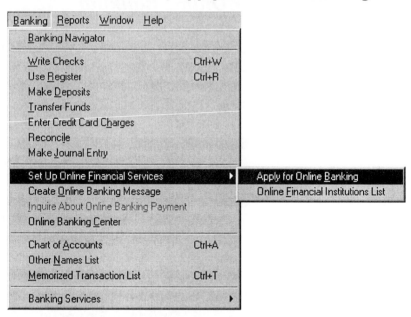

- Complete the Online Banking Setup Interview to set up your QuickBooks accounts. You will need to enter information from your financial institution.

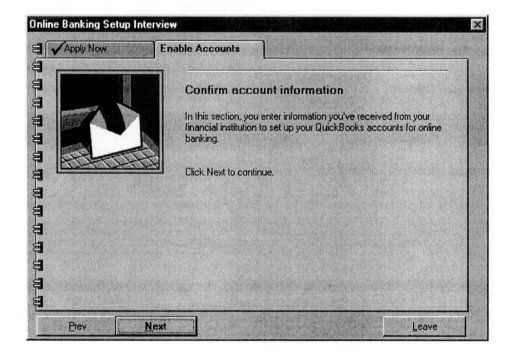

Step 5: Click **Leave** to close the Online Banking Setup Interview if you are not setting up your online account at this time.

✔ *View Online Account Balances*

After your QuickBooks account is set up for online banking, you can use two different online banking features:

1. Online account access: permits you to download transaction information about your account from your financial institution and view your online account balance.

2. Online payment: pay your bills online. Online payment services, such as those offered by Intuit, allow you to pay bills online for a fee.

If you have set up your QuickBooks accounts for online banking, to use the online account access feature:

Step 1: From the Banking Navigator, click the **Online Banking** icon to display the *Online Banking Center*.

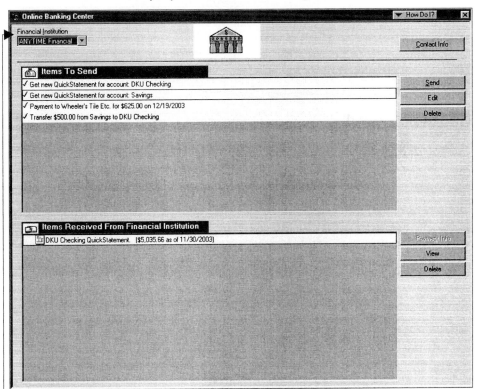

Step 2: Select Financial Institution: **ANYTIME Financial**.

Step 3: Click **Send** to download transactions that have occurred in your account since your last download. Your Checking QuickStatement should appear under *Items Received From Financial Institution*.

Step 4: Select your Checking QuickStatement, then click **View**, to view your online account balance.

✔ Reconcile Online Bank Accounts

To reconcile online bank accounts:

Step 1: With the *Match Transactions* window open from Step 4 above, select the **Show Register** checkbox.

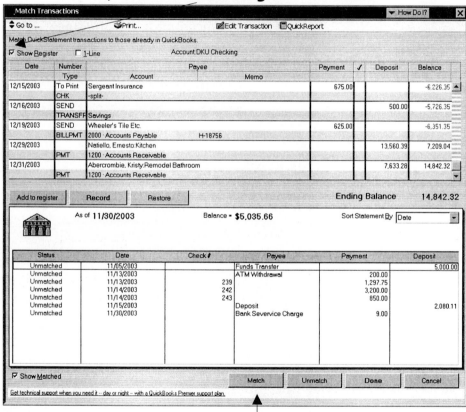

Step 2: Next, click **Match** to match downloaded transactions on the QuickStatement to transactions recorded in your QuickBooks accounts.

    ◆ Matched transactions: downloaded transactions that match transactions recorded in your QuickBooks accounts.

    ◆ Unmatched transactions: downloaded transactions that do not match your QuickBooks records. Unmatched transactions result when: (1) the transaction has not been entered in your QuickBooks records, or (2) the transaction has been entered in your QuickBooks records but the amount or check number does not match.

Step 3: Adjust your QuickBooks records to account for any unmatched transactions. Check for incorrect amounts or check numbers and make corrections as needed to your records. Enter any unmatched and unrecorded transactions in your QuickBooks records as follows:

    ◆ record unmatched transactions in your QuickBooks account register (Click the Record button on *the Match Transactions* window), or

    ◆ enter the unmatched transactions in the *Pay Bills* or *Make Deposits* windows.

Step 4: Reconcile your bank statement. When you receive your paper bank statement, reconcile your statement using the Banking *Reconcile* window. QuickBooks does not have the capability to do online bank reconciliation; therefore, you must reconcile using your paper bank statement. From the Banking *Reconcile* window, click the **Matched** button to mark matched online transactions from Step 2 as cleared.

Back Up Chapter 3

Back up your Chapter 3 file to your floppy disk. Use the file name: [your name] Chapter 3. For more information about backing up company files, see backup instructions in Chapter 1.

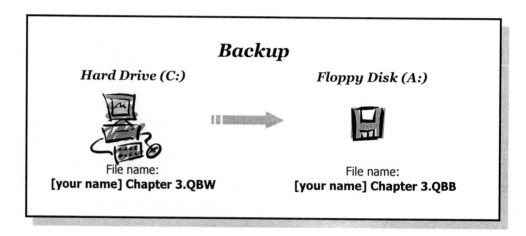

Backup

Hard Drive (C:)	Floppy Disk (A:)
File name:	File name:
[your name] Chapter 3.QBW	**[your name] Chapter 3.QBB**

Step 1: ⊞ Insert the **Chapter 3** backup disk in drive A.

Step 2: Click **File**, **Back Up**.

Step 3: Enter the file name: **[your name] Chapter 3**. Enter location: **A:**.

Step 4: Click **Back Up**.

You have now backed up the Chapter 3.QBW file to your Chapter 3 floppy disk.

If you are continuing your computer session, close the company file, then proceed to Activity 3.1.

If you are quitting your computer session now, (1) close the company file and (2) exit QuickBooks.

Assignments

Activity 3.1:
Make Deposit, Void Check, and Write Check

Scenario

As you glance up from your work, you notice Mr. Castle charging past your cubicle with more documents in hand. He tosses a hefty stack of papers into your creaking inbox. *"Here is another deposit to record. Also, Washuta called to say they did not receive the check we sent them. You will need to void that check—I believe it was check no. 263. I have already called the bank and stopped payment. Also, here are more bills to pay."*

Task 1: Restore Company File

Retrieve the Chapter 3 backup file from the A drive to the C drive, changing the file name to Activity 3.1. Changing the file name enables you to enter the information for this activity without overwriting the Chapter 3 file.

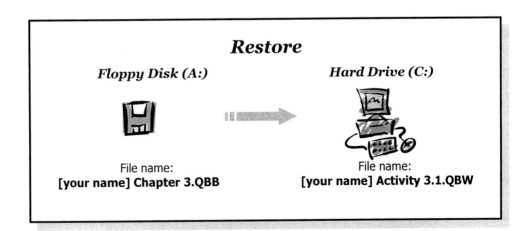

Restore

Floppy Disk (A:)

Hard Drive (C:)

File name:
[your name] Chapter 3.QBB

File name:
[your name] Activity 3.1.QBW

Step 1: 💾 Insert the **Chapter 3** backup disk into drive A.

Step 2: Click **Restore a backup file** (or click **File**, **Restore**).

Step 3: Identify the backup file:

    ◆ Filename: **[your name] Activity 3.1.QBB**.

    ◆ Location: **A:**.

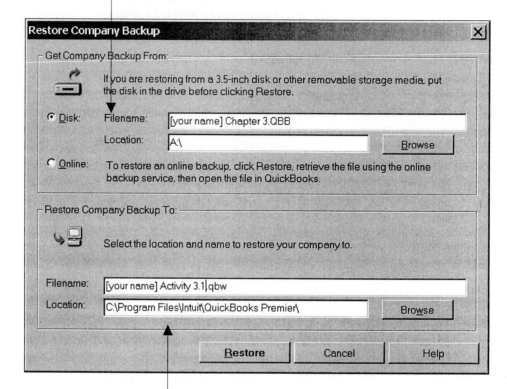

Step 4: Identify the restored file:

    ◆ Filename: **[your name] Activity 3.1.QBW**.

    ◆ Location: **C:\Program Files\Intuit\QuickBooks Premier**.

Step 5: Click **Restore.** On your C drive, you should now have a Chapter 3.QBW file and an Activity 3.1.QBW file. If prompted, enter your User ID and Password.

Step 6: Change the company name to: **[your name] Activity 3.1 Rock Castle Construction**. (To change the company name, select Company (menu), Company Information.)

Task 2: Make Deposit

Record the deposit for Mr. Castle's $1,000 check (No. 556). Record the deposit in Account 3100 Owner's Contributions with a deposit date of 12/15/2003. Print the deposit summary.

Task 3: Find Check

Find Check No. 263 made out to Washuta & Son in the QuickBooks Check Register by completing the following steps.

Step 1: View the Check Register. (Click Banking to open the Banking Navigator, then click the Check Register icon.)

Step 2: Next, search the Check Register for Check No. 263 using the Go To feature. Click the **Go To** button in the upper left corner of the *Check Register* window.

Step 3: In the *Go To* window:

- Select Which Field: **Number/Ref**.
- Enter Search For: **263**.

Step 4: Click the **Next** button. If asked if you want to search from the beginning, click **Yes**.

Step 5: Check No. 263 on 11/28/2003 to Washuta & Son Painting should appear in the *Check Register* window.

Step 6: Close the *Go To* window.

Step 7: To view Check No. 263, double-click on the Check Register entry for Washuta & Son Painting to drill down to the check. After viewing the check, close the *Check* window.

Task 4: Void Check

The next task is to void Check No. 263. There are two ways to remove a check amount from the check register:
(1) *Delete* the check: This removes all record of the transaction.
(2) *Void* the check: QuickBooks changes the amount deducted in the check register to zero, but the voided check still appears in the check register, thus leaving a record of the transaction. Should questions arise later about the transaction, a voided check provides a better record then a deleted check.

For Check No. 263, you want to maintain a record of the transaction; therefore, you want to void the check rather than delete it.

Void Check No. 263 by completing the following steps:

Step 1: Select Check No. 263 in the check register, then click **Edit *on the menu bar*. (*Note:* There is an Edit Transaction button in the *Checking* window and an Edit button on the menu bar. Use the *Edit button on the menu bar*.)

Step 2: Select **Void Bill Pmt - Check**. VOID should now appear next to Check No. 263 in the Check Register.

Step 3: Click the **Record** button in the lower right corner of the *Check Register* window.

Step 4: When asked if you are sure you want to record the voided check, click **Yes**.

Step 5: Print the Check Register for 11/28/2003. Verify that Check No. 263 has been voided and shows a check amount of $0.00.

Step 6: Close the *Check Register* window.

Task 5: Write Check

Write checks to pay the following bills, then print the checks in a batch (Click the down arrow by the **Print** button in the *Write Checks* window, then select **Print Batch**.)

Check No.	Select: To be printed
Date	12/15/2003
Vendor	Express Delivery Service
Amount	$45.00
Expense Account	6400 Freight & Delivery

Check No.	Select: To be printed
Date	12/15/2003
Vendor	Davis Business Associates
Amount	$200.00
Expense Account	6041 Advertising Expense

Task 6: Back Up Activity 3.1 File

Back up the Activity 3.1 file to a floppy disk.

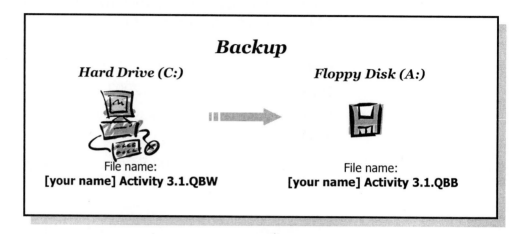

Step 1: 💾 Insert the **Chapter 3** backup disk in drive A.

Step 2: Click **File**, **Back Up**.

Step 3: Specify the backup file name: **[your name] Activity 3.1.QBB**. Specify location: **A:**.

Step 4: Click **Back Up** to backup Activity 3.1 to your backup floppy disk. Close the company file. (From the File menu, select Close Company.)

You should now have an Activity 3.1.QBB file on your floppy disk.

Activity 3.2: Bank Reconciliation

When you arrive at work the next morning, Rock Castle Construction's December bank statement is on your desk with the following note from Mr. Castle attached.

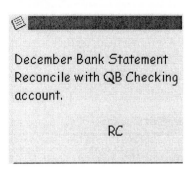

December Bank Statement
Reconcile with QB Checking
account.

RC

Task 1: Restore Company File

Retrieve the backup for Activity 3.1, restoring it to the hard drive and changing the file name to Activity 3.2.

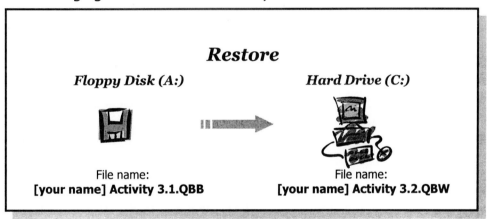

Step 1: 💾 Insert the **Chapter 3** backup disk into drive A.

Step 2: Click **Restore a backup file** (or click **File, Restore**).

Step 3: Identify the backup file:

  * Filename: **[your name] Activity 3.2.QBB**.

  * Location: **A:**.

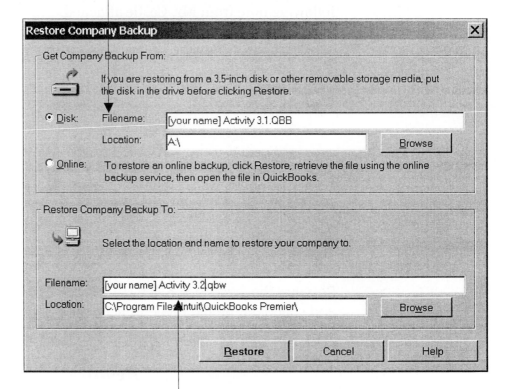

Step 4: Identify the restored file:

  * Filename: **[your name] Activity 3.2.QBW**.

  * Location: **C:\Program Files\Intuit\QuickBooks Premier**.

Step 5: Click **Restore.** Your backup file will be restored to the C drive. If prompted, enter your User ID and Password.

Step 6: Change the company name to:
[your name] Activity 3.2 Rock Castle Construction.
(To change the company name, select Company (menu), Company Information.)

Task 2: Reconcile Bank Statement

Reconcile Rock Castle's December bank statement that appears on the following page. *Reminder: Change the Service Charge Date to 12/20/2003.*

> ✓ **In the Reconcile window (lower left corner) "Items you have marked cleared" should agree with the December bank statement:**
>
> **13 Deposits**   **$81, 035.62**
> **16 Checks, Payments, and Service Charges**   **$64,405.42**

Task 3: Print Bank Reconciliation Report

Print a full reconciliation report.

BANK STATEMENT

Rock Castle Construction Company	12-20-03	Checking Account
Previous Balance	11-20-03	$22,698.89
+ Deposits	13	81,035.62
- Checks	15	64,395.42
- Service Charge	1	10.00
+ Interest Paid		0.00
Current Balance	12-20-03	$39,329.09

Deposits

Date	Amount
11-21-03	5,912.93
11-25-03	4,732.75
11-25-03	10,000.00
11-25-03	3,750.00
11-25-03	14,500.00
11-25-03	1,200.00
11-25-03	4,264.78
11-25-03	4,225.41
11-29-03	446.25
11-30-03	4,135.50
12-02-03	1,668.00
12-03-03	1,200.00
12-05-03	25,000.00

Checks Paid

Date	No.	Amount
11-15-03	247	3,000.00
11-17-03	248	311.00
11-21-03	250	4,984.65
11-25-03	251	37.85
11-25-03	252	97.53
11-25-03	253	72.18
11-25-03	Transfer	42,300.00
11-27-03	256	1,297.76
11-28-03	257	300.00
11-28-03	258	500.00
11-28-03	259	600.00
11-28-03	260	800.00
11-28-03	261	6,790.00
11-28-03	262	2,000.00
11-30-03	264	1,304.45

Thank you for banking with us!

Task 4: Back Up Activity 3.2 File

Back up the Activity 3.2 file to a floppy disk.

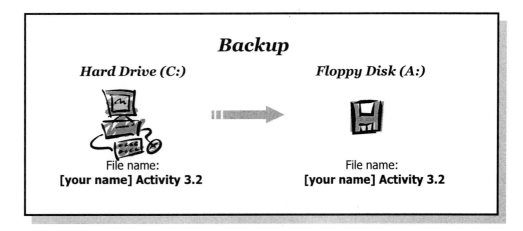

Step 1:   Insert the **Chapter 3** backup disk in drive A.

Step 2:   Click **File, Back Up**.

Step 3:   Specify the backup file name: **[your name] Activity 3.2**. Specify location: **A:**.

Step 4:   Click **Back Up** to backup Activity 3.2 to your backup floppy disk. Close the company file. (From the File menu, select Close Company.)

You have now backed up Activity 3.2 file to your floppy disk.

Activity 3.3: Web Quest

Various preprinted check forms and deposit slips are available from Intuit. These preprinted forms can be used with your printer to create checks and deposit slips.

The Web information listed is subject to change.

Step 1: Go to the www.intuitmarketplace.com.

Step 2: Locate and print information about preprinted checks and deposits slips.

Step 3: 📧 Prepare a short e-mail to Mr. Castle recommending which check forms and deposit slips Rock Castle Construction should purchase for use with QuickBooks.

Computer Accounting with QuickBooks 2002
Chapter 3 Printout Checklist
Name: _____ Date:_____

Instructions:
1. **Check off the printouts you have completed.**
2. **Staple this page to your printouts.**

☑	*Printout Checklist – Chapter 3*
☐	Check Register
☐	Deposit Summary
☐	Deposit Detail
☐	Check
☐	Journal
☐	Bank Reconciliation Report
☑	*Printout Checklist – Activity 3.1*
☐	Task 2: Deposit Summary
☐	Task 4: Check Register
☐	Task 5: Checks
☑	*Printout Checklist – Activity 3.2*
☐	Task 3: Bank Reconciliation Report
☑	*Printout Checklist – Activity 3.3*
☐	QuickBooks Preprinted Forms Printouts

Notes:

4 Customers and Sales

Scenario

Just as you are finishing the last bank reconciliation, Mr. Castle reappears. He always seems to know just when you are about to finish a task.

"While cash flow is crucial to our survival," he says, *"we also need to keep an eye on profits. We are in the business of selling products and services to our customers. We have to be certain that we charge customers enough to cover our costs and make a profit."*

Mr. Castle pulls out a pen and begins scribbling on a sheet of paper on your desk:

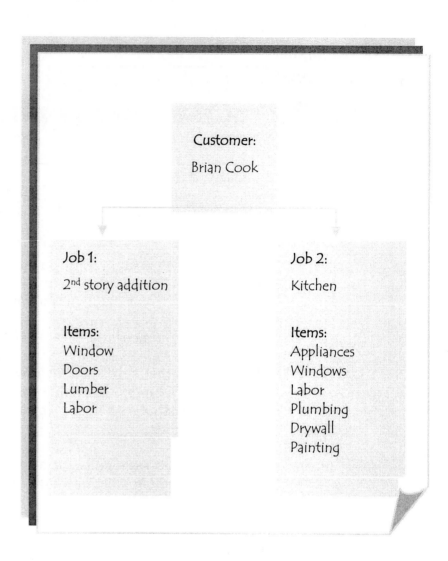

Customer:

Brian Cook

Job 1:

2nd story addition

Items:
Window
Doors
Lumber
Labor

Job 2:

Kitchen

Items:
Appliances
Windows
Labor
Plumbing
Drywall
Painting

"We track the costs of each job we work on. A job is a project for a specific customer. For example, we are working on two jobs for Brian Cook: Job 1 is a 2nd story addition and Job 2 is remodeling his kitchen."

"In QuickBooks we use items to track the products and services we use on each project. On the 2nd Story Addition job we used four different items."

Pushing a stack of papers toward you, Mr. Castle says, *"Here are some customer transactions that need to be recorded in QuickBooks."*

Learning Objectives

In Chapter 4, you will learn the following QuickBooks features:

Introduction

To begin Chapter 4, first start QuickBooks software and then restore your backup file.

Start QuickBooks software by clicking on the QuickBooks desktop icon or click **Start**, **Programs**, **QuickBooks Premier**, **QuickBooks Premier**.

Restore your Activity 3.2 backup from your floppy disk to the C: drive, renaming the file Chapter 4.QBW.

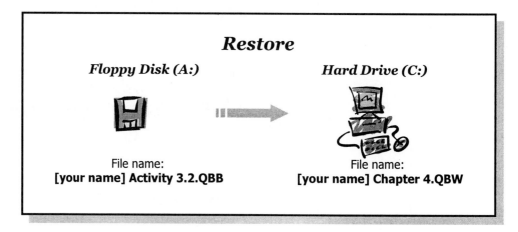

Step 1:   🖫 Insert the **Chapter 3** backup disk into drive A.

Step 2:   Click **Restore a backup file** (or click **File, Restore**).

Step 3:   Identify the backup file:

  ♦ Filename: **[your name] Chapter 4.QBB**.

  ♦ Location: **A:**.

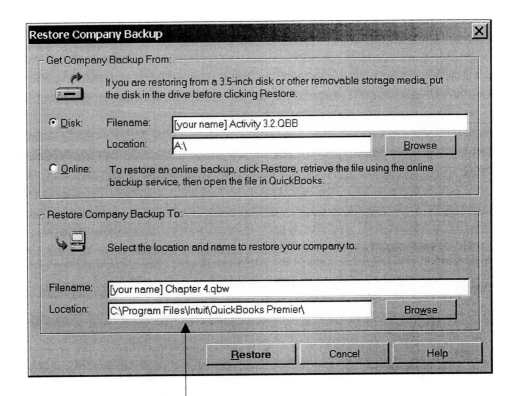

Step 4: Identify the restored file:

- Filename: **[your name] Chapter 4.QBW**.

- Location: **C:\Program Files\Intuit\QuickBooks Premier**.

Step 5: Click **Restore**. Your file will be restored to the C drive with a new filename, Chapter 4.QBW.

Step 6: Change the company name to: **[your name] Chapter 4 Rock Castle Construction**.

(To change the company name, click Company (menu), Company Information.)

After restoring your backup file for Rock Castle Construction, click **Customers** in the *Navigators* window to open the Customers Navigator shown below.

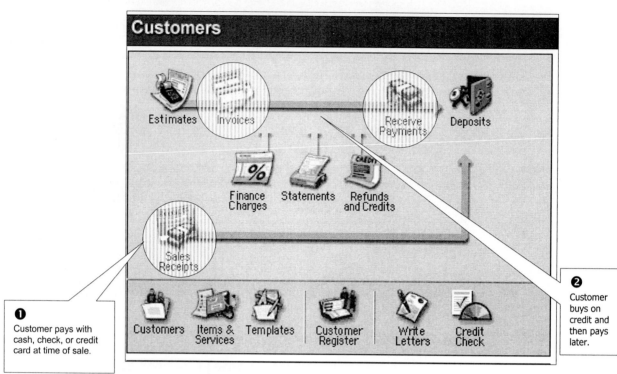

❶ Customer pays with cash, check, or credit card at time of sale.

❷ Customer buys on credit and then pays later.

The Customer Navigator is a flowchart of customer transactions. As the flowchart indicates, Rock Castle Construction can record a customer sale in two different ways:

❶ Sales Receipts: Customer pays when Rock Castle Construction provides the good or service to the customer. The customer pays with cash, check, or credit card at the time of sale. The sale is recorded on a Sales Receipt.

❷ Invoice/Receive Payment: The sale is recorded on an Invoice when the good or service is provided to the customer. The customer promises to pay later. These customer promises are called accounts receivable—amounts that Rock Castle Construction expects to *receive* in the future. The customer may pay its account with cash, check, credit card or online payment.

Other QuickBooks features available from the *Customers Navigator* window include:

* **Finance Charges**: Add finance charges to customer bills whenever bills are not paid by the due date.

* **Refunds and Credits**: Record refunds and credits for returned or damaged merchandise.

* **Statements**: Prepare billing statements to send to customers.

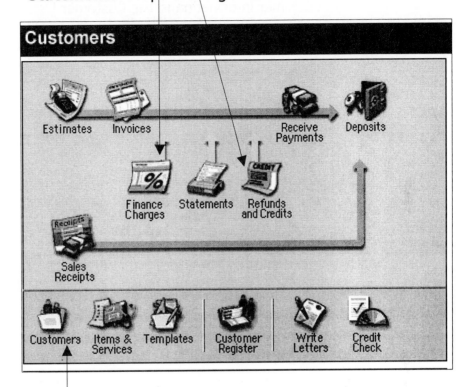

The lower section of the *Customers Navigator* window includes:

Customer List: The Customer List contains customer information, such as address and payment terms.

Items and Services: The Items List summarizes all goods and services that Rock Castle Construction sells to customers, such as Repair Labor, Lumber, Windows, and Doors.

Customer Register: The Customer Register tracks customer charges, payments, and customer account balances. The accounts receivable (A/R) balance is the amount Rock Castle Construction expects to *receive* from the customer in the future.

Write Letters: Prepare business letters to customers including collection letters to customers with overdue balances.

Credit Check: Check a customer's credit rating online with QuickBooks Credit Check Services using credit reports from Dun & Bradstreet or verify a commercial customer's address.

The first step in working with customer transactions is to enter customer information in the Customer List.

Customer List

The Customer List contains customer information such as address, telephone number, and credit terms. Once customer information is entered in the Customer List, QuickBooks automatically transfers the customer information to the appropriate forms, such as Sales Invoices and Sales Returns. This feature enables you to enter customer information only once instead of entering the customer information each time a form is prepared.

The Customer List in QuickBooks also tracks projects (jobs) for each customer. For example, Rock Castle Construction is working on two projects for Brian Cook:

Job 1: 2nd Story Addition

Job 2: Kitchen

View Customer List

To view the Customer List for Rock Castle Construction:

Step 1: Click the **Customers** icon in the lower left the *Customers Navigator* window. (Or click Customers on the Iconbar or the Shortcut List.)

Step 2: The following *Customer: Job List* window appears listing customers and jobs. Notice the two jobs listed for Brian Cook: (1) 2nd story addition and (2) Kitchen.

The *Customer: Job List* window displays:

- ◆ The balance for each job.

- ◆ The job status (not awarded, pending, in progress, or closed).

- ◆ The estimate total (if an estimate for the job was prepared).

- ◆ Notes about the job. (The Notepad icon appears if notes are entered.)

Step 3: To view additional information about a customer or job, double-click the item.

Name	Balance	Notes	Job Status	Estimate Total
◆2nd story addition	0.00		Closed	13,136.67
◆Bristol, Sonya	0.00			
◆Utility Shed	0.00			
◆Repairs	0.00		Closed	
◆Burch, Jason	1,005.00			
◆Room Addition	1,005.00		Closed	
◆Burney, Tony	0.00			
◆Repairs	0.00		Closed	
◆Cook, Brian	7,812.63	▨		35,594.54
◆2nd story addition	5,003.30		In progress	22,427.44
◆Kitchen	2,809.33		In progress	13,167.10
◆Change Order #1	0.00		Closed	4,225.41
◆Craven, Pam	0.00			602.40
◆Duct Work	0.00		Closed	602.40
◆Cuddihy, Matthew	0.00			
◆Utility Room	0.00		Closed	
◆Duncan, Dave	0.00			
◆Utility Shed	0.00			
◆Dunn, Eric C.W.	0.00			
◆Utility Shed	0.00			

Customer:Job ▼ Activities ▼ Reports ▼ ☐ Show All

Step 4: Activities that can be accessed from the Customers Navigator can also be accessed from the *Customer: Job List* window by clicking the **Activities** button.

Step 5: Customer reports can be accessed by clicking the **Reports** button in the *Customer: Job List* window.

Step 6: To make changes to the Customer List, use the **Customer: Job** button.

> *Tip:* You can import customer information using files with .iif extensions (Intuit Interchange File). See QuickBooks Help for more information.

Add New Customer

Rock Castle Construction needs to add a new customer, Tom Whalen, to the Customer List.

To add a new customer to the Customer List:

Step 1: Click the **Customer: Job** button near the bottom of the *Customer: Job List* window.

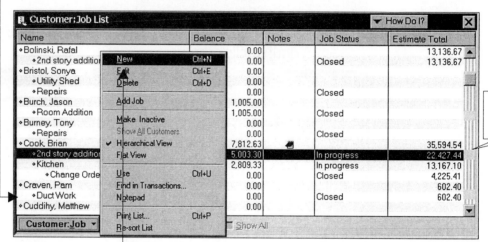

Right-click to open a pop-up menu.

Step 2: Click **New** on the drop-down menu.

Step 3: A blank *New Customer* window should appear. Enter the information shown below in the *New Customer | Address Info* window.

Customer	Whalen, Tom
First Name	Tom
M.I.	M
Last Name	Whalen
Contact	Tom
Phone	415-555-1234
Alt. Ph.	415-555-5678
Addresses Bill To:	Tom M. Whalen 100 Sunset Drive Bayshore, CA 94326

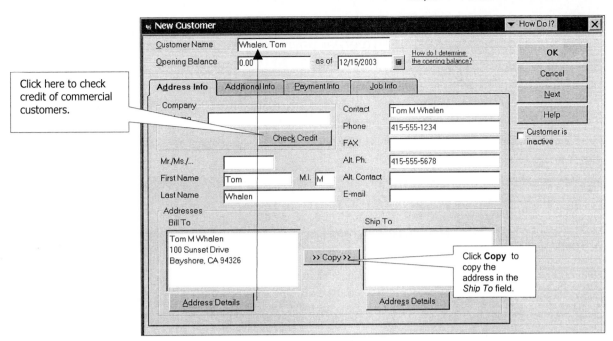

Click here to check credit of commercial customers.

Step 4: Click the **Additional Info** tab to display another customer information window. Enter the information shown below into the *Additional Info* fields.

Type	Residential
Terms	Net 30
Tax Item	San Tomas
Tax Code	Tax

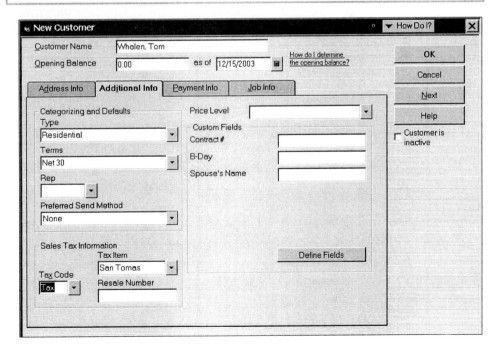

Step 5: To enter payment information for the customer, click the **Payment Info** tab.

Step 6: Enter the following information in the *Payment Info* fields:

Account	7890
Credit Limit	50,000
Preferred Payment	Check

Step 7: Click **OK** to add the new customer to Rock Castle Construction's Customer List.

Edit Customer Information

Enter the e-mail address for Tom Whalen by editing the customer information as follows:

Step 1: Select the customer or job in the *Customer:Job List* window.

Step 2: Display the *Edit Customer* window. Click the **Customer: Job** button near the bottom of the *Customer: Job List* window. (Or you can right-click to display the pop-up menu.) Then click **Edit** to display the *Edit Customer* window.

Step 3: Enter the new information or revise the current customer or job information as needed. In this instance, click the **Address Info** tab. Then enter the e-mail address: **twhalen@www.com**.

Step 4: Click **OK** to record the new information and close the *Edit Customer* window.

Add A Job

To add the Screen Porch Job for Tom Whalen, complete the following steps:

Step 1: Click on the customer, **Tom Whalen**, in the *Customer: Job List* window.

Step 2: Click the **Customer: Job** button in the bottom left corner of the *Customer: Job List* window. Then select **Add Job** from the menu.

Step 3: Enter the Job Name: **Screen Porch**. Then enter the Beginning Balance: **0.00**.

Step 4: Click the **Job Info** tab.

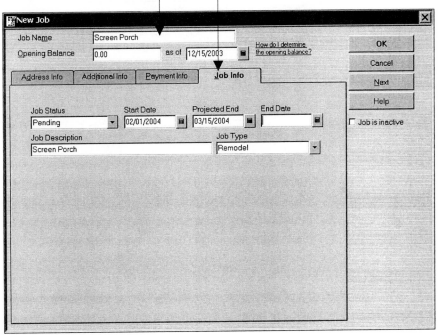

Step 5: Enter the following information in the *Job Info* fields:

Job Status	Pending
Start Date	02/01/2004
Projected End	03/15/2004
Job Description	Screen Porch
Job Type	Remodel

Tom Whalen told Rock Castle Construction that he would hire them to do the screen porch job on one condition—he needed Rock Castle Construction as soon as possible to replace a damaged exterior door that will not close.

To add the Exterior Door job:

Step 1: From the Screen Porch job window, click **Next** to add another job.

Step 2: In the Job Name field at the top of the *New Job* window, enter: **Exterior Door**. Enter Opening Balance: **0.00**.

Step 3: Click the **Job Info** tab, then enter the following information in the *New Job* window:

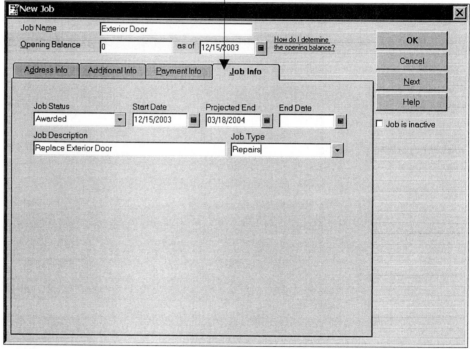

Job Name	Exterior Door
Job Status	Awarded
Start Date	12/15/2003
Projected End	12/18/2003
Job Description	Replace Exterior Door
Job Type	Repairs

Step 4: Click **OK** to record the new job and close the *New Job* window.

Step 5: Rock Castle Construction's Customer List should now list two jobs for Tom Whalen: Screen Porch and Exterior Door. Close the *Customer: Job List* window.

Recording Sales in QuickBooks

How you record a sale in QuickBooks depends upon how the customer pays for the goods or services.

There are three possible ways for a customer to pay for goods and services:

- Cash sale: Customer pays cash (or check) at the time of sale.

- Credit sale: Customer promises to pay later.

- Credit card sale: Customer pays using a credit card.

The diagram on the next page summarizes how to record sales transactions in QuickBooks. This chapter will cover how to record cash sales and credit sales and Chapter 12 covers credit card sales.

Cash Sales

❶ **Cash Sales:** Record sale and cash collected from customer.

❷ **Deposit:** Deposit cash in your bank account.

Credit Sales

❶ **Invoices**: Prepare customer invoices with charges for products and services provided to customers.

❷ **Receive Payments:** Record payments received from customers (undeposited funds).

❸ **Deposit:** Record deposit in bank account.

Cash Sales

When a customer pays for goods or services at the time the good or service is provided, it is typically called a cash sale.

Recording a cash sale in QuickBooks requires two steps:

❶ Create a sales receipt to record the cash sale.

❷ Record the bank deposit.

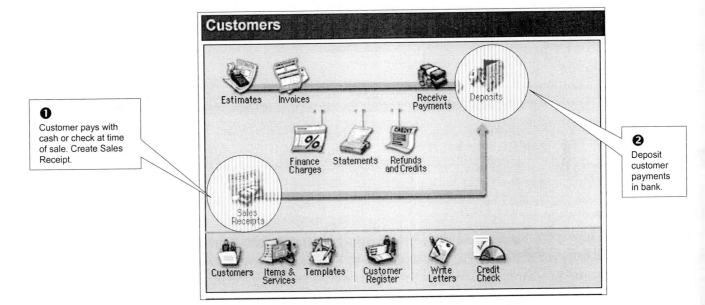

❶ Customer pays with cash or check at time of sale. Create Sales Receipt.

❷ Deposit customer payments in bank.

One of Rock Castle Construction's customers, Ernesto Natiello, wants to purchase an extra set of cabinet pulls that match the cabinets that Rock Castle Construction installed. Ernesto pays $10 in cash for the extra cabinet pulls.

To record the cash sale in QuickBooks:

Step 1: From the Customer Navigator, click **Sales Receipts** to display the *Enter Sales Receipts* window.

Step 2: Enter the following information in the *Enter Sales Receipts* window:

- Enter Customer name: **Natiello, Ernesto**.
- Select Date: **12/15/2003**.

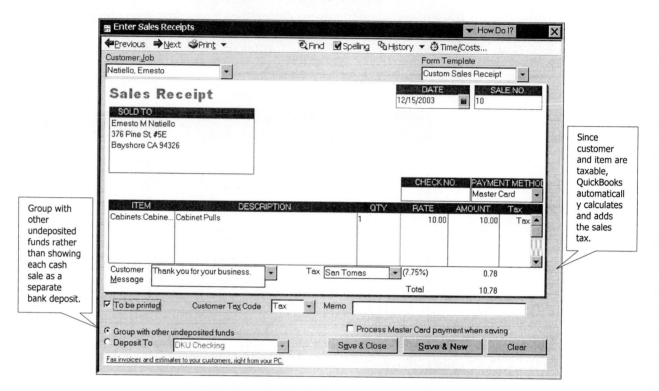

- Select Payment Method: **Cash**.
- Select Item: **Cabinet Pulls**.
- Select Quantity: **1**.
- Enter Rate: **10.00**.
- Select Customer Message: **Thank you for your business**.
- Select **To be printed** checkbox.
- Select **Group with other undeposited funds**.

Step 3: To print the Sales Receipt:

- Click the **Print** button at top of window.

- Select Print on: **Blank paper**.

- Select: **Print lines around each field**.

- Click **Print**.

Step 4: Click **Save & Close** to record the cash sale and close the *Enter Sales Receipts* window.

QuickBooks will record the $10.78 as undeposited funds. Later, you will record this as a bank deposit to Rock Castle's Checking Account.

Credit Sales

Credit sales occur when Rock Castle Construction provides goods and services to customers and in exchange receives a promise that the customers will pay later. This promise to pay is called an Account Receivable because Rock Castle expects to *receive* the account balance in the future.

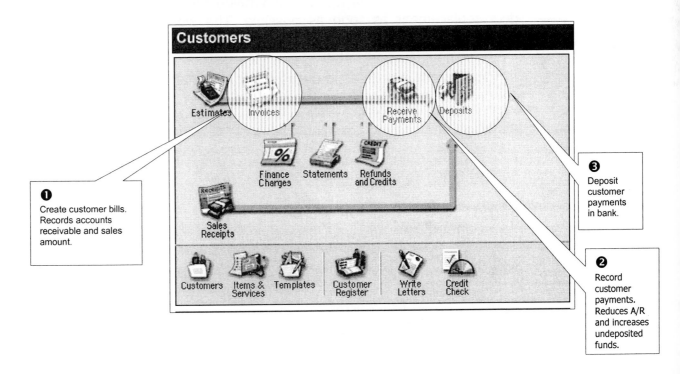

❶ Create customer bills. Records accounts receivable and sales amount.

❸ Deposit customer payments in bank.

❷ Record customer payments. Reduces A/R and increases undeposited funds.

Recording a credit sale in QuickBooks requires three steps:

❶ Create an Invoice to record the product or service provided to the customer and to bill the customer.

❷ Receive payment from the customer.

❸ Deposit the payment in the bank.

> A **Progress Invoice** is used if the customer is billed as the work progresses rather than when the work is fully completed.

Credit Sales: Create Invoices

An Invoice is used to record sales on credit when the customer will pay later. An Invoice is a bill that contains detailed information about the items (products and services) provided to a customer.

> For more information about time tracking, see Chapter 6.

If QuickBooks' time tracking feature (tracking time worked on each job) is *not* used, then time worked on a job is entered directly on the Invoice. In this chapter, assume that time tracking is not used and that time worked on a job is entered on the Invoice form.

Next, you will create an Invoice for Rock Castle Construction. Rock Castle sent a workman to the Whalen Residence immediately after receiving the phone call from Tom Whalen requesting an exterior door replacement as soon as possible. The workman spent one hour at the site the first day.

> Click the **Estimates** icon on the Customers Navigator to create a customer estimate using QuickBooks.

In this instance, Rock Castle Construction was not asked to provide an estimate before starting the work. Charges for products and labor used on the Whalen door replacement job will be recorded on an Invoice.

To create an Invoice to record charges:

Step 1: Click the **Invoices** icon on the Customers Navigator to display the *Create Invoices* window.

> Invoice templates can be customized.

Step 2: Select the invoice template: **Custom Invoice**.

Step 3: Enter the Customer:Job by selecting **Whalen, Tom: Exterior Door** from the drop-down Customer: Job list.

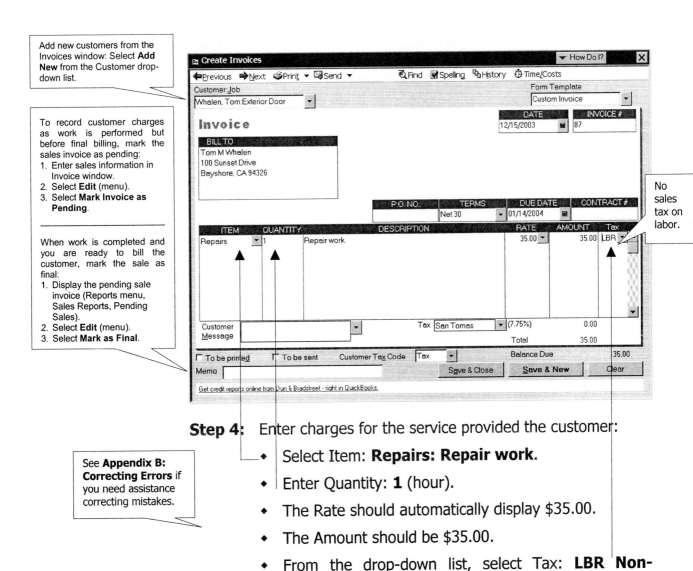

Add new customers from the Invoices window: Select **Add New** from the Customer drop-down list.

To record customer charges as work is performed but before final billing, mark the sales invoice as pending:
1. Enter sales information in Invoice window.
2. Select **Edit** (menu).
3. Select **Mark Invoice as Pending**.

When work is completed and you are ready to bill the customer, mark the sale as final:
1. Display the pending sale invoice (Reports menu, Sales Reports, Pending Sales).
2. Select **Edit** (menu).
3. Select **Mark as Final**.

No sales tax on labor.

See **Appendix B: Correcting Errors** if you need assistance correcting mistakes.

Step 4: Enter charges for the service provided the customer:

◆ Select Item: **Repairs: Repair work**.

◆ Enter Quantity: **1** (hour).

◆ The Rate should automatically display $35.00.

◆ The Amount should be $35.00.

◆ From the drop-down list, select Tax: **LBR Non-Taxable Labor**.

Step 5: You will wait until the job is complete to print the Invoice. If you wanted to enter another Invoice, you would click Next. Instead, click **Save & Close** to close the *Invoice* window.

The next day, December 16, 2003, Rock Castle Construction finished installing a new exterior door at the Whalen residence. The following products and services were used:

Exterior wood door	1 @ $120	Taxable Sales
Repair Labor	4 hours	Non-Taxable Labor

Step 1: Record the above items on Invoice No. 87 for the Whalen Exterior Door job.

(To display the invoice for the Exterior Door Repair job again, click on the **Invoices** icon. When the blank *Invoice* window appears, click the **Prev** button, and Invoice No. 87 for the Exterior Door Repair job will reappear. Or use the Edit, Find command.)

Step 2: With Invoice No. 87 displayed, print the invoice as follows:

+ Select **Print**.

+ Select Print on: **Blank paper**.

+ Select: **Print lines around each field**.

+ Click **Print**.

Step 3: Click **Save & Close** to close the *Invoice* window. When asked if you want to record your changes, select **Yes**.

✓ *The invoice total is $304.30. Notice that the Exterior Door is a taxable item and QuickBooks automatically calculates and adds sales tax of $9.30 for the door.*

QuickBooks will record the sale and record an account receivable for the amount to be received from the customer in the future.

Online Billing

QuickBooks has the capability to E-mail and fax invoices to customers. Customer E-mail and fax numbers are filled in automatically from the Customer List information. You can E-mail or fax single invoices or send a batch of invoices.

To email Invoice No. 87 which you just prepared:

Step 1: Open Invoice No. 87 on your screen. (Click the **Invoices** icon, then click **Previous**.)

Step 2: Click the **arrow** beside the **Send** button at the top of the *Invoices* window.

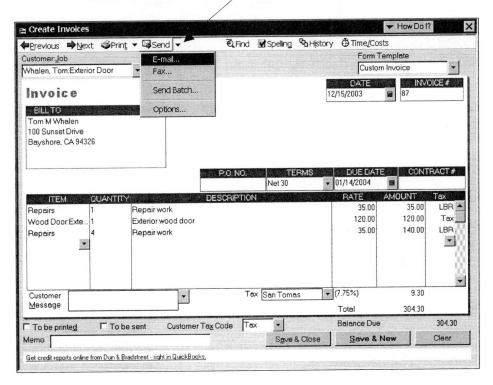

Step 3: Select **E-mail**.

Step 4: When the following *Edit E-mail Information* appears, notice that both Rock Castle Construction's E-mail address and the customer's E-mail address are automatically completed from the E-mail information contained in the Customer List.

> Click **Tell Me More** to learn more about Online Billing.

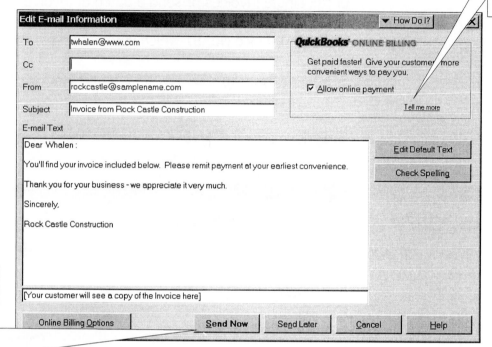

> Click **Send Now** to E-mail the individual invoice or click **Send Later** to send the invoice in a batch with other invoices later.

Step 5: Modify the E-mail text to read: **Dear Mr. Whalen:**.

Step 6: Click **Send Later** to send the E-mail later in a batch. Complete the spell check of the E-mail. Then click **Save & Close** to close the *Invoice* window.

After additional invoices are prepared, a batch of invoices can be sent at the same time using E-mail (Click Send, Send Batch.)

If you sign up for Online Bill Paying services, after receiving your E-mail invoices, customers can pay you online as well.

To learn more about online billing:

Step 1: From the *Navigators* window click **Business Services**. At the bottom of the Business Services Navigator, click **Featured Service Online Billing Click here to find out more**.

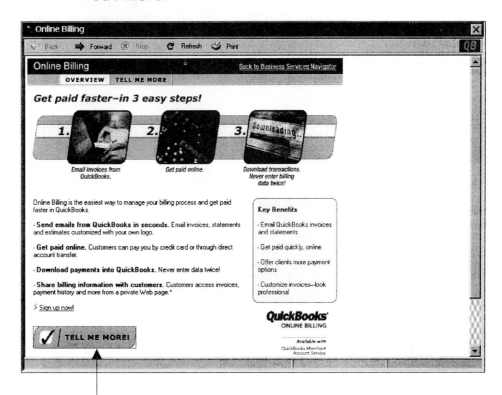

Step 2: To learn more about receiving payments online, click **Tell Me More**.

Step 3: Read the information about receiving online payments.

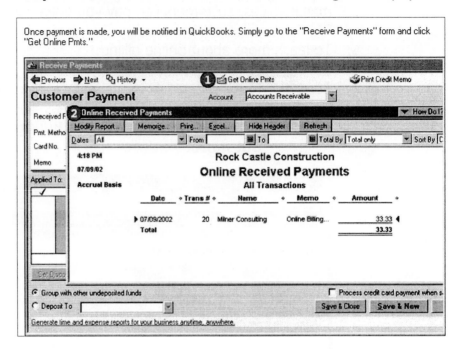

Step 4: In order to receive customer payments online, you must use either a Merchant Account or PayPal. To learn more about these options, read the Business Services information on the following page.

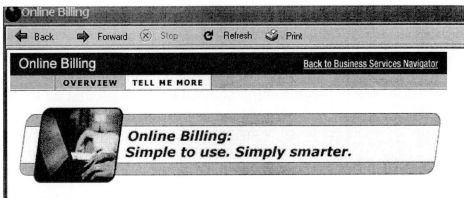

QUICKBOOKS ONLINE BILLING IS EASY TO USE:

In just three easy steps, you will be on your way to getting paid faster!

Step 1: Email invoices and statements from QuickBooks.

Step 2: Be sure the box entitled "Allow Online Payment" is checked before you send your email. This will allow you to post billing information to a private Web page and receive online payment. Click here to see how.

When this box is checked for the first time, you will be directed to sign up for Online Billing and choose a payment option.

After you've signed up, customers can pay you online by credit card or direct account transfer. Just check the same box each time you email billing information, and this information will be posted to a private Web page, hosted by Intuit, where your customers can make payments, view payment history and print forms. You can also add your logo to invoices, statements and estimates you send when you select this option.

Step 3: Once payment is made, you will be notified in QuickBooks. You can download transactions and view all payment information in one, easy-to-read report. Simply go to the "Receive Payments" form and click "Get Online Payments" to download transactions. Click here to see how.

PAYMENT OPTIONS AT-A-GLANCE
To get started, decide which payment option is right for you—a QuickBooks merchant account, a PayPal account, or both. Either service allows you to easily accept credit cards. However, you can also accept direct transfers with a PayPal account, provided your customer also has a PayPal account.

See which solution is right for you.

	QuickBooks Merchant Account Service	**PayPal**
Best if...	Your customers want to pay you by credit card. Your customers want the option of paying you by phone, fax or mail, as well as over the Internet.	Your customers want to transfer funds and/or pay by credit card. Your customers are comfortable primarily paying over the Internet.
How Customers Pay You	Most major credit cards	Most major credit cards, direct bank account transfer (eCheck), or PayPal account balance transfer
Requirements	You have a QuickBooks Merchant Account with Wells Fargo or Chase Merchant Services. Credit approval required.	You and your customers open or have a PayPal account. No Credit approval required.
Fees	Fees vary by Financial Institution. ⚡ Click here for fees.	Fees vary by payment option. ⚡ Click here for fees.

⚡ Sign up now!

I have questions—tell me more.

Credit Sales: Create Reminder Statements

> QuickBooks offers two different statements: **Reminder Statements** summarize invoices. **Billing Statements** are used *instead* of invoices. Billing statement charges are entered in the Customer Register.

Reminder statements are sent to remind customers to pay their bill. A reminder statement summarizes invoice charges. It does not provide the detailed information that an invoice provides.

If a company wants to provide a customer with detailed information about charges, a copy of the invoice should be sent instead of a reminder statement.

Reminder statements summarize:

- The customer's previous account balance.

- Charges for sales during the period.

- Payments received from the customer.

- The customer's ending account balance.

To print a QuickBooks reminder statement for the Whalen Exterior Door job:

Step 1: Click the **Statements** icon on the Customer Navigator to display the *Create Statements* window.

Step 2: Select Print format: **Intuit Standard Statement**.

Step 3: Select Print Statement for Transactions With Dates From: **11/17/2003** To: **12/16/2003**.

Step 4: Select Statement Date: **12/16/2003**.

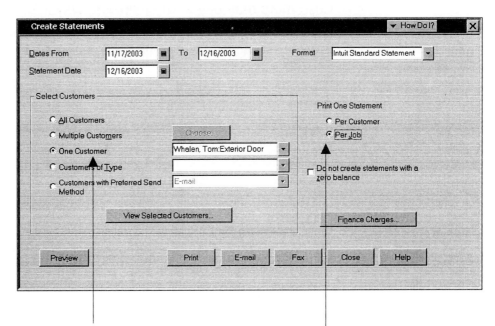

Step 5: In the *Select Customers* section, select **One Customer**. From the drop-down list, select: **Whalen, Tom: Exterior Door**.

Step 6: Select Print One Statement: **Per Job**.

Step 7: Click **Print** to print the reminder statement, then click **Close**.

Credit Sales: Record Customer Payments

Recall that when recording credit sales in QuickBooks, you first create an Invoice and then record the customer's payment. When a credit sale is recorded on an Invoice, QuickBooks records (debits) an account receivable—an amount to be received from the customer in the future. When the customer's payment is received, the account receivable is reduced (credited).

Customers may pay in the following ways:

1. **Online** using a credit card or bank account transfer. (See previous section regarding Online Billing.)

2. **Credit Card** using Visa, Master Card, American Express or Diners Club to pay over the phone, in-person, or by mail. Using QuickBooks' Merchant Account Service, you can obtain online authorization and then download payments directly into QuickBooks. (To learn more about the Merchant Account Service, click **Business Services** in the *Navigators* window, then in the Use Financial Management Tools, click **Accept Credit Cards in QB**.)

3. **Customer Check** received either in person or by mail.

To record Tom Whalen's payment by check for the Exterior Door job, complete the following steps:

Step 1: Click the **Receive Payments** icon on the Customers Navigator to display the *Receive Payments* window.

Step 2: Select Date: **12/17/2003**.

Step 3: Select Received From: **Whalen, Tom: Exterior Door**.

Invoice No. 87 for $304.30 should appear as an outstanding invoice near the bottom of the window.

Step 4: Enter Amount: **$304.30**.

QuickBooks will automatically apply this payment to an outstanding invoice. A check mark should appear before the outstanding invoice of $304.30.

Click **Get Online Pmts** to download online customer payments.

Step 5: Select: Pmt. Method: **Check**. Enter Check No. **1005**.

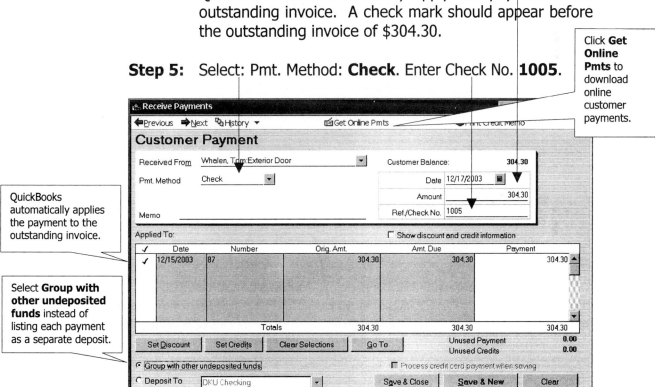

QuickBooks automatically applies the payment to the outstanding invoice.

Select **Group with other undeposited funds** instead of listing each payment as a separate deposit.

Step 6: Select: **Group with other undeposited funds**.

QuickBooks offers two ways for you to record the customer's payment as a bank deposit:

> Use whichever method your bank statement uses. If your bank statement groups deposits together, use this approach in QuickBooks to make it easier to match deposits on your bank statement with your QuickBooks records.

- *Group with other undeposited funds*: The customer's payment is held in an undeposited funds account with other undeposited customer payments. When the funds are deposited at the bank, they are recorded as one deposit and the funds are moved from the undeposited funds account to the bank checking or savings account.

- *Deposit to Checking*: This method records each payment as a separate deposit in the company's checking or savings account.

Step 7: Click **Save & Close** to record the payment and close the *Receive Payments* window.

QuickBooks will increase undeposited funds and decrease (credit) the customer's account receivable.

Record Bank Deposits

After recording a customer's payment in the *Receive Payments* window, the next step is to indicate which payments will be deposited in which bank accounts.

To select customer payments to deposit:

Step 1: Click the **Deposits** icon in the Customer Navigator to display the *Payments to Deposit* window.

> Two payments were added to undeposited funds in this chapter.

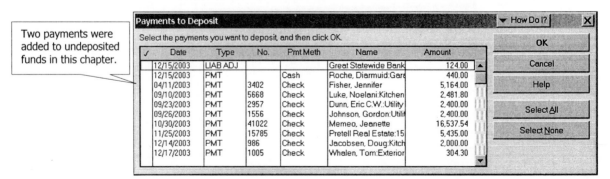

Step 2: The *Payments to Deposit* window lists undeposited funds that have been received but not yet deposited in the bank. Click **Select All** to select all listed payments to deposit.

Step 3: Click **OK** to display the following *Make Deposits* window.

Step 4: Select Deposit To: **Checking**. Select Date: **12/17/2003**.

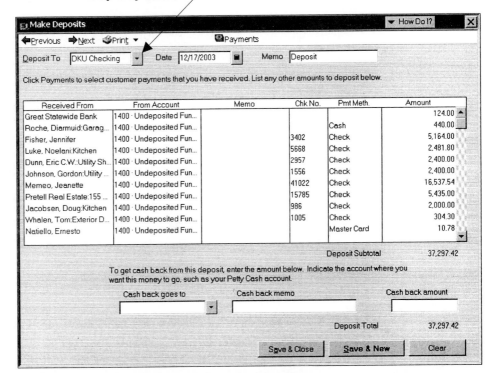

Step 5: Click **Print**. When the *Print Deposit* window appears, select **Deposit summary only**. Then click **OK**. Select printer settings, then click **Print**.

Step 6: Click **Save & Close** to record the deposit and close the *Make Deposits* window.

✓ **_Deposit Total is $37,297.42._**

Print Customer Register

Just as the Checking Register lists the transactions affecting the checking account, the Customer Register lists transactions affecting a customer's account.

Amounts owed Rock Castle Construction by customers are called accounts receivable. Accounts receivable are amounts that Rock Castle Construction will *receive* in the future.

In QuickBooks, the Accounts Receivable Register (A/R Register) shows *all* transactions that affect accounts receivable. The Customer Register, however, shows only transactions for a specific individual customer.

To print the Customer Register:

Step 1: Click the **Customer Register** icon in the Customers Navigator to display the following customer *Accounts Receivable* window.

Step 2: The Customer Register shows an individual customer's accounts receivable and lists only transactions for that specific customer.

To view Brian Cook's account, select Customer: **Cook, Brian**.

Select customer name from drop-down list or type a few letters of the name and QuickBooks will automatically complete the name.

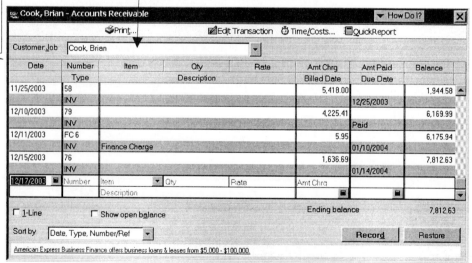

Two ways to print the customer's Account Receivable Register are:
1. Using the QuickReport.
2. Using the Customer Register (Print button).

Step 3: To print Brian Cook's Customer QuickReport:

- Click the **QuickReport** button at the top of the *Accounts Receivable* window.

- Select Dates: **All**.

- Insert **your name** and **Chapter 4** in the report footer. (Hint: Click Modify Report, Header/Footer.)

- Click **Print**. Select the printer settings. Then click **Print** again.

- Close the *Customer QuickReport* window.

Step 4: To print Brian Cook's Customer Register:

- Display Brian Cook's Customer Register.

- Click the **Print** button at the top of the *Customer* window.

- Enter the Date Range: From **10/01/2003** To **12/15/2003**.

- Select the **Print splits detail** checkbox, then click **OK**.

- Select Orientation: **Landscape**. Click **Print** to print the Customer Register.

> ✓ *The Customer Register provides more detail than the Customer QuickReport. The $3,100 charge to Brian Cook's account on 10/15/2003 for the Kitchen Job consists of Removal Labor of $980, Framing Labor of $440, and Installation Labor of $1,680.*

Step 5: Close the *Customer Register* window.

Print Journal Entries

As you entered transaction information into QuickBooks' onscreen forms, QuickBooks automatically converted the transaction information into journal entries.

To print the journal entries for the transactions you entered:

Step 1: Display the *Report Finder.* (Click Reports in the *Navigators* window.)

Step 2: Select Type of Report: **Accountant & Taxes.**

Step 3: Select Report: **Journal**.

Step 4: Select Dates From: **12/15/2003** To: **12/16/2003**.

Step 5: Click the **Display** button to display the Journal report. This Journal report lists all transactions recorded on 12/15/2003 and 12/16/2003.

Step 6: To filter for Invoice transactions only:

- Click the **Modify Reports** button, then click the **Filters** tab.

- Select Choose Filter: **Transaction Type**.

- Select Transaction Type: **Invoice**, then click **OK**.

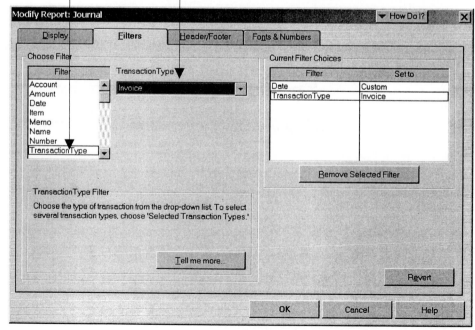

Step 7: Click the **Header/Footer** tab and insert **your name** and **Chapter 4** in the report footer.

Step 8: Print the Journal.

The Journal should list the journal entry that corresponds to Invoice No. 87. Notice that the journal entry records an increase (debit) to Accounts Receivable for $304.30, the net amount of the invoice.

Customer Center

While the Customer Register provides information about a single customer's account, there are many different customer reports that a business may find useful.

QuickBooks creates reports to answer the following questions:

◆ Which customers owe us money?

◆ Which customers have overdue balances?

◆ Which customers are profitable?

◆ Which jobs are profitable?

Customer reports can be accessed in QuickBooks in several different ways:

1. Customer Center: summarizes customer information in one location (Customer Navigator).

2. *Customer Reports* window on the Customer Navigator.

3. Report Finder: permits you to locate reports by type of report (*Navigators* window, Reports).

4. Report Menu: Reports on the Report menu are grouped by type of report.

In this chapter, you will use the Customer Center to access customer reports.

Display the Customer Center by clicking the **Customer Center** icon on the Customers Navigator. (You can also open the Customer Center from the Customers menu.)

View relevant and timely customer information, such as open balances and customers with overdue balances.

Select different activities and dates.

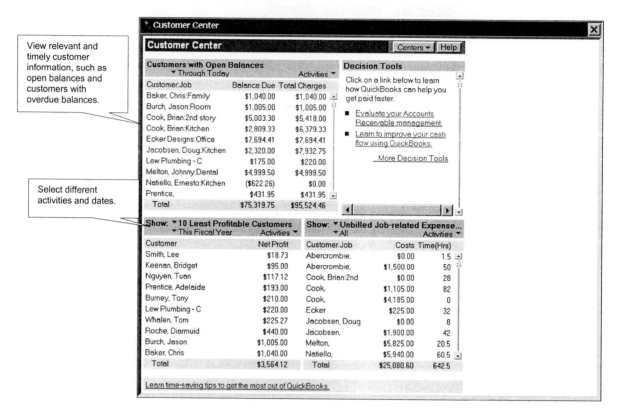

The Customer Center permits you to customize the customer information displayed by selecting different activities and dates. Double-click to drill down for more detail or print reports from the Customer Center.

Accounts Receivable Reports: Which Customers Owe Us Money?

Accounts Receivable reports can be accessed from the Customer Center, from the Reports menu or from the *Customer Reports* window on the Customers Navigator. When Rock Castle Construction makes a credit sale, the company provides goods and services to a customer in exchange for a promise that the customer will pay later. Sometimes the customer breaks the promise and does not pay. Therefore, a business should have a credit policy to ensure that credit is extended only to customers who are likely to keep their promise and pay their bills.

After credit has been extended, a business needs to track accounts receivable to determine if accounts are being collected in a timely manner. The following reports provide information useful in tracking accounts receivable.

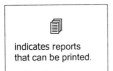

indicates reports that can be printed.

1. Customers with Open Balances (Open Invoices Report).

2. Accounts Receivable Aging Summary.

3. Customers with Overdue Balances.

4. Collections Report.

Customers with Open Balances

Customers with open balances (also called open invoices) are customer invoices with an unbilled or unpaid balance.

Customers with open balances are displayed in the upper left quadrant of the Customer Center.

Change the date to customize your view.

Access Activities, such as Manage Your Receivables.

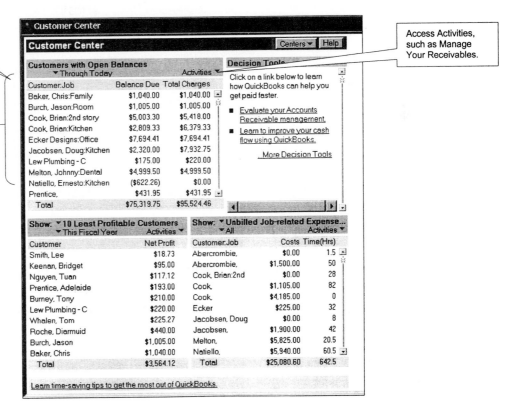

It is important to track the status of open accounts to determine:

♦ Are these amounts unbilled? The sooner the balances are billed, the sooner your company receives cash to pay your bills.

♦ Are these amounts billed but not yet due?

♦ Are these amounts billed and overdue? These accounts should be monitored closely with an action plan for collecting the accounts.

📑 *Open Invoices Report*

The Open Invoices report lists all customers with open balances and can be printed as follows:

Step 1: From the Customer Center, Customers with Open Balances section, click the **Activities** arrow **[▾]** to display the menu.

Customers with Open Balances ▾Through Today	Balance Due To	Activities ▾
Customer:Job		Receive Payments
Baker, Chris:Family	$1,040.00	Create Statements...
Burch, Jason:Room	$1,005.00	Write Letters...
Cook, Brian:2nd story	$5,003.30	
Cook, Brian:Kitchen	$2,809.33	Manage Your Receivables
Ecker Designs:Office	$7,694.41	
Jacobsen, Doug:Kitchen	$2,320.00	**Open Invoices Report**
Lew Plumbing - C	$175.00	Collections Report
Melton, Johnny:Dental	$4,999.50	A/R Aging Summary Report
Natiello, Ernesto:Kitchen	($622.26)	Customer Balance Summary Report
Prentice,	$431.95	
Total	$75,319.75	Help...

Step 2: Select **Open Invoices Report**.

Step 3: Select Date: **Today**.

Step 4: Enter **your name** and **Chapter 4** in the report footer.

Step 5: Print the Open Invoices report using **Landscape** orientation.

Step 6: ✏ Notice the *Aging* column in the report. This column indicates the age of overdue accounts. Circle all overdue customer accounts.

Step 7: Close the *Open Invoices* window.

 *Accounts Receivable Aging Summary Report*

Another report that provides information about the age of customer accounts is the A/R Aging Summary report. This report lists the age of accounts receivable balances. In general, the older an account, the less likely the customer will pay the bill. Therefore, it is important to monitor the age of accounts receivable and take action to collect old accounts.

To print the Accounts Receivable Aging Summary:

Step 1: From the Customer Center, click the **Activities [▾]** to display the following menu (or click the A/R Aging Summary from the *Customers* Navigator Report window.

Step 2: Select **A/R Aging Summary Report**.

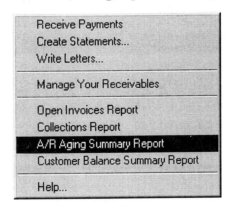

Step 3: Select Date: **Today**.

Step 4: Enter **your name** and **Chapter 4** in the report footer.

Step 5: If necessary, adjust the column widths by clicking and dragging.

Step 6: Print the report using **Landscape** orientation.

Step 7: Close the *A/R Aging Summary* window.

Customers with Overdue Balances

When reviewing the age of accounts receivable, a business should monitor overdue accounts closely and maintain ongoing collection efforts to collect its overdue accounts.

To customize the Customer Center to obtain more information about customers with overdue balances:

Step 1: In the lower left quandrant of the Customer Center, select Show: **Customers with Overdue Balances**.

Step 2: Select: **Through Today**.

Step 3: Seven customers have overdue balances. To obtain more information about a specific customer, simply double-click on the customer's name.

Double-click on **Brian Cook**. The following Customer Detail Center will display detailed information about the customer.

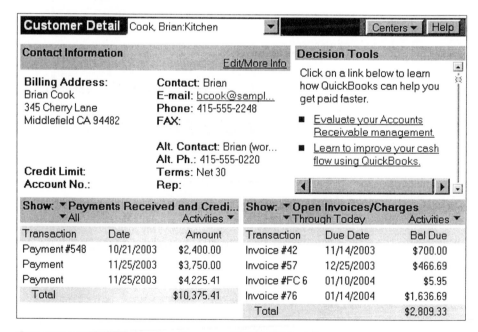

Step 4: Close the **Customer Detail Center**.

📑 *Collections Report*

The Collections Report lists customers with overdue account balances. In addition, the collection report includes a contact phone number for convenience in contacting the customer.

To view a Collections Report for a specific customer, simply double-click on the customer's name in the Customers with Overdue Accounts section of the Customer Center.

To view the Collections Report for Brian Cook:

Step 1: From the Customer Center, Show: **Customers with Overdue Balances** in one of the two lower quandrants.

Step 2: Double-click on the customer's account balance: **$700.00**.

> Click on the account balance to display the Collections Report; click on the customer name to display the Customer Detail Center.

Show: ▼ Customers with Overdue Balan...	
▼ Through Today	Activities ▼
Customer:Job	Bal. Overdue
Cook, Brian:Kitchen	$700.00
Jacobsen, Doug:Kitchen	$75.00
Lew Plumbing - C	$175.00
Prentice,	$431.95
Pretell Real Estate:155	$2,239.00
Teschner, Anton:Sun Room	$565.95
Total	$4,186.90

Step 3: Select Date: **Today**.

Step 4: Insert **your name** and **Chapter 4** in the report footer.

Step 5: Print the Collections Report for Brian Cook using **Portrait** orientation.

To print the Collections Report summarizing information for all Customers with Overdue Balances:

Step 1: Click the **Activities [▼]** to display the following menu.

Step 2: Select **Collections Report**.

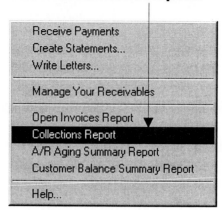

Step 3: Select Date: **Today**.

Step 4: Insert **your name** and **Chapter 4** in the report footer.

Step 5: Print the Collections Report.

Step 6: Close the *Collections Report* window.

The Collections Report provides the information necessary to monitor and contact overdue accounts and should be prepared on a regular basis.

Profit and Loss Reports: Which Customers and Jobs are Profitable?

To improve profitability in the future, a business should evaluate which customers and jobs have been profitable in the past. This information permits a business to improve profitability by:

1. Focusing on profitable areas.

2. Increasing business in profitable areas.

3. Improving performance in unprofitable areas.

4. Discontinuing unprofitable areas.

The Customer Center allows you to view:

- 10 Most Profitable Customers
- 10 Least Profitable Customers

- 10 Most Profitable Jobs
- 10 Least Profitable Jobs

- 10 Most Profitable Products
- 10 Least Profitable Products

- 10 Most Profitable Services
- 10 Least Profitable Services

In addition, you can print the following QuickBooks reports:
- Job Profitability Summary Report
- Job Profitability Detail Report

To view the 10 most profitable customers for Rock Castle Construction:

Step 1: In either of the lower quandrants of the Customer Center, select Show: **10 Most Profitable Customers**.

Step 2: Select Date: **This Fiscal Year**.

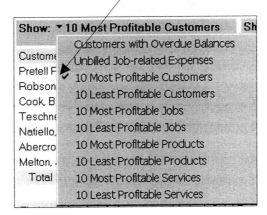

📰 *Job Profitability Summary Report*

To print the Job Profitabilty Summary Report:

Step 1: Click the **Activities** ▼ to display the following menu.

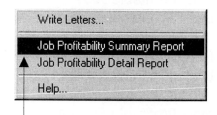

Step 2: Select **Job Profitability Summary Report**.

Step 3: Select Date: **This Fiscal Year**.

Step 4: Enter **your name** and **Chapter 4** in the report footer.

Step 5: Print the report using **Landscape** orientation.

Step 6: Close the *Job Profitabillty Summary* window.

QuickBooks offers other additional reports about customers that provide information useful to a business. These reports can be accessed from the Reports menu or from the Customer Report section of the Customers Navigator.

Back Up Chapter 4

Back up your Chapter 4 file to your floppy disk. Use the file name: [your name] Chapter 4.

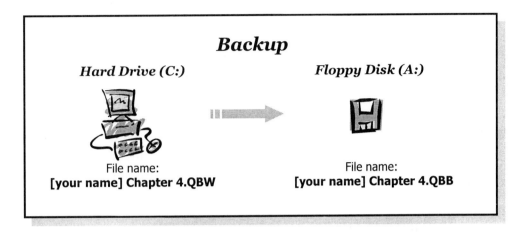

Step 1: 💾 Insert the **Chapter 4** backup disk in drive A.

Step 2: Click **File**, **Back Up**.

Step 3: Enter the file name: **[your name] Chapter 4.QBB**. Enter location: **A:**.

Step 4: Click **Back Up**.

You have now backed up the Chapter 4 file to your Chapter 4 floppy disk.

If you are continuing your computer session, close the company file then proceed to Activity 4.1.

If you are quitting your computer session now (1) close the company file and (2) exit QuickBooks.

Assignments

Activity 4.1: Bill Customer

Scenario

"I just finished the Flowers job, Mr. Castle." A workman tosses a job ticket over your cubicle wall into your inbox as he walks past. *"Mrs. Flowers' pet dog, Zander, really did a number on that door. No wonder she wanted it replaced before her party tonight. Looks better than ever now!"*

You hear Mr. Castle reply, *"We want to keep Mrs. Flowers happy. She will be a good customer."*

Task 1: Restore Company File

The first task is to restore your backup for Chapter 4 to the hard drive, changing the file name to Activity 4.1.

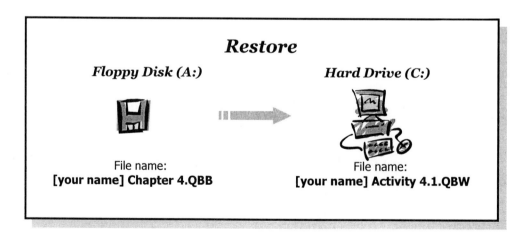

Step 1: 🖫 Insert the **Chapter 4** backup disk into drive A.

Step 2: Click **Restore a backup file** (or click **File**, **Restore**).

Step 3: Identify the backup file:

* Filename: **[your name] Activity 4.1.QBB**.

* Location: **A:**.

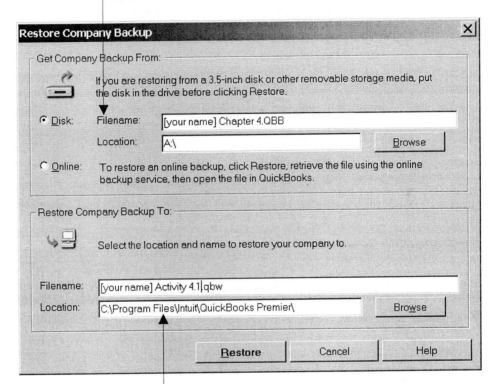

Step 4: Identify the restored file:

* Filename: **[your name] Activity 4.1.QBW**.

* Location: **C:\Program Files\Intuit\QuickBooks Premier**.

Step 5: Click **Restore.** Your backup file will be restored to the C drive. If prompted, enter your User ID and Password.

Step 6: Change the company name to:
[your name] Activity 4.1 Rock Castle Construction.
(To change the company name, select Company (menu), Company Information.)

You can add a new customer from the *Customer List* window or open the *Invoices* window and then from the Customer:Job drop-down list, select **Add New**.

Task 2: Add New Customer

Add Mrs. Flowers as a new customer and add a new job.

Address Info:	
Customer	Flowers, Diane
Mr./Ms./...	Mrs.
First Name	Diane
M.I.	L.
Last Name	Flowers
Contact	Diane
Phone	415-555-1078
Alt. Ph.	415-555-3434
Alt. Contact	Tad (spouse)
Addresses: **Bill To**	10 Tee Drive Bayshore, CA 94326

Additional Info:	
Type	Residential
Terms	Net 30
Tax Code	Tax
Tax Item	San Tomas

Payment Info:	
Account No.	78910
Credit Limit	2,000
Preferred Payment Method	VISA

Job Name: Door Replacement	
Job Status	Closed
Start Date	12/17/2003

Projected End	12/17/2003
End Date	12/17/2003
Job Description	Interior Door Replacement
Job Type	Repairs

Task 3: Create Invoice

Step 1: Create an invoice for an interior door replacement using the following information:

Customer: Job	Flowers, Diane: Door Replacement
Customer Template	Custom Invoice
Date	12/17/2003
Invoice No.	88
Items	1 Wood Door: Interior @ $72.00 1 Hardware: Standard Doorknob @ 30.00 Installation Labor: 3 hours

Step 2: Print the invoice.

> ✓ **The Invoice Total is $214.91.**

Task 4: Print Reminder Statement

Print a reminder statement for Diane Flowers on 12/20/2003.

Task 5: Back Up Activity 4.1

Back up the Activity 4.1 file to a floppy disk.

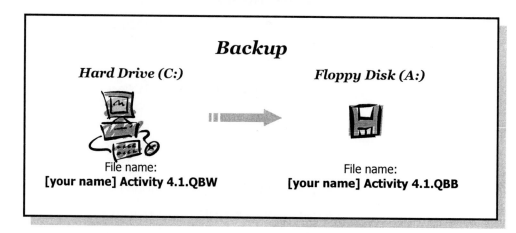

Step 1: 🖫 Insert the **Chapter 4** backup disk in drive A.

Step 2: Click **File**, **Back Up**.

Step 3: Specify the backup file name: **[your name] Activity 4.1.QBB**. Specify location: **A:**.

Step 4: Click **Back Up** to backup Activity 4.1 to your backup floppy disk. Close the company file. (From the File menu, select Close Company.)

Activity 4.2:
Record Customer Payment and Customer Credit

"It's time you learned how to record a credit to a customer's account." Mr. Castle groans, then rubbing his temples, he continues, *"Mrs. Flowers called earlier today to tell us she was very pleased with her new bathroom door. However, she ordered locking hardware for the door and standard hardware with no lock was installed instead. Although she appreciates our prompt service, she would like a lock on her bathroom door. We sent a workman over to her house, and when the hardware was replaced, she paid the bill.*

"We need to record a credit to her account for the standard hardware and then record a charge for the locking hardware set. And we won't charge her for the labor to change the hardware."

Task 1: Restore Company File

Restore your backup for Activity 4.1 to the hard drive, changing the file name to Activity 4.2.

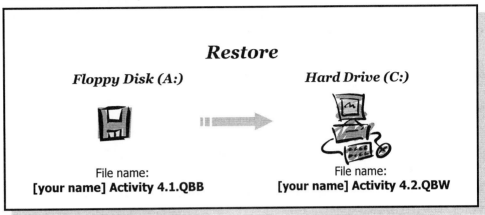

Restore

Floppy Disk (A:)   Hard Drive (C:)

File name: File name:
[your name] Activity 4.1.QBB   **[your name] Activity 4.2.QBW**

Step 1: 🖫 Insert the **Chapter 4** backup disk into drive A.

Step 2: Click **Restore a backup file** (or click **File, Restore**).

Step 3: Identify the backup file:

- Filename: **[your name] Activity 4.1.QBB**.
- Location: **A:**.

Step 4: Identify the restored file:

- Filename: **[your name] Activity 4.2.QBW**.
- Location: **C:\Program Files\Intuit\QuickBooks Premier**.

Step 5: Click **Restore.** Your backup file will be restored to the C drive. If prompted, enter your User ID and Password.

Step 6: Change the company name to:
[your name] Activity 4.2 Rock Castle Construction.
(To change the company name, select Company (menu), Company Information.)

Task 2: Record Customer Credit

Record a credit to Mrs. Flowers' account for the $30.00 she was previously charged for standard door hardware by completing the following steps:

Step 1: Click the **Refunds and Credits** icon on the Customer Navigator.

Step 2: Select Customer:Job: **Flowers, Diane: Door Replacement.**

Step 3: Select Date: **12/20/2003**.

Step 4: Select Item: **Hardware Standard Doorknobs**.

Step 5: Enter Quantity: **1**.

Step 6: Print the Credit Memo.

Step 7: Click **Save & Close** to close the *Create Credit Memos/Refunds* window.

✓   *The Credit Memo No. 89 totals $-32.33 ($30.00 plus $2.33 tax).*

Task 3: Create Invoice

Step 1: Create a new invoice (Invoice No. 90) for Diane Flowers on 12/20/2003 to record the charges for the interior door locking hardware.

Step 2: Print the invoice.

> ✓ **Invoice No. 90 totals $40.95.**

Task 4: Print Reminder Statement

Print a reminder statement for the Flowers account for 12/20/2003.

> ✓ **The Reminder Statement shows a total amount due of $223.53.**

Task 5: Receive Payment

Record Mrs. Flowers' payment by VISA credit card for $223.53 on 12/20/2003.

- Card No.: **4444-5555-6666-7777**
- Exp. Date: **07/04**
- Check: **Show discount and credit information**
- To record the credit, select an invoice, then select the **Set Credits** button.
- Select: **Group with Other Undeposited Funds**.

Task 6: Record Bank Deposit

Step 1: Record the deposit for $223.53 on 12/20/2003.

Step 2: Print a deposit summary.

Task 7: Back Up Activity 4.2

Step 1: 💾 Insert the **Chapter 4** backup disk in drive A.

Step 2: Click **File**, **Back Up**.

Step 3: Specify the backup file name: **[your name] Activity 4.2.QBB**. Specify location: **A:**.

Step 4: Click **Back Up** to backup Activity 4.2 to your backup floppy disk. Close the company file. (From the File menu, select Close Company.)

Activity 4.3: Customer Reports

In this activity, you will create additional customer reports that a business might find useful.

Task 1: Restore Company File

Restore your backup for Activity 4.2 to the hard drive, changing the file name to Activity 4.3.

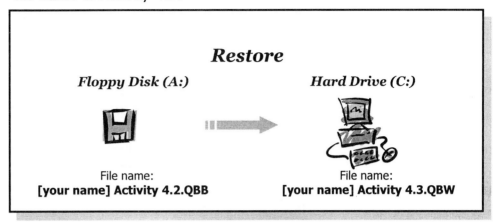

Restore

Floppy Disk (A:)	Hard Drive (C:)
File name:	File name:
[your name] Activity 4.2.QBB	**[your name] Activity 4.3.QBW**

Step 1: ⊞ Insert the **Chapter 4** backup disk into drive A.

Step 2: Click **Restore a backup file** (or click **File, Restore**).

Step 3: Identify the backup file:

- Filename: **[your name] Activity 4.2.QBB**.
- Location: **A:**.

Step 4: Identify the restored file:

- Filename: **[your name] Activity 4.3.QBW**.
- Location: **C:\Program Files\Intuit\QuickBooks Premier**.

Step 5: Click **Restore.** Your backup file will be restored to the C drive. If prompted, enter your User ID and Password.

Step 6: Change the company name to:
[your name] Activity 4.3 Rock Castle Construction.
(To change the company name, select Company (menu), Company Information.)

Task 2: Edit Customer List

Edit Ecker Designs' E-mail address in the Customer List.

Step 1: Open the Customer List.

Step 2: Select customer: **Ecker Designs**.

Step 3: Right-click to display the onscreen menu, then click **Edit** to display the _Edit Customer window_ for Ecker Designs.

Step 4: Edit the E-mail address for Ecker Designs: **decker@www.com**.

Step 5: Click **OK** to save the customer information and close the _Edit Customer_ window.

Step 6: Leave the _Customer: Job List_ window open to use for the next task.

Task 3:
Print Customer Account Receivable Register

Print the customer account register for Ecker Designs.

Step 1: Click the **Customer Register** icon in the Customer Navigator.

(Since Ecker Designs is currently selected when you click the Customer Register icon, the customer account register for Ecker Designs should display on your screen. If not, select Customer:Job: Ecker Designs.)

Step 2: When the _Ecker Designs – Accounts Receivable_ window appears, click the **QuickReport** button to display the _Customer QuickReport_ window for Ecker Designs.

Step 3: Insert **your name** and **Activity 4.3** in the report footer.

Step 4: Select Dates From: **11/01/2003** To: **12/31/2003**.

Step 5: Print the Customer QuickReport for Ecker Designs.

✓   ***The last amount charged to Ecker Design's account was $1,468.30 on December 15, 2003.***

Step 6: Close the *Customer QuickReport* window and the *Customer: Job List* window.

Task 4: Manage Your Receivables

From the Customer Center read how to improve credit management (More Decision Tools, Customers and Sales, Manage Your Receivables).

📧 Prepare an E-mail to Mr. Castle with your specific recommendations regarding how Rock Castle Construction can improve credit management.

Task 5: Customer Center

Using the Customer Center determine the following for Rock Castle Construction:

10 Most Profitable Products
10 Least Profitable Products
10 Most Profitable Services
10 Least Profitable Services

📧 Prepare an E-mail to Mr. Castle summarizing your recommendations as to how Rock Castle Construction can improve profitability in the future.

Task 6: Back Up Activity 4.3

Backup

Hard Drive (C:)		Floppy Disk (A:)

File name:
[your name] Activity 4.3.QBW

File name:
[your name] Activity 4.3.QBB

Step 1: Insert the **Chapter 4** backup disk in drive A.

Step 2: Click **File**, **Back Up**.

Step 3: Specify the backup file name: **[your name] Activity 4.3** Specify location: **A:**.

Step 4: Click **Back Up** to backup Activity 4.3 to your backup floppy disk. Close the company file. (From the File menu, select Close Company.)

Activity 4.4: Web Quest

Before extending credit to customers, it is often wise to investigate their credit history. Credit reports for businesses are now available online from Dun & Bradstreet.

Step 1: From the Customer Navigator, click the **Credit Check** icon. Read about QuickBooks Credit Check Service.

Step 2: Click the **New Customer** tab. Click **Look Up Commercial Customer Address**.

Step 3: Enter the name of a real commercial company in the *Company Name* field, then select the state in which the company is located.

Step 4: Click the **Start** button to verify the company address against the online Dun & Bradstreet database. Print your results.

Verifying a commercial customer's address is a free service. To obtain credit reports requires a subscription to the Dun & Bradstreet credit services. For a sample credit report, from the Business Services Navigator, click **Get a D&B Credit Report**, then click **See a sample credit report**.

Computer Accounting with QuickBooks 2002
Chapter 4 Printout Checklist
Name:_____ Date:_____

☑	***Printout Checklist – Chapter 4***
☐	Cash Sales Receipt
☐	Invoice No. 87
☐	Reminder Statement
☐	Deposit Summary
☐	Customer QuickReport
☐	Customer Register
☐	Journal
☐	Open Invoices Report
☐	Accounts Receivable Aging Summary Report
☐	Collections Report
☐	Job Profitability Summary Report
☑	***Printout Checklist – Activity 4.1***
☐	Task 3: Invoice No. 88
☐	Task 4: Reminder Statement
☑	***Printout Checklist – Activity 4.2***
☐	Task 2: Credit Memo No. 89
☐	Task 3: Invoice No. 90
☐	Task 4: Reminder Statement
☐	Task 6: Deposit Summary

☑	***Printout Checklist – Activity 4.3***
☐	Task 3: Customer QuickReport
☐	Task 4: E-mail Subject: Credit Management Recommendation
☐	Task 5: E-mail Subject: Improved Profitability Recommendation
☑	***Printout Checklist – Activity 4.4***
☐	Online Credit History Information
☐	Task 2: Verify Commercial Customer Address

Notes:

5

Vendors, Purchases, and Inventory

Scenario

As you work your way through stacks of paper in your inbox, you hear Mr. Castle's rapid footsteps coming in your direction. He whips around the corner of your cubicle with another stack of papers in hand.

In his usual rapid-fire delivery, Mr. Castle begins, *"This is the way we do business."* He quickly sketches the following:

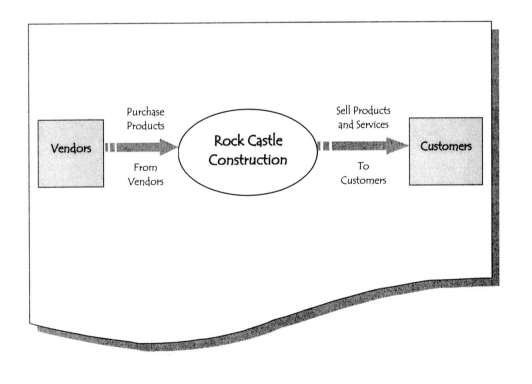

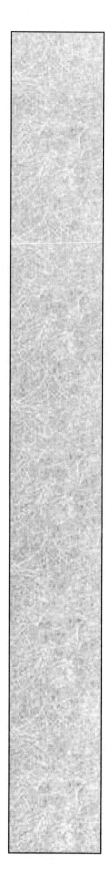

"*We purchase products from our vendors and suppliers, and then we sell those products and provide services to our customers. We use QuickBooks to track the quantity and cost of items we purchase and sell.*"

Mr. Castle tosses the papers into your inbox. "*Here are vendor and purchase transactions that need to be recorded.*"

5   *Learning Objectives*

In Chapter 5, you will learn the following QuickBooks features:

Introduction

To begin Chapter 5, first start QuickBooks software and then restore your backup file.

Start QuickBooks software by clicking on the QuickBooks desktop icon or click **Start**, **Programs**, **QuickBooks Premier**, **QuickBooks Premier**.

Restore your backup for Activity 4.3 to the C drive, renaming the file Chapter 5.QBW.

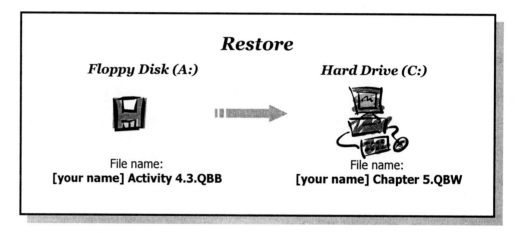

Step 1: 🖫 Insert the **Chapter 4** backup disk into drive A.

Step 2: Click **Restore a backup file** (or click **File**, **Restore**).

Step 3: Identify the backup file:

   ♦ Filename: **[your name] Chapter 5.QBB**.

   ♦ Location: **A:**.

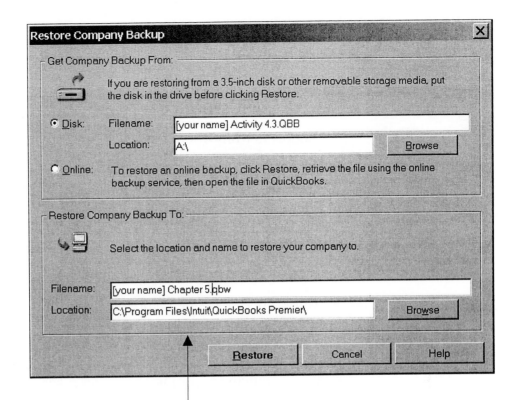

Step 4: Identify the restored file:

- Filename: **[your name] Chapter 5.QBW**.
- Location: **C:\Program Files\Intuit\QuickBooks Premier**.

Step 5: Click **Restore**.

Step 6: Change the company name to:
[your name] Chapter 5 Rock Castle Construction.

(To change the company name, click Company (menu), Company Information.)

In this chapter you will focus on recording vendor transactions. QuickBooks considers a vendor to be any individual or organization that provides products or services to your company.

QuickBooks considers all of the following to be vendors:

- Suppliers from whom you buy inventory or supplies.

- Service companies that provide services to your company, such as cleaning services or landscaping services.

- Financial institutions, such as banks, that provide financial services including checking accounts and loans.

- Tax agencies such as the IRS. The IRS is considered a vendor because you pay taxes to the IRS.

- Utility and telephone companies.

If your company is a merchandising business that buys and resells goods, then you must maintain inventory records to account for the items you purchase from vendors and resell to customers.

The following diagram summarizes vendor and customer transactions.

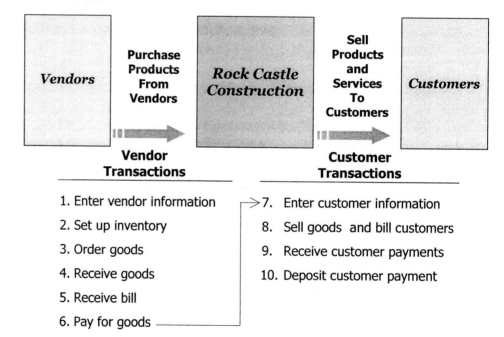

Vendor Transactions	Customer Transactions
1. Enter vendor information	7. Enter customer information
2. Set up inventory	8. Sell goods and bill customers
3. Order goods	9. Receive customer payments
4. Receive goods	10. Deposit customer payment
5. Receive bill	
6. Pay for goods	

The following table summarizes how to record Rock Castle Construction's business operations using QuickBooks.

Activity	Record Using QuickBooks Window
1. Record vendor information.	*Vendor List*
2. Record inventory information: Set up inventory records to track the quantity and cost of items purchased.	*Items List*
3. Order goods: Forms called Purchase Orders (PO's) are used to order goods from vendors.	*Purchase Order*
4. Receive goods: Goods are received and recorded as inventory.	*Receive Items*
5. Receive bill: Record an obligation to pay a bill later (Accounts Payable).	*Enter Bill*
6. Pay for goods: Bills for the goods are paid.	*Pay Bills*
7. Record customer information.	*Customer List*
8. Sell goods and bill customers: Record customer's promise to pay later (Account Receivable).	*Invoice*
9. Receive customer payment: Record cash collected and customer's Account Receivable is decreased.	*Receive Payments*
10. Deposit customers' payments in bank account.	*Deposit*

Vendor Transactions (rows 1–6)

Customer Transactions (rows 7–10)

Click **Vendors** in the *Navigators* window to open the Vendors Navigator shown below.

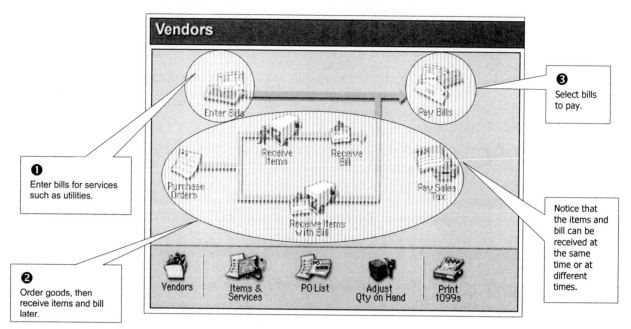

❸ Select bills to pay.

❶ Enter bills for services such as utilities.

❷ Order goods, then receive items and bill later.

Notice that the items and bill can be received at the same time or at different times.

The Vendors Navigator is a flowchart of vendor transactions. As the flowchart indicates, Rock Castle Construction can record bills in QuickBooks as follows:

❶ Record services received: Use the *Enter Bills* window to record bills for services received. Examples include rent, utilities expense, insurance expense, accounting and professional services. QuickBooks will record an obligation (Accounts Payable liability) to pay the bill later.

❷ Record goods purchased: Purchase Orders record an order to purchase goods. Use the *Receive Items* window (or *the Receive Items with Bill* window) to record goods received. If the bill is received after the goods, use the *Receive Bill* window to record the bill. Again, when the bill is entered, QuickBooks records Accounts Payable to reflect the obligation to pay the bill later.

❸ Select bills to pay. Use the *Pay Bills* window to select the bills that are due and you are ready to pay.

Other QuickBooks features available from the Vendors Navigator window include:

◆ **Pay Sales Tax**: Sales taxes is charged on retail sales to customers. The sales tax collected from customers must be paid to the appropriate state agency.

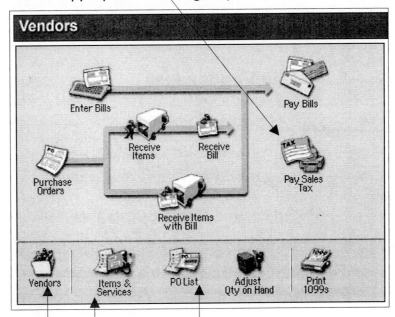

The lower section of the Navigator includes the following lists:

Vendor List: The Vendor List contains vendor information, such as address and payment terms.

Items and Services: A list of items (goods and services) that Rock Castle Construction buys from vendors (utilities, inventory items) as well as items sold to customers.

PO List: A list of all outstanding Purchase Orders for items that have not been received yet.

Vendor List

The first step in working with vendor transactions is to enter vendor information in the Vendor List.

The Vendor List contains information for each vendor, such as address, telephone number, and credit terms. Vendor information is entered in the Vendor List and then QuickBooks automatically transfers the vendor information to the appropriate forms, such as purchase orders and checks. This feature enables you to enter vendor information only once in QuickBooks instead of entering the vendor information each time a form is prepared.

View Vendor List

To view the Vendor List for Rock Castle Construction:

Step 1: Click on the **Vendors** icon in the lower section of the *Vendor Navigator* window.

Step 2: The following *Vendor List* window appears listing vendors with whom Rock Castle Construction does business. The Vendor List also displays the balance currently owed each vendor.

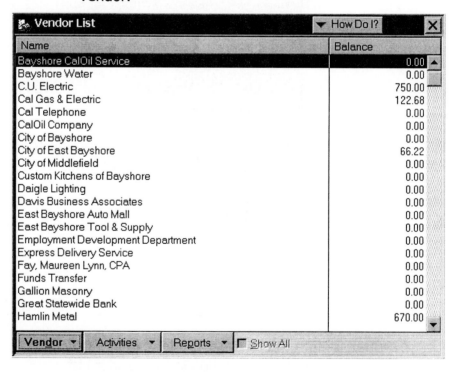

Name	Balance
Bayshore CalOil Service	0.00
Bayshore Water	0.00
C.U. Electric	750.00
Cal Gas & Electric	122.68
Cal Telephone	0.00
CalOil Company	0.00
City of Bayshore	0.00
City of East Bayshore	66.22
City of Middlefield	0.00
Custom Kitchens of Bayshore	0.00
Daigle Lighting	0.00
Davis Business Associates	0.00
East Bayshore Auto Mall	0.00
East Bayshore Tool & Supply	0.00
Employment Development Department	0.00
Express Delivery Service	0.00
Fay, Maureen Lynn, CPA	0.00
Funds Transfer	0.00
Gallion Masonry	0.00
Great Statewide Bank	0.00
Hamlin Metal	670.00

Step 3: To view additional information about a vendor, double-click the vendor's name.

Step 4: Activities that can be accessed from the Vendor Navigator can also be accessed from the *Vendor List* window by clicking the **Activities** button.

Step 5: Vendor reports can be accessed by clicking the **Reports** button in the *Vendor List* window.

Step 6: To make changes to the Vendor List, use the **Vendor** button or right-click over the Vendor window and an onscreen menu will appear.

Add New Vendor

Rock Castle Construction needs to add a new vendor, Koch Window & Door, to the Vendor List.

To add a new vendor to the Vendor List:

Step 1: Click the **Vendor** button near the bottom of the *Vendor List* window.

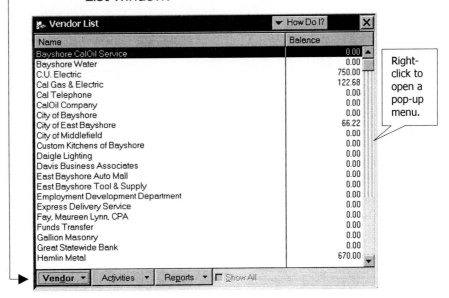

Step 2: Click **New** on the drop-down menu.

Step 3: A blank *New Vendor* window should appear. Enter the information shown below into the *New Vendor | Address Info* window.

Vendor	Koch Window & Door
Address	10 Dorsett Lane Bayshore, CA 94326
Contact	Alex Koch
Phone	415-555-9979
Print on check as	Koch Window & Door

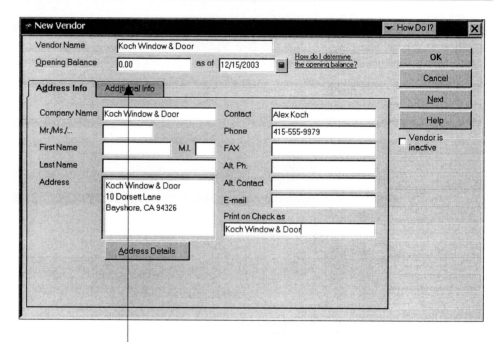

Step 4: Click the **Additional Info** tab to display another vendor information window. Enter the information shown below into the *Additional Info* fields.

Account	78789
Type	Materials
Terms	Net 30
Vendor eligible for 1099	Yes
Vendor Tax ID	37-1890123

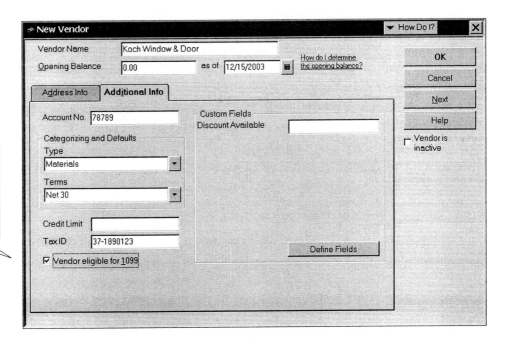

IRS Form 1099 must be completed for each business (other than corporations) to whom you paid $600 or more in a year. The vendor's Tax ID No. is required to complete the 1099.

Step 5: Click **OK** to add the new vendor and close *the New Vendor* window.

To edit vendor information, simply double-click the vendor's name in the *Vendor List* window. Make the necessary changes in the *Edit Vendor* window that appears, then click OK to close the *Edit Vendor* window.

Print Vendor List

To print the Vendor List:

Step 1: Click the **Reports** button in the lower left corner of the *Vendor List* window.

Step 2: Select **Contact List** from the drop-down menu.

Step 3: Insert [your name] and Chapter 5 in the report footer. Select **Landscape** print settings, then click **Print**.

Step 4: Close the *Vendor Contact List* window.

The Items and Services List, discussed next, is used to record information about goods and services purchased from vendors.

> Items provide supporting detail for accounts.

Items: Inventory Items, Non-Inventory Items, and Services

QuickBooks defines an item as anything that your company buys, sells, or resells including products, shipping charges and sales taxes. QuickBooks classifies goods and services purchased and sold into three different categories of items:

> ***Important!***
> QuickBooks tracks inventory costs using the weighted-average method. QuickBooks does not use FIFO (First-in, First-out) or LIFO (Last-in, First-out) inventory costing. The average cost of an inventory item is displayed in the *Edit Item* window.

1. **Service Items:** Service items can be services that are purchased *or* sold. For example, service items include:
   - Services you *buy* from vendors, such as cleaning services.
   - Services you *sell* to customers, such as installation labor.

2. **Inventory Items:** Inventory items are goods that a business purchases, holds as inventory, and then resells to customers. QuickBooks traces the quantity and cost of inventory items in stock.

> QuickBooks does *not* track the **quantity** of non-inventory items. If it is important for your business to know the quantity of an item on hand, record the item as an inventory item.

   For consistency, the *same* inventory item is used when recording *sales* and *purchases*. QuickBooks has the capability to track both the cost and the sales price for inventory items. For example, in Chapter 4, you recorded the *sale* of an inventory item, an interior door. When the interior door was recorded on a sales invoice, QuickBooks automatically updated your inventory records by reducing the quantity of doors on hand. If you *purchased* an interior door, then you would record the door on the purchase order using the same inventory item number as you used on the invoice, except the purchase order uses the door cost while the invoice uses the door selling price.

3. **Non-Inventory Items:** QuickBooks does not track the quantity on hand for non-inventory items. Non-inventory items include:
   - Items purchased for a specific customer job, such as a custom counter top.
   - Items purchased and used by your company instead of resold to customers, such as office supplies or carpentry tools.
   - Items purchased and resold (if the quantity on hand does not need to be tracked).

Items and Services List

The Items and Services List (Item List) summarizes information about items (inventory items, non-inventory items, and service items) that a company purchases or sells.

To view the Item List in QuickBooks:

Step 1: Click the **Items and Services** icon in the lower section of the Vendor Navigator.

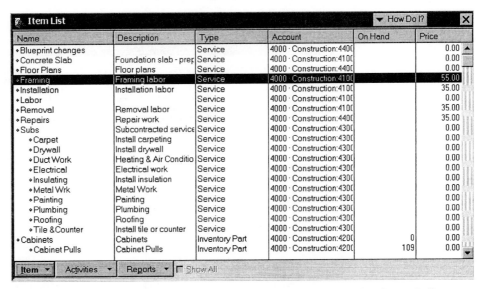

Step 2: Notice that the Item List contains the following information:

  ◆ Item name

  ◆ Item description

  ◆ Item type (service, inventory, non-inventory, other charge, discount, sales tax item)

  ◆ Account used

  ◆ Quantity on hand

  ◆ Price of the item

  Scroll down through the list to view the inventory and non-inventory items for Rock Castle Construction.

Add New Item to Item List

Rock Castle Construction needs to add two new items to the Item List: bifold doors and bifold door hardware. Because Rock Castle Construction wants to track the quantity of each item, both will be inventory items.

To add an inventory item to the Item List:

Step 1: If it is not already open, display the *Item List* window.

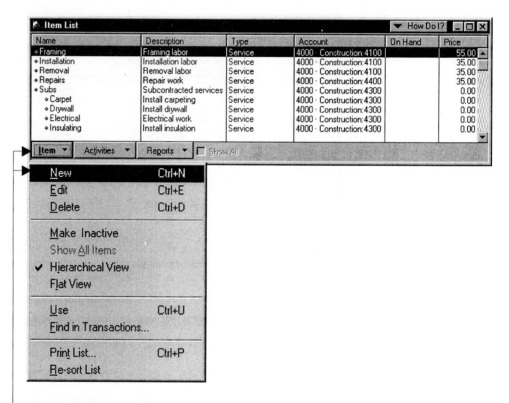

Step 2: Click the **Item** button, then select **New**.

Step 3: In the *New Item* window that appears, you will enter information about the bifold door inventory item. From the Type drop-down list, select **Inventory Part**.

Use **Group** if the same group of items are bought or sold as a package.

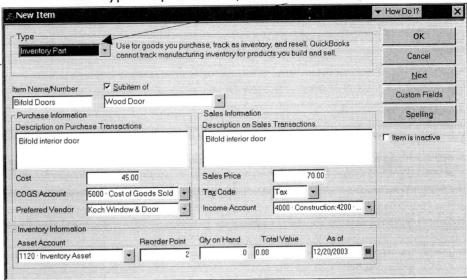

Step 4: Enter the following information in the *New Item* window.

Item Name/Number	Bifold Doors
Subitem of	Wood Door
Description on Purchase Transactions	Bifold interior door
Description on Sales Transactions	Bifold interior door
Cost	45.00
COGS Account	5000 – Cost of Goods Sold
Preferred Vendor	Koch Window & Door
Sales Price	70.00
Tax Code	Tax
Income Account	4000 – Construction: 4200 Materials
Asset Account	1120 – Inventory Asset
Reorder Point	2
Qty on Hand	0
Total Value	0.00
As of	12/20/2003

If spell checker starts, click **Ignore**.

Step 5: Click **Next** to record this inventory item and clear the fields to record another inventory item.

Step 6: Enter bifold door knobs as an inventory item in the Item List using the following information:

Item Name/Number	Bifold Knobs
Subitem of	Hardware
Description on Purchase Transactions	Bifold door hardware
Description on Sales Transactions	Bifold door hardware
Cost	6.00
Sales Price	10.00
Tax Code	Tax
COGS Account	5000 – Cost of Goods Sold
Preferred Vendor	Patton Hardware Supplies
Income Account	4000 – Construction: 4200 Materials
Asset Account	1120 – Inventory Asset
Reorder Point	2
Qty on Hand	0
Total Value	0.00
As of	12/20/2003

Step 7: Click **OK** to record the item and close the *New item* window.

Print the Item List

To print the Item List:

Step 1: Click the **Reports** button in the lower left corner of the *Item List* window.

Step 2: Select **Item Listing**.

Step 3: Insert your name in the report footer.

Step 4: Select the **Landscape** print settings, then click **Print**.

Step 5: Close the *Item List* window.

Purchase and Vendor Preferences

To set preferences to customize QuickBooks for your specific needs:

Step 1: Click **Company** in the *Navigators* window to open the Company Navigator.

Step 2: Click the **Preferences** icon in the Company Navigator.

Step 3: Preferences are grouped by area as listed in the left scrollbar of the *Preferences* window. Select **Purchases & Vendors**.

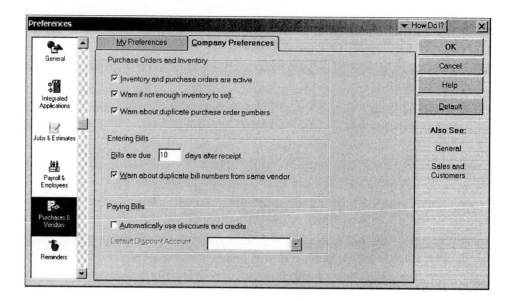

Step 4: Select the **Company Preferences** tab to display purchase and vendor preference settings. From this screen, you would select preferences for your company.

Step 5: Click **OK** to close the *Preferences* window.

Vendor Transactions

After creating a Vendor List and an Item List, you are ready to enter vendor transactions.

The diagram on the following page summarizes how to use QuickBooks to record different vendor transactions.

Enter Bills for Services Received

❶ **Enter Bills**

Enter Bills

Pay Bills

❷ **Pay Bills:** Select bills to pay, then print checks.

Order Goods, Receive Items, Receive Bill Later

❶ **Purchase Order:** Prepare an order to purchase items from vendors.

Purchase Orders

Receive Items

❷ **Receive Items:** Record inventory items received.

❸**Record Bill:** Record bill received as accounts payable.

Receive Bill

Pay Bills

❹ **Pay Bills:** Select bills to pay, then print checks.

Order Goods, Receive Items with Bill

❶ **Purchase Order**

Purchase Orders

Receive Items with Bill

❷ **Receive Items with Bill**

❸ **Pay Bills**

Pay Bills

Order Goods, Receive Items, then Receive Bill

Display the Vendors Navigator to view the flowchart of transactions with vendors. Recording the purchase of goods using QuickBooks involves the following steps:

❶ Create a Purchase Order to order items from vendors.

❷ Receive item and record as an inventory or non-inventory part.

❸ Receive bill and record an obligation to pay the vendor later (accounts payable).

❹ Pay bill by selecting bills to pay.

❺ Print checks to vendors. Since the obligation is fulfilled, accounts payable is reduced.

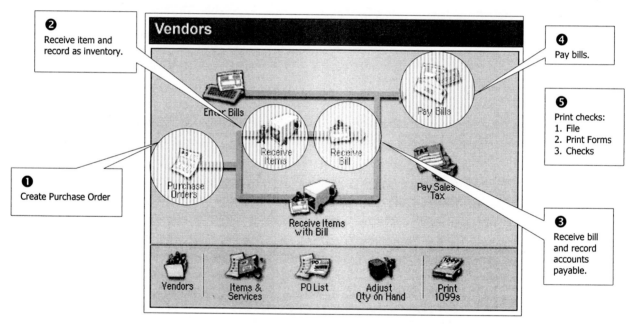

Create Purchase Orders

A Purchase Order is a record of an order to purchase inventory from a vendor.

Rock Castle Construction wants to order 6 bifold interior doors and 6 sets of bifold door hardware to stock in inventory.

To create a Purchase Order:

Step 1: Click the **Purchase Orders** icon in the Vendor Navigator.

Step 2: From the drop-down vendor list, select the vendor name: **Koch Window & Door**.

Step 3: Select Form Template: **Custom Purchase Order**.

Step 4: Enter the purchase order date: **12/20/2003**

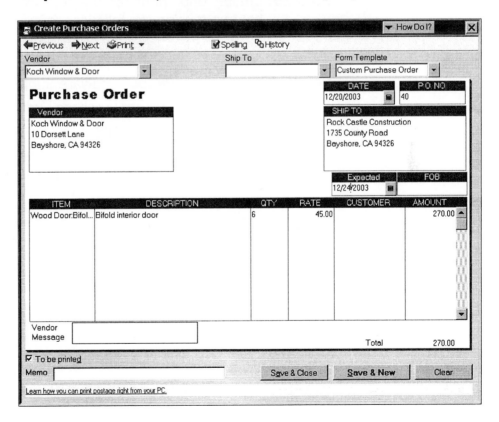

Step 5: Enter the Expected Date: **12/24/2003**.

Step 6: Select item ordered: **Wood Doors: Bifold Doors**. ($45.00 now appears in the Rate column.)

Step 7: Enter Quantity: **6**. ($270.00 should now appear in the Amount column.)

Step 8: Print the Purchase Order as follows:

   ♦ Click **Print**.

   ♦ Select Print on: **Blank paper**.

   ♦ Check **Print lines around each field**.

   ♦ Click **Print**.

Step 9: Click **Save & New** (or **Next**) to record the Purchase Order and clear the fields in the *Purchase Order* window.

Step 10: Create and print a purchase order for bifold door hardware using the following information.

Vendor	Patton Hardware Supplies
Custom Template	Custom Purchase Order
Date	12/20/2003
Expected Date	12/24/2003
Item	Hardware: Bifold knobs
QTY	6

> ✓ **The Purchase Order total for bifold door hardware is $36.**

Step 11: Click **Save & Close** to record the purchase order and close the *Purchase Order* window.

Receive Items

To record items received on 12/22/2003 that were ordered from the vendor, Koch Window & Door, complete the following steps:

Step 1: Click the **Receive Items** icon in Vendor Navigator.

Step 2: In the *Create Item Receipts* window, select vendor: **Koch Window & Door**.

Step 3: If a purchase order for the item exists, QuickBooks will display the following *Open PO's Exist* window.

  ♦ Click **Yes**.

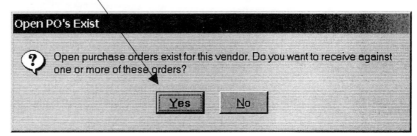

  ♦ When the following *Open Purchase Orders* window appears, select the Purchase Order for the items received, then click **OK**.

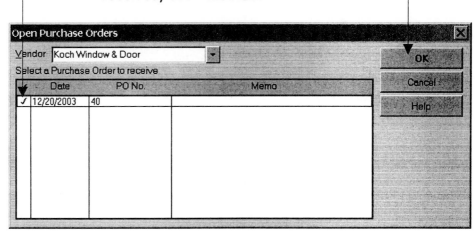

Step 4: The *Create Item Receipts* window will appear with a total of $270. If necessary, change the Date to: **12/22/2003.**

Although Rock Castle Construction ordered 6 bifold doors, only 5 were received. Change the quantity from 6 to **5**.

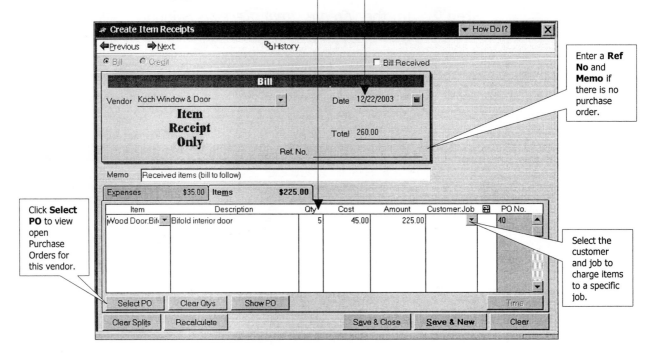

Click **Select PO** to view open Purchase Orders for this vendor.

Enter a **Ref No** and **Memo** if there is no purchase order.

Select the customer and job to charge items to a specific job.

Step 5: To record expenses associated with the items received, such as freight charges:

- Click the **Expenses** tab in the *Create Item Receipts* window.

- To record $35.00 in freight charges on the bifold doors received, select Account: **6400 Freight & Delivery**.

- Enter Amount: $**35.00**.

- Click the **Recalculate** button.

✓ ***The Total on the Create Item Receipts window is now $260.00.***

Step 6: Click **Save & New** (or **Next)** to record the bifold doors received and clear the window.

Step 7: Record the receipt of the bifold door hardware using the following information:

Vendor	Patton Hardware Supplies
Date	12/22/2003
PO No.	41
Item	Bifold door hardware
Qty	6

Step 8: Click **Save & Close** to record the items received and close the *Create Item Receipts* window.

Receive Bills

Bills for items purchased may be received at three different times:

1. You receive the bill for services (no items will be received), as for example, if the bill is for janitorial services. (Use *Enter Bills* window.)

2. You receive the bill at the same time you receive the items. (Use *Receive Items with Bill* window.)

3. You receive the bill after you receive the items. (Use *Receive Bill* window.)

Later, you will learn how to record bills for situation 1 and 2 above. Next, you will record the bill received for the bifold doors ordered from Koch Window & Door (situation 3 above).

To record a bill received after items are received:

Step 1:   Click the **Receive Bill** icon on the Vendor Navigator.

Step 2:   When the *Select Item Receipt* window appears:

- Select Vendor: **Koch Window & Door**. If necessary, press **Tab**.
- Select the Item Receipt that corresponds to the bill.
- Click **OK**.

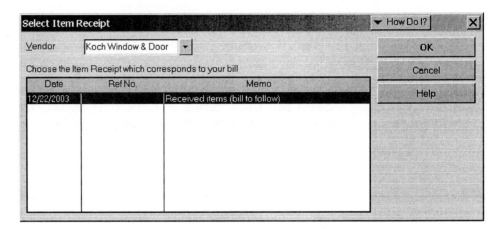

Step 3:   The following *Enter Bills* window will appear. Notice that the *Enter Bills* window is the same as the *Create Item Receipts* window except: (1) Item Receipt Only stamp does not appear, and (2) Bill Received in the upper right corner is checked.

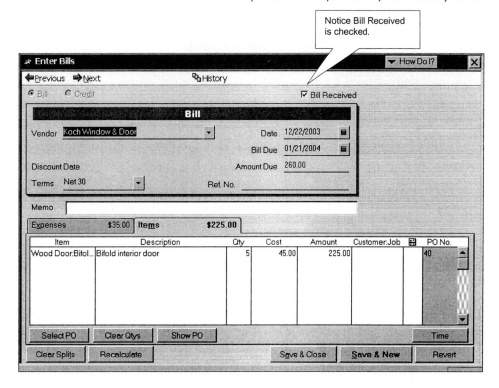

Notice Bill Received is checked.

Step 4: At this point, you can make any changes necessary, such as:

- ◆ Change the date if the bill is received on a date different from the date the item was received. In this instance, the item and bill are both received on **12/22/2003**.

- ◆ Terms

- ◆ Ref No.

- ◆ Memo

- ◆ Expenses, such as freight charges

Step 5: The Amount Due of $260.00 should agree with the amount shown on the vendor's bill.

Step 6: Click **Next** to advance to the Item Receipt for the bifold door hardware purchased from Patton Hardware Supplies.

Step 7: To record the bill received for the bifold door hardware, check **Bill Received** in the upper right corner of the window. Notice that the Item Receipt Only stamp is no longer displayed and the window name changed from *Create Item Receipts* to *Enter Bills*.

Step 8: Use the following information to record the bill for the bifold door hardware.

Vendor	Patton Hardware Supplies
Date Bill Received	12/22/2003
PO No.	41
Terms	Net 30
Item	Bifold door hardware
Qty	6

Step 9: Click **Save & Close** to record the bill and close the *Enter Bills* window.

When you enter a bill, QuickBooks automatically adds the bill amount to your Accounts Payable account balance.

Pay Bills

After receiving the items and entering the bill, the next step is to pay the bill.

To select the bills to pay:

Step 1: Click the **Pay Bills** icon from the Vendor Navigator.

Step 2: Select the bills to display. You can select to show all bills or only bills due before a specified date. In this instance, select: **Show all bills**.

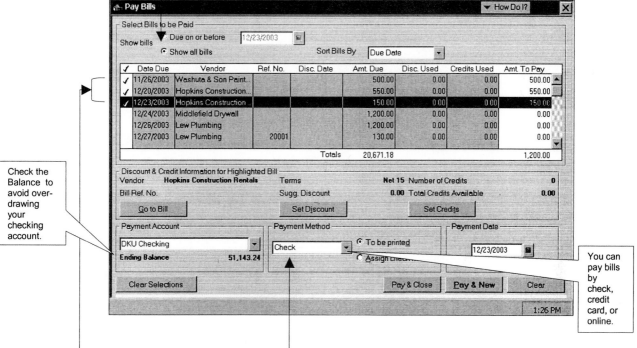

Check the Balance to avoid over-drawing your checking account.

You can pay bills by check, credit card, or online.

Step 3: In the *Payment Method* section, select: **Check**. Then select: **To be printed**.

Step 4: Select the bills you want to pay. In this case, select **bills with due dates on or before December 23, 2003**.

Step 5: Select Payment Date: **12/23/2003**.

Step 6: Scroll to the last two bills. Notice that the last two bills are the ones you just recorded for Koch Window & Door and Patton Hardware Supplies.

Step 7: Click **Pay & Close** to close the *Pay Bills* window.

✓   ***Bills selected for payment total $1,200.00.***

To print checks complete the following steps:

Step 1: Select **File** (Menu).

Step 2: Select **Print Forms** command.

Step 3: Select **Checks**.

Step 4: When the *Select Checks to Print* window appears, select Bank Account: **Checking**.

Step 5: Select First Check Number: **298.**

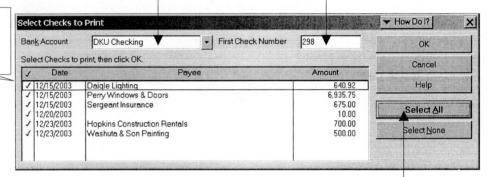

QuickBooks prints one check for each vendor, combining all amounts due to the same vendor.

Step 6: Click **Select All** checks to print.

Step 7: Click **OK**.

Step 8: Select Check Style: **Standard**. Select: **Print company name and address**.

Step 9: If you use Intuit's preprinted check forms, you would now insert the check forms in your printer. Then click **Print**.

Receive Items with Bill

If you receive the bill and the items at the same time, record both the items and the related bill by completing the following steps:

Step 1: Click the **Receive Items with Bill** icon from the Vendor Navigator.

Step 2: In the following *Enter Bills* window, you would:

- ◆ Enter the vendor and date.
- ◆ Select the purchase order that corresponds to the bill received.
- ◆ Make any necessary changes to quantity or cost.

Notice that the *Enter Bills* window is the same window that appeared when you clicked the *Receive Bill* icon.

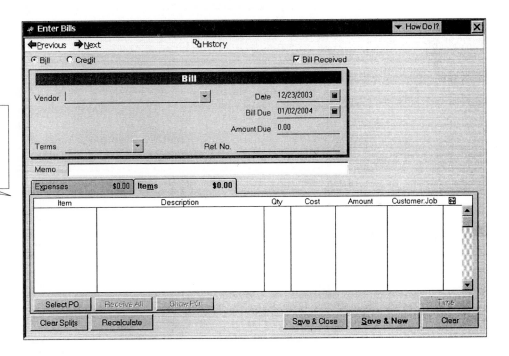

Step 3: Then click **Save & Close** to close the *Enter Bills* window.

Enter Bills

When you received items (goods) from vendors, you recorded those items using the *Receive Items* window or *Receive Items with Bill* window.

To record services (instead of goods) received, use the Enter Bills icon. Expenses that can be recorded using the *Enter Bills* window include utilities, insurance, and rent.

To enter bills for expenses:

Step 1: Click the **Enter Bills** icon from the Vendors Navigator.

Step 2: The following *Enter Bills* window will appear. Click the **Expenses** tab.

Notice that the *Enter Bills* window is the same window that appeared when you clicked the *Receive Bill* icon or the *Receive Items with Bill* icon.

You can record a bill as an Expense or an Item (inventory or non-inventory).

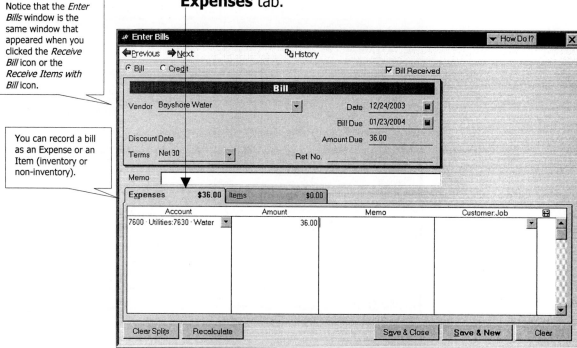

Step 3: Enter the following information for Rock Castle's water bill in the *Enter Bills* window.

Vendor	Bayshore Water
Date	12/24/2003
Amount Due	$36.00
Terms	Net 30
Account	7630: Water

Step 4: Click **Save & Close** to close the *Enter Bills* window.

Step 5: The next time you pay bills in QuickBooks, the water bill will appear on the list of bills to pay.

Pay Sales Tax

QuickBooks tracks the sales tax that you collect from customers and must remit to governmental agencies. When you set up a new company in QuickBooks, you identify which items and customers are subject to sales tax. In addition, you must specify the appropriate sales tax rate. Then whenever you prepare sales invoices, QuickBooks automatically calculates and adds sales tax to the invoices.

Rock Castle Construction is required to collect sales tax from customers on certain items sold. Rock Castle then must pay the sales tax collected to the appropriate governmental tax agency.

QuickBooks uses a two-step process to remit sales tax:

1. The *Pay Sales Tax* window lists the sales taxes owed and allows you to select the individual sales tax items you want to pay.

2. Print the check to pay the sales tax.

To select the sales tax to pay:

Step 1: Click the **Pay Sales Tax** icon on the Vendors Navigator.

Step 2: When the following *Pay Sales Tax* window appears:

- ◆ Select Pay From Account: **Checking**
- ◆ Select Check Date: **12/31/2003**.
- ◆ Show sales tax due through: **12/31/2003**.
- ◆ Check **To be printed**.

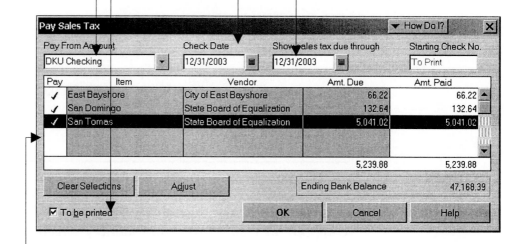

Step 3: Click in the Pay column to select the 3 tax items listed for payment.

Step 4: Click **OK**.

To print the check to pay sales tax to a governmental agency:

Step 1: Click **File** (Menu).

Step 2: Select **Print Forms**.

Step 3: Select **Checks**.

Step 4: When the following *Select Checks to Print* window appears, select **City of East Bayshore** and **State Board of Equalization**.

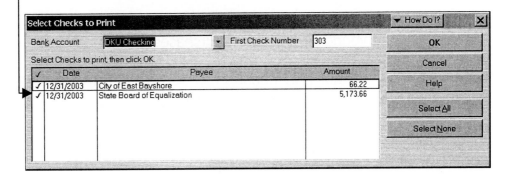

Step 5: Select Bank Account: **Checking**. Select First Check Number: **303**.

Step 6: Click **OK**.

Step 7: Select print settings, then click **Print**.

Vendor Reports

QuickBooks provides vendor reports to answer the following questions:

◆ How much do we owe? (Accounts Payable reports)

◆ How much have we purchased? (Purchase reports)

◆ How much inventory do we have? (Inventory reports)

QuickBooks offers several different ways to access vendor reports:

1. Vendor Detail Center: Summarizes vendor information in one location (Access the Vendor Detail Center from the Vendor Navigator or from the Vendors menu).

2. Vendor Navigator: Vendor Reports lists four vendor reports: A/P Aging Summary, Unpaid Bills Detail, Vendor Balance Detail, and Vendor Balance Summary.

3. Report Finder: Permits you to locate reports by type of report (Click Reports in the *Navigators* window; in the Report Finder, see Vendors & Payables, Purchases, and Inventory reports).

4. Report Menu: Reports are grouped by type of report (See Vendors & Payables, Purchases, and Inventory reports).

5. Vendor List: Reports can be accessed from the Reports button on the *Vendor List* window.

Vendor Detail Center

The Vendor Detail Center summarizes vendor information in one convenient location. Display the Vendor Detail Center as follows:

Step 1: From the Vendor Navigator under Related Activities, select: **Vendor Detail Center**.

Step 2: Select Vendor: **Koch Window & Door**.

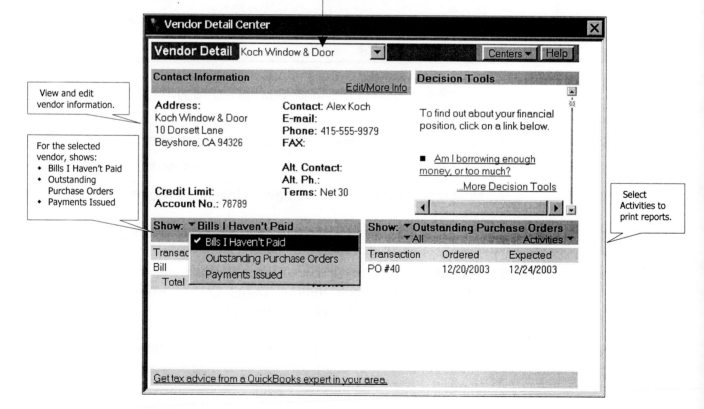

The Vendor Detail Center permits you to customize the vendor information displayed by selecting different activities and dates. Double-click to drill down for more detail or to print reports from the Vendor Center.

Notice that the Vendor Detail Center provides information in the four quadrants about one selected vendor rather than all vendors.

Accounts Payable Reports: How Much Do We Owe?

Accounts Payable are amounts that your company is obligated to pay in the future. Accounts Payable reports tell you how much you owe vendors and when amounts are due.

indicates reports that can be printed.

The following Accounts Payable reports provide information useful when tracking amounts owed vendors:

1. 📄 Accounts Payable Aging Summary

2. 📄 Accounts Payable Aging Detail

3. Bills I Haven't Paid (📄 Unpaid Bills Detail)

📄 *Accounts Payable Aging Summary*

The Accounts Payable Aging Summary summarizes accounts payable balances by the age of the account. This report helps to track any past due bills as well as provides information about bills that will be due shortly.

Although you can access the vendor reports in several different ways, we will access this report from the Reports menu.

To print the A/P Aging Summary report:

Step 1: From the **Reports** menu, select: **Vendors & Payables**.

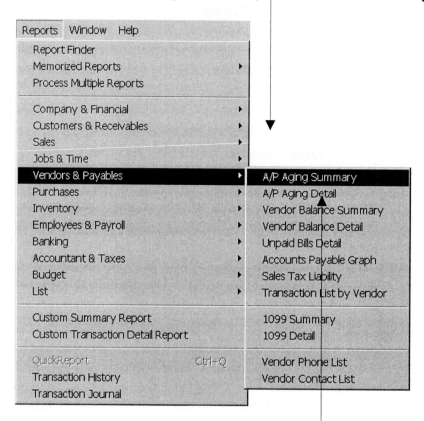

Double-click an entry to drill down to display transaction detail. Double-click again to view the bill.

Step 2: Select: **A/P Aging Summary**.

Step 3: Select Date: **12/22/2003**. Click **Refresh**.

Step 4: Insert **your name** and **Chapter 5** in the report footer.

Step 5: Print the report using the **Portrait** orientation.

Step 6: ✎ Circle the vendors and amounts of any account payable that is 31-60 days past due.

Step 7: Close the *A/P Aging Summary* window.

✓ **$4,125 is 31-60 days past due.**

📘 *Accounts Payable Aging Detail*

The Accounts Payable Aging Detail report lists the specific bills that make up the account payable balances.

To print the A/P Aging Detail report:

Step 1: From the **Reports** menu, select: **Vendors & Payables**.

Step 2: Select: **A/P Aging Detail**.

Step 3: When the *A/P Aging Detail* window appears, select Date: **12/22/2003**. Click **Refresh**.

> Double-click on an entry to drill down to the related bill.

Step 4: Insert **your name** and **Chapter 5** in the report footer. Print the report using **Portrait** orientation.

Step 5: Close the *A/P Aging Detail* window.

Bills I Haven't Paid (📘 Unpaid Bills Detail)

QuickBooks permits you to view unpaid bills for a specific vendor or all of your unpaid bills.

To view unpaid bills for a specific vendor onscreen:

Step 1: Display the **Vendor Detail Center** and select Vendor: **Koch Window & Door**.

Step 2: In one of the lower quandrants, select Show: **Bills I Haven't Paid**. Select: **All**.

Step 3: One bill for $260.00 for Koch Window & Door should be listed.

If you wanted to view all of your unpaid bills, use the Unpaid Bills Detail report:

Step 1: From the **Reports** menu, select: **Vendors & Payables**.

Step 2: Select **Unpaid Bills Detail**.

Step 3: When the *Unpaid Bills Detail* window appears, select Date: **12/22/2003**. Click **Refresh**. All of the unpaid bills will appear.

Step 4: Insert **your name** and **Chapter 5** in the report footer. Print the Unpaid Bills Detail report.

Step 5: Close the *Unpaid Bills Detail* window.

Purchase Reports: How Much Have We Purchased?

Purchase reports provide information about purchases by item, by vendor, or by open purchase orders. Purchase reports include:

1. Open Purchase Orders Report (Outstanding Purchase Orders).

2. Purchases by Vendor Summary.

3. Purchases by Item Summary.

Open Purchase Orders Report

Open purchase orders are purchase orders for items ordered but not yet received. QuickBooks permits you to view open purchase orders for a specific vendor or to view all open purchase orders. Open purchase orders for specific vendors can be viewed from the Vendor Detail Center.

To print the Open Purchase Orders Report that lists all open purchase orders:

Step 1: From the **Reports** menu, select: **Purchases**.

Step 2: Select: **Open Purchase Orders**.

Step 3: Select Dates: **All**. Click **Refresh**.

Step 4: Insert **your name** and **Chapter 5** in the report footer.

Step 5: Print the report using **Portrait** orientation.

Step 6: Close the *Open Purchase Orders* window.

Inventory Reports: How Much Inventory Do We Have?

Inventory reports list the amount and status of inventory. Inventory reports include:

1. ▥ Inventory Valuation Summary.

2. ▥ Inventory Stock Status By Item.

3. ▥ Inventory Stock Status By Vendor.

4. ▥ Physical Inventory Worksheet.

▥ *Inventory Stock Status By Item*

This report lists quantity of inventory items on hand and on order. This information is useful when planning when and how many units to order.

To print the Inventory Stock Status By Item report:

Step 1: From the **Reports** menu, select: **Inventory**.

Step 2: Select: **Inventory Stock Status By Item**.

Step 3: Enter Date: From: **12/22/2003** To: **12/22/2003**. Click **Refresh**.

Step 4: Insert **your name** and **Chapter 5** in the report footer.

Step 5: Print the report using **Landscape** orientation.

Step 6: ✎ Circle all Hardware inventory items that need to be reordered.

Step 7: Close the *Stock Status By Item* window.

✓   **On 12/22/2003, 5 bifold wood doors are on hand and 1 more is on order.**

📋 *Physical Inventory Worksheet*

The Physical Inventory Worksheet is used when taking a physical count of inventory on hand. The worksheet lists the quantity of inventory items on hand and provides a blank column in which to enter the quantity counted during a physical inventory count.

To print the Physical Inventory Worksheet:

Step 1: From the **Reports** menu, select: **Inventory**.

Step 2: Select: **Physical Inventory Worksheet**.

Step 3: Insert **your name** and **Chapter 5** in the report footer.

Step 4: Print the worksheet using **Portrait** orientation. Then close the *Physical Inventory Worksheet* window.

QuickBooks offers other additional vendor reports that provide useful information to a business. These reports can also be accessed from the Reports menu or from the Report Finder in the Navigators window.

Back Up Chapter 5

Back up your Chapter 5 file to your floppy disk. Use the file name: [your name] Chapter 5.

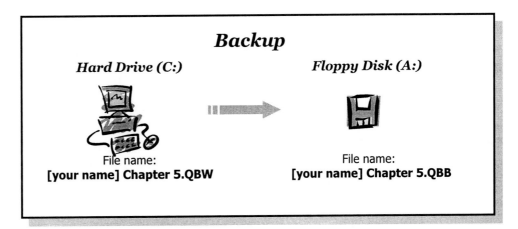

Backup

Hard Drive (C:)

File name:
[your name] Chapter 5.QBW

Floppy Disk (A:)

File name:
[your name] Chapter 5.QBB

Step 1:   Insert the **Chapter 5** backup disk in drive A.

Step 2:   Click **File, Back Up**.

Step 3:   Enter the file name: **[your name] Chapter 5.QBB**. Enter location: **A:**.

Step 4:   Click **Back Up**.

You have now backed up the Chapter 5 file to your Chapter 5 floppy disk.

If you are continuing your computer session, close the company file then proceed to Activity 5.1.

If you are quitting your computer session now (1) close the company file and (2) exit QuickBooks.

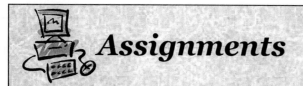

Assignments

Activity 5.1: Purchase Inventory

Scenario

Mr. Castle tosses you a document as he charges past your cubicle, shouting over his shoulder, *"That's info about our new supplier. From now on, Rock Castle will install closet shelving instead of waiting on unreliable subcontractors. We do a better job and we get it done on time!"*

Vendor:	Claire's Closets
Contact:	Claire Koch
Address:	91 Sunshine Lane
	Bayshore, CA 94326
Phone:	415-555-0414
Account:	78790
Type:	Materials
Terms:	Net 30
Vendor 1099:	No

New Inventory Item: Closets

New Subitems:

6' Closet Shelving	Cost: $11.00	Sales Price: $15.00
12' Closet Shelving	Cost: $18.00	Sales Price: $25.00
Closet Installation Kit	Cost: $ 5.00	Sales Price: $ 8.00

Reorder Point: 2 each item

Task 1: Restore Company File

The first task is to restore your backup for Chapter 5 to the hard drive, changing the file name to Activity 5.1. Changing the file name enables you to enter the information for this activity without overwriting the Chapter 5 file.

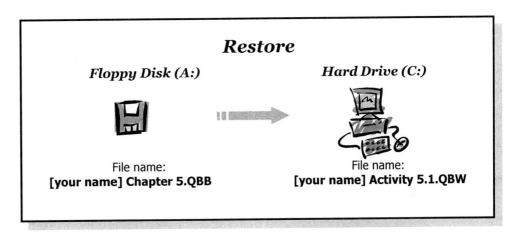

Restore

Floppy Disk (A:)

Hard Drive (C:)

File name:
[your name] Chapter 5.QBB

File name:
[your name] Activity 5.1.QBW

Step 1: 💾 Insert the **Chapter 5** backup disk into drive A.

Step 2: Click **Restore a backup file** (or click **File**, **Restore**).

Step 3: Identify the backup file:

- Filename: **[your name] Chapter 5.QBB**.
- Location: **A:**.

Step 4: Identify the restored file:

- Filename: **[your name] Activity 5.1.QBW**.
- Location: **C:\Program Files\Intuit\QuickBooks Premier**.

Step 5: Click **Restore.** Your backup file will be restored to the C drive. If prompted, enter your User ID and Password.

Step 6: Change the company name to:
[your name] Activity 5.1 Rock Castle Construction.
(To change the company name, select Company (menu), Company Information.)

Task 2: Add New Vendor

Add Claire's Closets as a new vendor. (Hint: Click the Vendor List icon on the Vendor Navigator.)

Task 3: Add New Inventory Item

Step 1: Add the new inventory item, Closets, to the Items List for Rock Castle Construction.

Item Name/Number	Closets
Item Type	Inventory Part
Item Description	Closet Materials
COGS Account	5000 – Cost of Goods Sold
Income Account	4200 – Materials
Asset Account	1120 – Inventory Asset
Tax Code	Tax

Step 2: Add the following three new inventory parts as subitems to Closet Materials. Use Claire's Closets as the preferred vendor.

Item Name	6' Closet Shelving
Item Description	6' Closet Shelving
Cost	$11.00
Sales Price	$15.00

Item Name	12' Closet Shelving
Item Description	12' Closet Shelving
Cost	$18.00
Sales Price	$25.00

Item Name	Closet Install Kit
Item Description	Closet Installation Kit
Cost	$5.00
Sales Price	$8.00

Task 4: Create Purchase Order

Step 1: Create a Purchase Order to order 6 each of the new inventory items from Claire's Closets on 12/23/2003. Expected delivery date: 12/24/2003.

Step 2: Print the Purchase Order.

> ✓ **The total amount of the purchase order is $204.00.**

Task 5: Receive Items

On 12/24/2003, record the receipt of the closet items ordered on 12/23/2003. There are no freight charges.

Task 6: Receive Bill

Record the receipt of the bill for the closet items on 12/27/2003.

Task 7: Back Up Activity 5.1

Back up the Activity 5.1 file to a floppy disk.

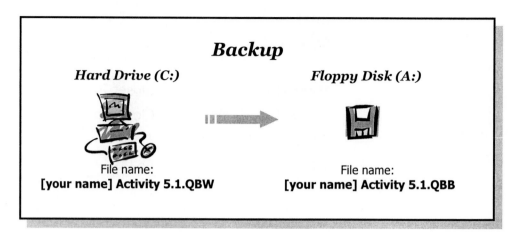

Backup

| Hard Drive (C:) | Floppy Disk (A:) |

File name:
[your name] Activity 5.1.QBW

File name:
[your name] Activity 5.1.QBB

Step 1: 🖫 Insert the **Chapter 5** backup disk in drive A.

Step 2: Click **File, Back Up**.

Step 3: Specify the backup file name: **[your name] Activity 5.1.QBB**. Specify location: **A**.

Step 4: Click **Back Up** to backup Activity 5.1 to your backup floppy disk. Close the company file. (From the File menu, select Close Company.)

Activity 5.2: Record Sale (Chapter 4 Review)

"I told you replacing Mrs. Flowers' door hardware would pay off. She is going to become one of our best customers. Just wait and see." Mr. Castle appears to be in a much better mood today. *"Diane Flowers just had us install new closet shelving in her huge walk-in closet. She said she wanted us to do it because we stand by our work."*

Task 1: Restore Company File

Restore your Activity 5.1 backup, changing the file name to Activity 5.2.

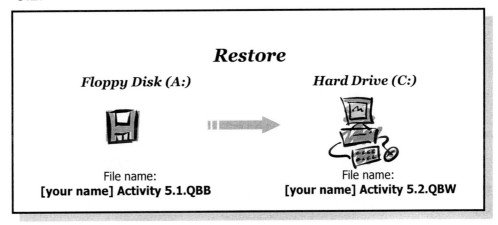

Restore

Floppy Disk (A:)		Hard Drive (C:)
File name:		File name:
[your name] Activity 5.1.QBB		**[your name] Activity 5.2.QBW**

Step 1: Insert the **Chapter 5** backup disk into drive A.

Step 2: Click **Restore a backup file** (or click **File**, **Restore**).

Step 3: Identify the backup file:

- Filename: **[your name] Activity 5.1.QBB**.

- Location: **A:**.

Step 4: Identify the restored file:

- Filename: **[your name] Activity 5.2.QBW**.

- Location: **C:\Program Files\Intuit\QuickBooks Premier**.

Step 5: Click **Restore.** Your backup file will be restored to the C drive. If prompted, enter your User ID and Password.

Step 6: Change the company name to:
[your name] Activity 5.2 Rock Castle Construction.
(To change the company name, select Company (menu), Company Information.)

Note: Use the Customer Navigator to record Tasks 2 – 5.

Task 2: Add Customer Job

Add the Closet Shelving job for Diane Flowers to the Customer: Job List. (Hint: From the Customer: Job list, right-click to display menu, select **Add Job**.)

Job Name	Closet Shelving
Job Status	Closed
Start Date	12/27/2003
Projected End	12/27/2003
End Date	12/27/2003
Job Description	Replace Closet Shelving
Job Type	Repairs

Task 3: Create Invoice

Step 1: Create an invoice for the Flowers closet shelving job using the following information.

Customer: Job	Flowers, Diane: Closet Shelving
Custom Template	Custom Invoice
Date	12/27/2003
Invoice No.	91
Items	(2) 12' Closet Shelves $25.00 each
	(1) 6' Closet Shelves $15.00 each
	(1) Closet Installation Kit $ 8.00 each
	Installation Labor 3 hours

Step 2: Print the invoice.

✓ **The invoice for the Closet Shelving job totals $183.66.**

Task 4: Receive Customer Payment

Record Diane Flowers' payment for the Closet Job (Check No. 625) for the full amount on 12/29/2003. Use the Group with Other Undeposited Funds selection.

Task 5: Record Bank Deposit

Step 1: Record the bank deposit for Diane Flowers' payment.

Step 2: Print a deposit summary.

Task 6: Back Up Activity 5.2

Backup

Hard Drive (C:)   **Floppy Disk (A:)**

File name: File name:
[your name] Activity 5.2.QBW   **[your name] Activity 5.2.QBB**

Step 1: Insert the **Chapter 5** backup disk in drive A.

Step 2: Click **File**, **Back Up**.

Step 3: Specify the backup file name: **[your name] Activity 5.2.QBB**. Specify location: **A**.

Step 4: Click **Back Up** to backup Activity 5.2 to your backup floppy disk. Close the company file. (From the File menu, select Close Company.)

Activity 5.3: Enter Bills

When you arrive at work, you decide to sort through the papers stacked in the corner of your cubicle. You discover two unpaid utility bills amid the clutter.

Task 1: Restore Company File

Restore your Activity 5.2 backup to the hard drive, changing the file name to Activity 5.3.

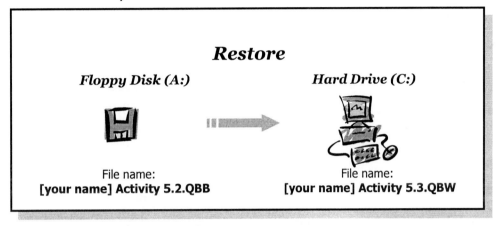

Restore

Floppy Disk (A:)   *Hard Drive (C:)*

File name: File name:
[your name] Activity 5.2.QBB   **[your name] Activity 5.3.QBW**

Step 1: 💾 Insert the **Chapter 5** backup disk into drive A.

Step 2: Click **Restore a backup file** (or click **File, Restore**).

Step 3: Identify the backup file:

- Filename: **[your name] Activity 5.2.QBB**.
- Location: **A:**.

Step 4: Identify the restored file:

- Filename: **[your name] Activity 5.3.QBW**.
- Location: **C:\Program Files\Intuit\QuickBooks Premier**.

Step 5: Click **Restore.** Your backup file will be restored to the C drive. If prompted, enter your User ID and Password.

Step 6: Change the company name to: **[your name] Activity 5.3 Rock Castle Construction**. (To change the company name, select Company (menu), Company Information.)

Task 2: Enter Bills

Using the Enter Bills icon on the Vendor Navigator, enter the following two utility bills for Rock Castle Construction.

Vendor	Cal Gas & Electric
Date	12/24/2003
Amount	$87.00
Account	7610: Gas and Electric

Vendor	Cal Telephone
Date	12/24/2003
Amount	$54.00
Account	7620: Telephone

Task 3: Pay Bills

On 12/24/2003, pay the two utility bills that you entered in Task 2. (Hint: Select **Show all bills**.) Print the checks.

> ✓ *The Amt. Paid on the Pay Bills window totals $141.00.*

Task 4: Back Up Activity 5.3

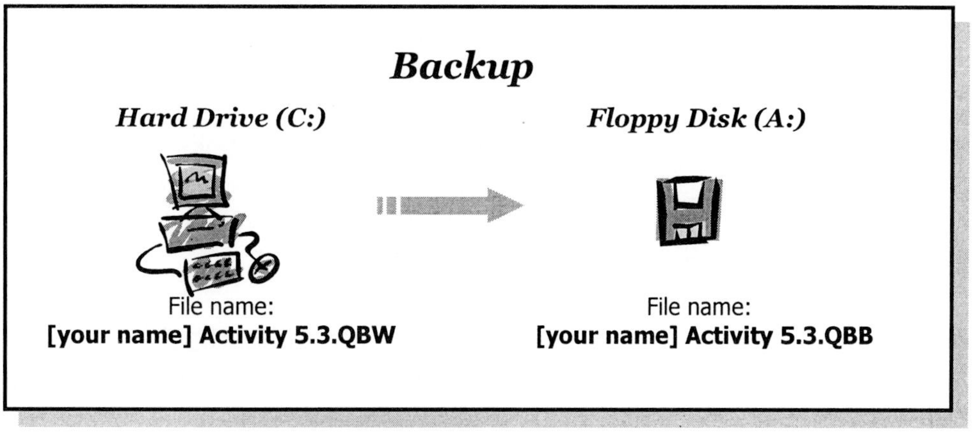

Backup

Hard Drive (C:)

File name:
[your name] Activity 5.3.QBW

Floppy Disk (A:)

File name:
[your name] Activity 5.3.QBB

Step 1: 🖫 Insert the **Chapter 5** backup disk in drive A.

Step 2: Click **Restore a backup file** (or click **File, Back Up**).

Step 3: Specify the backup file name: **[your name] Activity 5.3.QBB**. Specify location: **A**.

Step 4: Click **Back Up**.

Activity 5.4: Vendor Report

Step 1: Print an Inventory Stock Status By Item report to check the status of the closet inventory items as of 12/31/2003. Insert **your name** and **Activity 5.4** in the report footer.

Step 2: ✎ Circle the closet inventory items on the Inventory Stock Status printout.

Step 3: Close the company file.

Activity 5.5: Web Quest

B2B (Business to Business) is the trend in e-commerce purchasing. Digital marketplaces permit businesses to purchase online from other businesses.

Step 1: From the QuickBooks Vendor Navigator in the *Vendor Solutions* window, click Automatically back up your important data online and have anytime, anywhere access.

Step 2: Read about online backups, then click **Tell Me More** to learn more about the various options available.

Step 3: Prepare an e-mail to Mr. Castle summarizing the advantages and disadvantages of online backups. Include your recommendations regarding whether Rock Castle Construction should use online backup and if so, which online backup option would be best.

Computer Accounting with QuickBooks 2002
Chapter 5 Printout Checklist
Name:_____ **Date:**_____

☑	***Printout Checklist – Chapter 5***
☐	Vendor List
☐	Item List
☐	Purchase Order No. 40 & 41
☐	Checks No. 298 – 302
☐	Check No. 303 – 304 for sales tax
☐	A/P Aging Summary Report
☐	A/P Aging Detail Report
☐	Unpaid Bills Detail Report
☐	Open Purchase Orders Report
☐	Inventory Stock Status By Item Report
☐	Physical Inventory Worksheet
☑	***Printout Checklist – Activity 5.1***
☐	Task 4: Purchase Order
☑	***Printout Checklist – Activity 5.2***
☐	Task 3: Customer Invoice
☐	Task 5: Bank Deposit Summary
☑	***Printout Checklist – Activity 5.3***
☐	Task 3: Checks No. 305 & 306
☑	***Printout Checklist – Activity 5.4***
☐	Inventory Stock Status By Item Report

☑	*Printout Checklist – Activity 5.5*
☐	E-mail Summarizing Online Backup Options and Recommendations

6 Employees and Payroll

Scenario

The next morning on your way to your cubicle, two employees ask you if their paychecks are ready yet. Apparently, Rock Castle employees expect their paychecks *today?!*

Deciding that you do not want all the employees upset with you if paychecks are not ready on time, you take the initiative and ask Mr. Castle about the paychecks.

His reply: *"Oops! I was so busy I almost forgot about paychecks."* He hands you another stack of documents. *"Here—you will need these. I'm sure you won't have any trouble using QuickBooks to print the paychecks. And don't forget to pay yourself!"* he adds with a chuckle as he rushes out the door.

6 *Learning Objectives*

In Chapter 6, you will learn the following QuickBooks features:

Introduction

To begin Chapter 6, first start QuickBooks software and then restore your backup file.

Start QuickBooks software by clicking on the QuickBooks desktop icon or click **Start**, **Programs**, **QuickBooks Premier** (or QuickBooks Pro), **QuickBooks Premier** (or QuickBooks Pro).

Restore your backup for Activity 5.3 on your floppy disk to the C: drive, renaming the file Chapter 6.

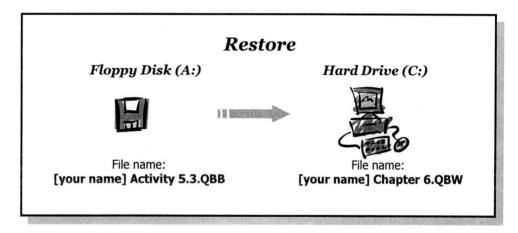

Restore

Floppy Disk (A:)	*Hard Drive (C:)*
File name: **[your name] Activity 5.3.QBB**	File name: **[your name] Chapter 6.QBW**

Step 1: 🖫 Insert the **Chapter 5** backup disk into drive A.

Step 2: Click **Restore a backup file** (or click **File**, **Restore**).

Step 3: Identify the backup file:

- Filename: **[your name] Chapter 6.QBB**.
- Location: **A:**.

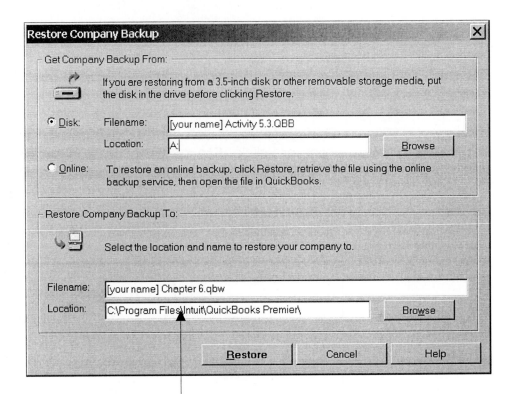

Step 4: Identify the restored file:

- Filename: **[your name] Chapter 6.QBW**.
- Location: **C:\Program Files\Intuit\QuickBooks Premier**.

Step 5: Click **Restore**.

Step 6: Change the company name to:
[your name] Chapter 6 Rock Castle Construction.

(To change the company name, click Company (menu), Company Information.)

In this chapter you will focus on recording employee and payroll transactions. To assist in processing payroll, QuickBooks offers a time tracking feature that permits you to track the amount of time worked. QuickBooks uses time tracked to:

1. Calculate employee paychecks.

2. Transfer time to sales invoices to bill customers for work performed.

Although this chapter focuses on time worked by employees, work can be performed by employees, subcontractors, or owners. The time tracking feature can be used to track time worked by any of the three. How you record the payment, however, depends upon who performs the work: employee, subcontractor, or business owner.

Employees complete Form W-4 when hired. Form W-2 summarizes annual wages and tax withholdings.

No tax withholdings if independent contractor status. Tax Form 1099-MISC summarizes payments.

If owner is also an employee, wages are recorded as payroll. If not wages, then payment to owner is a withdrawal (sole proprietorship) or dividends (corporation).

Status	Pay using QB Window....	Navigator
Employee	*Pay Employees* Window	Employee Navigator
Subcontractor (Vendor)	*Enter Bills* Window *Pay Bills* Window	Vendor Navigator
Owner	*Write Checks* Window	Banking Navigator

It is important that you determine the status of the individual performing work. The status determines whether you record payments to the individual as an employee paycheck, vendor payment, or owner withdrawal.

After you determine the status of persons performing work, the next step is to set up the time tracking and payroll features of QuickBooks. The following table summarizes the steps to set up QuickBooks payroll and time tracking.

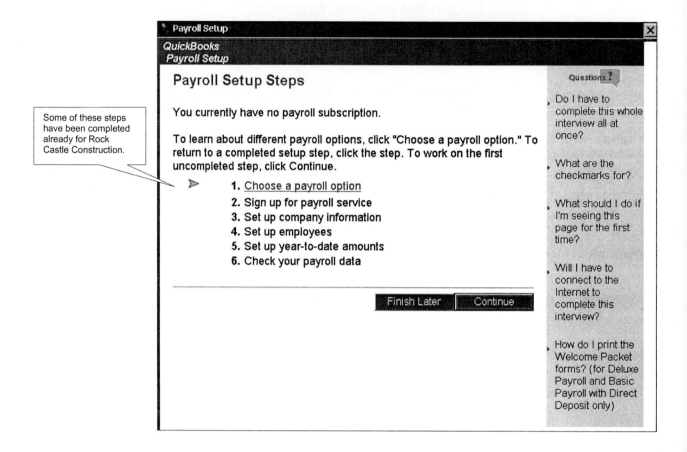

QuickBooks Time Tracking and Payroll Setup

Action	Using QB...
1. Set up payroll.	Employees Navigator, Set Up Payroll
2. Turn on time tracking.	Preferences, Time Tracking
3. Turn on payroll, enter Payroll and Employee Preferences.	Preferences, Payroll & Employees
4. Enter customer and jobs on which time will be worked.	Customer: Job List
5. Record labor as a service item.	Item List
6. Enter employees and nonemployees whose time will be tracked:	
▶ Employee information	Employee List
▶ Subcontractors	Vendor List
▶ Owners	Other List

QuickBooks automatically creates a chart of accounts with payroll liability and payroll expense accounts. QuickBooks also uses Payroll Items to track supporting detail for the payroll accounts.

Payroll accounts for Rock Castle Construction have already been established. To learn more about payroll setup, see Chapter 11.

To track time and process payroll in QuickBooks you will use the Employee Navigator. After restoring your backup file for Rock Castle Construction, click **Employees** in the *Navigators* window to open the Employees Navigator shown below.

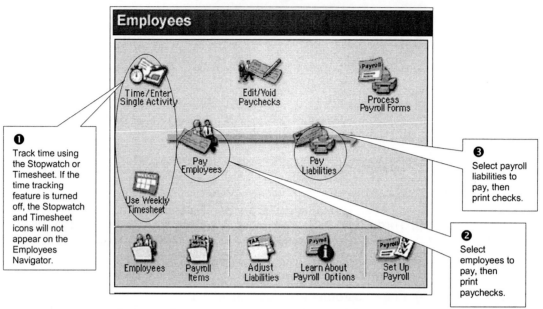

The Employee Navigator is a flowchart of payroll transactions. As the flowchart indicates, there are three main steps to processing payroll using QuickBooks:

❶ **Track time**: QuickBooks Pro and QuickBooks Premier permits you to track employee time in the following ways:

    ♦ **Stopwatch**: Use the Stopwatch to time an activity and enter the time data. QuickBooks automatically records the time on the employee's weekly timesheet.

    ♦ **Timesheet**: Use the weekly Timesheet to enter time worked by each employee on various jobs during the week.

    ♦ **QuickBooks Timer**: QuickBooks Timer is a separate computer program. Employees and subcontractors can track time with the Timer program without access to QuickBooks software or your QuickBooks company data file. Then you can import Timer files (*.iif files) into QuickBooks to process payroll. (Click Start, Programs, QuickBooks Premier, Install QuickBooks Pro Timer.)

❷ **Pay Employees**: Select employees to pay and create their paychecks.

❸ **Pay payroll liabilities**: Pay payroll tax liabilities due governmental agencies such as the IRS. Payroll tax liabilities include federal income taxes withheld, state income taxes withheld, FICA (Social Security and Medicare), and unemployment taxes.

Other QuickBooks features available from the Employee Navigator include:

◆ **Learn About Payroll Options**: QuickBooks offers basic and deluxe payroll services.

◆ **Set Up Payroll**: Set up QuickBooks to process your company payroll.

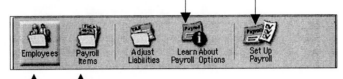

The Employee Navigator includes the following lists:

Employee List: The Employee List contains employee information, such as address and social security number.

Payroll Items List: The Payroll Items List contains information about wages, benefits, and withholding.

Next, you will set Quickbooks preferences for time tracking and payroll.

Time Tracking and Payroll Preferences

Use QuickBooks Preferences to customize time tracking and payroll to suit your company's specific needs. There are two types of preferences that affect payroll:

1. Time Tracking Preferences.

2. Payroll and Employees Preferences.

Time Tracking Preferences

To turn on the QuickBooks time tracking feature, complete the following steps:

Step 1: Click **Company** in the *Navigators* window to display the Company Navigator.

Step 2: Click the **Preferences** icon to display the *Preferences* window.

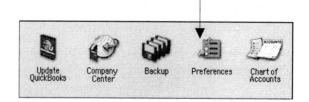

Step 3: Select **Time Tracking** from the scrollbar on the left of the *Preferences* window.

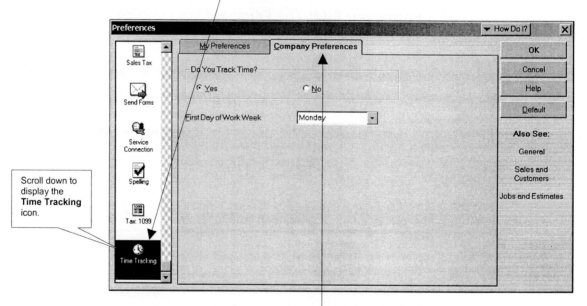

Scroll down to display the **Time Tracking** icon.

Step 4: Select the **Company Preferences** tab.

Step 5: Select Do You Track Time: **Yes**. Select First Day of Work Week: **Monday**.

Step 6: Leave the *Preferences* window open.

Payroll and Employees Preferences

Next, select QuickBooks Payroll and Employees Preferences for your company.

With the *Preferences* window open:

Step 1: From the left scrollbar of the *Preferences* window, click on the **Payroll & Employees** icon.

Step 2: Select the **Company Preferences** tab.

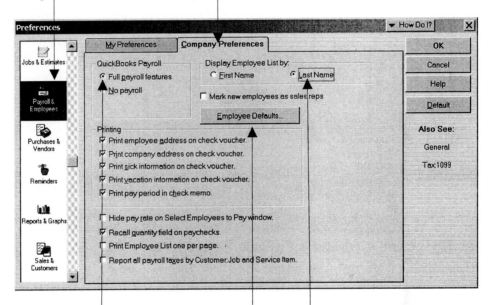

Step 3: Select **Full payroll features**.

Step 4: Select Display Employee List by: **Last Name**.

Step 5: Click the **Employee Defaults** button to select payroll defaults.

Step 6: Select the checkbox: **Use time data to create paychecks**. Now QuickBooks will automatically use tracked time to calculate payroll.

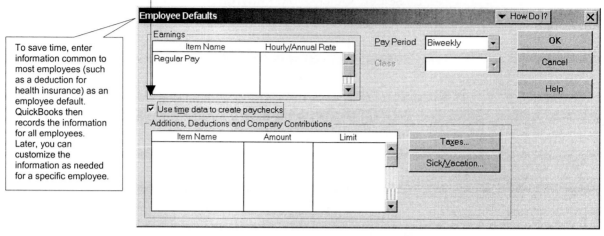

To save time, enter information common to most employees (such as a deduction for health insurance) as an employee default. QuickBooks then records the information for all employees. Later, you can customize the information as needed for a specific employee.

Step 7: Click **OK** to close the *Employee Defaults* window. Click **OK** again to close the *Preferences* window.

Step 8: When the following warning message appears, click **OK**.

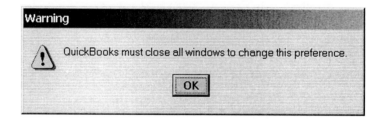

Next, you will edit and print the Employee List.

Employee List

The Employee List contains employee information such as address, telephone, salary or wage rate, and social security number.

To view the Employee List for Rock Castle Construction:

Step 1: Open the Employee Navigator, then click the **Employees** icon in the lower left corner of the Navigator.

Step 2: The following *Employee List* window should appear listing employees and their social security numbers. Click the **Name** bar to sort employee names in alphabetical order.

To view or edit employee information, double-click the employee's name.

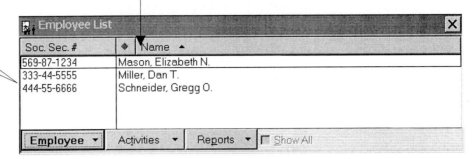

Add New Employee

To enter your name as a new employee in the Employee List:

Step 1: Click the **Employee** button in the lower left corner of the *Employee List* window.

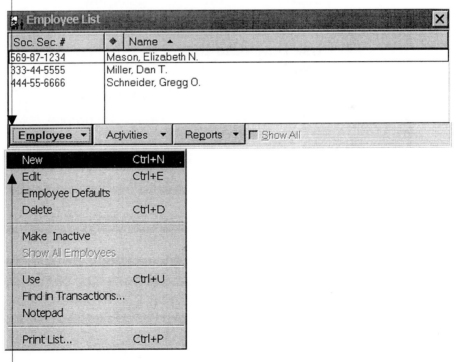

Step 2: Click **New**.

Step 3: A blank *New Employee* window should appear. Enter **your name** and the following information into *the New Employee* window.

Address Info:	
Address	555 Sundown Lane Bayshore, CA 94326
Phone	415-555-6677
SS No.	333-22-4444
E-mail	[enter your email address]
Type	Regular
Hired	12/15/2003

Payroll Info:	
Earnings Name	Regular Pay
Hour/Annual Rate	$7.00
Use time data to create paychecks	Yes
Pay Period	Biweekly
Deductions	Health Insurance
Amount	-25.00
Limit	-1200.00

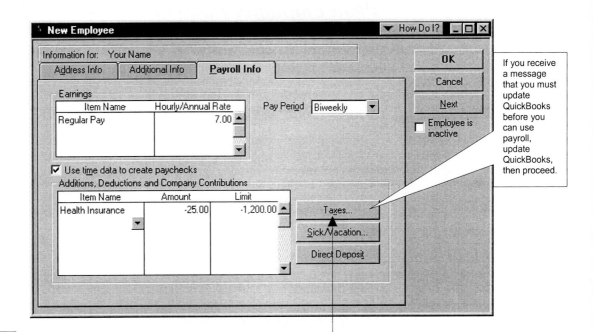

New employees complete Form W-4 to indicate filing status and allowances.

Step 4: Click the **Taxes** button to view federal, state, and other tax information related to your employment, such as filing status and allowances. Leave the number of allowances at 0 for both **federal** and **state** taxes. Click **OK** to close the *Taxes* window.

Step 5: Click **OK** again to add your name to Rock Castle Construction's Employee List.

If you start using QuickBooks midyear, enter year-to-date amounts for payroll *before* you start using QuickBooks to process paychecks.

Step 6: When asked if you want to set up payroll information for sick leave and vacation, click **Leave As Is** to use the employee default information for these items.

Step 7: Leave the *Employee List* window open.

Print Employee List

To print the Employee List:

Step 1: Click the **Employee** button in the lower left corner of the *Employee List* window.

Step 2: Select **Print List**.

Step 3: Select appropriate printer settings, then click **Print**.

Step 4: ✎ On the Employee List printout, circle your information on the Employee List.

Step 5: Close the *Employee List* window.

For more information about payroll setup, see Chapter 11. The remainder of this chapter will cover time tracking, payroll processing and payroll reports.

Time Tracking

QuickBooks Pro and QuickBooks Premier permits you to track time worked on various jobs. As mentioned earlier, time can be tracked for employees, subcontractors, or owners.

When employees use time tracking, the employee records the time worked on each job. The time data is then used to:

1. Prepare paychecks.
2. Bill customers for time worked on specific jobs.

QuickBooks Pro and QuickBooks Premier provides three different ways to track time.

1. **Stopwatch**: Use the Stopwatch to time an activity and enter the time data. QuickBooks automatically records the time on the employee's weekly timesheet.

2. **Timesheet**: Use the weekly Timesheet to enter time worked by each employee on various jobs during the week.

3. **QuickBooks Timer**: QuickBooks Timer is a separate computer program. Employees and subcontractors can track time with the Timer program. Then you can import Timer files (*.iif files) into QuickBooks to process payroll. The advantage to using the QuickBooks Timer is that employees and subcontractors do not need access to QuickBooks or your company data file to enter time worked.

Stopwatch

You will use the QuickBooks stopwatch feature to time how long it takes you to complete payroll activities in this chapter.

To start the Stopwatch:

Step 1: From the Employee Navigator, click the **Time/Enter Single Activity** icon.

Step 2: When the following window appears:

- Select Date: **12/15/2003**.

- Select Name: **Your Name**.

You can only use the Stopwatch to time activities for today's date. However, for this activity, use the programmed date for the sample company: 12/15/2003.

- If the work was for a particular job or customer, you would enter the job or customer name and the service item, then click Billable. In this case, your time is not billable to a particular customer's job, so **uncheck Billable**.

- Select Payroll Item: **Regular Pay**.

- Enter Notes: **Process payroll**.

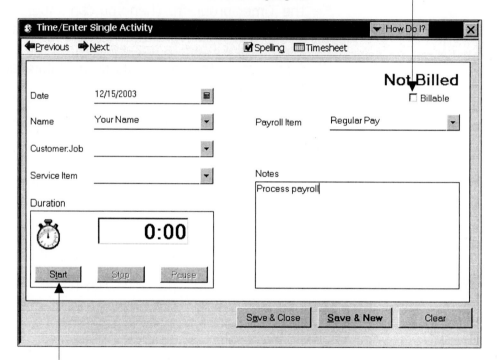

Step 3: Click the **Start** button to start the stopwatch.

Step 4: Leave the window open while you complete the following payroll activities.

Timesheet

Rock Castle Construction pays employees biweekly. Checks are issued on Wednesday for the pay period ending that day.

Use the timesheet to enter the hours you worked for Rock Castle Construction during the last pay period.

To use QuickBooks timesheet feature:

Step 1: Click on the **Use Weekly Timesheets** icon on the Employee Navigator.

Step 2: Select Name: **[Your Name]**.

Step 3: From the Payroll Item drop-down list, select **Regular Pay**.

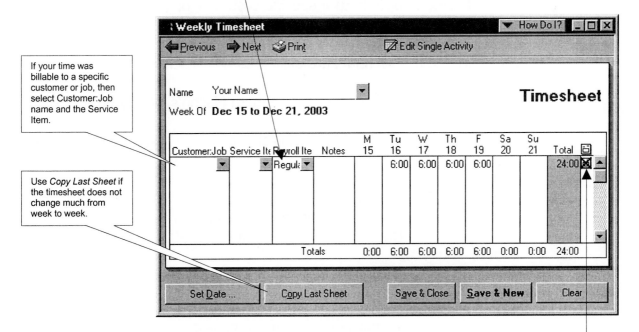

If your time was billable to a specific customer or job, then select Customer:Job name and the Service Item.

Use *Copy Last Sheet* if the timesheet does not change much from week to week.

Step 4: Because your time is not billable to a specific customer or job, click the white **Invoice** icon in the last column to indicate these charges will not be transferred to an invoice. A red ⊠ should appear over the Invoice icon.

Step 5: Enter **6** hours each for Tuesday (December 16th), Wednesday (December 17th), Thursday (December 18th), and Friday (December 19th) for a total of 24 hours for the week.

Step 6: Click the **Next** button in the upper left corner of the *Weekly Timesheet* window to advance to the timesheet for the week of December 22.

> Remember to enter **Regular Pay** and click the **Invoice icon** to mark your hours as nonbillable.

Step 7: The Timesheet date should change to December 22 through December 28. Enter **6** hours each for Monday (22nd), Tuesday (23rd), and Wednesday (24th) for a total of 18 hours.

Step 8: Click **Save & New** to record your hours and display a new timesheet.

If time is billable to a specific customer or job, this is indicated on the weekly timesheet. For example, Elizabeth Mason, a Rock Castle Construction employee, worked on the Teschner sunroom; therefore, her hours are billable to the Teschner sunroom job.

To enter billable hours on Elizabeth Mason's weekly timesheet:

Step 1: On the new timesheet, select Name: **Elizabeth N. Mason**.

Step 2: Click the **Previous** button in the upper left corner of the *Timesheet* window to change the timesheet dates to December 15 to December 21, 2003.

Step 3: To record time billable to a specific customer:

- Select Customer: Job: **Teschner, Anton: Sunroom**.
- Select Service Item: **Framing**.

Step 4: Enter the following hours into the weekly timesheet to record time Elizabeth worked framing the sunroom:

Monday December 15	8 hours
Tuesday December 16	8 hours
Wednesday December 17	8 hours
Thursday December 18	6 hours

Notice that if the customer: job or service item changes, the time is entered on a new line in the timesheet.

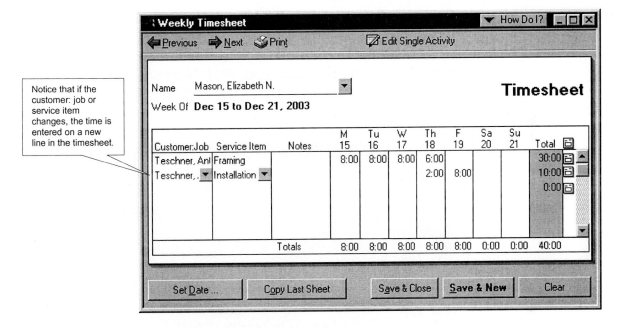

Step 5: Move to the next line in the timesheet to enter the *installation* work that Elizabeth performed on the Teschner sunroom.

- Select Customer: Job: **Teschner, Anton: Sunroom**.

- Select Service Item: **Installation**.

- Enter hours worked:

| Thursday December 18 | 2 hours |
| Friday December 19 | 8 hours |

Step 6: Click the **Next** button to record Elizabeth's hours and display a new timesheet.

Step 7: Record **8** hours for Monday (22nd), Tuesday (23rd), and Wednesday (24th) that Elizabeth worked on installing the Teschner sunroom.

Step 8: Leave the *Weekly Timesheets* window open.

To print the weekly timesheets for yourself and Elizabeth Mason, complete the following steps:

Step 1: From the the *Weekly Timesheet* window, click the **Print** button.

Step 2: When the following *Print Timesheets* window appears, select Dated: **12/15/2003** thru **12/24/2003**. If necessary, press **Tab**.

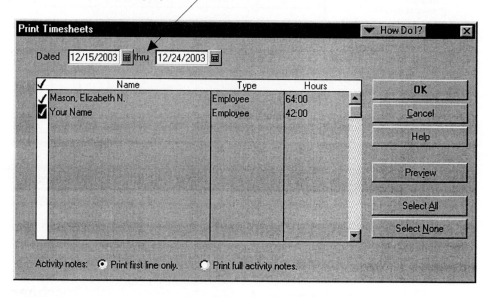

Step 3: Select **Elizabeth Mason** and **your name**.

Step 4: Click **OK**, then print the timesheets.

Step 5: ✒ Sign the timesheets.

Step 6: Click **Save & Close** to close the *Weekly Timesheet* window.

Transfer Time to Sales Invoices

Billable time can be transferred to a specific customer's invoice. First open the *Create Invoices* window for the customer, then select the time billable to that specific customer.

To transfer billable time to the Teschner sales invoice:

Step 1: Open the *Create Invoices* window by clicking the **Invoices** icon on the Customer Navigator.

Step 2: From the *Create Invoices* window, select the customer job to be billed. In this instance, select Customer: Job: **Teschner, Anton: Sunroom**.

Step 3: Select Date: **12/24/2003**.

Step 4: Click the **Time/Costs** button on the upper right of the *Create Invoices* window.

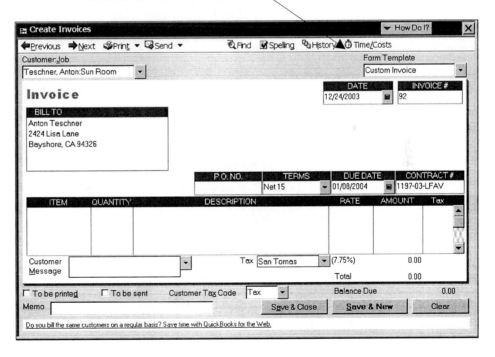

Step 5: When the *Choose Billable Time and Costs* window appears, click the **Time** tab.

Notice that items and expenses can also be tracked and billed to specific customer' jobs.

Total billable time should be $8,680.

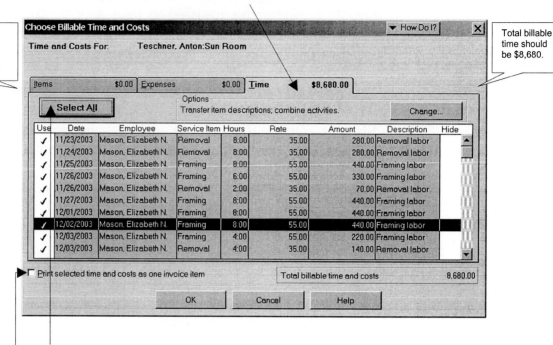

Step 6: Click the **Select All** button to select all the billable times listed for the Teschner Sunroom job.

Step 7: You can transfer time to an invoice in three different ways:

(1) Combine all the selected times and costs into *one* entry on the invoice.
(2) List a *subtotal* for each *service* item on the invoice, or
(3) List a separate invoice line item for each *activity* you check.

In this instance, you will list a separate invoice line item for each activity you check, so:

- *Uncheck* **Print selected time and costs as one invoice item** in the lower left corner of the *Billable Time and Costs* window, *and*
- Click the **Change** button, then select **Do not combine activities** from the *Options for Transferring Billable Time* window.

To create a report detailing time spent on a specific job:
1. Report Finder
2. Jobs & Time
3. Time by Job Detail
4. Filter for Customer & Job

Step 8: Click **OK** to close the *Billable Time and Costs* window and add the labor cost to the Teschner sales invoice.

Step 9: Print the invoice. Select blank paper and print lines around fields.

Step 10: Click **Save & Close** to record the invoice and close the *Create Invoices* window.

🕐 ***Stop the Stopwatch now, by clicking the Stop button and then clicking Clear. Close the Stopwatch window.***

Print Paychecks

> Intuit provided tax tables with QuickBooks 99; however, to receive tax table updates with QuickBooks 2001 and 2002, you must subscribe to one of the payroll tax services.

After entering time worked, the next step is to create employee paychecks.

There are two ways that a company can perform payroll calculations.
1. Use QuickBooks Payroll Services: Basic, Deluxe, or Premier.
2. Manually calculate payroll taxes.

1. **Use QuickBooks Payroll Services**.

> If you receive a message about updating QuickBooks before using payroll, update QuickBooks and then proceed. If you are not able to use QB payroll tax tables, then enter amounts shown on the following pages manually in the *Create Paychecks* window.

QuickBooks offers three levels of payroll services: Basic Payroll, Deluxe Payroll, and Premier Payroll. When you subscribe to a payroll service, QuickBooks automatically calculates tax deductions. The Deluxe Payroll Service offers the additional feature of preparing federal and state payroll forms and electronically paying federal and state payroll taxes. Both Basic and Deluxe Payroll Services require an Internet connection. You can receive the first payroll update free for the Basic Payroll Service.

For more information about QuickBooks Payroll Services, see *Learn About Payroll Options* on the Employee Navigator.

Click here to see the comparison chart for the Basic, Deluxe and Premier Payroll services.

	Integrates with QuickBooks		
	Basic	**Deluxe**	**Premier**
Payroll Services Comparison			
Integrates with QuickBooks	x	x	
Earnings and deductions calculations	x	x	x
Federal and state tax table updates	x	x	x
Federal payroll tax forms[1]	x	x	x
Electronic direct deposit of paychecks[2]	optional	x	x
Automatic federal and state payroll tax deposits		x	x
Electronic payroll tax filings		x	x
W-2 printing and mailing		x	x
"No Penalties" Guarantee[3]		x	x
Submit payroll by phone or PC, or set up to process payroll automatically			x
Paycheck delivery to your office			x
Preparation of 1099-MISC forms for contractors and vendors			x
Preparation of state new hire reporting forms			x

2. **Calculate payroll taxes manually**. If you do not use a payroll tax service, you must calculate tax withholdings and payroll taxes manually using IRS Circular E. Then enter the amounts in QuickBooks to process payroll.

To use the manual payroll option:
♦ From the Employee Navigator, click **Set Up Payroll**.
♦ Click **Choose a Payroll Option**.
♦ Scroll to the bottom of the page and click **Learn more about manual payroll calculation**.
♦ Click **I choose to manually calculate payroll taxes** button.

To create paychecks for Rock Castle Construction:

Step 1: From the Employee Navigator, click the **Pay Employees** icon to display the *Select Employees to Pay* window.

Step 2: When the following *Select Employees to Pay* window appears, select Employees: **Elizabeth N. Mason** and **your name**.

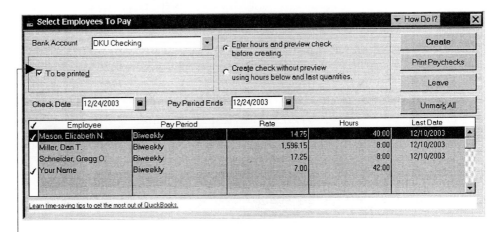

Step 3: Select **To be printed**. This indicates that you will print the checks. Uncheck this box if you want to record the paychecks but not print them.

Step 4: Select Bank Account: **Checking**.

Step 5: Select Check Date: **12/24/2003**. This date will print on each check.

Step 6: Select Pay Period Ends: **12/24/2003**. This is the last day of this pay period.

Step 7: Select **Enter hours and preview check before creating**. This permits you to preview the check and make any necessary changes.

Step 8: Click **Create**.

If you use a QuickBooks payroll service, payroll taxes and deductions would automatically be calculated and appear in the *Preview Paycheck* window.

Step 9: When the *Preview Paycheck* window appears, the Regular pay amount will appear automatically. If you are calculating payroll taxes manually, you must calculate tax withholding amounts and enter them in this window.

Step 10: Click **Create** to create Elizabeth Mason's paycheck.

Payroll deductions may vary based upon which payroll update you are using.

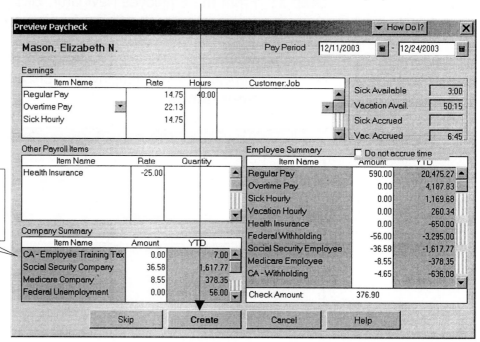

Step 11: The *Preview Paycheck* window should now display your paycheck information. Click **Create**.

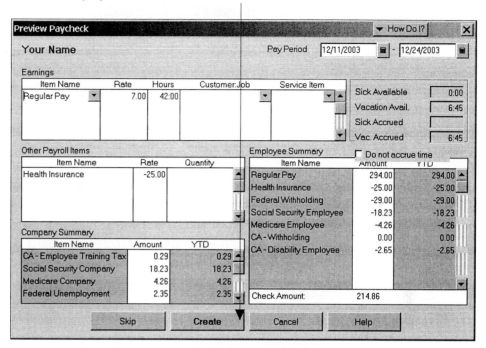

✓ **Mason's net pay is $376.90 and your net pay is $214.86. (Note: These amounts may vary depending upon your payroll update.)**

> Some businesses use a separate Payroll Checking account instead of using the regular Checking account.

To print your paycheck and Mason's paycheck:

Step 1: Click the **Print Paychecks** button on the right side of the *Select Employees to Pay* window.

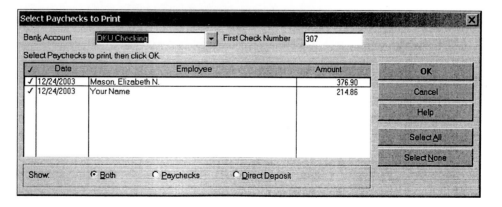

> If voucher checks are used, the paystub information is printed on the check voucher.

In the *Select Paychecks to Print* window shown above, select **Elizabeth Mason (12/24/2003)** and **your name (12/24/2003)**.

Step 2: Select Bank Account: **Checking**, then click **OK**.

Step 3: Select Check Style: **Standard**, then click **Print**.

Step 4: Click **Leave** to close the *Select Employees to Pay* window.

If a company uses standard checks for payroll, print paystubs as follows:

Step 1: From the **File** menu, select **Print Forms**, **Paystubs**.

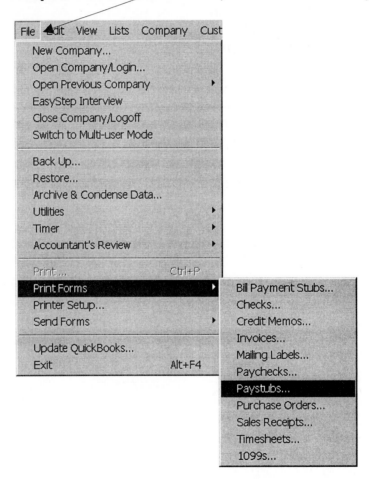

Step 2: Select Date: **12/11/2003** thru **12/24/2003**.

Step 3: Select **Your Name**.

Step 4: Click **OK**. Then click **Print**.

Pay Payroll Liabilities

Payroll liabilities include amounts for:

Tip: To help you keep track of filing dates, see the IRS Tax Calendar at www.irs.gov, Tax Info for Business, Tax Calendar.

- ◆ Federal income taxes withheld from employee paychecks.

- ◆ State income taxes withheld from employee paychecks.

- ◆ FICA (Social Security and Medicare, including both the employee and the employer portions).

- ◆ Unemployment taxes.

Federal income taxes, state income taxes, and the employee portion of FICA are withheld from the employee and the company has an obligation (liability) to remit these amounts to the appropriate tax agency. The employer share of FICA and unemployment taxes are payroll taxes the employer owes.

To pay the payroll tax liability:

Step 1: Click the **Pay Liabilities** icon on the Employee Navigator.

Step 2: If the payroll liabilities were due, you would select dates and amounts to pay, then click Create. At this time, Rock Castle Construction is not paying payroll liabilities, so click **Cancel**.

Payroll Reports

QuickBooks provides payroll reports that answer the following questions:

- ◆ How much did we pay our employees and pay in payroll taxes? (Payroll reports)

- ◆ How much time did we spend classified by employee and job? (Project reports)

Payroll reports can be accessed in the following ways:

1. Reports menu (select Employees & Payroll from the Reports menu).

2. Report Finder (click Reports in the *Navigators* window, then select Employees & Payroll).

3. Employee List window (click the Reports button on the *Employee List* window).

Payroll Reports: How Much Did We Pay for Payroll?

The payroll reports list the amounts paid to employees and the amounts paid in payroll taxes.

To print the Payroll Summary report:

Step 1: Open the **Employee List** window. (Click Employees in the *Navigators* window, then click the Employees icon on the Employee Navigator.)

Step 2: Click the **Reports** button.

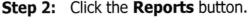

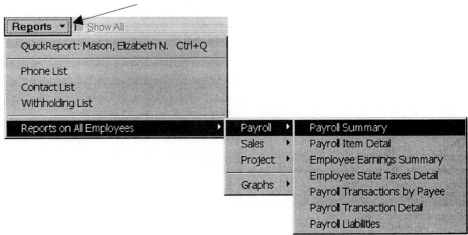

Step 3: Select **Reports on All Employees, Payroll, Payroll Summary**.

Step 4: Select Dates: **Last Month** From: **11/01/2003** To: **11/30/2003**.

Step 5: Insert **your name** and **Chapter 6** in the report footer.

Step 6: Select **Landscape** orientation, then click **Print**.

✓ *Net pay for Dan Miller for November was $2,595.51.*

Project Reports: How Much Time Did We Use?

Projects reports are accessed from the *Employee List* window as follows:

Step 1: Click the **Reports** button.

Step 2: Click **Reports on All Employees**.

Step 3: Click **Project** to display the project reports.

Two projects reports are:

1. Time by Name Report: Lists the amount of time worked by each employee.
2. Time by Job Detail Report: Lists the time worked on a particular job.

Step 4: Print the **Time by Job Detail** report for **This Month** from **12/01/2003** To: **12/31/2003**. Insert **your name** and **Chapter 6**. Select **Portrait** orientation.

✓ *Notice the Billing Status column indicates whether the time is billed, unbilled, or not billable.*

Summarize Payroll Data in Excel

This activity requires Microsoft Excel software.

To export and summarize payroll data in a Microsoft Excel spreadsheet:

Step 1: From the Employees menu, select **Summarize Payroll Data in Excel**.

Step 2: Microsoft Excel will automatically open and create an Excel spreadsheet. If a macro warning message appears, click **Enable Macros**.

Step 3: The payroll data is exported into an Excel spreadsheet in a pivot table format.

Step 4: When the following *Options* window appears, select dates: **10/01/2003** to **12/31/2003**.

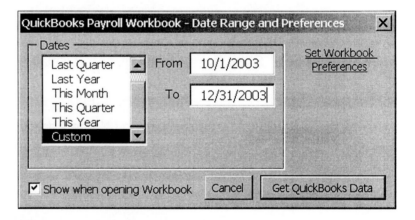

Step 5: Click **Get QuickBooks Data**. When requested, enter your User ID and Password.

Step 6: Print the Active Sheet in Excel.

Step 7: Close the Excel spreadsheet without saving and then close Excel.

Back Up Chapter 6

Back up your Chapter 6 file to a floppy disk. Use the file name: [your name] Chapter 6.

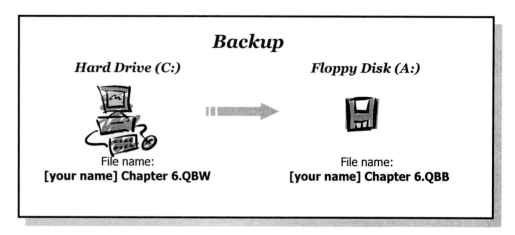

Step 1: Insert the **Chapter 6** backup disk in drive A.

Step 2: Click **Restore a backup file** (or click **File, Back Up**).

Step 3: Enter the file name: **[your name] Chapter 6.QBB**. Enter location: **A:**.

Step 4: Click **Back Up**.

You have now backed up the Chapter 6 file to your Chapter 6 floppy disk.

If you are continuing your computer session, close the company file and then proceed to Activity 6.1.

If you are quitting your computer session now (1) close the company file and (2) exit QuickBooks.

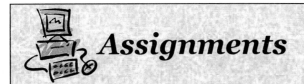

Assignments

Activity 6.1: Track Time and Print Paychecks

Scenario

When sorting through the payroll documents that Mr. Castle gave you, you find the following timesheets for Dan Miller and Greg Schneider.

				Timesheet		
Dan Miller	**Salary**	**Dec 15**	**Dec 16**	**Dec 17**	**Dec 18**	**Dec 19**
Cook: 2nd Story	Installation	8	8	2		4
Pretell: 75 Sunset	Framing			6	7	4

				Timesheet		
Dan Miller	**Salary**	**Dec 22**	**Dec 23**	**Dec 24**	**Dec 25**	**Dec 26**
Pretell: 75 Sunset	Framing	8	8	3		
Pretell: 75 Sunset	Installation			5		

Timesheet						
Gregg Schneider	**Regular Pay**	**Dec 15**	**Dec 16**	**Dec 17**	**Dec 18**	**Dec 19**
Jacobsen: Kitchen	Installation	8	8	8	2	
Pretell: 75 Sunset	Framing				6	8

Timesheet						
Gregg Schneider	**Regular Pay**	**Dec 22**	**Dec 23**	**Dec 24**	**Dec 25**	**Dec 26**
Pretell: 75 Sunset	Framing	8	8			
Pretell: 75 Sunset	Installation			8		

Task 1: Restore Company File

The first task is to restore your backup for Chapter 6 to the hard drive, changing the file name to Activity 6.1.

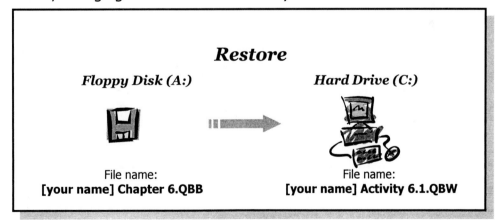

Restore

Floppy Disk (A:)   *Hard Drive (C:)*

File name: **[your name] Chapter 6.QBB**

File name: **[your name] Activity 6.1.QBW**

Step 1: 🖫 Insert the **Chapter 6** backup disk into drive A.

Step 2: Click **Restore a backup file** (or click **File, Restore**).

Step 3: Identify the backup file:

- Filename: **[your name] Chapter 6.QBB**.
- Location: **A:**.

Step 4: Identify the restored file:

- Filename: **[your name] Activity 6.1.QBW**.
- Location: **C:\Program Files\Intuit\QuickBooks Premier**.

Step 5: Click **Restore**.

Step 6: Change the company name to:
[your name] Activity 6.1 Rock Castle Construction.

(To change the company name, select Company (menu), Company Information.)

Task 2: Timesheet

Step 1: Enter the hours **Dan Miller** worked using QuickBooks weekly timesheet.

Step 2: Enter the hours **Gregg Schneider** worked using QuickBooks weekly timesheet.

Step 3: Print timesheets for Dan Miller and Gregg Schneider.

Task 3: Print Paychecks

Step 1: Create paychecks for **Dan Miller** and **Gregg Schneider**. Select Check Date: **12/24/2003**. Select Pay Period Ends: **12/24/2003**.

Step 2: Print paychecks for **Dan Miller** and **Gregg Schneider** dated: **12/24/2003**.

Task 4: Print Paystubs

Print the paystubs dated **12/24/2003** for **Dan Miller** and **Gregg Schneider**.

Task 5: Back Up Activity 6.1

Back up Activity 6.1 to a floppy disk.

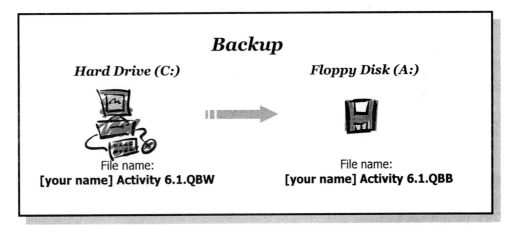

Step 1: 💾 Insert the **Chapter 6** backup disk in drive A.

Step 2: Click **Restore a backup file** (or click **File, Back Up**).

Step 3: Enter the filename: **[your name] Activity 6.1.QBB**. Enter location: **A:**.

Step 4: Click **Back Up**.

Step 5: Click **OK** after the backup is complete. Then close the company file. (Click File, Close Company.)

Activity 6.2: Transfer Time to Sales Invoice

"By the way, did I mention that I need a current sales invoice for the Jacobsen Kitchen job? Make sure all labor charges have been posted to the invoice," Mr. Castle shouts over the top of your cubicle as he rushes past.

Task 1: Restore Company File

Restore the Activity 6.1 backup to the hard drive, changing the file name to Activity 6.2.

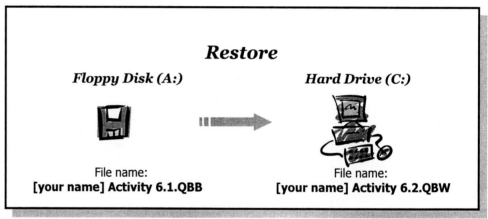

Restore

Floppy Disk (A:)   **Hard Drive (C:)**

File name: File name:
[your name] Activity 6.1.QBB   **[your name] Activity 6.2.QBW**

Step 1: 💾 Insert the **Chapter 6** backup disk into drive A.

Step 2: Click **Restore a backup file** (or click **File**, **Restore**).

Step 3: Identify the backup file:

* Filename: **[your name] Activity 6.1.QBB**.
* Location: **A:**.

Step 4: Identify the restored file:

* Filename: **[your name] Activity 6.2.QBW**.
* Location: **C:\Program Files\Intuit\QuickBooks Premier**.

Step 5: Click **Restore.**

Step 6: Change the company name to:
[your name] Activity 6.2 Rock Castle Construction.

(To change the company name, select Company (menu), Company Information.)

> Note: To record Task 2, click **Create Invoices** on the Customer Navigator.

Task 2: Transfer Time to Sales Invoice

> Recall that subcontractors are considered vendors, not employees. Subcontractor payments are entered using the *Enter Bills* window.

Step 1: Click the **Time/Costs** button to transfer time data to a sales invoice dated **12/24/2003** for the Jacobsen Kitchen job.

Step 2: From the *Choose Billable Time & Costs* window, click the **Items** tab. Click the **Select All** button to transfer subcontractors work to the invoice.

Step 3: From the *Choose Billable Time & Costs* window, click the **Time** tab, then click the **Select All** button to transfer employee time worked to the invoice.

> ✓ ***Items total $1,900. Time totals $2,380.***

Step 4: Print the invoice.

> ✓ ***Invoice No. 93 totals $4,280.***

Task 3: Back Up Activity 6.2

Backup

Hard Drive (C:)

Floppy Disk (A:)

File name:
[your name] Activity 6.2.QBW

File name:
[your name] Activity 6.2.QBB

Step 1: 🖫 Insert the **Chapter 6** backup disk in drive A.

Step 2: Click **Restore a backup file** (or click **File**, **Back Up**).

Step 3: Enter the file name: **[your name] Activity 6.2**. Enter location: **A:**.

Step 4: Click **Back Up**.

Step 5: Click **OK** after the backup is complete. Close the company file.

Activity 6.3: QuickBooks Payroll Services

To learn more about the payroll services offered by QuickBooks:

Step 1: From the Employee Navigator, click the **Learn About Payroll Options** icon.

Step 2: Print information summarizing the differences between the Basic, Deluxe and Premier Payroll Service.

Step 3: 📝 Prepare a short e-mail to Mr. Castle recommending which payroll service Rock Castle Construction should use.

Activity 6.4: Web Quest

The IRS prepares a publication, the Employer's Tax Guide, that summarizes information about payroll taxes.

To obtain a copy of the Employer's Tax Guide:

Step 1: Go to the www.irs.gov web site, Forms & Pubs.

Step 2: Select and print *two* of the following sections of the **Employer's Tax Guide, IRS Publication 15, Circular E**:
- ◆ Employee's Social Security Number (SSN)
- ◆ Employer Identification Number (EIN)
- ◆ Wages and Other Compensation
- ◆ Depositing Taxes
- ◆ Percentage Method 1
- ◆ Wage Bracket 3

Activity 6.5: Web Quest

When hiring individuals to perform work for a business, it is important to identify the status of the individual as either an employee or independent contractor. For an employee, your business must withhold taxes and provide a W-2. For an independent contractor, your business does not have to withhold taxes. Instead of a W-2, you provide a contractor with a Form 1099-MISC. To learn more about whether a worker is classified for tax purposes as an employee or independent contractor, visit the IRS web site.

Step 1: Go to the www.irs.gov web site.

Step 2: Search for requirements that determine employee status and contractor status and print your search results.

Step 3: To learn more about employee versus contractor status, in QuickBooks click **Company**, **Decision Tools**, then **Employee, Contractor, or Temp?**.

Computer Accounting with QuickBooks 2002
Chapter 6 Printout Checklist
Name:_____ Date:_____

☑	**Printout Checklist – Chapter 6**
☐	Employee List
☐	Timesheets
☐	Invoice No. 92
☐	Paychecks & Paystub
☐	Payroll Summary Report
☐	Time by Job Detail Report
☐	Excel Payroll Report
☑	**Printout Checklist – Activity 6.1**
☐	Task 2: Timesheets
☐	Task 3: Paychecks
☐	Task 4: Paystubs
☑	**Printout Checklist – Activity 6.2**
☐	Task 2: Customer Invoice No. 93
☑	**Printout Checklist – Activity 6.3**
☐	QuickBooks Payroll Service Printouts
☑	**Printout Checklist – Activity 6.4**
☐	IRS Publication 15, Circular E, Employer's Tax Guide
☑	**Printout Checklist – Activity 6.5**
☐	IRS Printouts for Employee Status and Independent Contractor

Reports and Graphs

Scenario

"I need an income tax summary report ASAP—" Mr. Castle barks as he races past your cubicle. In a few seconds he charges past your cubicle again. *"Don't forget to adjust the accounts first. You'll need to use those confounded debits and credits!"*

"Also, I need a P&L, balance sheet, and cash flow statement for my meeting with the bankers this afternoon. Throw in a graph or two if it'll make us look good."

7

Learning Objectives

In Chapter 7, you will learn the following QuickBooks features:

The accounting cycle is a series of activities that a business performs each accounting period.

The Accounting Cycle

Financial reports are the end result of the accounting cycle. The accounting cycle usually consists of the following steps:

Chart of Accounts

The chart of accounts is a list of all accounts used to accumulate information about assets, liabilities, owners' equity, revenues, and expenses. Create a chart of accounts when the business is established and modify the chart of accounts as needed over time.

Record Transactions

During the accounting period, record transactions with customers, vendors, employees and owners.

An accounting period can be one month, one quarter, or one year.

Trial Balance

A trial balance lists each account and the account balance at the end of the accounting period. Prepare a trial balance to verify that the accounting system is in balance—total debits should equal total credits. An *unadjusted* trial balance is a trial balance prepared *before* adjustments.

Adjustments

At the end of the accounting period before preparing financial statements, make any adjustments necessary to bring the accounts up to date. Adjustments are entered in the Journal using debits and credits.

Adjusted Trial Balance

Prepare an *adjusted* trial balance (a trial balance *after* adjustments) to verify that the accounting system still balances. If additional account detail is required, print the General Ledger (the collection of all the accounts listing the transactions that affected the accounts).

Financial Statements and Reports

Prepare financial statements for external users (profit & loss, balance sheet, and statement of cash flows). Prepare income tax summary reports and reports for managers.

> The objective of financial reporting is to provide information to external users for decision making. The rules followed when preparing financial statements are called GAAP (Generally Accepted Accounting Principles.)

> Financial statements can be prepared monthly, quarterly, or annually. Always make adjustments *before* preparing financial statements.

Three types of reports that a business prepares are:

1. **Financial Statements**: Financial reports used by investors, owners, and creditors to make decisions. A banker might use the financial statements to decide whether to make a loan to a company. A prospective investor might use the financial statements to decide whether to invest in a company.

   The three financial statements most frequently used by external users are:

   - Profit & loss (also called the income statement): lists income and expenses.

   - Balance sheet: lists assets, liabilities, and owners' equity.

   - Statement of cash flows: lists cash flows from operating, investing, and financing activities.

2. **Tax Forms**: The objective of the tax form is to provide information to the Internal Revenue Service and state tax authorities. When preparing tax returns, a company uses different rules from those used to prepare financial statements. When preparing a federal tax return, use the Internal Revenue Code.

   Tax forms include the following:
   - IRS Income Tax Return
   - State Tax Return
   - Forms 940, 941, W-2, W-3, 1099

3. **Management Reports**: Financial reports used by internal users (managers) to make decisions regarding company operations. These reports do not have to follow a particular set of rules and can be created to satisfy a manager's information needs.

Examples of reports that managers use include:

- Cash forecast
- Cash budget
- Accounts Receivable Aging Summary
- Accounts Payable Aging Summary

In this chapter, you will prepare some of these reports for Rock Castle Construction. First, you will prepare a trial balance and adjustments.

Restore Back Up

To begin Chapter 7, first start QuickBooks software and then restore your backup file.

Start QuickBooks software by clicking on the QuickBooks desktop icon or click **Start**, **Programs**, **QuickBooks Premier**, **QuickBooks Premier**.

Restore your Activity 6.2 backup to the C drive, renaming the file Chapter 7.

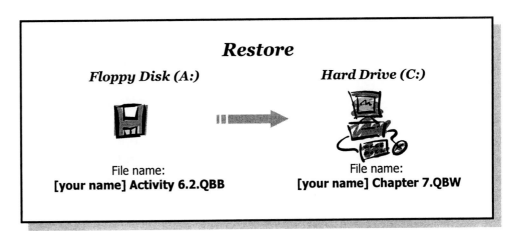

Step 1: ⊟ Insert the **Chapter 6** backup disk into drive A.

Step 2: Click **Restore a backup file** (or click **File**, **Restore**).

Step 3: Identify the backup file:

- ◆ Filename: **[your name] Activity 6.2.QBB**.
- ◆ Location: **A:**.

Step 4: Identify the restored file:

- ◆ Filename: **[your name] Chapter 7.QBW**.
- ◆ Location: **C:\Program Files\Intuit\QuickBooks Premier**.

Step 5: Click **Restore.** If prompted, enter your User ID and Password.

Step 6: Change the company name to: **[your name] Chapter 7 Rock Castle Construction**. (To change the company name, select Company (menu), Company Information.)

Trial Balance

A trial balance is a listing of all of a company's accounts and the ending account balances. A trial balance is often printed both before and after making adjustments. The purpose of the trial balance is to verify that the accounting system balances.

On a trial balance, all debit ending account balances are listed in the debit column and credit ending balances are listed in the credit column. If the accounting system balances, total debits equal total credits.

To print the trial balance for Rock Castle Construction:

Step 1: Click **Reports** in the *Navigators* window to display the *Report Finder* window.

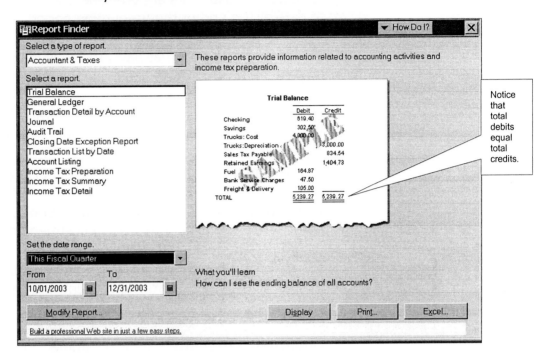

Step 2: Select Type of Report: **Accountant & Taxes**.

Step 3: Select Report: **Trial Balance**.

Step 4: Select Date Range: **This Fiscal Quarter** From: **10/01/2003** To: **12/31/2003**.

Step 5: Click the **Display** button.

Step 6: Print the report using a **Portrait** print setting.

Step 7: To memorize the report, click the **Memorize** button. In the name field, enter: **Trial Balance**, then click **OK**.

Step 8: Close the *Trial Balance* window.

✓ **Total debits and total credits equal $347,718.92.**

Adjusting Entries

In QuickBooks, the journal is used to record adjustments (and corrections). Adjustments are often necessary to bring the accounts up to date at the end of the accounting period.

If you are using the accrual basis to measure profit, the following five types of adjusting entries may be necessary.

Financial statements for external users use straight-line depreciation. For tax forms, MACRS (Modified Accelerated Cost Recovery System) is usually used. See your accountant for more information about calculating depreciation.

1. **Depreciation**: Depreciation has several different definitions. When conversing with an accountant it is important to know which definition of depreciation is used. See the table on the following page for more information about depreciation.

2. **Prepaid Items**: Items that are prepaid, such as prepaid insurance or prepaid rent. An adjustment may be needed to record the amount of the prepaid item that has not expired at the end of the accounting period. For example, an adjustment may be needed to record the amount of insurance that has not expired as Prepaid Insurance (an asset with future benefit).

3. **Unearned Revenue**: If a customer pays in advance of receiving a service, such as when a customer makes a deposit, your business has an obligation (liability) to either provide the service in the future or return the customer's money. An adjustment may be necessary to bring the revenue account and unearned revenue (liability) account up to date.

A small business may want to hire an outside accountant to prepare adjusting entries at year-end. You can create a copy of your company data file for your accountant to use when making adjustments. For more information about creating an Accountant's Review Copy, see Chapter 12.

4. **Accrued Expenses**: Expenses that are incurred but not yet paid or recorded. Examples of accrued expenses include accrued interest expense (interest expense that you have incurred but have not yet paid).

5. **Accrued Revenues**: Revenues that have been earned but not yet collected or recorded. Examples of accrued revenues include interest revenue that has been earned but not yet collected or recorded.

Depreciation

> The accounting definitions of depreciation differ from the popular definition of depreciation as a decline in value.

Depreciation is listed on....	Report Objective	Reporting Rules	Definition of Depreciation	Depreciation Calculation
Financial statements Profit & Loss, Balance Sheet, Statement of Cash Flows	Provide information to external users (bankers and investors)	GAAP (Generally Accepted Accounting Principles)	*Financial Accounting Defintion:* Allocation of asset's cost to periods used.	Straight-line depreciation = (Cost – Salvage)/Useful life
Income tax returns	Provide information to the Internal Revenue Service	Internal Revenue Code	*Tax Definition:* Recovery of asset's cost through depreciation deductions on return	MACRS (See IRS Publication 946 on depreciation)

Record Journal Entries

In a traditional accounting system, transactions are recorded using journal entries with debits and credits. QuickBooks uses onscreen forms instead of the journal to record transactions. In QuickBooks the journal is used to record adjustments and corrections. QuickBooks also permits you to record adjustments directly in the accounts.

Rock Castle Construction needs to make an adjustment to record $3,000 of depreciation expense on its truck.

To make the adjusting journal entry in QuickBooks:

Step 1: From the **Company** menu, select **Make Journal Entry**.

You can also access the journal from the Banking Navigator.

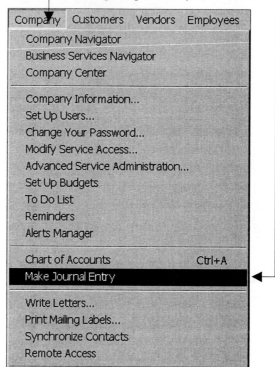

Step 2: When the following window appears, click **OK**.

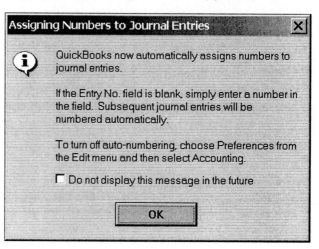

Step 3: When the following *General Journal Entry* window appears, select Date: **12/31/2003**.

Adjusting entries are dated the last day of the accounting period.

Type the Account No. **6200** and QuickBooks will automatically complete the account title.

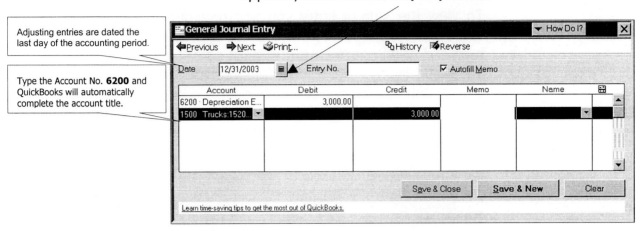

Step 4: Select Account to debit: **6200 Depreciation Expense**.

Tip: Memorize the journal entry to reuse each accounting period:
1. With the Journal Entry displayed, click **Edit** (menu).
2. Select **Memorize General Journal**.
To use the memorized transaction, select Memorized Transactions from the Lists menu.

Step 5: Enter Debit amount: **3000.00**.

Step 6: Select Account to credit: **1520 Depreciation Fixed Asset**.

Step 7: If it does not appear automatically, enter Credit amount: **3000.00**.

Step 8: Click **Save & Close** to record the journal entry and close the *General Journal Entry* window.

Print Journal Entries

To view the journal entry you just recorded, display the journal. The journal also contains journal entries for all transactions recorded using onscreen forms, such as sales invoices. QuickBooks automatically converts transactions recorded in onscreen forms into journal entries with debits and credits.

To display and print the General Journal:

Step 1: Click **Reports** in the *Navigators* window to display the Report Finder.

Step 2: Select Type of Report: **Accountant & Taxes**.

Step 3: Select Report: **Journal**.

Step 4: Select Dates From: **12/15/2003** To: **12/31/2003**.

Step 5: Click the **Display** button to display the Journal.

Notice that the sales invoice you recorded on 12/24/2003 for the Jacobsen Kitchen job has now been converted to a journal entry.

Notice the adjusting entry for depreciation.

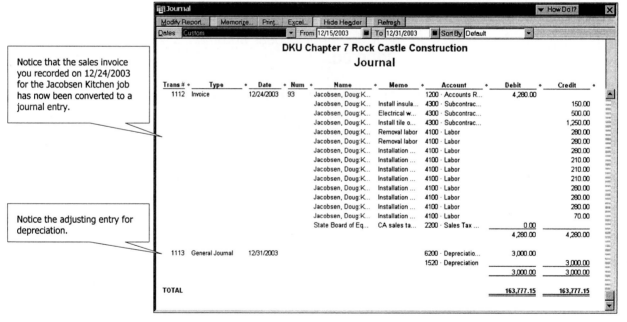

Step 6: Insert **your name** and **Chapter 7** in the report footer.

Step 7: Print the journal using **Portrait** orientation.

Step 8: Close the *Journal* window.

Adjusted Trial Balance

The adjusted trial balance is prepared to verify that the accounting system still balances after adjusting entries are made.

Step 1: Print an adjusted trial balance as of December 31, 2003 using the **Portrait** orientation. Insert **your name**, **Chapter 7 Adjusted Trial Balance** in the report footer.

Step 2: ✒ Circle the account balances that are different from the trial balance amounts.

✓	**Total debits and total credits equal $350,718.92.**

General Ledger

The General Ledger is a collection of all of the company's accounts and account activity. While the trial balance lists only the ending balance for each account, the general ledger provides detail about all transactions affecting the account during a given period.

Each account in the General Ledger lists:

- Beginning balance.
- Transactions that affected the account for the selected period.
- Ending balance.

Normally, the General Ledger is not provided to external users, such as bankers. However, the General Ledger can provide managers with supporting detail needed to answer questions bankers might ask about the financial statements.

To print the General Ledger:

Step 1: If the Report Finder is not open, click **Reports** in the *Navigators* window to open the Report Finder.

Step 2: Select Type of Report: **Accountant & Taxes**.

Step 3: Select Report: **General Ledger**.

Step 4: Select Date Range: **This Fiscal Quarter**.

Step 5: Click the **Display** button to display the *General Ledger* window.

Step 6: The General Ledger report lists each account and all the transactions affecting the account. **Double-click on any transaction listed in the Checking account** to drill down to the original source document, such as a check or an invoice. Close the source document window.

Step 7: Use a filter to view only selected accounts in the General Ledger. For example, to view only the Savings account, complete the following steps:

- Click the **Modify Report** button at the top of the *General Ledger* window. Then click the **Filters** tab.

- Select Filter: **Account**.

- Select Account: **All bank accounts**.

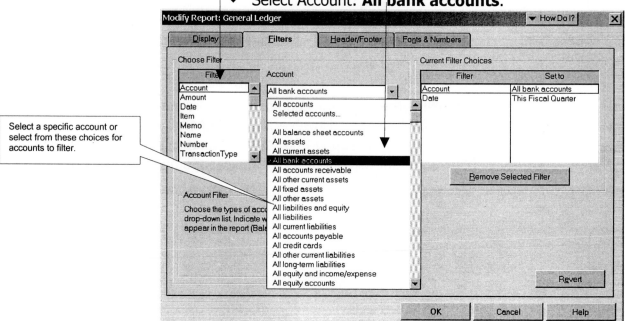

Select a specific account or select from these choices for accounts to filter.

Step 8: To omit accounts with zero balances in the General Ledger report, from the *Modify Report* window:
  - Click the **Display** tab, then click the **Advanced** button.
  - Select Include: **In Use**.
  - Click **OK**.

Step 9: Click the **Header/Footer** tab to insert **your name** and **Chapter 7** in the report footer.

Step 10: Click **OK** to close the *Modify Report* window.

Step 11: Print the selected General Ledger account using **Portrait** orientation. Select **Fit to 1 page(s) wide**.

Step 12: Close the *General Ledger* window.

Financial Statements

Financial statements are standardized financial reports given to bankers and investors. The three main financial statements are the profit and loss, balance sheet, and statement of cash flows. The statements are prepared following Generally Accepted Accounting Principles (GAAP).

> The profit & loss statement is also called P&L or income statement.

Profit and Loss

The profit and loss statement lists sales (sometimes called revenues) and expenses for a specified accounting period. Profit, or net income, can be measured two different ways:

> GAAP requires the accrual basis for the profit and loss statement because it provides a better matching of income and expenses.

1. **Cash basis**: A sale is recorded when cash is collected from the customer. Expenses are recorded when cash is paid.

2. **Accrual basis**: Sales are recorded when the good or service is provided regardless of whether the cash is collected from the customer. Expenses are recorded when the cost is incurred or expires, even if the expense has not been paid yet.

QuickBooks permits you to prepare the profit and loss statement using either the accrual or the cash basis. QuickBooks also permits you to prepare profit and loss statements monthly, quarterly, or annually.

To prepare a quarterly profit and loss statement for Rock Castle Construction using the accrual basis:

Step 1: Display the **Report Finder**.

Step 2: Select Type of Report: **Company & Financial**.

Step 3: Select Report: **Profit & Loss Standard**.

Step 4: Select Date Range: **This Fiscal Quarter**.

> *Tip:* To turn off account numbers before printing reports for external users:
> 1. Click **Company** in the Navigators window.
> 2. Click the **Preferences** icon.
> 3. Select the **Accounting** icon.
> 4. Select **Company Preferences** tab.
> 5. *Uncheck* **account numbers**.

Step 5: Click the **Modify Report** button in the lower left corner of the *Report Finder* window. Click the **Display** tab, then select Report Basis: **Accrual**. Click **OK**.

Step 6: Click the **Header/Footer** button. Insert **your name** and **Chapter 7** in the report footer.

Step 7: Click the **Display** button to display the profit and loss statement.

Step 8: Print the profit and loss statement using **Portrait** orientation.

Step 9: Close the *Profit and Loss* window.

Income and Expense Graph

QuickBooks provides you with the ability to easily graph profit and loss information. A graph is simply another means to communicate financial information.

To create an income and expense graph for Rock Castle Construction:

Step 1: From the *Report Finder*, select Type of Report: **Company & Financial**.

Step 2: Select Report: **Income and Expense Graph**.

Step 3: Select Date Range: **This Fiscal Quarter** then click the **Display** button to display the following *QuickInsight: Income and Expense Graph* window.

Step 4: Click the **By Account** button. The income and expense graph depicts a bar chart of income and expense for the three months in the fiscal quarter. The pie chart in the lower section of the window displays the relative proportion of each expense as a percentage of total expenses.

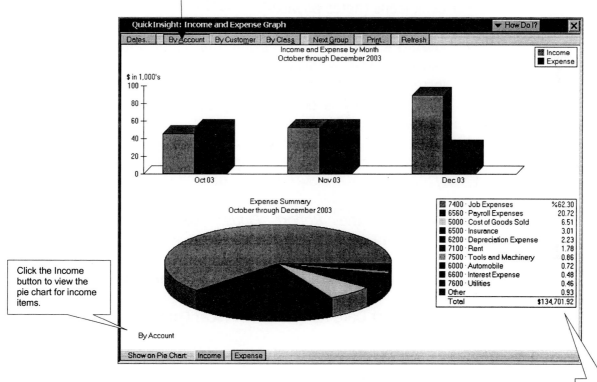

Click the Income button to view the pie chart for income items.

Percentages for the pie chart are also displayed.

Step 5: Print the income and expense graph.

Step 6: Close the *QuickInsight: Income and Expense Graph* window.

Balance Sheet

The balance sheet presents a company's financial position on a particular date. The balance sheet can be prepared at the end of a month, quarter, or year. The balance sheet lists:

1. **Assets**: What a company owns. On the balance sheet, assets are recorded at their historical cost, the amount you paid for the asset when you purchased it. Note that historical cost can be different from the market value of the asset, which is the amount the asset is worth now.

2. **Liabilities**: What a company owes. Liabilities are obligations which include amounts owed vendors (accounts payable) and bank loans (notes payable).

3. **Owner's equity**: The residual that is left after liabilities are satisfied. This is also called net worth. Owner's equity is increased by the owner's contributions and net income. Owner's equity is decreased by the owner's withdrawals (or dividends) and net losses.

To prepare a balance sheet for Rock Castle Construction at 12/31/2003:

Step 1: From the *Report Finder*, select Type of Report: **Company & Financial**.

Step 2: Select Report: **Balance Sheet Standard**.

Step 3: Select Date Range: **This Fiscal Quarter**.

Step 4: Click the **Display** button to display the *Balance Sheet* window.

Step 5: Insert **your name** and **Chapter 7** in the report footer.

Step 6: Print the balance sheet using the **Portrait** orientation.

Step 7: Close the *Balance Sheet* window.

Step 8: ✏ Circle the single largest asset listed on the balance sheet.

Net Worth Graph

QuickBooks provides you with the ability to graph net worth, assets, and liabilities.

To create a net worth graph for Rock Castle Construction:

Step 1: From the *Report Finder*, select Type of Report: **Company & Financial**.

Step 2: Select Report: **Net Worth Graph**.

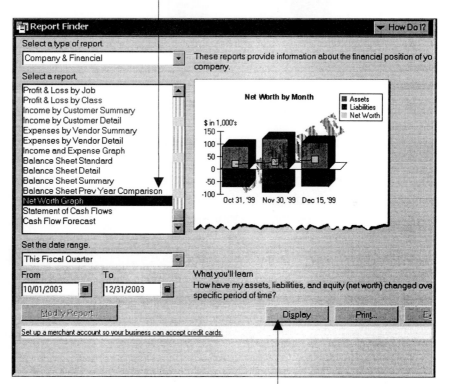

Step 3: Select Date Range: **This Fiscal Quarter**.

Step 4: Click the **Display** button to display the following *QuickInsight: Net Worth Graph* window.

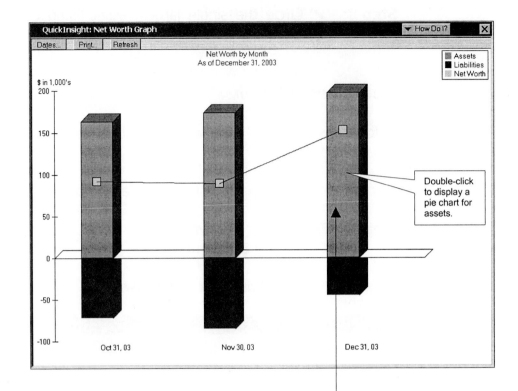

Step 5: Print the Net Worth Graph.

Step 6: To view a pie chart of assets, double-click on the asset column for December 31, 2003. The following *QuickZoom Graph* window appears.

Notice that the largest asset is A/R.

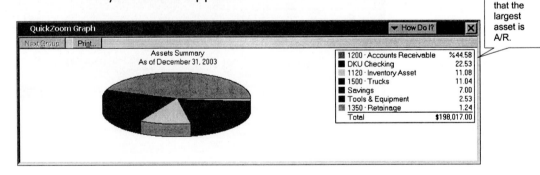

Step 7: Print the QuickZoom Graph for assets.

Step 8: Close the *QuickZoom Graph* window and the *QuickInsight: Net Worth Graph* window.

Statement of Cash Flows

The Statement of Cash Flows summarizes cash inflows and cash outflows for a business over a period of time. Cash flows are grouped into three categories:

1. **Cash flows from Operating Activities**: Cash inflows and outflows related to the company's primary business, such as cash flows from sales and operating expenses.

2. **Cash flows from Investing Activities**: Cash inflows and outflows related to acquisition and disposal of long-term assets.

3. **Cash flows from Financing Activities**: Cash inflows and outflows to and from investors and creditors (except for interest payments). Examples include: loan principal repayment and investments by owners.

To set preferences for the Statement of Cash Flows:

Step 1: Open the *Preferences* window by clicking **Company** in the *Navigators* window, then clicking **Preferences**.

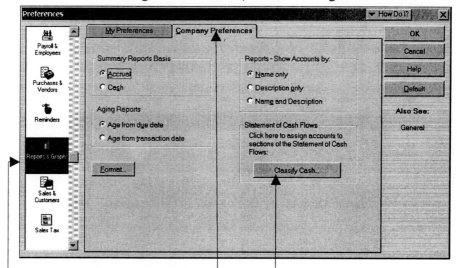

Step 2: Click the **Reports & Graphs** icon on the left scrollbar.

Step 3: Click the **Company Preferences** tab.

Step 4: Click the **Classify Cash** button to assign accounts to appropriate sections in the Statement of Cash Flows.

Step 5: From the *Classify Cash* window you can assign accounts to sections of the Statement of Cash Flows.

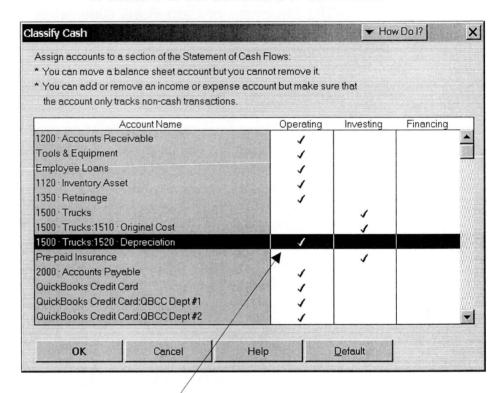

Step 6: For 1500-Truck:1520-Depreciation, click to check **Operating** (instead of Investing). Click **OK** to close the *Classify Cash* window. Then click **OK** to close the *Preferences* window.

To view the Statement of Cash Flows for Rock Castle Construction:

Step 1: From the Report Finder, select Type of Report: **Company & Financial**.

Step 2: Select Report: **Statement of Cash Flows**.

Step 3: Select Date Range: **This Fiscal Quarter**.

Step 4: Click the **Display** button to display the Statement of Cash Flows.

Step 5: Insert **your name** and **Chapter 7** in the report footer.

Step 6: Print the Statement of Cash Flows using the **Portrait** orientation.

Step 7: Close the *Statement of Cash Flows* window.

Tax Reports

QuickBooks provides two different approaches that you can use when preparing your tax return.

(1) Print QuickBooks income tax reports and then manually enter the tax information in your income tax return.

(2) Export your QuickBooks accounting data to TurboTax software and then use TurboTax to complete your income tax return.

Three different income tax reports are provided by QuickBooks:

1. **Income Tax Preparation Report**: lists the assigned tax line for each account.

2. **Income Tax Summary Report**: summarizes income and expenses that should be listed on a business income tax return.

3. **Income Tax Detail Report**: provides more detailed information about the income or expense amount appearing on each tax line of the income tax summary.

Income Tax Preparation Report

Before printing the Income Tax Summary report, check your QuickBooks accounts to see that the correct Tax Line is selected for each account. An easy way to check the Tax Line specified for each account is to print the Income Tax Preparation report as follows.

Step 1: From the Report Finder, select Type of Report: **Accountant & Taxes**.

Step 2: Select Report: **Income Tax Preparation**.

Step 3: Click the **Display** button to display the *Income Tax Preparation* window.

Recall that when you create a new account, you specify a Tax Line for the account. The Tax Line determines the tax line of the Income Tax Summary that the account balance will be appear. See Chapter 2 for more information about account Tax Lines.

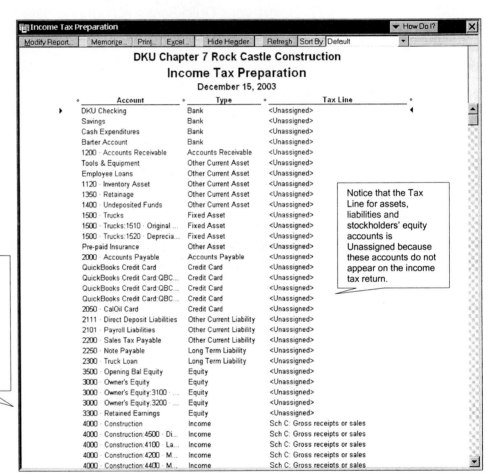

Notice that the Tax Line for assets, liabilities and stockholders' equity accounts is Unassigned because these accounts do not appear on the income tax return.

Step 4: Insert **your name** and **Chapter 7** in the report footer.

Step 5: Print the Income Tax Preparation Report.

Step 6: Close the *Income Tax Preparation* window.

To determine if the correct tax line has been entered for each account, compare the tax lines listed on the Income Tax Preparation report with your business income tax return.

If you need to change the Tax Line for an account:

Step 1: Open the *Chart of Accounts* window. (Company Navigator, Chart of Accounts icon.)

Step 2: Select the account then right-click to display a popup menu. Select **Edit** on the popup menu to edit the account.

Step 3: When the following *Edit Account* window appears, change the Tax Line as needed.

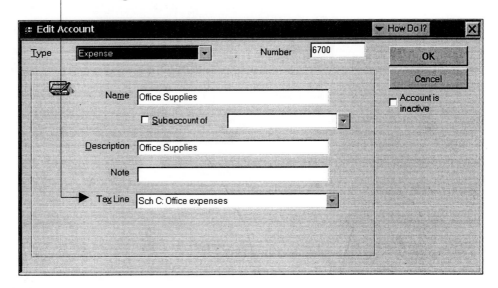

Step 4: To save the changes, you would click OK. In this activity, click **Cancel** to close the *Edit Account* window.

A sole proprietorship files Schedule C (attached to the owner's personal 1040 tax return). A corporation files Form 1120; a subchapter S corporation files Form 1120S.

Income Tax Summary Report

After you have confirmed the Tax Line for each account is correct, you are ready to print an Income Tax Summary Report. The Income Tax Summary report lists sales and expenses which should appear on the business federal tax return filed with the IRS.

To print the Income Tax Summary report:

Step 1: From the Report Finder, select Type of Report: **Accountant & Taxes**.

Step 2: Select Report: **Income Tax Summary**.

Step 3: Select Date: **This Tax Year** From: **01/01/2003** To: **12/31/2003**.

Step 4: Click the **Display** button to display the *Income Tax Summary* window.

QuickZoom:
Double-click to drill down and view more detail about the tax line. Double-click on **Other costs, COGS** to reveal that the other costs are permits and licenses.

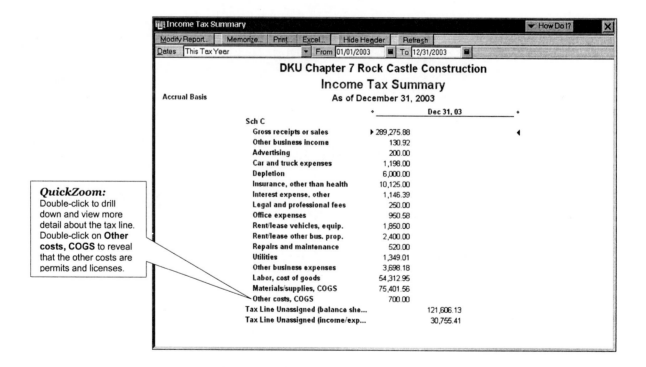

Step 5: Insert **your name** and **Chapter 7** in the report footer.

Step 6: Print the Income Tax Summary report.

Step 7: Close the *Income Tax Summary* window.

A business can use the information on the Income Tax Summary report to manually complete its income tax return.

Income Tax Detail Report

If you want to view detail for the line items shown on the Income Tax Summary report, display the Income Tax Detail report as follows:

Step 1: From the Report Finder, select Type of Report: **Accountant & Taxes**.

Step 2: Select Report: **Income Tax Detail**.

Step 3: Select Date Range: **This Tax Year**.

Step 4: Click the **Display** button to display the *Income Tax Detail* window. Detailed information is then listed for each line item.

Step 5: Close the *Income Tax Detail* window.

Export to TurboTax

TurboTax for Home and Business is used for a sole proprietorship Schedule C. TurboTax for Business is for corporations, S corporations, and partnerships.

Another approach to preparing a tax return is to export the account information from QuickBooks into TurboTax software.

To import your QuickBooks tax data into TurboTax software:

Step 1: Make a copy of your QuickBooks company data file.

Step 2: Start TurboTax software.

Step 3: Import your QuickBooks company file into TurboTax.

Management Reports

Reports used by management do not have to follow a specified set of rules such as GAAP or the Internal Revenue Code. Instead, management reports are prepared as needed to provide management with information for making operating and business decisions.

Management reports include:

1. Cash flow forecast.

2. Budgets (See Chapter 12).

3. Accounts Receivable Aging (See Chapter 4).

4. Accounts Payable Aging (See Chapter 5).

5. Inventory Reports (See Chapter 5).

Cash Flow Forecast

QuickBooks permits you to forecast cash flows. This enables you to project whether you will have enough cash to pay bills when they are due. If it appears that you will need additional cash, then you can arrange for a loan or line of credit to pay your bills.

To print a cash flow forecast for Rock Castle Construction:

Step 1: From the Report Finder, select Type of Report: **Company & Financial**.

Step 2: Select Report: **Cash Flow Forecast**.

Step 3: Select Date Range: **Next 4 Weeks**.

Step 4: Click the **Display** button to display the *Cash Flow Forecast* window.

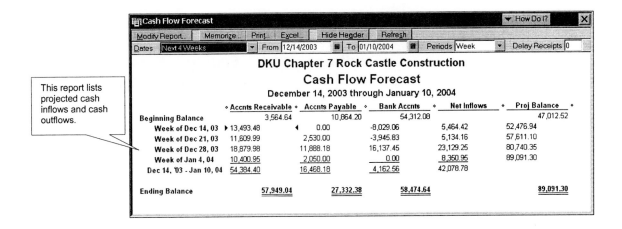

This report lists projected cash inflows and cash outflows.

Step 5: Print the Cash Flow Forecast using **Portrait** orientation.

Step 6: Leave the *Cash Flow Forecast* window open.

Export Reports to Microsoft® Excel®

QuickBooks permits you to export a report to Microsoft Excel spreadsheet software. In order to use this feature of QuickBooks, you must have Microsoft Excel software installed on your computer.

To export the Cash Flow Forecast report to Excel:

Step 1: With the *Cash Flow Forecast* window still open, click the **Excel** button at the top of the window.

Step 2: When the *Export Report to Excel* window appears, select **Send report to a new Excel spreadsheet**. Then click **OK** to export the QuickBooks report to Excel.

To export to an existing Excel spreadsheet, select: Send report to an existing Excel spreadsheet. Click **Browse** to select the file.

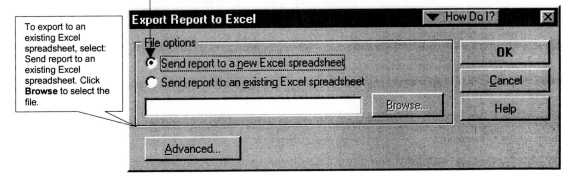

Step 3: Excel will automatically open. When the spreadsheet appears on your screen, **click on the cell that contains the Ending Balance of Accounts Receivable**. Notice that Excel has already entered a formula into the cell.

Step 4: To save the Excel file to the A drive:

- In Excel, click **File** on the menu bar.
- Select **Save As**.
- Select drive **A**.
- Enter File name: **Cash Forecast**.
- Click **Save**.

Step 5: Print the Excel spreadsheet.

Step 6: Close the Cash Forecast Excel workbook, then close Excel software by clicking the ⊠ in the upper right corner of the Excel window.

Step 7: Leave the *Cash Flow Forecast* window open.

Save Reports to Disk

QuickBooks permits you to save a report to a file instead of printing the report. You can select from the following file formats:

- ASCII text file: After saving as a text file, the file can be used with word processing software.

- Comma delimited file: Comma delimited files can be imported into word processing, spreadsheet, or database software. Commas identify where columns begin and end.

- Tab delimited file: Tab delimited files can be used with word processing or database software. Tabs identify where columns begin and end.

To save the cash flow forecast report as a text file:

Step 1: With the *Cash Flow Forecast* window still open, click the **Print** button at the top of the window.

Step 2: When the following *Print Reports* window appears, click Print to: **File**.

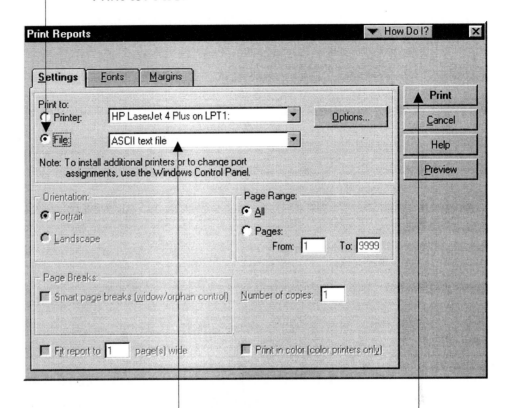

Step 3: Select file type: **ASCII text file**.

Step 4: Click **Print**.

Step 5: Insert a floppy disk in drive **A**.

Step 6: When the following *Create Disk File* window appears, select Save in: **3 ½ Floppy (A:)**.

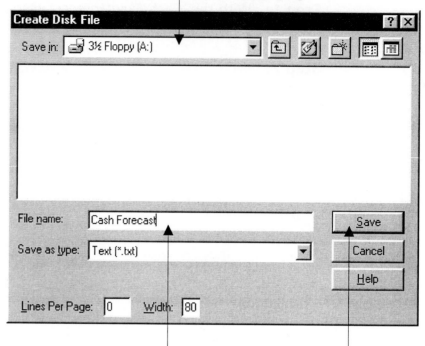

Step 7: Enter File name: **Cash Forecast**.

Step 8: Click **Save** to save the Cash Forecast report to a text file on your floppy disk. This file can now be used with word processing software.

Step 9: Close the *Cash Flow Forecast* window. Then close the Report Finder.

Company Center

The Company Center summarizes selected company reports in one convenient location in QuickBooks.

To open the Company Center:

Step 1: Click **Company** on the Navigation Bar.

Step 2: Click the **Company Center** icon on the Company Navigator.

Step 3: .The Company Center contains four quandrants. You can also customize the reports that appear in the Company Center by selecting Activities and Dates.

Step 4: Close the *Company Center* window.

Back Up Chapter 7

Back up your Chapter 7 file, using the file name: [your name] Chapter 7.

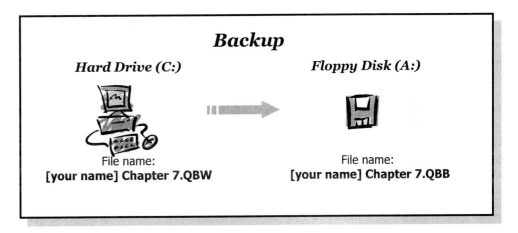

Step 1: 🖫 Insert the **Chapter 7** backup disk in drive A.

Step 2: Click **Restore a backup file** (or click • **File, Back Up**).

Step 3: Enter the file name: **[your name] Chapter 7.QBB**.
Enter location: **A:**.

Step 4: Click **Back Up**.

If you are continuing your computer session, close the company file and then proceed to Activity 7.1.

If you are quitting your computer session now (1) close the company file and (2) exit QuickBooks.

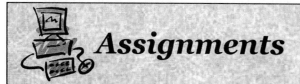

Assignments

Activity 7.1: Profit & Loss: Vertical Analysis

Scenario

You vaguely recall from your college accounting course that performing financial statement analysis can reveal additional useful information. Since Mr. Castle asked for whatever additional information he might need, you decide to print a vertical analysis of the income statement using QuickBooks.

Task 1: Restore Company File

The first task is to restore Chapter 7 to the hard drive, changing the file name to Activity 7.1.

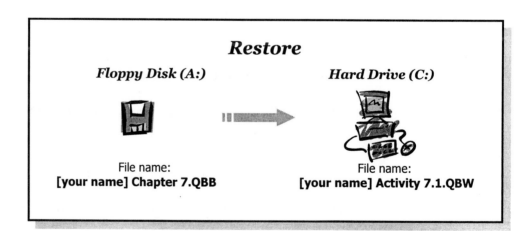

Step 1: ⊞ Insert the **Chapter 7** backup disk into drive A.

Step 2: Click **Restore a backup file** (or click **File, Restore**).

Step 3: Identify the backup file:

- Filename: **[your name] Chapter 7.QBB**.
- Location: **A:**.

Step 4: Identify the restored file:

- Filename: **[your name] Activity 7.1.QBW**.
- Location: **C:\Program Files\Intuit\QuickBooks Premier**.

Step 5: Click **Restore.** If prompted, enter your User ID and Password.

Step 6: Change the company name to: **[your name] Activity 7.1 Rock Castle Construction**. (To change the company name, select Company (menu), Company Information.)

Task 2: Profit & Loss: Vertical Analysis

Prepare a customized profit and loss statement that shows each item on the statement as a percentage of sales (income):

Step 1: Open the Report Finder (click **Reports** on the Navigation Bar).

Step 2: Select Type of Report: **Company & Financial**.

Step 3: Select Report: **Profit & Loss Standard**.

Step 4: Select Date Range: **This Fiscal Quarter**.

Step 5: To customize the report, click the **Modify Report** button in the lower left corner of the *Report Finder* window.

Step 6: When the following *Modify Report* window appears, select: **% of Income**. Then click **OK**.

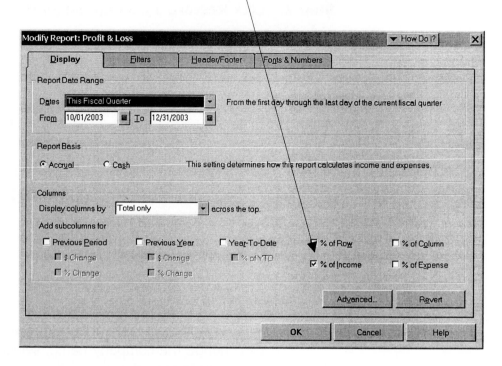

Step 7: Click the **Header/Footer** tab and insert **your name** and **Activity 7.1** in the report footer.

Step 8: Click the **Print** button to print the report using the **Portrait** orientation.

Step 9: ✎ On the printout, circle or highlight the single largest expense as a percentage of income.

Step 10: ✎ On the printout, circle or highlight the profit margin (income as a percentage of sales).

Task 3: Back Up Activity 7.1

Back up the Activity 7.1 file to a floppy disk.

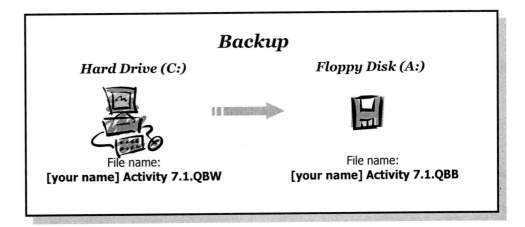

Step 1: ▫ Insert the **Chapter 7** backup disk in drive A.

Step 2: Click **File, Back Up**.

Step 3: Enter the file name: **[your name] Activity 7.1.QBB**. Enter location: **A:**.

Step 4: Click **Back Up**.

Step 5: Click **OK** after the backup is complete. Then close the company file. (Click File, Close Company.)

Activity 7.2: Balance Sheet: Vertical Analysis

You decide to also prepare a customized balance sheet that displays each account on the balance sheet as a percentage of total assets. This vertical analysis indicates the proportion of total assets that each asset represents. For example, inventory might be 30 percent of total assets. Vertical analysis also helps to assess the percentage of assets financed by debt versus owner's equity.

Task 1: Restore Company File

Restore your Activity 7.1 backup, changing the file name to Activity 7.2.

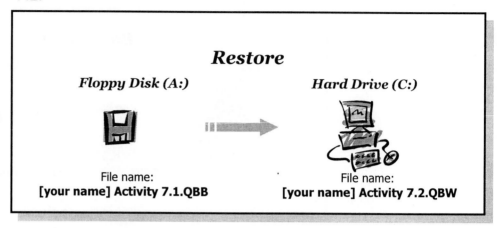

Step 1: Insert the **Chapter 7** backup disk into drive A.

Step 2: Click **Restore a backup file** (or click **File**, **Restore**).

Step 3: Identify the backup file:

- Filename: **[your name] Activity 7.1.QBB**.
- Location: **A:**.

Step 4: Identify the restored file:

- Filename: **[your name] Activity 7.2.QBW**.
- Location: **C:\Program Files\Intuit\QuickBooks Premier**.

Step 5: Click **Restore.** If prompted, enter your User ID and Password.

Step 6: Change the company name to:
[your name] Activity 7.2 Rock Castle Construction.
(To change the company name, select Company (menu), Company Information.)

Task 2:
Balance Sheet: Vertical Analysis, Export to Excel

Prepare a customized balance sheet that shows each account as a percentage of total assets.

Step 1: From the Report Finder, select Type of Report: **Company & Financial**.

Step 2: Select Report: **Balance Sheet Standard**.

Step 3: Select Date Range: **This Fiscal Quarter**.

Step 4: Click the **Display** button to display the balance sheet report.

Step 5: Click the **Modify Report** button and select: **% of Column**.

Step 6: Insert **your name** and **Activity 7.2** in the report footer.

Step 7: Print the customized balance sheet using the **Portrait** orientation.

Step 8: ✎ On the printout, circle or highlight the asset that represents the largest percentage of assets.

Step 9: ✎ On the printout, circle or highlight the percentage of assets financed with debt. (Hint: What is the percentage of total liabilities?)

Step 10: Export the customized balance sheet to Excel by clicking the **Excel** button in the *Balance Sheet* window. Print the Excel spreadsheet and compare it to your QuickBooks printout.

Task 3: Back Up Activity 7.2

Backup

Hard Drive (C:)   Floppy Disk (A:)

File name: File name:
[your name] Activity 7.2.QBW   **[your name] Activity 7.2.QBB**

Step 1: ⊞ Insert the **Chapter 7** backup disk in drive A.

Step 2: Click **File, Back Up**.

Step 3: Enter the file name: **[your name] Activity 7.2.QBB**. Enter location: **A:**.

Step 4: Click **Back Up**.

Step 5: Click **OK** after the backup is complete.

Activity 7.3: Depreciation Decision Tool

To learn more about depreciation, see the QuickBooks Decision Tools.

Step 1: Click **Company** on the menu bar, then click **Decision Tools**.

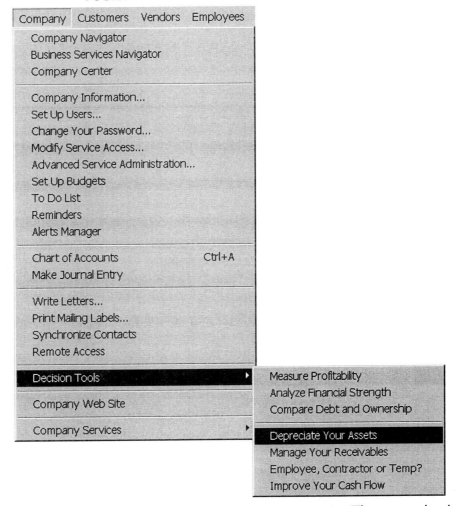

Step 2: Select: **Depreciate Your Assets**. Then read about depreciation basics.

Step 3: 📧 Prepare a short e-mail to Mr. Castle that summarizes depreciation basics and answers the following questions:

- ♦ What set of accounting rules are followed when preparing financial statements for bankers?

- What set of rules are followed when preparing federal income tax forms?

- What is the popular definition of depreciation?

- What is the financial accounting definition of depreciation?

- What is the tax definition of depreciation?

Activity 7.4: Web Quest

The IRS provides Publication 946 on depreciation to summarize information about depreciation for tax purposes.

To view Publication 946:

Step 1: Go to the www.irs.gov web site.

Step 2: Print the information that you find the most useful from **Publication 946.**

Activity 7.5: Web Quest

To learn more information about TurboTax software, visit Intuit's TurboTax web site.

Step 1: Go to www.intuit.com/turbotax or www.turbotax.com web sites.

Step 2: Prepare a short e-mail to Mr. Castle summarizing the difference between TurboTax for Home and Business and TurboTax for Business. Which TurboTax would you recommend for Rock Castle Construction?

Computer Accounting with QuickBooks 2002
Chapter 7 Printout Checklist
Name:_____ **Date:**_____

☑	***Printout Checklist – Chapter 7***
☐	Trial Balance
☐	Journal
☐	Adjusted Trial Balance
☐	General Ledger
☐	Profit & Loss
☐	Income and Expense Graph
☐	Balance Sheet
☐	Net Worth Graph
☐	Asset Pie Chart
☐	Statement of Cash Flows
☐	Income Tax Preparation Report
☐	Income Tax Summary
☐	Cash Flow Forecast
☐	Excel Spreadsheet Cash Flow Forecast
☑	***Printout Checklist – Activity 7.1***
☐	Task 2: Profit & Loss: Vertical Analysis
☑	***Printout Checklist – Activity 7.2***
☐	Task 2: Balance Sheet: Vertical Analysis & Excel Spreadsheet
☑	***Printout Checklist – Activity 7.3***
☐	Depreciation Basics e-mail

☑	***Printout Checklist – Activity 7.4***
☐	IRS Publication 946 on depreciation
☑	***Printout Checklist – Activity 7.5***
☐	TurboTax Recommendation e-mail

Part

II

Small Business Accounting
with
QuickBooks 2002

8

Creating a Service Company in QuickBooks

Scenario

Lately, you've considered starting your own business and becoming an entrepreneur. You have been looking for a business opportunity that would use your talents to make money.

While working at Rock Castle Construction, you have overheard conversations that some of the customers have been dissatisfied with the quality of the paint jobs. In addition, you believe there is a demand for custom painting. You know that Rock Castle Construction lost more than one job because it could not find a subcontractor to do custom painting.

One morning when you arrive at work, you hear Mr. Castle's voice booming throughout the office. *"That's the second time this month!"* he roars into the telephone. *"How are we supposed to finish our jobs on time when the painting subcontractor doesn't show up?!"* Mr. Castle slams down the phone.

That morning you begin to seriously consider the advantages and disadvantages of starting your own painting service business. Perhaps you could pick up some work from Rock Castle Construction. You could do interior and exterior painting for homes and businesses, including custom-painted murals while continuing to work part-time for Rock Castle Construction maintaining its accounting records. Now that you have learned QuickBooks, you can quickly enter transactions and create the reports Mr. Castle needs, leaving you time to operate your own painting service business.

When you return from lunch, you notice Diane Flowers in Mr. Castle's office. Then you overhear Mr. Castle telling her, *"We would like to help you, Mrs. Flowers, but we don't have anyone who can do a custom-painted landscape on your dining room wall. If I hear of anyone who does that type of work, I will call you."*

You watch as the two of them shake hands and Mrs. Flowers walks out the front door. Sensing a window of opportunity, you pursue Mrs. Flowers into the parking lot. *"Mrs. Flowers—"*

She stops and turns to look at you. *"Mrs. Flowers—I understand that you are looking for someone to paint a landscape mural in your home. I would like to bid on the job."*

With a sparkle in her eye, Mrs. Flowers asks, *"How soon can you start?"*

"As soon as I get off work this afternoon!" you reply as the two of you shake hands. *"Would you like a bid on the job?"*

Without hesitation, Mrs. Flowers replies, *"I trust you will be fair to your first customer."*

When you reenter the office building, Mr. Castle is waiting for you. You can feel Mr. Castle's gaze as you debate how best to tell him about your business plans.

Finally, Mr. Castle speaks. *"Give Tom Whalen a call. He would like you to do marbled faux painting in his home's foyer."*

"Thanks, Mr. Castle. I'll do that right away," you reply as you head toward your cubicle, wondering how Mr. Castle knew about your business plans.

Walking back to your cubicle, you quickly make three start-up decisions:

1. To use the sole proprietorship form of business.

2. To name your business Fearless Painting Service.

3. To invest in a computer so that you can use QuickBooks to maintain the accounting records for your business.

Now you will have two sources of income:

$ Wages from Rock Castle Construction reported on your W-2 and attached to your 1040 tax return.

$ Income from your painting business reported on a Schedule C attached to your 1040 tax return.

8

Learning Objectives

In Chapter 8, you will learn the following QuickBooks activities:

Introduction

In this chapter, you will set up a new service company in QuickBooks by completing the following steps:

1. Easy Step Interview

Use the EasyStep Interview to enter information and preferences for the new company. Based on the information entered, QuickBooks automatically creates a chart of accounts.

2. Customize the Chart of Accounts

Modify the chart of accounts to customize it for your business.

3. Customer List

In the Customer List, enter information about customers to whom you sell products and services.

4. Vendor List

In the Vendor List, enter information about vendors from whom you buy products, supplies, and services.

5. Item List

In the Item List, enter information about (1) products and services you *sell to customers* and (2) products and services you *buy from vendors*.

If you hired employees, you would also enter information into the Employee List. In this case, Fearless Painting Service has no employees.

To begin Chapter 8, start QuickBooks software by clicking on the QuickBooks desktop icon or click **Start**, **Programs**, **QuickBooks Premier**, **QuickBooks Premier**.

Create a New Company Using EasyStep Interview

To create a new company data file in QuickBooks, use the EasyStep Interview. The EasyStep Interview asks you a series of questions about your business. Then QuickBooks uses the information to customize QuickBooks to fit your business needs.

> To open the EasyStep Interview later:
> 1. Click **File**.
> 2. Click **EasyStep Interview**.

Open the EasyStep Interview as follows:

Step 1: Select the **File** menu.

Step 2: Select **New Company**.

> The top tabs change depending on the selected tab along the right.

The following *EasyStep Interview* window will appear.

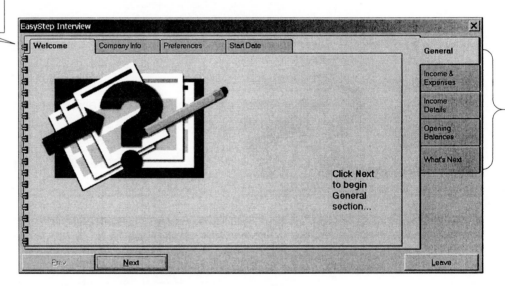

EasyStep Interview consists of five sections listed on the tabs on the right side of the *EasyStep Interview* window:

- **General:** Enter company information and customize QuickBooks for your company preferences. QuickBooks will automatically set up a chart of accounts for the type of business you select.

- **Income and Expenses:** Customize income and expense accounts for your business.

- **Income Details:** Enter the items (products and services) that you sell, such as products that you buy from vendors, hold as inventory, and then resell to customers.

- **Opening Balances:** Enter beginning balances for:

  - Customers who owe you money.

  - Vendors to whom you owe money.

  - Balance sheet accounts.

- **What's Next:** QuickBooks lists the items you have not completed in the EasyStep Interview and permits you to finish entering the items later.

General Company Information

> If you wanted to skip the EasyStep Interview, you would click the Skip Interview button.

To enter General Company Information about Fearless Painting Service, complete the following steps:

Step 1: Click the **General** tab along the right side of the *EasyStep Interview* window, then click **Next** *twice*.

Step 2: In the *Welcome* windows that follow, QuickBooks provides general information about setting up a company. Read the information on each of the windows, clicking **Next** to move to the next window. When you have completed the *Welcome* windows, click **Next** to move to the *Company Info* window.

Step 3: When the *General: Company Information* window appears, read the information on the window, then click **Next**.

Step 4: When the following *Your Company Name* window appears:

- Enter Company Name: **[your initials] Fearless Painting Service**.

- Press the **Tab** key and QuickBooks will automatically enter the Company Name in the *Legal Name* field. Since your company will do business under its legal name, the *Company Name* and *Legal Name* fields are the same.

- Click **Next**.

This is your DBA (Doing Business As) name. This name is used to identify your company for sales, advertising, and marketing.

Your company's Legal Name is used on all legal documents, such as contracts, tax returns, licenses, and patents.

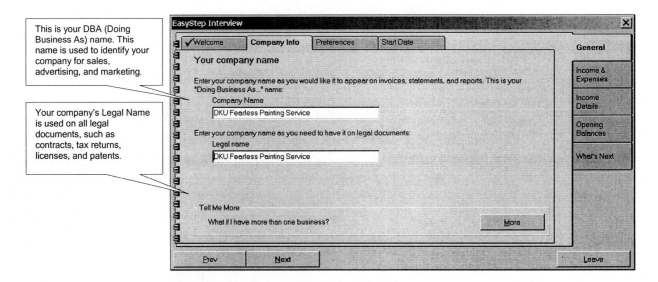

Step 5: When the *Company Address* window appears, enter the following information, then click **Next**.

Address	1230 Olive Boulevard
City	Bayshore
State	CA
Zip	94326
Phone #	800.555.3344
Email	<Enter your own email address>

Since your company is a sole proprietorship, the business income is reported on Schedule C which is attached to your 1040 tax return. Accordingly, you use your social security number for the business federal tax ID number.

Step 6: In the following *Other Company Information* window:

♦ Enter the Federal Tax ID number that will appear on your federal tax return: **333-22-4444**.

♦ Enter the first month of your Income Tax Year: **January**. For tax purposes, you will report income and expenses for the 12-month period beginning January 1 and ending December 31.

♦ Enter the first month of your Fiscal Year: **January**. The fiscal year is the 12-month period for which a business reports income and expenses for financial statements given to investors and creditors. Your fiscal year will coincide with your tax year, beginning on January 1 and ending December 31.

♦ Click **Next**.

For a Federal Tax ID number:
1. A sole proprietorship uses the owner's social security number.
2. A corporation uses an EIN (Employer Identification Number).

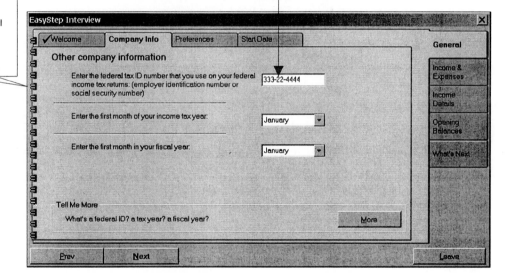

Step 7: In the *Your Company Income Tax Form* window:

- Select: **Form 1040 (Sole Proprietorship)**.
- Click **Next**.

Business tax returns:
1. A sole proprietorship files Schedule C which is attached to the owner's Form 1040 tax return.
2. A corporation files a Form 1120.
3. An S corporation files Form 1120S.
4. A partnership files Form 1065.

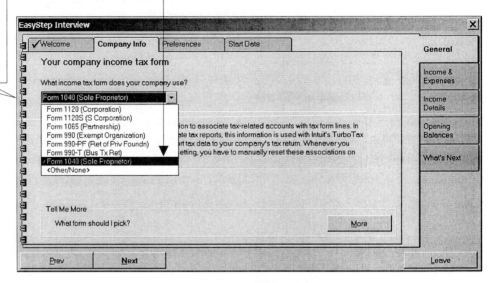

Step 8: In the following *Select Your Type of Business* window, select **Service Business**. QuickBooks will automatically create a chart of accounts for a service business. Later, you can customize the chart of accounts to suit your specific business needs. Click **Next**.

Warning!
You **cannot** change type of business later.

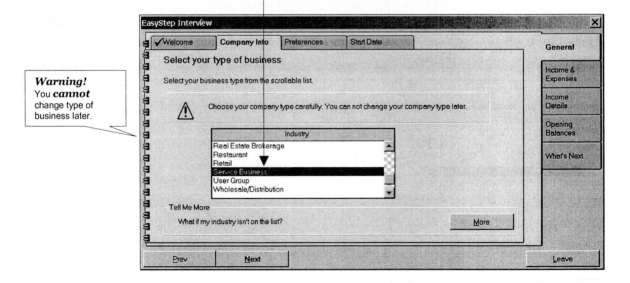

Step 9: Read the information on the *Setup Tips For Your Business* window. Then click **Next**.

Step 10: Next, you will save your company data file, specifying a file name and where the file will be saved. When the *We're Ready To Create Your Company File Now* window appears, click **Next**. When the following *Save As* window appears:

- Save in: **QuickBooks Premier** folder.

- Enter File Name: **[your initials] Fearless Painting Service Chapter 8**.

- Click **Save**.

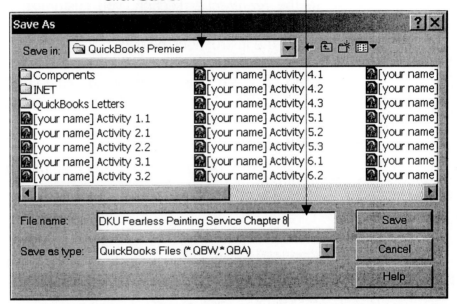

Step 11: When *Your Income and Expense Accounts* window appears:

- Click **Yes** to use the accounts that QuickBooks automatically creates for a service business.

- Click **Next**.

Step 12: When the *Accessing Your Company* window appears:

- Select **0** when asked: "How many people (besides yourself) will have access to your QuickBooks company?"

- Click **Next**.

Step 13: When the *Company Info Completed* window appears, click **Next** to proceed to the *Preferences* section.

General Information: Preferences

In the *Preferences* section, you customize QuickBooks to fit your company's specific needs. To complete the *Preferences* section, follow the instructions below:

Step 1: Read the information contained in the *What are Preferences?* window, then click **Next**.

Step 2: When the *Inventory* window appears:

- "Does your company maintain inventory?" Select **No**.

- Click **Next**.

Step 3: When the *Sales Tax* window appears:

- "Do you collect sales tax from your customers?" Select **No**.

- Click **Next**.

Step 4: When *Your Invoice Format* window appears:

- Select Invoice Format: **Service**.

- Click **Next**.

Note: You are not considered an employee because you are the owner.

Step 5: When the *Using QuickBooks for Payroll* window appears:

- "Do you want to use the QuickBooks Payroll feature?" Select **No**.

- Click **Next**.

Step 6: When the *Estimates* window appears:

- ◆ "Do you prepare written or verbal estimates for your customers?" Select **Yes**.
- ◆ Click **Next**.

> Fearless Painting will always invoice the job in full when the job is completed rather than using progress billings for partial completion of the job.

Step 7: When the *Progress Invoicing* window appears:

- ◆ "Do you ever issue more than one invoice for one estimate?" Select **No**.
- ◆ Click **Next**.

Step 8: When the *Time Tracking* window appears:

- ◆ "Would you like to track the time that you or your employees spend on each job or project?" Select **Yes**.
- ◆ Click **Next**.

> Classes can be used to track income and expenses for different departments or locations.

Step 9: When the *Tracking Segments of Your Business with Classes* window appears:

- ◆ "Do you want to use classes?" Select **No**.
- ◆ Click **Next**.

Step 10: When the *Two Ways to Handle Bills and Payments* window appears:

- ◆ Select **Enter the bills first and then enter the payments later**.
- ◆ Click **Next**.

Step 11: When the *Reminders List* window appears:

- ◆ "How often would you like to see your Reminders List?" Select: **When I ask for it**.
- ◆ Click **Next**.

> Recall that the cash basis of accounting records sales when the cash is received in contrast to the accrual basis that records sales when the goods or services are provided to the customer. The cash basis records expenses when they are paid and the accrual basis records expenses when incurred.

Step 12: When the *Accrual or Cash Based Reporting* window appears:

- "Do you prefer to view reports on an accrual or cash basis?" Select: **Accrual-based reports**.
- Click **Next**.

Step 13: When the *Preferences Completed!* window appears, click **Next** to proceed to the *Start Date* section.

General Information: Start Date

The Start Date is the date that you will start entering transactions in QuickBooks. For a new business, this is the first day of business. For an existing business, the Start Date is the day you switch to using QuickBooks for your accounting.

Step 1: Read the information on *the Understanding Your QuickBooks Start Date* window, then click **Next**.

Step 2: Read the *Information for Your Start Date* window, then click **Next**. Because you are starting a new company, you will not have any prior bank statements, invoices, or bills.

Step 3: When the *Choose Your QuickBooks Start Date* window appears:

- Enter your company start date: **01/01/2002**.
- Click **Next**.

Step 4: When the *General Section Completed!* window appears, click **Next** to proceed to the *Income and Expenses* tab of the EasyStep Interview.

Income and Expenses

The *Income and Expenses* section permits you to view the chart of accounts that QuickBooks has created and to add any additional income or expenses accounts that you may need. You will not add any income accounts for Fearless Painting, but you will add a Supplies Expense account to the chart of accounts.

Step 1: When the *Income Accounts* window appears, click **Next** *twice*.

Step 2: When the *Here Are Your Income Accounts* window appears, four income accounts are listed.

> You can add additional income accounts now or later after exiting the EasyStep Interview.

- ◆ "Do you want to add an income account now?" Select **No**.

- ◆ Click **Next**.

Step 3: When the *Income Accounts Completed!* window appears, click **Next** to move to the next section.

Step 4: When the *Expense Accounts* window appears:

- ◆ "Would you like a more detailed explanation of expense accounts and subaccounts?" Select **No Thank You**.

- ◆ Click **Next**.

Step 5: When the *Here Are Your Expense Accounts* window appears:

- ◆ "Do you want to add an expense account now?" Select **Yes**.

- ◆ Click **Next**.

Step 6: When the following *Adding an Expense Account* window appears:

- Enter Account Name: **Supplies Expense**.

- Select Tax Line: **Sch C: Supplies (not from COGS)**.

- Click **Next**.

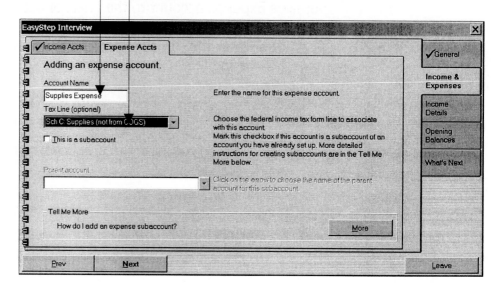

Step 7: When the *Add Another Expense Account* window appears:

- "Do you want to add an expense account now?" Select **No**.

- Click **Next**.

Step 8: When the *Expense Accounts Completed!* window appears, click **Next** to proceed to the *Income Details* tab.

Income Details

In this section, QuickBooks asks you questions about:

1. Customer accounts receivable.

2. Services you sell to customers.

3. Inventory that you sell to customers.

This information permits QuickBooks to select the QuickBooks features that you need.

> This tells QuickBooks that you need to track accounts receivable (the amount customers owe you).

Step 1: Click **Next** *twice* to view the *Receipt of Payment* window.

- "Do you receive full payment at the time you provide a service or sell a product?" Select **Sometimes**.

- Click **Next**.

> This indicates that Fearless Painting will not be sending monthly bills to customers. Instead, Fearless will bill customers when work is completed.

Step 2: When the *Statement Charges* window appears:

- "Will you be using statement charges?" Select **No**.

- Click **Next**.

Step 3: When the *Introduction Completed!* Window appears, click **Next** to proceed to the *Items* tab.

Income Details: Items

QuickBooks considers an item to be anything that you sell to a customer. An item can be:

1. Service Item: A service you provide customers.

2. Non-inventory Item: A product that you sell to customers, but do not track the quantity as inventory.

3. Inventory Item: A product that you buy, stock as inventory, and then resell to customers.

Items can be entered when completing the EasyStep Interview or entered later when entering the Item List.

For Fearless Painting Service, you will enter items after exiting the EasyStep Interview.

Step 1:   When the *Income Details: Items* window appears, read the information on the window, then click **Next**.

Step 2:   When the *Service Item* window appears:

- "Do you want to set up a service item for any work or service?" Select **No**. (You will enter service items later after exiting the EasyStep Interview.)
- Click **Next**.

Step 3:   When the *Non-Inventory Parts* window appears:

- "Do you want to set up a non-inventory part item for any material or product?" Select **No**.
- Click **Next**

Step 4:   When the *Other Charges* window appears:

> Other Charges include such items as shipping charges.

- "Do you want to set up an Other Charge item for any miscellaneous charges?" Select **No**.
- Click **Next**.

Step 5: When the *Items Completed!* Window appears, click **Next** to proceed to the *Inventory* section.

Income Details: Inventory

Because Fearless Painting Service provides a service, it will not hold and sell inventory items.

Step 1: When the *Income Details: Inventory* window appears, click **Next**.

Step 2: Select **Skip Inventory Items**, then click **Next**.

Opening Balances

In the Opening Balances section, QuickBooks permits you to enter the following opening balances:

1. Opening balances for accounts receivable, indicating the amounts that customers owe you as of the start date.

2. Opening balances for accounts payable, indicating the amounts that you owe vendors as of the start date.

3. Opening balances for the remaining balance sheet accounts (assets, liabilities, and owner's equity accounts) as of your start date. In this section, you can create bank accounts and loan accounts.

Because Fearless Painting Service is a new company, there are no opening balances for any of the accounts. All of the balance sheet accounts will have beginning balances of zero; however, Fearless needs to create a bank account.

To complete the *Opening Balances* section:

Step 1: When the *Opening Balance Introduction* window appears, read the information on the screen, then click **Next** until the *Enter Customers* window appears.

Step 2: When the *Enter Customers* window appears:

♦ "Do you have any customers who owed you money on your start date to add?" Select **No**.

♦ Click **Next**.

Step 3: When the *Opening Balances: Vendors* window appears, click **Next**.

Step 4: When the *Adding Vendors with Open Balances* window appears:

♦ "Do you have any vendors whom you owed money on your start date to add?" Select **No**.

♦ Click **Next**.

Step 5: When the *Vendors Completed!* window appears, click **Next**.

Step 6: When the *Opening Balances: Accounts* window appears, click **Next**.

Step 7: When the *Credit Card Accounts* window appears:

♦ "Would you like to set up a credit card account?" Select **No**.

♦ Click **Next**.

> A line of credit is the ability to borrow from the bank as needed up to a specified amount.

Step 8: When the *Adding Lines of Credit* window appears:

♦ "Do you have any lines of credit?" Select **No**.

♦ Click **Next**.

Step 9: When the *Loans and Notes Payable* window appears:

♦ "Would you like to set up an account to track a loan or note payable?" Select **No**.

♦ Click **Next**.

Step 10: When the *Bank Accounts* window appears:

- ◆ "Would you like to set up a bank account?" Select **Yes**.
- ◆ Click **Next**.

Step 11: When the *Adding a Bank Account* window appears:

- ◆ Enter the Bank Account Name: **[your initials] Checking**.
- ◆ Click **Next**.

Step 12: When the *Last Statement Date and Balance* window appears:

- ◆ Enter Statement Ending Date: **01/01/2002**.
- ◆ Enter Statement Ending Balance: **0.00**.
- ◆ Click **Next**.

Step 13: When the *Adding Another Bank Account* window appears:

- ◆ Select **No** when asked if you want to add another bank account.
- ◆ Click **Next**.

Step 14: When the *Introduction to Assets* window appears, read the information on the screen and then click **Next**.

Step 15: When the *Assets Account* window appears:

- ◆ "Would you like to set up an asset account?" Select **No**.
- ◆ Click **Next** *4* times to proceed to the *What's Next* section.

What's Next

Step 1: When the *What's Next* window appears, click **Next**.

Step 2: Read the What's Next Recommendations.

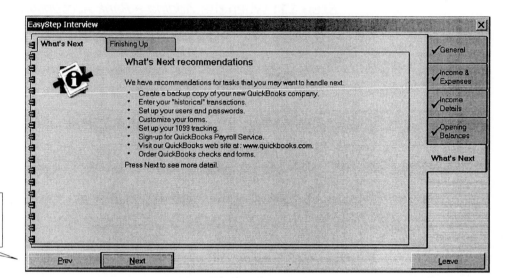

Click **Next** to view more information about the recommendations.

Step 3: Click the **Leave** button to exit the EasyStep Interview.

Edit the Chart of Accounts

The Chart of Accounts is a list of all the accounts Fearless Painting Service will use when maintaining its accounting records. The chart of accounts is like a table of contents for accounting records.

In the EasyStep Interview, when you selected service company as the type of business, QuickBooks automatically created a chart of accounts for Fearless Painting. QuickBooks permits you to customize the chart of accounts to fit your accounting needs.

Display Chart of Accounts

To display the following *Chart of Accounts* window, click **Chart of Accounts** on the Company Navigator.

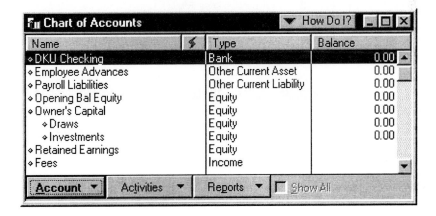

Display Account Numbers

Notice that the Chart of Accounts does not list the account numbers. Display account numbers in the Chart of Accounts by completing the following steps:

Step 1: Click the **Preferences** icon on the Company Navigator.

Step 2: When the following *Preferences* window appears:

- Click the **Accounting** icon on the left scrollbar.
- Click the **Company Preferences** tab.
- Select **Use account numbers**.

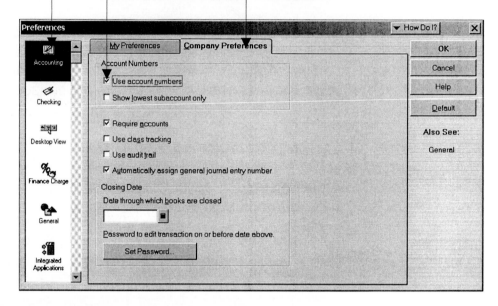

Step 3: Click **OK** to close the *Preferences* window.

The Chart of Accounts should now display account numbers.

Add New Accounts

Fearless Painting needs to add the following accounts to its Chart of Accounts:

Account	Computer
Subaccount	Computer Cost
Subaccount	Accumulated Depreciation Computer

You can also add a new account as follows:
1. Holding the mouse pointer over the Chart of Accounts window, right-click.
2. Select **New**.

To add new accounts to the Chart of Accounts for Fearless Painting:

Step 1: From the following *Chart of Accounts* window:

- ◆ Click the **Account** button.

- ◆ Select **New**.

The chart of accounts now lists account numbers.

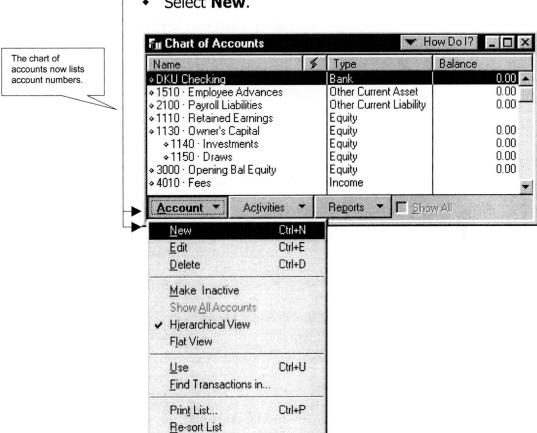

Step 2: When the following *New Account* window appears:

> The Tax Line determines where QuickBooks lists the account balance on the Income Tax Summary report. Only income and expense accounts are assigned a Tax Line. Because asset, liability, and equity accounts are not listed on the tax return, use Unassigned Tax Line for these accounts.

- ◆ Select Account Type: **Fixed Asset**.
- ◆ Enter Account Number: **1410**.
- ◆ Enter Name: **Computer**.
- ◆ Enter Description: **Computer**.
- ◆ Select Tax Line: **<Unassigned>**.
- ◆ Enter Opening Balance: **0** as of **01/01/2002**.

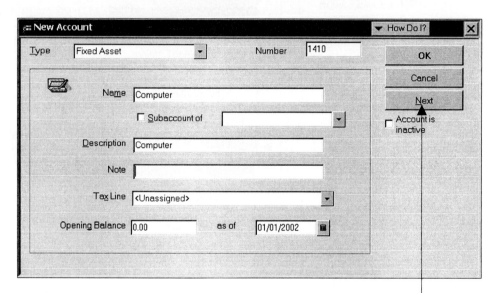

Step 3: Click **Next** to enter another account.

To enter new subaccounts, complete the following steps.

Step 1: Add the Computer Cost subaccount by entering the following information when a blank *New Account* window appears:

- Select Account Type: **Fixed Asset**.
- Enter Account Number: **1420**.
- Enter Name: **Computer Cost**.
- Check ✓ Subaccount of: **1410 – Computer**.
- Enter Description: **Computer Cost**.
- Select Tax Line: **<Unassigned>**.
- Enter Opening Balance: **0.00** as of **01/01/2002**.

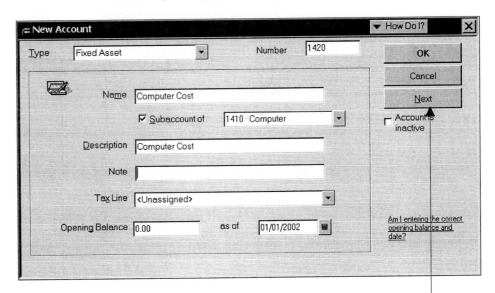

Step 2: Click **Next** to add another subaccount.

Step 3: Add the Accumulated Depreciation Computer subaccount by entering the following information in the *New Account* window:

Account No.	1430
Account Type	Fixed Asset
Account Name	Accumulated Depr Computer
Subaccount of	1410 Computer
Account Description	Accumulated Depr Computer
Tax Line	Unassigned
Opening Balance	0 as of 01/01/2002

Step 4: Click **OK** to close the *New Account* window.

Print the Chart of Accounts

To print the chart of accounts complete the following steps:

Step 1: From the *Chart of Accounts* window:

- Click the **Reports** button.
- Select **Account Listing**.
- Insert **your name** and **Chapter 8** in the report footer. (Modify Report, Header/Footer tab.)
- Click **Print**. Select **Portrait** orientation and **Fit report to 1 page(s) wide**. Click **Print** again.
- Close the *Account Listing* window.

Step 2: Close the *Chart of Accounts* window.

Create a Customer List

As you learned in Chapter 4, the Customer List contains information about the customers to whom you sell services. In addition, the Customer List also contains information about jobs or projects for each customer.

Fearless Painting has two customers:

1. Diane Flowers, who wants a custom landscape mural painted on her dining room wall.

2. Tom Whalen, who wants marbled faux painting in his home's foyer.

Tip: You can import list information using files with .iif extensions (Intuit Interchange File). See QuickBooks Help for more information.

To add the new customers to Fearless Painting's Customer List:

Step 1: Click **Customers** on the Customer Navigator.

Step 2: To add a new customer, when the *Customer:Job List* window appears, click the **Customer:Job** button.

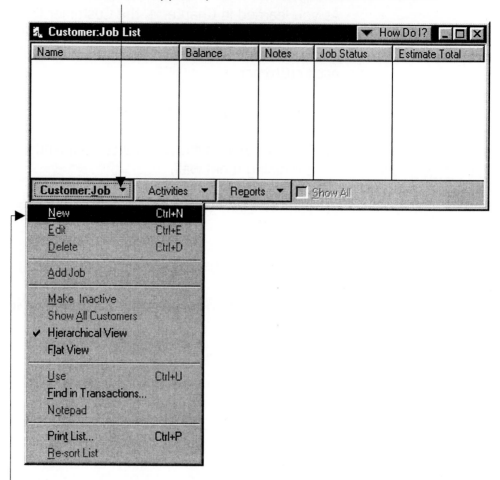

Step 3: Click **New** to add a new Customer.

Step 4: When the *New Customer* window appears, enter the following information about your first customer, Diane Flowers.

Customer	Flowers, Diane
Address Info:	
Mr./Ms./...	Mrs.
First Name	Diane
M.I.	L.
Last Name	Flowers
Contact	Diane
Phone	415-555-1078
Alt. Ph.	415-555-3434
Alt. Contact	Tad (spouse)
Address	10 Tee Drive Bayshore, CA 94326

Select **Add New**.

Additional Info:	
Type	Residential
Terms	Net 30

Payment Info:	
Account	1001
Preferred Payment Method	Check

Select **Add New**.

Job Info:	
Job Status	Awarded
Start Date	01/03/2002
Job Description	Dining Room Landscape Mural
Job Type	Mural

From the *Customer: Job List* window:
1. Click **Reports** button.
2. Click **Contact List**.
3. Select **Landscape**.

Step 5:   Click **OK** to close the *New Customer* window.

Step 6:   Print the Customer List.

Step 7:   Close the *Customer: Job List* window.

Create a Vendor List

As you learned in Chapter 5, the Vendor List contains information about vendors from whom you buy products and services.

To add vendors to the Vendor List for Fearless Painting:

Step 1:   Click **Vendors** on the Vendor Navigator.

Step 2:   When the following *Vendor List* window appears, click the **Vendor** button.

Step 3: Click **New** to add a new vendor.

Step 4: When the *New Vendor* window appears, enter the following information about Garrison Paint Supplies.

Vendor	Garrison Paint Supplies
Opening Balance	0
As of	01/01/2002
Address Info:	
Company Name	Garrison Paint Supplies
Address	200 Clay Street Bayshore, CA 94326
Contact	Cheryl
Phone	415-555-6039
Print on Check as	Garrison Paint Supplies

Additional Info:	
Account	2002
Type	Supplies
Terms	Net 30
Credit Limit	3000.00
Tax ID	37-7832541
Vendor Eligible for 1099	No

From the *Vendor List* window:
1. Click **Reports** button.
2. Click **Contact List**.
3. Select **Landscape**.

Step 5: Click **OK** to close the *New Vendor* window.

Step 6: Print the Vendor List.

Step 7: Close the *Vendor List* window.

Create an Item List

As you learned in Chapter 5, the Item List contains information about service items, inventory items, and non-inventory items sold to customers. Fearless Painting plans to sell four different service items to customers:

1. Labor: mural painting

2. Labor: faux painting

3. Labor: interior painting

4. Labor: exterior painting

To add a service item to the Item List:

Step 1: Click the **Items & Services** icon in the Vendors Navigator.

Step 2: When the *Item List* window appears, click the **Item** button.

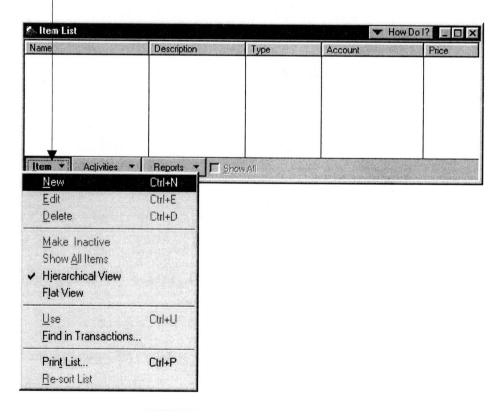

Step 3: Click **New** to add new items to the Items List.

Step 4: When the following *New Item* window appears:
- ◆ Enter Type: **Service**
- ◆ Enter Item Name: **Labor**
- ◆ Enter Description: **Painting Labor**
- ◆ Select Account: **4070 - Services**

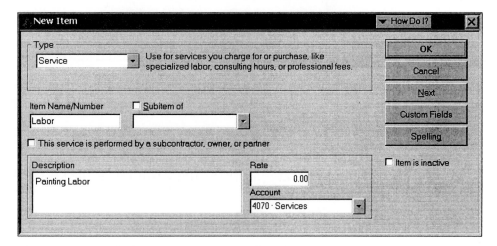

Step 5: Click **OK** to close the *New Item* window.

Step 6: Print the Item List at January 1, 2002. (Hint: Click the **Reports** button, then click **Item Listing**. Remember to insert **your name** and **Chapter 8** in the report footer.)

Step 7: Close the *Item List* window.

Back Up Chapter 8

Back up your Chapter 8 file to your floppy disk. Use the file name: [your name] Chapter 8.

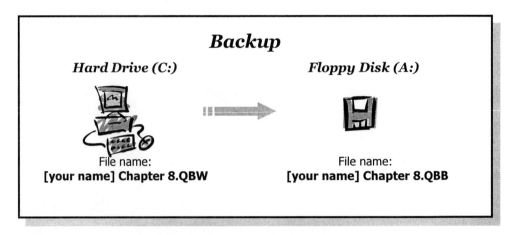

Backup

Hard Drive (C:)   **Floppy Disk (A:)**

File name:
[your name] Chapter 8.QBW

File name:
[your name] Chapter 8.QBB

Step 1:   Insert the **Chapter 8** backup disk in drive A.

Step 2:   Click **File**, **Back Up**.

Step 3:   Enter the file name: **[your name] Chapter 8.QBB**. Enter location: **A:**.

Step 4:   Click **Back Up**.

Step 5:   Click **OK** after the backup is complete.

You have now backed up the Chapter 8 file to your Chapter 8 floppy disk.

If you are continuing your computer session, close the company file and then proceed to Activity 8.1.

If you are quitting your computer session now, (1) close the company file and (2) exit QuickBooks.

Assignments

Activity 8.1: Edit Chart of Accounts

In this activity, you will add new accounts and subaccounts to Fearless Painting's chart of accounts.

Task 1: Restore Company File

The first task is to restore the Chapter 8 backup to the hard drive, changing the file name to Activity 8.

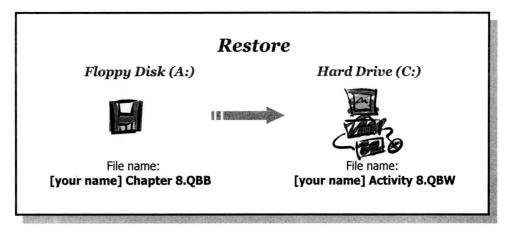

Step 1:   Insert the **Chapter 8** backup disk into drive A.

Step 2:   Click **Restore a backup file** (or click **File, Restore**).

Step 3:   Identify the backup file:

  ♦ Filename: **[your name] Fearless Painting Service Chapter 8.QBB**.

  ♦ Location: **A:**.

Step 4: Identify the restored file:

- Filename: **[your name] Fearless Painting Service Activity 8.QBW**.

- Location: **C:\Program Files\Intuit\QuickBooks Premier**.

Step 5: Click **Restore.** If prompted, enter your User ID and Password.

Step 6: Change the company name to:
[your name] Fearless Painting Service Activity 8.
(To change the company name, select Company (menu), Company Information.)

Task 2: Edit Account

Notice on your Account Listing printout from Chapter 8 that the Supplies Expense account that you added during the EasyStep Interview does not have an account number. Edit the account to add the account number: **6552**. (Hint: Open the Company Navigator, click Chart of Accounts, select Supplies Expense, click Account, and click Edit.)

Task 3: Add Accounts

Add the following new accounts and subaccounts to the chart of accounts for Fearless Painting Service. Click **Next** after entering each account.

Account No.	1100
Account Type	Accounts Receivable
Account Name	Accounts Receivable
Account Description	Accounts Receivable
Tax Line	Unassigned

Account No.	1310
Account Type	Other Current Asset
Account Name	Paint Supplies
Account Description	Paint Supplies
Tax Line	Unassigned

Account No.	1440
Account Type	Fixed Asset
Account Name	Equipment
Account Description	Equipment
Tax Line	Unassigned

Account No.	1450
Account Type	Fixed Asset
Account Name	Equipment Cost
Account Description	Equipment Cost
Subaccount of	1440 Equipment
Tax Line	Unassigned

Account No.	1460
Account Type	Fixed Asset
Account Name	Accumulated Depreciation
Account Description	Accumulated Depreciation
Subaccount of	1440 Equipment
Tax Line	Unassigned

Account No.	2110
Account Type	Accounts Payable
Account Name	Accounts Payable
Account Description	Accounts Payable
Tax Line	Unassigned

Account No.	6430
Account Type	Expense
Account Name	Depr Expense-Computer
Account Description	Depr Expense-Computer
Tax Line	Unassigned

Account No.	6460
Account Type	Expense
Account Name	Depr Expense-Equipment
Account Description	Depr Expense-Equipment
Tax Line	Unassigned

Account No.	6551
Account Type	Expense
Account Name	Paint Supplies Expense
Account Description	Paint Supplies Expense
Tax Line	Sch C: Supplies (not from COGS)

Task 4: Print Chart of Accounts

Print the chart of accounts (Reports button, Account Listing). Remember to insert Activity 8.1 and your name in the report footer.

Leave the company file open for the next activity.

Activity 8.2: Customer List

In this activity, you will enter a new customer in Fearless Painting's Customer List.

Task 1: Add Customer

Add Tom Whalen to the Customer List.

Customer	Whalen, Tom
Address Info:	
Mr./Ms./...	Mr.
First Name	Tom
M.I.	M.
Last Name	Whalen
Contact	Tom
Phone	415-555-1234
Alt. Ph.	415-555-5678
Alt. Contact	Work phone
Address	100 Sunset Drive Bayshore, CA 94326

Additional Info:	
Type	Residential
Terms	Net 30

Payment Info:	
Account	1002
Preferred Payment	Check

Job Info:	
Job Status	Pending
Job Description	Foyer Marbled Faux Painting
Job Type	Faux Painting

Select **Add New.**

Task 2: Print Customer List

Print the Customer List. (Click the Reports button, then click Contact List. Insert **your name** and **Activity 8.2** in the report footer. Use Landscape orientation.)

Leave the company file open for the next activity.

Activity 8.3: Vendor List

In this activity, you will add vendors to Fearless Painting's Vendor List.

Task 1: Add Vendors

Add the following vendors to the Vendor List.

Vendor	Cornell Computers
Opening balance	0
As of	01/01/2002
Address Info:	
Company Name	Cornell Computers
Address	218 Business Parkway Bayshore, CA 94326
Contact	Becky
Phone	415-555-7507
Additional Info:	
Account	2002
Type	Supplies
Terms	Net 30
Credit Limit	3000.00
Tax ID	37-4356712
Vendor eligible for 1099	No

Click **Next** to add another vendor.

Vendor	Hartz Leasing
Opening balance	0
As of	01/01/2002
Address Info:	
Company Name	Hartz Leasing
Address	13 Appleton Drive Bayshore, CA 94326
Contact	Joe
Phone	415-555-0412
Additional Info:	
Account	2003
Type	Leasing
Terms	Net 30
Tax ID	37-1726354
Vendor eligible for 1099	No

Select **Add New**.

Task 2: Print Vendor List

Print the Vendor List. (Click the Reports button, then click Contact List. Insert **your name** and **Activity 8.3** in the report footer. Use Landscape orientation.)

Leave the company file open for the next activity.

Activity 8.4: Item List

In this activity, you will add items to Fearless Painting's Item List.

Task 1: Add Items

Add the following items to Fearless Painting's Item List. Click **Next** after entering each item.

Item Type	Service
Item Name	Labor Mural
Subitem of	Labor
Description	Labor: Mural Painting
Rate	40.00
Account	4070 – Services

Item Type	Service
Item Name	Labor Faux
Subitem of	Labor
Description	Labor: Faux Painting
Rate	40.00
Account	4070 – Services

Item Type	Service
Item Name	Labor Interior
Subitem of	Labor
Description	Labor: Interior Painting
Rate	20.00
Account	4070 – Services

Item Type	Service
Item Name	Labor Exterior
Subitem of	Labor
Description	Labor: Exterior Painting
Rate	30.00
Account	4070 - Services

Task 2: Print Item List

Print the Item List. (From the *Item List* window, click the Reports button, then click Item Listing. Insert **your name** and **Activity 8.4** in the report footer. Use Landscape orientation.)

Task 3: Back Up Activity 8

Backup

Hard Drive (C:)   Floppy Disk (A:)

File name: File name:
[your name] Activity 8.QBW   [your name] Activity 8.QBB

Step 1: 🖫 Insert the **Chapter 8** backup disk in drive A.

Step 2: Click **File, Back Up**.

Step 3: Enter the file name: **[your name] Activity 8.QBB**.
Enter location: **A:**.

Step 4: Click **Back Up**.

Step 5: Click **OK** after the backup is complete. Close the company file.

Activity 8.5: Web Quest

When launching a small business, a business plan is essential. To assist entrepreneurs in writing a business plan, Intuit provides sample business plans on its Quicken Small Business web site.

Step 1: Go to the www.quicken.com web site, Small Business, Business Plan Template.

Step 2: Print one of the sample business plans and business plan financials listed on the web site.

Activity 8.6: Web Quest

The Small Business Administration (SBA) summarizes government resources available to the small business owner.

Step 1: Go to www.sbaonline.sba.gov web site.

Step 2: Print two resources on the SBA web site that you find the most useful to the small business owner.

Activity 8.7: Web Quest

The IRS provides an IRS Small Business Corner that summarizes tax information for the small business.

Step 1: Go to the www.irs.gov web site. Click:

- **Tax Information For Business**
- **Small Business Corner**
- **Operating Your Business**
- **Business Taxes**

> The IRS and Small Business Administration offer a FREE Small Business Resource Guide CD.

Step 2: Print the list of tax forms a business must file.

Computer Accounting with QuickBooks 2002
Chapter 8 Printout Checklist
Name:_____ Date:_____

☑	***Printout Checklist – Chapter 8***
☐	Chart of Accounts (Account Listing)
☐	Customer List
☐	Vendor List
☐	Item List
☑	***Printout Checklist – Activity 8.1***
☐	Task 4: Chart of Accounts
☑	***Printout Checklist – Activity 8.2***
☐	Task 2: Customer List
☑	***Printout Checklist – Activity 8.3***
☐	Task 2: Vendor List
☑	***Printout Checklist – Activity 8.4***
☐	Task 2: Item List
☑	***Printout Checklist – Activity 8.5***
☐	Business Plan
☑	***Printout Checklist – Activity 8.6***
☐	Small Business Administration Resources
☑	***Printout Checklist – Activity 8.7***
☐	Business Taxes

Accounting for a Service Company

Scenario

Preferring to use your savings rather than take out a bank loan, you invest $6,000 of your savings to launch Fearless Painting Service.

You prepare the following list of items your business will need.

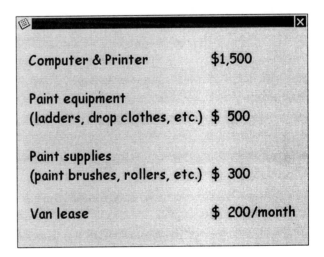

Computer & Printer	$1,500
Paint equipment (ladders, drop clothes, etc.)	$ 500
Paint supplies (paint brushes, rollers, etc.)	$ 300
Van lease	$ 200/month

9

Learning Objectives

In Chapter 9, you will learn the following QuickBooks activities:

Introduction

In this chapter, you will enter business transactions for Fearless Painting's first year of operations. These include transactions with the owner, customers, and vendors.

To begin Chapter 9, first start QuickBooks software and then restore your backup file.

Start QuickBooks software by clicking on the QuickBooks desktop icon or click **Start**, **Programs**, **QuickBooks Premier**, **QuickBooks Premier**.

Restore Back Up

Restore your Activity 8 backup to the C drive, renaming the file Chapter 9.

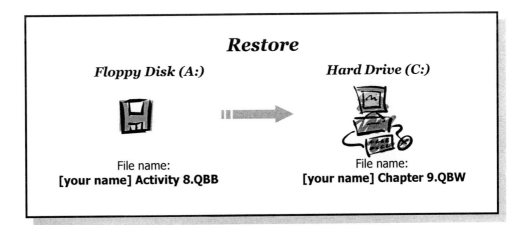

Restore

Floppy Disk (A:)	*Hard Drive (C:)*
File name:	File name:
[your name] Activity 8.QBB	**[your name] Chapter 9.QBW**

Step 1: ⎙ Insert the **Chapter 8** backup disk into drive A.

Step 2: Click **Restore a backup file** (or click **File**, **Restore**).

Step 3: Identify the backup file:

- Filename: **[your name] Fearless Painting Service Activity 8.QBB**.
- Location: **A:**.

Step 4: Identify the restored file:

- Filename: **[your name] Fearless Painting Service Chapter 9.QBW**.
- Location: **C:\Program Files\Intuit\QuickBooks Premier**.

Step 5: Click **Restore.** If prompted, enter your User ID and Password.

Step 6: Change the company name to:
[your name] Fearless Painting Service Chapter 9.
(To change the company name, select Company (menu), Company Information.)

Record Owner's Investment in the Company

To launch your new business, you invest $6,000 in Fearless Painting. In order to keep business records and your personal records separate, you open a business checking account at the local bank for Fearless Painting. You then deposit your personal check for $6,000 in the business checking account.

In Chapters 3 and 4 you recorded deposits using the Deposits icon on the Banking Navigator (Chapter 3) and the Customer Navigator (Chapter 4).

You can also record deposits directly in the Check Register. QuickBooks then transfers the information to the *Make Deposits* window.

To record the deposit to Fearless Painting's checking account using the *Make Deposits* window, complete the following steps:

Step 1: After restoring the Fearless Painting Service backup file, click **Banking** on the Navigation Bar. The following Banking Navigator will appear.

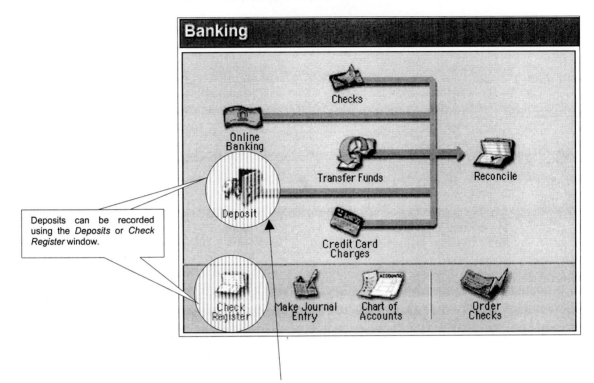

Deposits can be recorded using the *Deposits* or *Check Register* window.

Step 2: Click the **Deposit** icon to display the *Make Deposits* window.

 ♦ Enter Date: **01/01/2002**.

 ♦ On the *Receive From* drop-down list, select **<Add New>**. Select **Other**, then click **OK**. Enter Name: **[Your Name]**. Click **OK**.

- Select Account: **1140: Owner's Capital: Investments**. Press the **Tab** key.

- Enter Memo: **Invested $6,000 in the business**.

- Enter Check No.: **1001**.

- Enter Payment Method: **Check**.

- Enter Amount: **6000.00**.

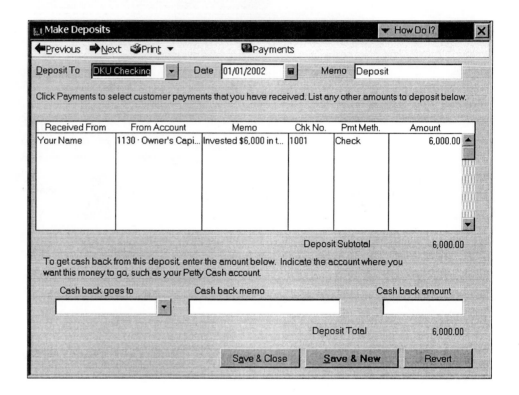

Step 3: To print the deposit slip:

- Click the **Print** button at the top of the *Make Deposits* window.

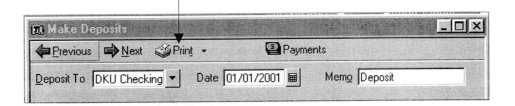

- Select **Deposit Summary Only**.

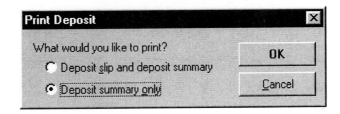

- Click **OK**.
- Select **Portrait** printer setting, then click **Print**.

Step 4: Click **Save & Close** to close the *Make Deposits* window.

Record Purchase Transactions

Purchases can be either cash purchases or credit purchases on account.

	Description	**Record Using QB...**
Cash Purchase	Pay cash at the time of purchase	*Write Checks* window
Credit Purchase	Pay for purchase at a later time	1. *Enter Bills* window 2. *Pay Bills* window 3. Print checks

Fearless Painting purchased a computer, painting equipment, and paint supplies. To record these purchases, complete the following steps.

Record Cash Purchases Using the Write Checks Window

Fearless Painting first purchased a computer and printer for $1,500 cash. Because Fearless Painting paid cash for the purchase, you can use the *Write Checks* window to record the purchase.

To record the computer and printer purchase using the *Write Checks* window:

Step 1: From the Banking Navigator, click the **Checks** icon.

Step 2: Enter the following information in the *Write Checks* window shown below:

To save time entering dates, change the Windows system date to the current date as follows:
1. Double-click on the time displayed in the lower right corner of your Windows taskbar.
2. Select Date: January 1, 2002.
3. Click OK to save.
4. Exit QuickBooks software
5. Restart QuickBooks. Now when opening the *Write Checks* window, the date displayed should be 01/01/2002.
6. Remember to reset to the current system date when finished with your QuickBooks assignments.

- ◆ Enter Date: **01/01/2002**.
- ◆ Pay to the Order of: **Cornell Computers**.
- ◆ Enter Amount: **1500.00**.

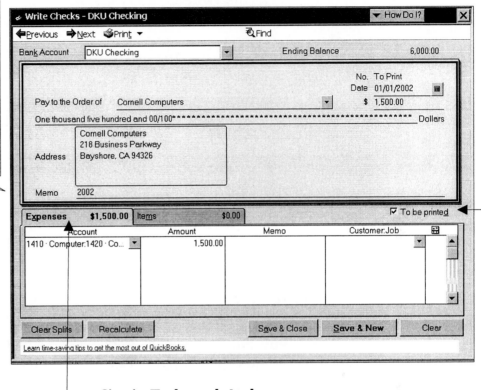

- ◆ Check: **To be printed**.
- ◆ Select the **Expenses** tab.
- ◆ Select Account: **1420 Computer Cost**.
- ◆ Enter Memo: **Purchased computer**.

Step 3: Print the check as follows:

- ◆ Click the **Print** button.
- ◆ When the *Print Check* window appears, enter Check No. **301**, then click **OK**.

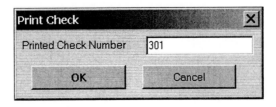

♦ Select **Print company name and address**.

♦ Select print settings, then click **Print**.

♦ When asked if the check(s) printed OK, select **OK**.

Step 4: Click **Save & Close** to record Check No. 301 and close the *Write Checks* window.

Record Credit Purchases Using the Enter Bills Window

When items are purchased on credit, a two-step process is used to record the purchase in QuickBooks.

	Action	Record Using QB...	Result
1	**Enter bill when received**	*Enter Bills* Window	QuickBooks records an expense (or asset) and records an obligation to pay the bill later (Accounts Payable)
2	**Pay bill when due**	*Pay Bills* Window Print Checks	QuickBooks reduces cash and reduces accounts payable

Next, you will enter bills for items Fearless Painting purchased on credit. The first bill is for paint and supplies that Fearless Painting purchased for the Flowers job.

Step 1: Click the **Enter Bills** icon on the Vendor Navigator.

Step 2: Enter the following information in the *Enter Bills* window:

  ♦ Select **Bill**.

  ♦ Enter Date: **01/03/2002**.

  ♦ Select Vendor: **Garrison Paint Supplies**.

  ♦ Enter Amount Due: **300.00**.

  ♦ Select Terms: **Net 30**.

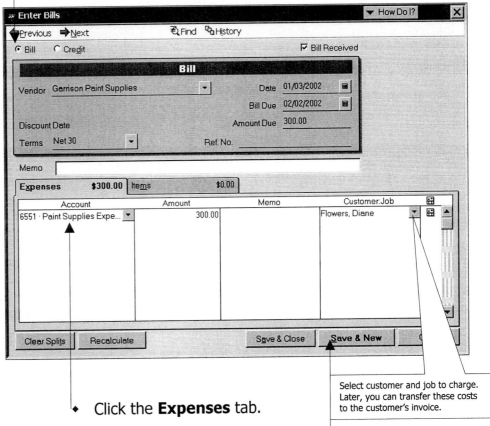

Select customer and job to charge. Later, you can transfer these costs to the customer's invoice.

  ♦ Click the **Expenses** tab.

  ♦ Select Account: **6551 Paint Supplies Expense**.

  ♦ Select Customer: Job: **Flowers, Diane**.

Step 3: Click **Save & New** to enter another bill.

Step 4: Fearless Painting made a credit purchase of painting equipment including ladders, drop clothes, etc. The painting equipment is recorded as an asset because it will benefit more than one accounting period. The painting equipment will be depreciated over the useful life of the equipment.

Enter the following bill for paint equipment purchased on credit.

Date	01/04/2002
Vendor	Garrison Paint Supplies
Amount Due	500.00
Terms	Net 30
Account	1450 Equipment Cost
Memo	Purchased paint equipment

Step 5: Click **Save & Close** to record the bill and close the *Enter Bills* window.

QuickBooks records these bills as accounts payable, indicating that Fearless Painting has an obligation to pay these amounts to vendors. QuickBooks increases liabilities (accounts payable) on the company's balance sheet.

To view the balance sheet:

Step 1: Click **Reports** in the *Navigators* window.

Step 2: Select Type of Report: **Company & Financial**.

Step 3: Select Report: **Balance Sheet Standard**.

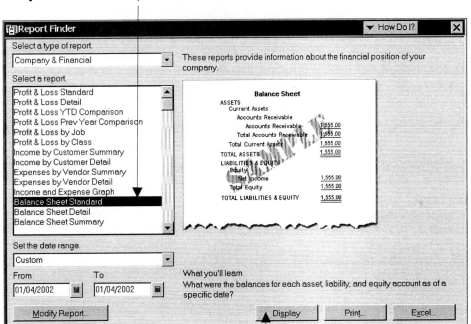

Step 4: Select Date Range: **Custom** From: **01/04/2002** To: **01/04/2002**.

Step 5: Click the **Display** button.

Step 6: Insert **your name** and **Chapter 9** in the report footer.

Step 7: Print the balance sheet using the Portrait setting.

Step 8: ✐ Circle the accounts payable balance.

Step 9: Close the *Balance Sheet* window and close the *Report Finder* window.

> ✓ *The Accounts Payable $800 balance consists of $500 owed for paint equipment and $300 owed for paint supplies. Also note that total fixed assets equal $2,000 (consisting of the Computer account of $1,500 and the Equipment account of $500).*

Record a Memorized Transaction

Often a transaction is recurring, such as monthly rent or utility payments. QuickBooks' memorized transaction feature permits you to memorize recurring transactions.

Fearless Painting Service leases a van for a monthly lease payment of $200. You will use a memorized transaction to reuse each month to record the lease payment.

To create a memorized transaction:

Step 1: First, enter the transaction in QuickBooks. You will enter the bill for the van lease payment for Fearless Painting.

- Click the **Enter Bills** icon on the Vendor Navigator.

- Enter the following information about the van lease bill.

Date	01/04/2002
Vendor	Hartz Leasing
Amount Due	200.00
Terms	Net 30
Account	6170 Equipment Rental
Memo	Van lease

Step 2: With the *Enter Bills* window still open, click **Edit** on the menu bar.

Step 3: Click **Memorize Bill** on the *Edit* menu.

Step 4: When the following *Memorize Transaction* window appears:

- Select **Remind Me**.
- Select How Often: **Monthly**.
- Enter Next Date: **02/01/2002**.
- Click **OK** to record the memorized transaction.

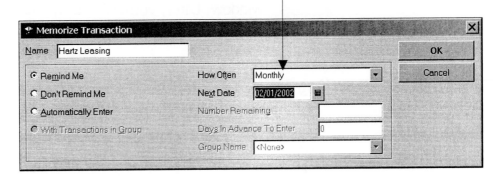

Step 5: Click **Save & Close** to close the *Enter Bills* window and record the van lease.

To use the memorized transaction at a later time:

Step 1: Click **Lists** on the menu bar.

Step 2: Click **Memorized Transaction List** from the *Lists* menu.

Step 3: When the following *Memorized Transactions List* window appears, double-click the memorized transaction you want to use.

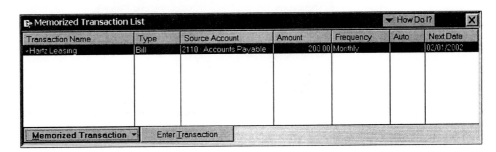

Step 4: QuickBooks displays the *Enter Bills* window with the memorized transaction data already entered. You can make any necessary changes on the form (such as changing the date). To record the bill in QuickBooks, you would click Save & Close.

At this time, **close the *Enter Bills* window without saving**. Then close the *Memorized Transaction List* window. Later, you will use the memorized transaction in *Activity 9.1* at the end of the chapter.

Pay Bills

To pay bills that have been recorded:

Step 1: Click the **Pay Bills** icon on the Vendor Navigator.

Step 2: When the following *Pay Bills* window appears:

♦ Select Show Bills: **Due on or before 02/04/2002**, then press the **Tab** key.

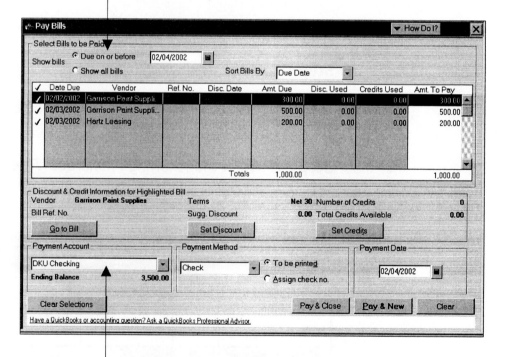

♦ Select Payment Account: **Checking**.

◆ Select Payment Method: **Check**.

◆ Select **To be printed**.

◆ Payment Date: **02/04/2002**.

◆ Click **Select All Bills** to pay all three bills listed.

Step 3: Click **Pay & Close** to record the bills selected for payment and close the *Pay Bills* window.

Print Checks

You can buy preprinted check forms to use with QuickBooks software.

After using the *Pay Bills* windows to select bills for payment, the next step is to print checks.

To print checks for the bills selected for payment:

Step 1: Select **File** from the menu bar.

Step 2: Select **Print Forms**.

Step 3: Select **Checks**.

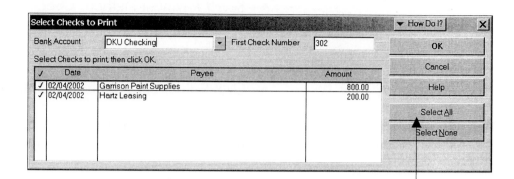

Step 4: When the above *Select Checks to Print* window appears:

- ◆ Select Bank Account: **Checking**.
- ◆ First Check Number: **302**.
- ◆ Click the **Select All** button.
- ◆ Click **OK**.
- ◆ Select print settings, then click **Print**.

✓ *Notice that QuickBooks combined the amounts due Garrison Paint Supplies and printed only one check for the total $800 due ($500 plus $300).*

✓ *After these bills are paid, QuickBooks reduces the accounts payable balance to zero.*

Additional Purchase Transactions

See *Activity 9.1* for additional purchase transactions for Fearless Painting Service.

Record Sales Transactions

When using QuickBooks, sales transactions are recorded using three steps.

Reminder statements sent to customers to remind them of the amount owed, contain less detail than invoices.

	Action	Record Using QB...	Result
1	**Prepare invoice to record charges for services provided customer**	*Invoice* Window	The invoice is used to bill the customer for services. QuickBooks records the services provided on credit as an account receivable (an amount to be received in the future).
2	**Receive customer payment**	*Receive Payments* Window	QuickBooks reduces accounts receivable and increases undeposited funds.
3	**Record bank deposit**	*Make Deposits* Window	QuickBooks transfers the amount from undeposited funds to the bank account.

To create an invoice to record painting services provided by Fearless Painting to Diane Flowers during January:

Step 1: Click the **Invoices** icon on the Customer Navigator.

Step 2: Select Customer: Job: **Flowers, Diane**.

Step 3: Select Form Template: **Intuit Service Invoice**.

Step 4: Enter Date: **01/31/2002**.

Step 5: Click the **Time/Costs** button.

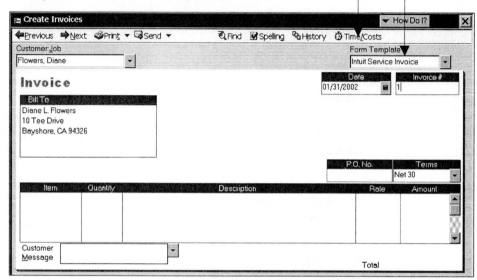

Step 6: Select billable costs to apply to the Flowers' invoice as follows:

- Click the **Expenses** tab.

- Enter Markup Amount: **40%**. Select Markup Account: **4050 – Sales**.

- Check ✓ to select: **Garrison Paint Supplies**.

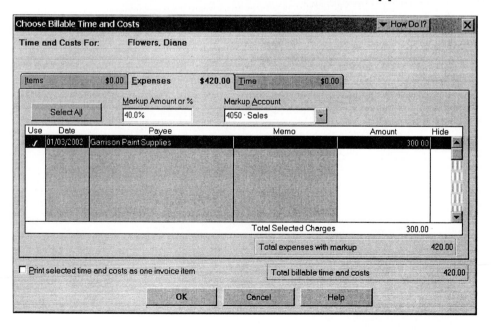

♦ Click **OK** to bill the Paint Supplies cost.

Step 7: The Flowers' Invoice will now list Total Reimbursable Expenses of $420.00. Enter the service provided in the *Create Invoices* window as follows:

♦ Select Item: **Labor Mural**.

> The Amount column will automatically display 3,280.00.

♦ Enter Quantity: **82** (hours).

Step 8: Click the **Print** button and print the invoice.

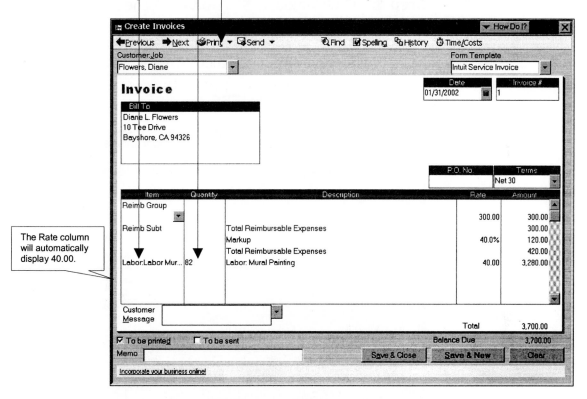

Step 9: To E-mail an invoice:

> For purposes of this exercise, E-mail the invoice to yourself.

♦ Click the **Send** button at the top of the *Invoices* window.

♦ In the *To* field, enter your E-mail address.

♦ In the *From* field, enter your E-mail address.

♦ Click **Send Now**.

Step 10: Click **Save & Close** to record the invoice and close the *Create Invoices* window.

To record Diane Flowers' payment for the $3,700.00 invoice:

Step 1: From the Customer Navigator, click the **Receive Payments** icon.

Step 2: Select Date: **02/04/2002**.

> Invoice No. 1 for $3,700 should appear as an outstanding invoice.

Step 3: Select Received From: **Flowers, Diane**.

> QuickBooks automatically applies the payment to the outstanding invoice.

Step 4: Enter Amount: **$3700.00**. A check mark will appear by the outstanding invoice listed.

Step 5: Select Payment Method: **Check**.

Step 6: Enter Check No. **555**.

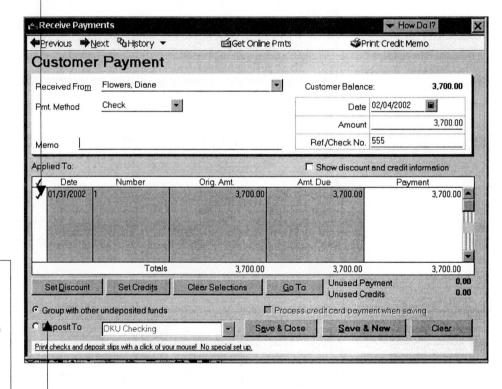

> QuickBooks will record the customer payment in an undeposited funds account. When the funds are deposited in the bank, they are moved from the undeposited funds account to the checking account.

Step 7: Select **Group with other undeposited funds**.

Step 8: Click **Save & Close** to record the payment and close the *Receive Payments* window.

When a customer makes a payment, the customer's account receivable is reduced by the amount of the payment. In this case, Flowers' account receivable is reduced by $3,700.00.

To record the deposit of the customer's payment in the bank:

Step 1: From the Customer Navigator, click the **Deposits** icon. The following *Payments to Deposit* window will appear.

The *Payments to Deposit* window lists undeposited funds that have been received, but not yet deposited in the bank.

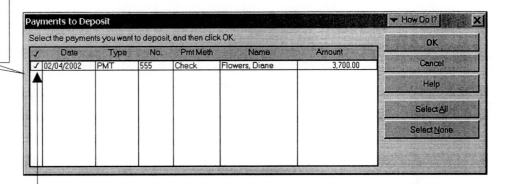

Step 2: Select the payment from Diane Flowers for deposit.

Step 3: Click **OK** and the following *Make Deposits* window appears.

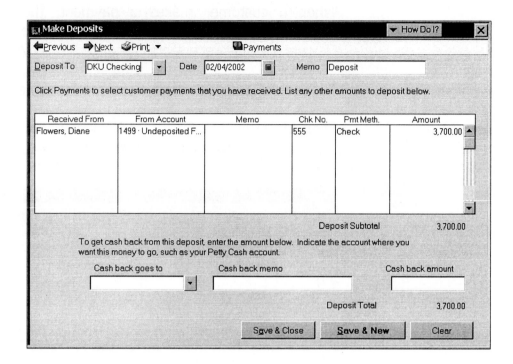

Step 4: Select Deposit To: **Checking.**

Step 5: Select Date: **02/04/2002.**

Step 6: Click **Print.**

Step 7: When the *Print Deposits* window appears, select **Deposit summary only.** Then click **OK.** Select printer settings, then click **Print.**

Step 8: Click **Save & Close** to record the deposit and close the *Make Deposits* window.

Additional Sales Transactions

See *Activity 9.2* for additional sales transactions for Fearless Painting Service.

Before making adjusting entries, prepare a trial balance to see if the accounting system is in balance (debits equal credits).

Make Adjusting Entries

At the end of Fearless Painting's accounting period, December 31, 2002, it is necessary to record adjustments to bring the company's accounts up to date as of year-end.

The following adjustments are necessary for Fearless Painting at December 31, 2002:

1. Record depreciation expense for the computer for the year.

QuickBooks permits you to record adjustments in two different ways:
1. Record the adjustment in the account register. (Example: Record Depreciation Expense in the Accumulated Depreciation account)
2. Use the general journal to record adjusting entries.

2. Record depreciation expense for the painting equipment for the year. (Complete in *Activity 9.3*.)

3. Record the amounts of paint supplies that are still on hand at year-end. Unused paint supplies should be recorded as assets because they have future benefit. (Complete in *Activity 9.3*.)

Use the General Journal to record the adjusting entry for computer depreciation expense on the computer for Fearless Painting at December 31, 2002. The $1,500 computer cost will be depreciated over a useful life of three years.

Step 1: Click **Banking** in the *Navigators* window.

Step 2: Click the **Make Journal Entry** icon on the Banking Navigator.

Step 3: Record the entry for depreciation on the computer equipment in the General Journal.

- Select Date: **12/31/2002**.

- Entry No.: **Adj Entry 1**.

- Enter Account: **6430**. Press the **Tab** key to advance the cursor to the Debit column.

- Next, use QuickMath calculator to calculate the amount of depreciation expense.

  - With the cursor in the Debit column, press the **=** key to display the QuickMath calculator.

  - Enter **1500.00**.

  - Press **/**.

  - Enter **3** to divide by the 3-year useful life.

  - Press the **Enter** key. $500 should now appear in the Debit column.

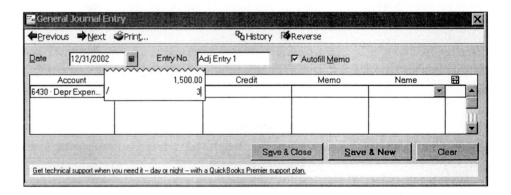

◆ Enter Account: **1430** Credit: **500.00**. Your journal entry should appear as shown below.

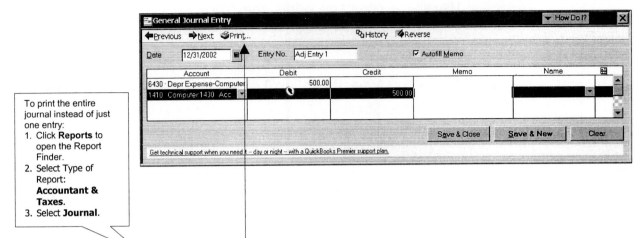

To print the entire journal instead of just one entry:
1. Click **Reports** to open the Report Finder.
2. Select Type of Report: **Accountant & Taxes**.
3. Select **Journal**.

Step 4: To print the adjusting journal entry, click the **Print** button.

Step 5: Click **Save & Close** to close the *General Journal Entry* window.

Print Reports

The next step in the accounting cycle is to print financial reports. Usually, a company prints the following financial reports for the year:

- General Ledger
- Profit & Loss (also known as the P & L or Income Statement)
- Balance Sheet
- Statement of Cash Flows

> To print financial statements, select **Reports** in the *Navigators* window, then select **Company, Financial** from the Report Finder.

The General Ledger is accessed from the Report Finder (click Reports in the *Navigators* window, then select Accountant & Taxes).

The Profit & Loss, the Balance Sheet, and the Statement of Cash Flows are financial statements typically given to external users, such as bankers and investors.

You will print financial statements for Fearless Painting Service for the year 2002 in *Activity 9.4*.

Close the Accounting Period

When using a manual accounting system, closing entries are made in the general journal to close the temporary accounts (revenues, expenses, and withdrawals or dividends). In a manual system, closing entries are used in order to start the new year with a zero balance in the temporary accounts.

QuickBooks automatically closes temporary accounts to start each new year with $-0- balances in all temporary accounts (revenues, expenses, and dividends).

To prevent changes to prior periods, QuickBooks permits you to restrict access to the accounting records for past periods that have been closed. See *Activity 9.5* for instructions on closing the accounting period in QuickBooks.

Back Up Chapter 9

Back up your Chapter 9 file to your floppy disk. Use the file name: [your name] Chapter 9.

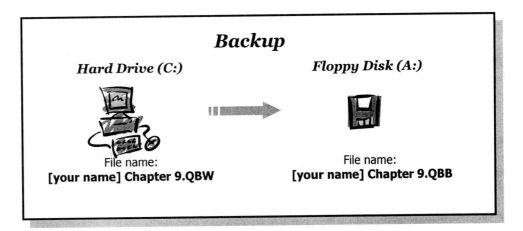

Backup

Hard Drive (C:)   Floppy Disk (A:)

File name:
[your name] Chapter 9.QBW

File name:
[your name] Chapter 9.QBB

Step 1:   Insert the **Chapter 9** backup disk in drive A.

Step 2:   Click **File, Back Up**.

Step 3:   Enter the file name: **[your name] Chapter 9.QBB**.
Enter location: **A:**.

Step 4:   Click **Back Up**.

Step 5:   Click **OK** after the backup is complete. Then close the company file. (Click File, Close Company.)

If you are continuing your computer session, close the company file and then proceed to Activity 9.1.

If you are quitting your computer session now, (1) close the company file and (2) exit QuickBooks.

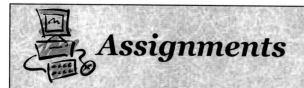

Assignments

Activity 9.1: Purchase Transactions

In this activity, you will enter purchase transactions for Fearless Painting Service.

Task 1: Restore Company File

The first task is to restore your Chapter 9 backup to the hard drive, changing the file name to Activity 9.

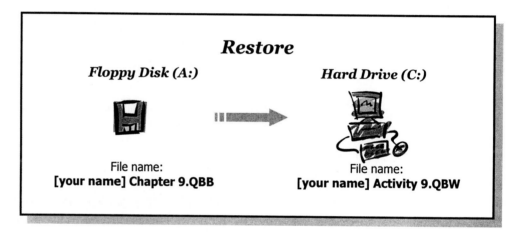

Restore

Floppy Disk (A:)   **Hard Drive (C:)**

File name:
[your name] Chapter 9.QBB

File name:
[your name] Activity 9.QBW

Step 1:   Insert the **Chapter 9** backup disk into drive A.

Step 2:   Click **Restore a backup file** (or click **File, Restore**).

Step 3:   Identify the backup file:

- Filename: **[your name] Chapter 9.QBB**.
- Location: **A:**.

Step 4: Identify the restored file:

- Filename: **[your name] Activity 9.QBW**.

- Location: **C:\Program Files\Intuit\QuickBooks Premier**.

Step 5: Click **Restore.** If prompted, enter your User ID and Password.

Step 6: Change the company name to:
[your name] Fearless Painting Service Activity 9.
(To change the company name, select Company (menu), Company Information.)

Your Chapter 9 backup file has now been restored to the C: drive as Activity 9.

Task 2: Record Purchase Transactions

Record the following purchase transactions for Fearless Painting Service during the year 2002. Print checks as appropriate.

> Memorized Transaction:
> 1. **Lists** (menu)
> 2. **Memorized Transactions List**
> 3. Double-click: **Hartz Leasing**

> To view the van lease bill, select **Show All Bills** in the *Pay Bills* window.

> Print Checks:
> 1. **File** (menu)
> 2. **Print Form**
> 3. **Checks**

Date	Purchase Transaction
02/01/2002	Use the memorized transaction to record the $200 bill for the February van lease.
02/28/2002	Paid van lease for February.
03/01/2002	Received $200 bill for van lease for March.
03/30/2002	Paid van lease for March. (Due: 03/31/2002)
04/01/2002	Received $200 bill for van lease for April.
04/04/2002	Purchased $50 of paint supplies on account from Garrison Paint Supplies. Record as Paint Supplies Expense and charge to Flowers job.

04/30/2002	Paid van lease for April. (Due: 05/01/2002) Paid for paint supplies purchased on April 4.
05/01/2002	Received $200 bill for van lease for May.
05/30/2002	Paid van lease for May. (Due: 05/31/2002)
06/01/2002	Received $200 bill for van lease for June.
06/30/2002	Paid van lease for June. (Due: 07/01/2002)
07/01/2002	Purchased $100 of paint supplies on account from Garrison Paint Supply.
07/01/2002	Received $200 bill for van lease for July.
07/30/2002	Paid van lease for July. (Due: 07/31/2002) Paid for paint supplies purchased on July 1.
08/01/2002	Received $200 bill for van lease for August.
08/30/2002	Paid van lease for August. (Due: 08/31/2002)
09/01/2002	Received $200 bill for van lease for September.
09/02/2002	Purchased $75 of paint supplies from Garrison Paint Supply.
09/30/2002	Paid van lease for September. (Due: 10/01/2002) Paid for paint supplies purchased on 09/02/2002.
10/01/2002	Received $200 bill for van lease for October.
10/30/2002	Paid van lease for October. (Due: 10/31/2002)
11/01/2002	Received $200 bill for van lease for November.

Record as Paint Supplies Expense. These items are not chargeable to a specific job.

11/30/2002	Paid van lease for November. (Due: 12/01/2002)
12/01/2002	Received $200 bill for van lease for December.
12/20/2002	Purchased $50 of paint supplies from Garrison Paint Supply.
12/30/2002	Paid van lease for December. (Due: 12/31/2002)

Leave the company file open for the next activity.

Activity 9.2: Sales Transactions

In this activity, you will record sales transactions for Fearless Painting Service.

Task 1:
Sales Transactions and Deposit Summaries

When necessary, add a new job. For more information, see Chapter 3.

Print invoices and deposit summaries for the following sales transactions for Fearless Painting Service during the year 2002.

Date	02/28/2002
Customer	Diane Flowers
Job	Dining room mural
Item	Labor: Mural
Hours	86
Payment Received & Deposited	03/15/2002
Check No.	675

Date	03/31/2002
Customer	Diane Flowers
Job	Dining room mural
Item	Labor: Mural
Hours	84
Payment Received & Deposited	04/15/2002
Check No.	690

Date	04/30/2002
Customer	Tom Whalen
Job	Entry, marbled faux
Item	Labor: Faux
Hours	80
Payment Received & Deposited	05/15/2002
Check No.	432

Date	05/31/2002
Customer	Tom Whalen
Job	Entry, marbled faux
Item	Labor: Faux
Hours	75
Payment Received & Deposited	06/15/2002
Check No.	455

Date	06/30/2002
Customer	Diane Flowers
Job	Vaulted kitchen
Item	Labor: Mural
Hours	100
Payment Received & Deposited	07/15/2002
Check No.	733

Date	07/31/2002
Customer	Diane Flowers
Job	Vaulted kitchen
Item	Labor: Mural
Hours	90
Payment Received & Deposited	08/15/2002
Check No.	750

Date	08/31/2002
Customer	Diane Flowers
Job	Vaulted kitchen
Item	Labor: Mural
Hours	92
Payment Received & Deposited	09/15/2002
Check No.	782

Date	10/31/2002
Customer	Tom Whalen
Job	Screen Porch
Item	Labor: Mural
Hours	85
Payment Received & Deposited	11/15/2002
Check No.	685

Date	11/30/2002
Customer	Tom Whalen
Job	Screen porch
Item	Labor: Mural
Hours	87
Payment Received & Deposited	12/15/2002
Check No.	725

Leave the company file open for the next activity.

Activity 9.3: Year-End Adjustments

In this activity, you will first print a trial balance and then record adjusting entries for Fearless Painting Service.

The purpose of the trial balance is to determine whether the accounting system is in balance (debits equal credits).

Task 1: Print Trial Balance

Print a trial balance for Fearless Painting at December 31, 2002.

Step 1: Click **Reports** in the *Navigators* window to open the *Report Finder* window.

Step 2: Select Type of Report: **Accountant & Taxes**.

Step 3: Select Report: **Trial Balance**.

Step 4: Select Dates From: **01/01/2002** To: **12/31/2002**.

Step 5: Click **Display** to display the *Trial Balance* window.

Step 6: Insert **your name** and **Activity 9** in the report footer.

Step 7: Print the trial balance for Fearless Painting.

Step 8: Close the *Trial Balance* window.

✓ **Total debits equal $41,110.**

Task 2: Record Adjusting Entries

At the end of the accounting period, it is necessary to make adjusting entries to bring a company's accounts up to date as of year-end. Two adjusting entries are needed for Fearless Painting as of December 31, 2002:

This adjusting entry was recorded in Chapter 9.

1. Record depreciation expense for the computer for the year.

Hint: Access the General Journal from the Banking Navigator. Debit: Acct No. 6460 Depr Expense-Equipment.

2. Record depreciation expense for the painting equipment for the year. The $500 paint equipment cost is depreciated using straight-line depreciation over five years with no salvage value.

Make the adjusting entry at 12/31/2002 to record depreciation expense for the painting equipment for the year.

Task 3: Print Adjusting Entries

Print the adjusting entries recorded on December 31, 2002 for Fearless Painting.

Step 1: Click **Reports** in the *Navigators* window to open the *Report Finder* window.

Step 2: Select Type of Report: **Accountant & Taxes**.

Step 3: Select Report: **Journal**.

Step 4: Select Dates From: **12/31/2002** To: **12/31/2002**.

Step 5: Click **Display** to display the *General Journal* window.

Step 6: Insert **your name** and **Activity 9** in the report footer.

Step 7: Print the Journal using **Portrait** orientation.

Step 8: Close the *General Journal Entry* window.

> An adjusted trial balance is printed after adjusting entries are made.

Task 4: Print Adjusted Trial Balance

Step 1: Print an adjusted trial balance at December 31, 2002. Insert **your name** and **Activity 9** in the report footer. Change the report title to: **Adjusted Trial Balance**. Use **Portrait** orientation.

Step 2: ✎ On the adjusted trial balance, circle the accounts affected by the adjusting entries.

Leave the company file open for the next activity.

Activity 9.4: Financial Reports

In this activity, you will print out financial statements for Fearless Painting Service for the year 2002.

> To eliminate the 0.00 appearing for accounts with zero balances, from the *General Ledger* report window, click the **Modify Reports** button, **Advanced, In Use, Report Date**.

Task 1: General Ledger

Print the General Ledger for Fearless Painting Service for the year 2002.

Task 2: Financial Statements

Print the following financial statements for Fearless Painting Service for the year 2002.

📄 Profit & Loss, Standard

📄 Balance Sheet, Standard

📄 Statement of Cash Flows

> ✓ **Net income for the year 2002 is $31,285.**

Leave the company file open for the next activity.

Activity 9.5: Close the Accounting Period

> The QuickBooks Administrator has access to all areas of QuickBooks and is established when a new company is set up. For more information about the QuickBooks Administrator, see Chapter 2.

To prevent changes to prior periods, QuickBooks permits you to restrict access to the accounting records for past periods that have been closed.

The QuickBooks Administrator can restrict user access to closed periods either at the time a new user is set up or later.

> ***Important! Do not complete this activity until after you have completed Activity 9.4.***

Task 1: Close the Accounting Period

To enter the closing date in QuickBooks:

Step 1: Click **Company** on the menu bar.

Step 2: Click **Set up Users** from the *Company* menu.

Step 3: Enter information for the QuickBooks Administrator, then click **OK**.

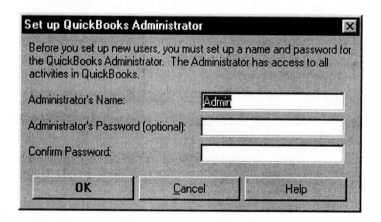

Step 4: When the following *User List* window appears, click the **Closing Date** button.

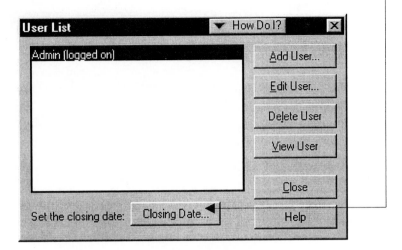

Step 5: Enter the closing date: **12/31/2002**.

Step 6: Click **OK** to close the *Set Closing Date* window.

If you wanted to track the time that your friend Max helps you with your business, you could permit Max to access the time tracking features of QuickBooks but restrict his access to other areas and to closed periods.

> If the *User List* window is not open, open the *User List* window by clicking **Company, Set up Users**.

To restrict access when setting up a new user (Max):

Step 1: From the *User List* window, click **Add** User.

Step 2: Enter User Name: **Max**.

Step 3: Enter Password: **Time**. Click **Next**.

Step 4: Select: **Selected areas of QuickBooks**. Click **Next**.

Step 5: For Time Tracking, make the following selections.

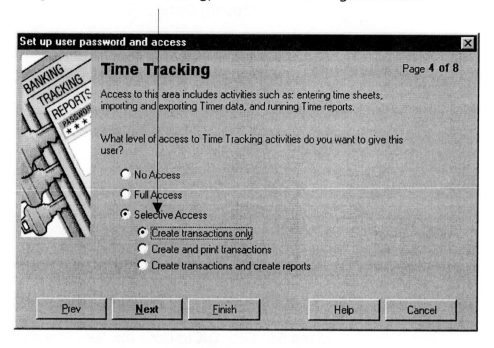

Step 6: To restrict access to closed periods, when the following window appears, select: **No.**

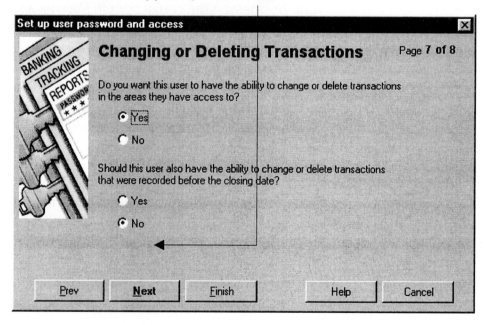

Step 7: Click **Finish** to set up Max as a new user.

Step 8: Close the *User List* window.

Max will have access to time tracking only and will not have access to other accounting functions or accounting periods prior to the closing date.

Task 2: Back Up Activity 9

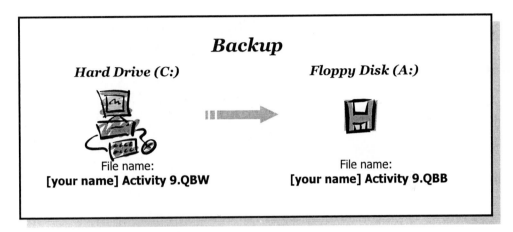

Step 1: Insert the **Chapter 9** backup disk in drive A.

Step 2: Click **File, Back Up**.

Step 3: Enter the file name: **[your name] Activity 9.QBB**.
Enter location: **A:**.

Step 4: Click **Back Up**.

Step 5: Click **OK** after the backup is complete. Close the company file.

Activity 9.6 Web Quest

The Internet provides a number of resources for the small business owner. You can find business forms to use when operating your business as well as legal and technology resources at allbusiness.com.

Step 1: Go to www.allbusiness.com web site.

Step 2: Print two business forms that you think might be useful to a small business.

Activity 9.7: Web Quest

In addition to its QuickBooks web site, Intuit also has a Quicken Small Business web site that contains tax, accounting, and legal information for the entrepreneur.

Step 1: Go to www.quicken.com/small_business.

Step 2: Print two resources on the web site that you find the most useful to the small business owner.

Computer Accounting with QuickBooks 2002
Chapter 9 Printout Checklist
Name:_____ Date:_____

☑	*Printout Checklist – Chapter 9*
☐	Deposit Summary
☐	Check No. 301
☐	Balance Sheet 01/04/2002
☐	Check No. 302
☐	Check No. 303
☐	Invoice No. 1
☐	Deposit Summary
☐	Adjusting Entry
☑	*Printout Checklist – Activity 9.1*
☐	Task 2: Checks
☑	*Printout Checklist – Activity 9.2*
☐	Task 2: Invoices and Deposit Summaries
☑	*Printout Checklist – Activity 9.3*
☐	Task 1: Trial Balance
☐	Task 3: Adjusting Entries
☐	Task 4: Adjusted Trial Balance
☑	*Printout Checklist – Activity 9.4*
☐	Task 1: General Ledger
☐	Task 2: Financial Statements

☑	***Printout Checklist – Activity 9.6***
☐	Business Forms
☑	***Printout Checklist – Activity 9.7***
☐	Quicken Small Business Resources

Virtual Company
Project 9.1

Project 9.1: Max's Lawn Service

Scenario

Your friend Max started a new lawn service business to help pay his college expenses. You and Max reach an agreement: you will help Max with his accounting records and provide customer referrals, and he will help you with your painting business.

Task 1: Set Up a New Company

Create a new company in QuickBooks for Max's Lawn Service. Use the following information.

Company name	[your initials] Max's Lawn Service
Legal name	[your initials] Max's Lawn Service
Address	2300 Olive Boulevard
City	Bayshore
State	CA
Zip	94326
E-mail	[enter your own email address]
Federal tax ID	314-14-7878
First month of income tax year	January
First month of fiscal year	January
Income tax form	Form 1040 (Sole Proprietorship)
Type of business	Service Business
Save in	C:/Program Files/Intuit/QuickBooks Premier folder
File name	[your name] Project9.1

Inventory	No
Sales tax	No
Invoice format	Service
Use payroll feature?	No
Estimates	No
Time tracking	No
Classes	No
Handle bills and payments	Enter bills first and payments later
Reminders list	At start up
Accrual or cash-based reporting	Accrual
Company start date	01/01/2002
Receipt of payment at time of service	Sometimes
Statement charges	No
Set up service item	No
Set up non-inventory item	No
Set up other charges	No
Inventory	Skip inventory items
Do any customers owe you money on your start date?	No
Do you owe any vendors money on your start date?	No
Would you like to set up a credit card account?	No
Any lines of credit	No
Loans and notes payable	No
Would you like to set up a bank account?	Yes
Name of bank	Checking [your initials] National Bank
Statement ending balance	0.00
Add another bank account	No

Click **Leave** to exit the EasyStep Interview.

To display
account numbers:
1. Click
   Company in
   the *Navigators*
   window.
2. **Preferences.**
3. **Accounting.**
4. **Company
   Preferences.**
5. **Display**

Task 2: Customize the Chart of Accounts

Customize the Chart of Accounts for Max's Lawn Service as follows:

Step 1: Display account numbers in the Chart of Accounts.

Step 2: Add the following accounts to the Chart of Accounts. Abbreviate account titles as necessary.

Account No.	1700
Account Type	Fixed Asset
Account Name	Mower
Account Description	Mower
Tax Line	Unassigned
Opening Balance	0 as of 01/01/2002

Account No.	1710
Account Type	Fixed Asset
Account Name	Mower Cost
Subaccount of	Mower
Account Description	Mower Cost
Tax Line	Unassigned
Opening Balance	0 as of 01/01/2002

Account No.	1720
Account Type	Fixed Asset
Account Name	Accumulated Depreciation-Mower
Account Description	Accumulated Depreciation-Mower
Subaccount of	Mower
Tax Line	Unassigned
Opening Balance	0 as of 01/01/2002

Account No.	1800
Account Type	Fixed Asset
Account Name	Trimmer Equipment
Account Description	Trimmer Equipment
Tax Line	Unassigned
Opening Balance	0 as of 01/01/2002

Account No.	1810
Account Type	Fixed Asset
Account Name	Trimmer Equipment Cost
Account Description	Trimmer Equipment Cost
Subaccount of	Trimmer Equipment
Tax Line	Unassigned
Opening Balance	0 as of 01/01/2002

Account No.	1820
Account Type	Fixed Asset
Account Name	Accumulated Depr Trimmer
Account Description	Accumulated Depr Trimmer
Subaccount of	Trimmer Equipment
Tax Line	Unassigned
Opening Balance	0 as of 01/01/2002

Account No.	6551
Account Type	Expense
Account Name	Supplies Expense
Account Description	Supplies Expense
Tax Line	Sch C: Supplies (not from COGS)

Step 3: Print the Chart of Accounts for Max's Lawn Service. (Click the Reports button in the *Chart of Accounts* window, then select Account Listing. Insert **your name** and **Project 9.1** in the report footer.)

Task 3: Customer List

Step 1: Create a Customer List for Max's Lawn Service using the following information.

Customer	Flowers, Diane
Opening Balance	0 as of 01/01/2002
Address Info:	
First Name	Diane
Last Name	Flowers
Contact	Diane
Phone	415-555-1078
Alt. Ph.	415-555-3434
Alt. Contact	Tad (spouse)
Address	10 Tee Drive Bayshore, CA 94326

Select **Add New**.

Additional Info:	
Type	Residential
Terms	Net 30

Payment Info:	
Account No.	3001
Preferred Payment Method	Check

Job Info:	
Job Status	Awarded
Job Description	Mow/Trim Lawn
Job Type	Lawn

Select **Add New**.

Customer	Whalen, Tom
Opening balance	0 as of 01/01/2002
Address Info:	
First Name	Tom
Last Name	Whalen
Contact	Tom
Phone	415-555-1234
Alt. Ph.	415-555-5678
Alt. Contact	Work phone
Address	100 Sunset Drive Bayshore, CA 94326

Additional Info:	
Type	Residential
Terms	Net 30

Payment Info:	
Account	3002
Preferred Payment Method	Check

Job Info:	
Job Status	Awarded
Job Description	Mow/Trim Lawn
Job Type	Lawn

Customer	Rock Castle Construction
Opening balance	0 as of 01/01/2002
Address Info:	
Company Name	Rock Castle Construction
First Name	Rock
Last Name	Castle
Contact	Rock
Phone	415-555-7878
Alt. Ph.	415-555-5679
Address	1735 County Road Bayshore, CA 94326

Additional Info:	
Type	Commercial
Terms	Net 30

Payment Info:	
Account No.	3003
Preferred Payment Method	Check

Job Info:	
Job Status	Awarded
Job Description	Mow/Trim Lawn & Shrubs
Job Type	Lawn & Shrubs

Step 2: Print the Customer List. (Click the Reports button, Contact List.)

Task 4: Vendor List

Step 1: Create a Vendor List for Max's Lawn Service using the following information.

Vendor	Ryan Gas Station
Opening Balance	0 as of 01/01/2002
Address Info:	
Company Name	Ryan Gas Station
Address	100 Manchester Road Bayshore, CA 94326
Contact	Ryan
Phone	415-555-7844
Print on Check as	Ryan Gas Station

Additional Info:	
Account	4001
Type	Fuel
Terms	Net 30
Credit Limit	500.00
Tax ID	37-8910541
Vendor Eligible for 1099	No

Vendor	Mower Sales & Repair
Opening Balance	0 as of 01/01/2002
Address Info:	
Company Name	Mower Sales & Repair
Address	650 Manchester Road Bayshore, CA 94326
Contact	Carol
Phone	415-555-8222
Print on Check as	Mower Sales & Repair

Additional Info:	
Account	4002
Type	Mower
Terms	Net 30
Credit Limit	1000.00
Tax ID	37-6510541
Vendor Eligible for 1099	No

Step 2: Print the Vendor List. (Click the Reports button, Contact List.)

Task 5: Item List

Step 1: Create an Item List for Max's Lawn Service using the following information.

Item Type	Service
Item Name	Mowing
Description	Lawn Mowing
Rate	25.00
Account	4070 - Services

Item Type	Service
Item Name	Trim Shrubs
Description	Trim Shrubs
Rate	30.00
Account	4070 - Services

Step 2: Print the Item List. (Click the Reports button in *the Item List* window. Then select Item Listing. Remember to include your name and Project 9.1 in the report footer.)

Task 6: Custom Invoice Template

Create a Custom Invoice Template with a *Service Date* column. This permits Max to bill customers once a month for all services provided during the month, listing each service date separately on the invoice.

To create a custom invoice, first you will create a duplicate of an existing invoice template, then customize the duplicate.

Step 1: Click **Lists** (menu).

Step 2: Select **Templates**.

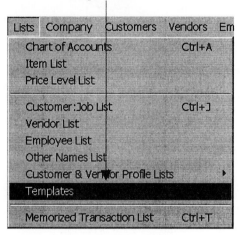

Step 3: Create a Duplicate Invoice as follows:

◆ When the following *Templates* window appears, select the **Intuit Service Invoice**.

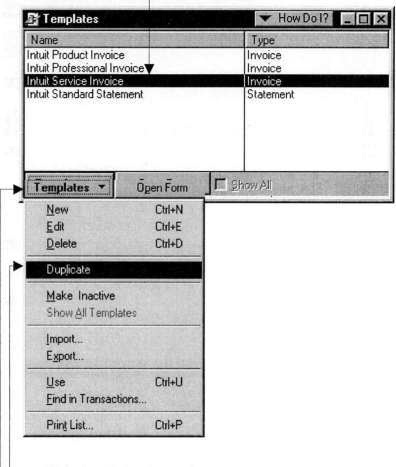

◆ Click the **Templates** button.

◆ Click **Duplicate** on the *Templates* menu.

- ◆ When the *Select Template Type* window appears, select **Invoice**, then click **OK**.

Step 4: To add a *Service Date* column to the duplicate invoice:

- ◆ Select **DUP: Intuit Service Invoice** from the *Template* window.

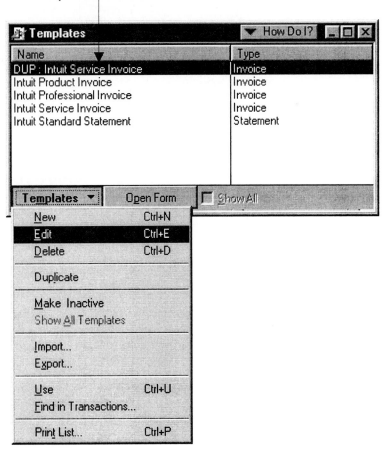

- ◆ Click the **Template** button.
- ◆ Click **Edit** to edit the duplicate invoice.
- ◆ When the following *Customize Invoice* window appears, change the Template Name: **Intuit Service Date Invoice**.
- ◆ Click the **Columns** tab.

Click the Options tab to customize the Invoice template using a Logo and the Layout Designer.

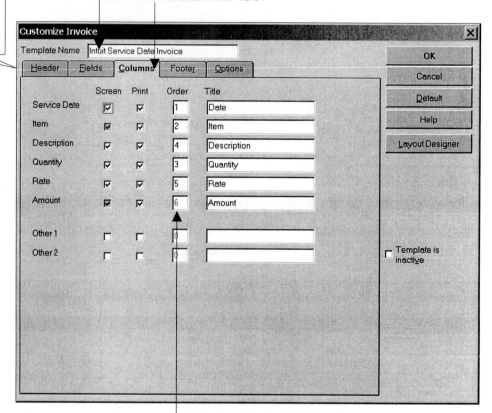

- ◆ ✓ Check **Service Date: Screen**.
- ◆ ✓ Check **Service Date: Print**.
- ◆ Enter Title: **Date**.
- ◆ Renumber the Order so they appear as shown above.
- ◆ Click **OK** to close the *Customize Invoice* window.

Step 5: To view the custom invoice:

- Click **Invoices** on the Customers Navigator.

- When the *Create Invoices* window appears, select Form Template: **Intuit Service Date Invoice**.

- Notice that the first column of the invoice is now the *Date* column.

Step 6: Close the *Create Invoices* window.

Task 7: Record Transactions

During the year, Max's Lawn Service entered into the transactions listed below.

Step 1: Record the following transactions for Max's Lawn Service. Customers are billed monthly. Print invoices, checks, and deposit summaries as appropriate. Use memorized transactions for recurring transactions.

Use *Make Deposits* window.

Use *Enter Bills* window.

Select Show All Bills in the *Pay Bills* window.

Use *Write Checks* window.

Record Supplies Expense.

Date	Transaction
01/01/2002	Max Milan invested $1,500 cash in the business.
02/01/2002	Purchased a mower for $800 cash from Mower Sales & Repair (Check No. 501).
02/20/2002	Purchased trimming equipment from Mower Sales & Repair for $200 on account.
03/01/2002	Purchased $100 of gasoline and supplies on account from Ryan Gas Station.
03/20/2002	Paid $200 on your account with Mower Sales & Repair. Paid $100 on your account with Ryan Gas Station.

Check **To be printed** on the *Invoice* window. Then print the invoices by selecting **File**, **Print Forms**, **Invoices**.

04/30/2002	Printed and mailed invoices to customers for the following work performed in April. Use the Intuit Service Date Invoice to record all work performed for the same customer on one invoice, indicating the date of service in the DATE column.	
	04/01/2002 04/15/2002	Mowed Diane Flowers' lawn Mowed Diane Flowers' lawn	6 hrs 6 hrs
	04/04/2002 04/19/2002	Mowed R.C. Construction's lawn Mowed R.C. Construction's lawn	8 hrs 8 hrs
	04/08/2002 04/22/2002	Mowed Tom Whalen's lawn Mowed Tom Whalen's lawn	4 hrs 4 hrs
05/01/2002	Purchased $100 of gasoline and supplies on account from Ryan Gas Station.	
05/15/2002	Received payments from Flowers (Check No. 755), Whalen (Check No. 645), and Rock Castle Construction (Check No. 1068) for April invoices.	
05/30/2002	Paid Ryan Gas Station bill.	
05/30/2002	Mailed invoices to customers for the following services provided during May.	
	05/01/2002 05/15/2002	Mowed Diane Flowers' lawn Mowed Diane Flowers' lawn	6 hrs 6 hrs
	05/04/2002 05/19/2002	Mowed R.C. Construction's lawn Mowed R.C. Construction's lawn	8 hrs 8 hrs
	05/08/2002 05/22/2002	Mowed Tom Whalen's lawn Mowed Tom Whalen's lawn	4 hrs 4 hrs
06/01/2002	Purchased $100 of gasoline and supplies on account from Ryan Gas Station.	
06/15/2002	Received payments from Flowers (Check No. 895), Whalen (Check No. 698), and Rock Castle Construction (Check No. 1100) for May services.	
06/30/2002	Paid Ryan Gas Station bill.	

06/30/2002	Mailed invoices to customers for the following services provided during June.		
	06/01/2002	Mowed Diane Flowers' lawn	6 hrs
	06/02/2002	Trimmed Diane Flowers' shrubs	7 hrs
	06/15/2002	Mowed Diane Flowers' lawn	6 hrs
	06/04/2002	Mowed R. C. Construction's lawn	8 hrs
	06/05/2002	Trimmed R.C. Construction's shrubs	9 hrs
	06/19/2002	Mowed R. C. Construction's lawn	8 hrs
	06/08/2002	Mowed Tom Whalen's lawn	4 hrs
	06/09/2002	Trimmed Tom Whalen's shrubs	3 hrs
	06/22/2002	Mowed Tom Whalen's lawn	4 hrs
07/01/2002	Purchased $100 of gasoline and supplies on account from Ryan Gas Station.		
07/15/2002	Received payments from Flowers (Check No. 910), Whalen (Check No. 715), and Rock Castle Construction (Check No. 1200) for June services.		
07/31/2002	Paid Ryan Gas Station bill.		
07/31/2002	Mailed invoices to customers for the following services provided during July.		
	07/01/2002	Mowed Diane Flowers' lawn	6 hrs
	07/15/2002	Mowed Diane Flowers' lawn	6 hrs
	07/04/2002	Mowed R.C. Construction's lawn	8 hrs
	07/19/2002	Mowed R.C. Construction's lawn	8 hrs
	07/08/2002	Mowed Tom Whalen's lawn	4 hrs
	07/22/2002	Mowed Tom Whalen's lawn	4 hrs
08/01/2002	Purchased $100 of gasoline and supplies on account from Ryan Gas Station.		
08/15/2002	Received payments from Flowers (Check No. 935), Whalen (Check No. 742), and Rock Castle Construction (Check No. 1300) for July services.		

08/31/2002	Paid Ryan Gas Station bill.		
08/31/2002	Mailed invoices to customers for the following services provided during August.		
	08/01/2002	Mowed Diane Flowers' lawn	6 hrs
	08/15/2002	Mowed Diane Flowers' lawn	6 hrs
	08/04/2002	Mowed R.C. Construction's lawn	8 hrs
	08/19/2002	Mowed R.C. Construction's lawn	8 hrs
	08/08/2002	Mowed Tom Whalen's lawn	4 hrs
	08/22/2002	Mowed Tom Whalen's lawn	4 hrs
09/01/2002	Purchased $100 of gasoline and supplies on account from Ryan Gas Station.		
09/15/2002	Received payments from Flowers (Check No. 934), Whalen (Check No. 746), and Rock Castle Construction (Check No. 1400) for August services.		
09/30/2002	Paid Ryan Gas Station bill.		
09/30/2002	Mailed invoices to customers for the following service provided during September.		
	09/01/2002	Mowed Diane Flowers' lawn	6 hrs
	09/15/2002	Mowed Diane Flowers' lawn	6 hrs
	09/04/2002	Mowed R.C. Construction's lawn	8 hrs
	09/19/2002	Mowed R.C. Construction's lawn	8 hrs
	09/08/2002	Mowed Tom Whalen's lawn	4 hrs
	09/22/2002	Mowed Tom Whalen's lawn	4 hrs
10/01/2002	Purchased $50 of gasoline on account from Ryan Gas Station.		
10/15/2002	Received payments from Flowers (Check No. 956), Whalen (Check No. 755), and Rock Castle Construction (Check No. 1500) for September services.		
10/31/2002	Paid Ryan Gas Station bill.		

10/31/2002	Mailed invoices to customers for the following services provided during October.		
	10/01/2002	Mowed Diane Flowers' lawn	6 hrs
	10/02/2002	Trimmed Diane Flowers' shrubs	7 hrs
	10/15/2002	Mowed Diane Flowers' lawn	6 hrs
	10/04/2002	Mowed R. C. Construction's lawn	8 hrs
	10/05/2002	Trimmed R.C. Construction's shrubs	9 hrs
	10/19/2002	Mowed R. C. Construction's lawn	8 hrs
	10/08/2002	Mowed Tom Whalen's lawn	4 hrs
	10/09/2002	Trimmed Tom Whalen's shrubs	3 hrs
	10/22/2002	Mowed Tom Whalen's lawn	4 hrs
11/15/2002	Received payments from Flowers (Check No. 967), Whalen (Check No. 765), and Rock Castle Construction (Check No. 1600) for October services.		

Step 2: Print the Check Register for January 1, 2002, to December 31, 2002.

Task 8: Adjusting Entries

Step 1: Make adjusting entries for Max's Lawn Service at December 31, 2002, using the following information.

- The mowing equipment cost $800 and has a four-year life and no salvage value.

- The trimming equipment cost $200 and has a two-year life and no salvage value.

Step 2: Print the Journal for the year.

Task 9: Financial Reports

Print the following reports for Max's Lawn Service. Remember to insert your name in the report footer.

- General Ledger
- Profit & Loss, Standard
- Balance Sheet, Standard
- Statement of Cash Flows

✓   ***Net income is $6,490.00.***

Task 10: Back Up Project 9.1

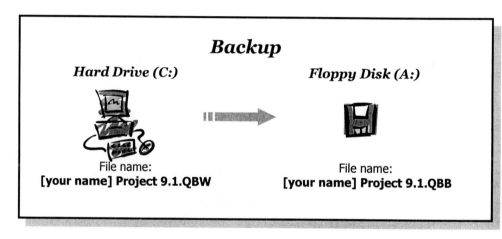

Backup

Hard Drive (C:)   **Floppy Disk (A:)**

File name: File name:
[your name] Project 9.1.QBW   **[your name] Project 9.1.QBB**

Step 1:   Insert the **Project 9.1** backup disk in drive A.

Step 2:   Click **File, Back Up**.

Step 3:   Enter the file name: **[your name] Project 9.1.QBB**. Enter location: **A:**.

Step 4:   Click **Back Up**.

Step 5:   Click **OK** after the backup is complete. Close the company file.

Task 11: Analysis and Recommendations

Step 1: Analyze the financial performance of Max's Lawn Service.

Step 2: What are your recommendations to improve the company's financial performance in the future?

Computer Accounting with QuickBooks 2002
Project 9.1 Printout Checklist
Name:_____ **Date:**_____

☑	*Printout Checklist – Project 9.1*
☐	Chart of Accounts
☐	Customer List
☐	Vendor List
☐	Item List
☐	Invoices
☐	Checks
☐	Deposit Summaries
☐	Check Register
☐	General Journal
☐	General Ledger
☐	Profit & Loss
☐	Balance Sheet
☐	Statement of Cash Flows

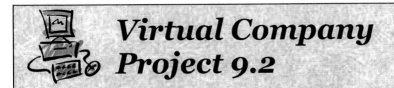

**Virtual Company
Project 9.2**

Project 9.2: Your Choice

Scenario

In this project you will create a service company that is a partnership. You will make decisions regarding the business, including creating transactions.

Additional information:

◆ To reduce costs, your new company will have no employees initially. The partners will perform all services provided to customers.

◆ Start date: 01/01/2002.

Task 1: Option 1

You can complete this project individually (Option 1A) or in teams (Option 1B). Ask your instructor whether you should use Option 1A or 1B to complete this project.

✎ Circle the option below that you are using for this project.

Option 1A: Complete Project 9.2 individually.

TEAMS   **Option 1B:** Complete Project 9.2 in teams.

Ask your instructor for the student password to access the remaining instructions for Virtual Company Project 9.2 at the following website:

www.mhhe.com/ulmer2002

Notes:

10 Merchandising Corporation: Sales, Purchases & Inventory

Scenario

After only one year of operation, your painting service is growing as more customers learn of your custom murals. You often suggest that your customers buy their paint from a small paint store owned and operated by Richard Batt because he provides excellent customer service. In addition, Richard will deliver paint to a job when you run short.

To your dismay, you discover that Richard Batt is planning to sell the store and retire, taking his first vacation since he opened the store 15 years ago. After your initial disappointment, however, you see a business opportunity.

Lately, you've noticed increased demand for custom paint colors to coordinate with furniture, fabrics, and various decorating accessories. If you owned the paint store, you could make a profit on the markup from paint sales made to Fearless Painting Service customers. In addition, you are certain you could land three large commercial customers for whom you have worked: Custom Interiors, The Decorating Center, and Rock Castle Construction. You could also sell paint to other customers, including paint contractors and homeowners.

Convinced there is a profitable market for custom-mixed paint, you approach Richard Batt about purchasing his store. Richard agrees to sell the business to you for $11,000 cash. In addition, you agree to assume a $1,000 bank loan as part of the purchase agreement. You have some extra cash you can invest, and you decide to seek other investors to finance the remainder.

Two of Rock Castle Construction's subcontractors, Alex Koch of Koch Window and Door and his sister, Claire Koch of Claire's Closets, are long-time customers of the paint store. When they learn of your plans to buy the paint store, both eagerly offer to invest.

Claire suggests that you investigate incorporating the new business to provide limited liability to the owners. You vaguely recall discussion of limited liability in your college accounting class and decide to e-mail your college accounting professor for more information.

The Professor's e-mail reply:

SUBJECT:RE:Limited Liability

Corporations provide investors with
limited liability; the most the investor
can lose is the amount invested in the
corporation's stock. If you invest in a
corporation, your personal assets are
protected from claims against the paint
store.

For tax purposes, there are two
different types of corporations: (1)
subchapter S corporation and (2) C
corporation. A C corporation's earnings
are subject to double taxation: the
profits of the corporation are taxed
(Form 1120) and then the dividends
received by investors are taxed on their
1040s.

To avoid double taxation, use an S
Corporation. (It appears you meet the
requirements.) An S Corporation files a
Form 1120S and its earnings appear on
your personal 1040 tax return, taxed at
your personal income tax rate.

Good Luck!

Claire, Alex, and yourself form an S Corporation. Claire and Alex each buy $3,000 of stock, and you buy $5,000 of stock. The stock proceeds are used to purchase the business from Richard Batt. Until you can hire a store manager, you will manage the store.

You prepare the following list of planned expenditures to launch the business:

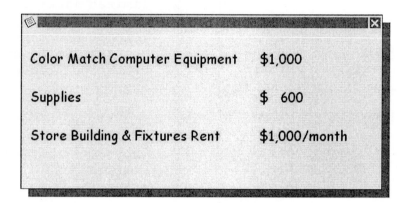

Color Match Computer Equipment	$1,000
Supplies	$ 600
Store Building & Fixtures Rent	$1,000/month

Fearless Paint Store opens for business on January 1, 2003.

10   *Learning Objectives*

In Chapter 10, you will learn the following QuickBooks activities:

Introduction

A company can sell customers either (1) a product or (2) a service.

In Chapters 8 and 9, you maintained accounting records for a company that sells a service to customers. In this chapter, you will maintain an accounting system for a company that sells a product to customers. In Chapter 10, you will complete the following:

1. Easy Step Interview

Use the EasyStep Interview to enter information and preferences for the new company. Based on the information entered, QuickBooks automatically creates a chart of accounts.

2. Customize the Chart of Accounts

Modify the chart of accounts to customize it for your business. Enter beginning account balances.

3. Create Lists

Enter information in the following lists:
* Customer List: Enter information about customers to whom you sell.
* Vendor List: Enter information about vendors from whom you buy.
* Item List: Enter information about products (inventory) you buy and resell to customers.
* Employee List: Enter information about employees. (See Chapter 11).

4. Record Transactions

Enter business transactions in QuickBooks using onscreen forms and the onscreen journal.

5. Reports

After preparing adjusting entries, print financial reports.

To begin Chapter 10, start QuickBooks software by clicking on the QuickBooks desktop icon or click **Start**, **Programs**, **QuickBooks Premier**, **QuickBooks Premier**.

Create a New Company Using EasyStep Interview

To open the EasyStep Interview later:
1. Click **File**.
2. Click **EasyStep Interview**.

If you are familiar with accounting, you can create a company in QuickBooks but skip the interview questions, by clicking **Skip Interview** in the Welcome section.

To create a new company data file in QuickBooks, use the EasyStep Interview. The EasyStep Interview will ask you a series of questions about your business. QuickBooks then uses the information to customize QuickBooks to fit your business needs.

Open the EasyStep Interview as follows:

Step 1: Select **File** (menu).

Step 2: Select **New Company**.

Step 3: Enter the following information for Fearless Paint Store in the EasyStep Interview.

Company name	[your initials] Fearless Paint Store
Legal name	[your initials] Fearless Paint Store
Address	2301 Olive Boulevard
City	Bayshore
State	CA
Zip	94326
Federal tax ID	37-9875602
First month of income tax year	January
First month of fiscal year	January
Income tax form	Form 1120S (S Corporation)
Type of business	Retail
Save in	QuickBooks Premier folder
File name	[your name] Chapter 10
Sales tax	Yes
Single or multiple sales tax rates	Single tax rate paid to a single tax agency
Short name for sales tax	San Tomas
Sales tax description	CA sales tax, San Tomas County
Sales tax rate	7.75%
Government agency to which sales tax is paid	State Board of Equalization
Invoice format	Product
Use payroll feature?	No
Estimates	No
Time tracking	No
Classes	Yes
Handle bills and payments	Enter bills first and enter payments later
Reminders list	At start up
Accrual or cash-based reporting	Accrual
Company start date	01/01/2003
Receipt of payment at time of service	Sometimes

Statement charges	No
Set up service item	No
Set up non-inventory item	No
Set up other charges	No
Inventory	I want to set up inventory items
Enter inventory part items now	No
Do any customers owe you money on your start date?	No
Do you owe any vendors money on your start date?	No
Would you like to set up a credit card account?	Yes
Name of credit card	Bank Visa
Statement ending balance	0.00 on 01/01/2003
Add another credit card account	No
Any lines of credit	No
Loans and notes payable	Yes
Name of loan	Notes Payable
Unpaid balance	1,000.00
Long-term liability	No
Add another loan?	No
Would you like to set up a bank account?	Yes
Name of bank	Checking [your initials] National Bank
Statement ending date	12/31/2002
Statement ending balance	2400.00
Add another bank account	No

> This loan will be paid in less than one year; therefore, it is a short-term or current liability.

Step 4: To close the EasyStep Interview, click the **Leave** button in the lower right corner of the *EasyStep Interview* window.

Customize the Chart of Accounts

Based on your answers in the EasyStep Interview, QuickBooks automatically creates a chart of accounts for Fearless Paint Store. You can customize the chart of accounts to suit your specific business needs.

Because you are purchasing an existing business, some accounts will have opening balances. The balance sheet with opening balances for Fearless Paint Store at January 1, 2003, appears below.

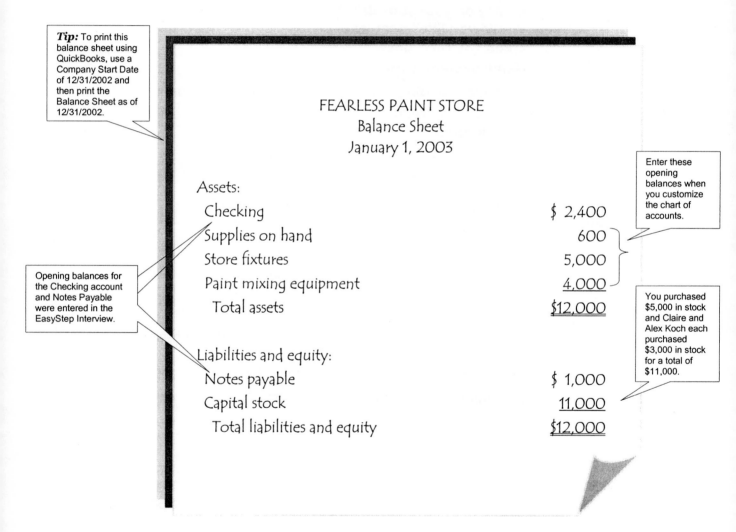

Tip: To print this balance sheet using QuickBooks, use a Company Start Date of 12/31/2002 and then print the Balance Sheet as of 12/31/2002.

Opening balances for the Checking account and Notes Payable were entered in the EasyStep Interview.

Enter these opening balances when you customize the chart of accounts.

You purchased $5,000 in stock and Claire and Alex Koch each purchased $3,000 in stock for a total of $11,000.

FEARLESS PAINT STORE
Balance Sheet
January 1, 2003

Assets:
Checking .... $ 2,400
Supplies on hand 600
Store fixtures 5,000
Paint mixing equipment 4,000
  Total assets $12,000

Liabilities and equity:
Notes payable .... $ 1,000
Capital stock 11,000
  Total liabilities and equity $12,000

To display account numbers:
1. Click **Company** in the *Navigators* window
2. **Preferences**
3. **Accounting**
4. **Company Preferences**

Edit the Chart of Accounts and enter opening balances as follows:

Step 1: Display account numbers in the Chart of Accounts.

Step 2: Add the following accounts and opening balances to the Chart of Accounts. Abbreviate account titles as necessary.

Account No.	1300
Account Type	Other Current Asset
Account Name	Supplies on Hand
Account Description	Supplies on Hand
Tax Line	Unassigned
Opening Balance	$600 as of 01/01/2003

Account No.	1600
Account Type	Fixed Asset
Account Name	Store Fixtures
Account Description	Store Fixtures
Tax Line	Unassigned
Opening Balance	0 as of 01/01/2003

Account No.	1610
Account Type	Fixed Asset
Account Name	Store Fixtures Cost
Subaccount of	Store Fixtures
Account Description	Store Fixtures Cost
Tax Line	Unassigned
Opening Balance	$5,000 as of 01/01/2003

Account No.	1620
Account Type	Fixed Asset
Account Name	Accumulated Depreciation-Store Fixtures
Subaccount of	Store Fixtures
Account Description	Accumulated Depreciation-Store Fixtures
Tax Line	Unassigned
Opening Balance	0 as of 01/01/2003

Account No.	1700
Account Type	Fixed Asset
Account Name	Paint Mixing Equipment
Account Description	Paint Mixing Equipment
Tax Line	Unassigned
Opening Balance	0 as of 01/01/2003

Account No.	1710
Account Type	Fixed Asset
Account Name	Paint Mixing Equipment Cost
Subaccount of	Paint Mixing Equipment
Account Description	Paint Mixing Equipment Cost
Tax Line	Unassigned
Opening Balance	$4,000 as of 01/01/2003

Account No.	1720
Account Type	Fixed Asset
Account Name	Accumulated Depreciation-Paint Mixing Equipment
Subaccount of	Paint Mixing Equipment
Account Description	Accumulated Depreciation-Paint Mixing Equipment
Tax Line	Unassigned
Opening Balance	0 as of 01/01/2003

Account No.	1800
Account Type	Fixed Asset
Account Name	Color Match Equipment
Account Description	Color Match Equipment
Tax Line	Unassigned
Opening Balance	0 as of 01/01/2003

Account No.	1810
Account Type	Fixed Asset
Account Name	Color Match Equipment Cost
Subaccount of	Color Match Equipment
Account Description	Color Match Equipment Cost
Tax Line	Unassigned
Opening Balance	0 as of 01/01/2003

Account No.	1820
Account Type	Fixed Asset
Account Name	Accumulated Depreciation-Color Match Equipment
Subaccount of	Color Match Equipment
Account Description	Accumulated Depreciation-Color Match Equipment
Tax Line	Unassigned
Opening Balance	0 as of 01/01/2003

Account No.	6551
Account Type	Expense
Account Name	Supplies Expense
Account Description	Supplies Expense
Tax Line	Deductions: Other Deductions

Click the **Reports** button in the *Chart of Accounts* window, then select **Account Listing**. Insert your name and Chapter 10 in the report footer.

Step 3: Print the Chart of Accounts with opening balances for Fearless Paint Store.

Create a Customer List

Next, enter customer information in the Customer List. When using QuickBooks to account for a merchandising company that sells a product to customers, you must indicate whether the specific customer is charged sales tax.

Fearless Paint Store will sell to:

1. Retail customers, such as homeowners who must pay sales tax.

2. Wholesale customers, such as The Decorating Center, who resell the product and do not pay sales tax.

Note: If customers had opening balances:
1. Enter the opening balances in the EasyStep Interview, or
2. Enter the opening balances using the Create Invoices window (select Item: **Opening Balance**).

Step 1: Create a Customer List for Fearless Paint Store using the following information.

Customer	Flowers, Diane
Address Info:	
Mr./Ms./...	Mrs.
First Name	Diane
M.I.	L.
Last Name	Flowers
Contact	Diane
Phone	415-555-1078
Alt. Ph.	415-555-3434
Alt. Contact	Tad (spouse)
Address	10 Tee Drive Bayshore, CA 94326

Select **Add New**.

Additional Info:	
Type	Residential
Terms	Net 30
Tax Code	Tax
Tax Item	San Tomas

Payment Info:	
Account	3001

Select **Add New**.

Job Info:	
Job Status	Awarded
Job Description	Custom Paint
Job Type	Custom Paint

Customer	Rock Castle Construction
Address Info:	
Company Name	Rock Castle Construction
Mr./Ms./...	Mr.
First Name	Rock
Last Name	Castle
Contact	Rock
Phone	415-555-7878
Alt. Ph.	415-555-5679
Address	1735 County Road Bayshore, CA 94326

Additional Info:	
Type	Commercial
Terms	Net 30
Tax Code	Non

Payment Info:	
Account	3003

Job Info:	
Job Status	Awarded
Job Description	Custom Paint
Job Type	Custom Paint

Customer	Custom Interiors
Address Info:	
Company Name	Custom Interiors
Contact	Suzanne
Phone	415-555-4356
Address	120 Ignatius Drive Bayshore, CA 94326

Additional Info:	
Type	Commercial
Terms	Net 30
Tax Code	Non

Payment Info:	
Account	3004

Job Info:	
Job Status	Awarded
Job Description	Custom & Stock Paint
Job Type	Custom & Stock Paint

Customer	The Decorating Center
Address Info:	
Company Name	The Decorating Center
Contact	Angie
Phone	415-555-9898
Address	750 Highland Road Bayshore, CA 94326

Additional Info:	
Type	Commercial
Terms	Net 30
Tax Code	Non

Payment Info:	
Account	3005

Job Info:	
Job Status	Awarded
Job Description	Custom & Stock Paint
Job Type	Custom & Stock Paint

Customer	Whalen, Tom
Address Info:	
Mr./Ms./...	Mr.
First Name	TomMike
M.I.	
Last Name	Whalen
Contact	Tom
Phone	415-555-1234
Address	100 Sunset Drive Bayshore, CA 94326

Additional Info:	
Type	Residential
Terms	Net 30
Tax Code	Tax
Tax Item	San Tomas

Payment Info:	
Account	3002

Job Info:	
Job Status	Awarded
Job Description	Custom Paint
Job Type	Custom Paint

Step 2:   Print the Customer List for Fearless Paint Store.

Create a Vendor List

Step 1: Create a Vendor List for Fearless Paint Store using the following information.

Vendor	Garrison Paint Supplies
Opening Balance	0 as of 01/01/2003
Address Info:	
Company Name	Garrison Paint Supplies
Address	200 Clay Street Bayshore, CA 94326
Contact	Cheryl
Phone	415-555-6039
Print on Check as	Garrison Paint Supplies

Additional Info:	
Account	4001
Type	Paint
Terms	Net 30
Credit Limit	15,000.00
Tax ID	37-7832541
Vendor Eligible for 1099	No

Vendor	Hartz Leasing
Opening Balance	0 as of 01/01/2003
Address Info:	
Company Name	Hartz Leasing
Address	13 Appleton Drive Bayshore, CA 94326
Contact	Joe
Phone	415-555-0412

Select **Add New**.

Additional Info:	
Account	4002
Type	Leasing
Terms	Net 30
Tax ID	37-1726354
Vendor Eligible for 1099	No

Vendor	Custom Color
Opening Balance	0 as of 01/01/2003
Address Info:	
Company Name	Custom Color
Address	650 Manchester Road Bayshore, CA 94326
Contact	Barb
Phone	415-555-0444

Select **Add New**.

Additional Info:	
Account	4003
Type	Inventory
Terms	Net 30
Tax ID	37-1726355
Vendor Eligible for 1099	No

Step 2: Print the Vendor List for Fearless Paint Store.

Create an Inventory List

Each of the inventory items that Fearless sells is entered in the QuickBooks Item List. Fearless Paint Store will stock and sell paint inventory to both retail and wholesale customers. Fearless will charge retail customers the full price and charge wholesale customers a discounted price for the paint. Because the sales price varies depending upon the type of customer, instead of entering the sales price in the Item List, you will enter the sales price on the invoice at the time of sale.

Step 1: Create an Item List for Fearless Paint Store inventory using the following information.

Item Type	Inventory Part
Item Name	Paint Base
Description	Paint Base
COGS Account	5000 – Cost of Goods Sold
Income Account	4010 – Sales
Asset Account	1120 – Inventory Assset
Qty on Hand	0 as of 01/01/2003

Item Type	Inventory Part
Item Name	IntBase 1 gal
Subitem of	Paint Base
Description	Interior Paint Base (1 gallon)
Cost	10.00
COGS Account	5000 – Cost of Goods Sold
Taxable	Tax
Income Account	4010 – Sales
Asset Account	1120 – Inventory Assset
Qty on Hand	0 as of 01/01/2003

Item Type	Inventory Part
Item Name	ExtBase 1 gal
Subitem of	Paint Base
Description	Exterior Paint Base (1 gallon)
Cost	10.00
COGS Account	5000 – Cost of Goods Sold
Taxable	Tax
Income Account	4010 – Sales
Asset Account	1120 – Inventory Assset
Qty on Hand	0 as of 01/01/2003

Item Type	Inventory Part
Item Name	Paint Color
Description	Paint Color
COGS Account	5000 – Cost of Goods Sold
Income Account	4010 – Sales
Asset Account	1120 – Inventory Assset
Qty on Hand	0 as of 01/01/2003

Item Type	Inventory Part
Item Name	Stock Color
Subitem of	Paint Color
Description	Stock Paint Color
Cost	2.00
COGS Account	5000 – Cost of Goods Sold
Taxable	Tax
Income Account	4010 – Sales
Asset Account	1120 – Inventory Assset
Qty on Hand	0 as of 01/01/2003

Item Type	Inventory Part
Item Name	Custom Color
Subitem of	Paint Color
Description	Custom Paint Color
Cost	8.00
COGS Account	5000 – Cost of Goods Sold
Taxable	Tax
Income Account	4010 – Sales
Asset Account	1120 – Inventory Assset
Qty on Hand	0 as of 01/01/2003

Note: Before entering transactions, you can transfer the Opening Balance-Equity account balance to the Capital Stock (and Retained Earnings) account(s) by making a journal entry:

Debit: Opening Balance
  Credit: Capital Stock
  Credit: Retained Earnings

Step 2: Print the Item List for inventory.

Record Purchase Transactions

Equipment Purchases

On January 1, 2003, Fearless Paint Store purchased computerized paint color matching equipment from Garrison Paint Supplies for $1,000 cash.

Step 1: Record the purchase using the *Write Checks* window.

Step 2: Print the check (Check No. 401).

The Purchasing Cycle

The purchasing cycle for a merchandising company consists of the following transactions:

1. Create a purchase order to order inventory.

2. Receive the inventory items ordered and record in the inventory account.

3. Enter the bill in QuickBooks when the bill is received.

4. Pay the bill.

5. Print the check.

Next, you will record each of the above transactions in the purchasing cycle for Fearless Paint Store.

Create a Purchase Order

The first step in the purchasing cycle is to create a Purchase Order which is sent to the vendor to order inventory. The Purchase Order provides a record of the type and quantity of item ordered.

Fearless Paint Store needs to order 50 gallons of Interior Base Paint. To order the paint, Fearless must create a purchase order indicating the item and quantity desired.

To create a Purchase Order in QuickBooks:

Step 1: Click **Vendors** on the Navigation Bar.

Step 2: Click the **Purchase Orders** icon on the Vendor Navigator.

Step 3: Select Vendor: **Garrison Paint Supplies**.

Step 4: Select Form Template: **Custom Purchase Order**.

Step 5: Enter Date: **01/03/2003**.

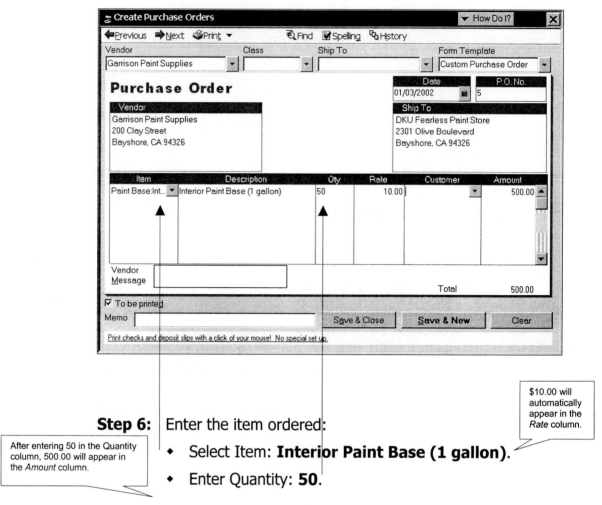

Step 6: Enter the item ordered:

After entering 50 in the Quantity column, 500.00 will appear in the *Amount* column.

$10.00 will automatically appear in the *Rate* column.

- ◆ Select Item: **Interior Paint Base (1 gallon)**.

- ◆ Enter Quantity: **50**.

Step 7: Select: **To be printed**.

Step 8: Click **Next** to record the purchase order and advance to a blank purchase order.

Step 9: Create purchase orders for the following inventory items for Fearless Paint Store.

Vendor	Garrison Paint Supplies
Date	01/05/2003
Item	Exterior Paint Base (1 gallon)
Quantity	40

Vendor	Custom Color
Date	01/10/2003
Item	Custom Color
Quantity	25 cartons
Item	Stock Color
Quantity	5 cartons

Vendor	Garrison Paint Supplies
Date	01/12/2003
Item	Stock Color
Quantity	10 cartons

Step 10: Click **Save & Close** to record the last purchase order and close the *Purchase Order* window.

Step 11: Print the Purchase Orders as follows:

- ◆ Click **File** (menu).
- ◆ Click **Print Forms**.
- ◆ Click **Purchase Orders**.
- ◆ Select the purchase orders to print.
- ◆ Select print settings: **Blank paper** and **Print lines around each field**.
- ◆ Click **Print**.

Receive Inventory Items

When the inventory items that have been ordered are received, record their receipt in QuickBooks. QuickBooks will then add the items received to the Inventory account.

On January 12, 2003, Fearless Paint Store received 40 gallons of interior paint base from Garrison Paint Supplies.

To record the inventory items received from Garrison Paint Supplies:

Step 1: Click the **Receive Items** icon in the Vendor Navigator.

Step 2: When the *Create Item Receipts* window, select Vendor: **Garrison Paint Supplies**.

Step 3: If a purchase order for the item exists, QuickBooks displays the following *Open PO's Exist* window.

   ◆ Click **Yes** to receive against an open purchase order for Garrison Paint Supplies.

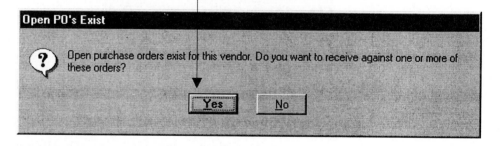

◆ When the following *Open Purchase Orders* window appears, select purchase order No. 1 dated **01/03/2003**, then click **OK**.

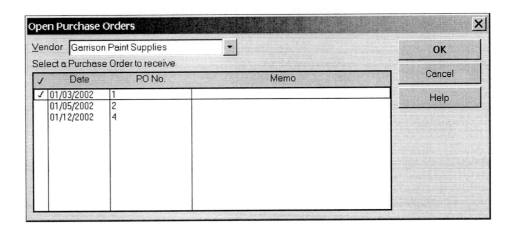

Step 4: The following *Create Item Receipts* window will appear. The quantity received (40 gallons) differs from the quantity ordered (50 gallons). Enter Quantity: **40**.

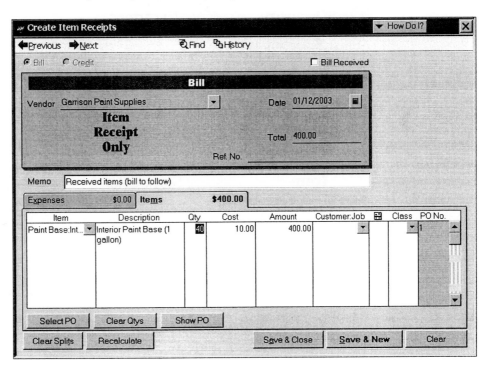

> ✓ **Total for Items Received is $400.00.**

Step 5: Click **Next** on the *Create Item Receipts* window to record the paint received and advance to a blank screen.

Step 6: Record the following inventory items received.

Vendor	Garrison Paint Supplies
Date	01/13/2003
Item	1 gallon Exterior Paint Base
Quantity	40

Vendor	Garrison Paint Supplies
Date	01/14/2003
Item	Stock Color
Quantity	10 cartons

Vendor	Custom Color
Date	01/15/2003
Item	Custom Color
Quantity	25 cartons
Item	Stock Color
Quantity	5 cartons

Step 7: Click **Save & Close** to record the items received and close the *Create Item Receipts* window.

Step 8: Print the Item List showing the quantity on hand for each item in inventory.

Enter Bills

You can enter bills in QuickBooks three different ways:
1. *Enter Bills* window: record services or if there is no purchase order.
2. *Receive Bill* window: record item and bill received at different times.
3. *Receive Item with Bill*: record item and bill received at the same time.

Bills can be entered in QuickBooks when the bill is received or when the bill is paid. (For more information, see Chapter 5.)

Fearless Paint Store will enter bills in QuickBooks when bills are received. At that time, QuickBooks records an obligation to pay the bill later (account payable). QuickBooks tracks bills due. If you use the reminder feature, QuickBooks will even remind you when it is time to pay bills.

Fearless Paint Store previously received 40 1-gallon cans of Interior Paint Base and received the bill later.

If the items and the bill were received at the same time, use the *Receive Item with Bill* window.

To record the bill received:

Step 1: Click the **Receive Bill** icon on the Vendor Navigator.

Step 2: The following *Select Item Receipt* window will appear.

- Select Vendor: **Garrison Paint Supplies**.
- Select Item Receipt corresponding to the bill.
- Click **OK**.

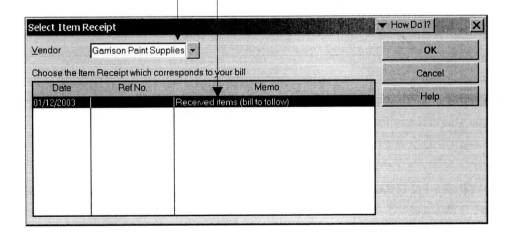

Step 3: When the following *Enter Bills* window appears, make any necessary changes. In this case, change the date to **01/14/2003** (the date the bill was received).

Note: The *Enter Bills* window is the same as the *Create Item Received* window except:
1. There is no *Item Receipt Only* stamp.
2. *Bill Received* in the upper right corner is checked.

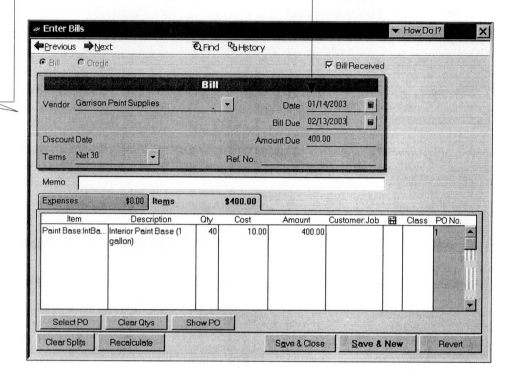

Step 4: The Amount Due of $400.00 should agree with the amount shown on the vendor's bill received.

Step 5: Click **Next** to record another bill.

Step 6: Record the following bills that Fearless Paint Store received.

Vendor	Garrison Paint Supplies
Date Bill Received	01/16/2003
Terms	Net 30
PO No.	2
Item	Exterior Paint Base (1 gallon)
Quantity	40

Vendor	Custom Color
Date Bill Received	01/16/2003
Terms	Net 30
PO No.	3
Item	Custom Color
Quantity	25 cartons
Item	Stock Color
Quantity	5 cartons

> You could also use the *Enter Bills* window because there was no purchase order for the transaction.

Step 7: Click **Next** to enter the Hartz Leasing bill for January rent.

Vendor	Hartz Leasing
Date Bill Received	01/16/2003
Terms	Net 30
Amount Due	1,000.00
Account	Rent Expense
Memo	Rent

> Click the **Expenses** tab to record.

With the *Enter Bills* window still open, click **Edit**, **Memorize Bill**.

Step 8: Record the bill for rent as a memorized transaction.

Step 9: Click **Save & Close** to record the bill and close the *Enter Bills* window.

When you enter bills, QuickBooks automatically adds the amount of the bill to Accounts Payable, reflecting your obligation to pay the bills later.

Pay Bills

After receiving an inventory item and entering the bill in QuickBooks, the next step is to pay the bill when due. To pay the bill, select bills to pay, then print the checks.

Fearless Paint Store will pay the bills for paint and paint color that have been received and recorded.

To pay bills in QuickBooks:

Step 1: Click the **Pay Bills** icon in the Vendor Navigator.

Step 2: When the *Pay Bills* window appears:

- ◆ Select Payment Date: **01/31/2003**.
- ◆ Select: **Show All Bills**.
- ◆ Select Pay By: **Check To be Printed**. Select **Checking** account.
- ◆ Select bills from **Garrison Paint Supply** and **Custom Color**.

Step 3: Click **Pay & Close** to close the *Pay Bills* window.

Print Checks

After selecting bills to pay, you can prepare checks in two different ways:

1. Write the checks manually, or

2. Print the checks using QuickBooks.

> If using QuickBooks to print checks, insert Intuit's preprinted check forms in your printer.

To print checks:

Step 1: Select **File** (menu).

Step 2: Select **Print Forms**.

Step 3: Select **Checks**.

Step 4: Select **Checking** account.

> QuickBooks prints one check for each vendor, combining all amounts due the same vendor.

Step 5: First Check Number: **402**.

Step 6: Select checks to print: **Garrison Paint Supply** and **Custom Color**. Then click **OK**.

Step 7: Select printer settings, then click **Print**.

Record Sales Transactions

The sales cycle for a merchandising company consists of the following transactions:

1. Create an invoice to record the sale and bill the customer.

2. Receive the customer payments.

3. Deposit the customer payments in the bank.

Next, you will record each of these transactions in QuickBooks for Fearless Paint Store.

Create Invoices

When inventory is sold to a customer, the sale is recorded on an invoice in QuickBooks. The invoice lists the items sold, the quantity, and the price. In addition, if the product is sold to a retail customer, sales tax is automatically added to the invoice.

To create an invoice:

Step 1: Click the **Invoices** icon in the Customer Navigator.

Step 2: Create and print invoices for the following sales made by Fearless Paint Store.

Sale of 3 gallons of custom color interior paint to Diane Flowers:

Date	01/20/2003
Customer	Diane Flowers
Terms	Net 30
Quantity	3 gallons
Item Code	Interior Paint Base (1 gallon)
Price Each	25.00
Quantity	3
Item Code	Custom Color
Price Each	6.00
To Be Printed	Yes
Tax Code	Tax

> ✓ ***The Invoice total for Diane Flowers is $100.21.***

Sale of 10 gallons of stock color interior paint to The Decorating Center:

Date	01/22/2003
Customer	The Decorating Center
Terms	Net 30
Quantity	10 gallons
Item Code	Interior Paint Base (1 gallon)
Price Each	20.00
Quantity	10
Item Code	Stock Color
Price Each	3.50
To Be Printed	Yes
Tax Code	Non

Sale of 5 gallons stock color interior paint and 2 gallons customer color exterior paint to Custom Interiors:

If a customer pays cash at the time of sale, it is recorded using the *Sales Receipts* window.

Date	01/25/2003
Customer	Custom Interiors
Terms	Net 30
Quantity	5 gallons
Item Code	Interior Paint Base (1 gallon)
Price Each	20.00
Quantity	5
Item Code	Stock Color
Price Each	3.50
Quantity	2 gallons
Item Code	Exterior Paint Base (1 gallon)
Price Each	22.00
Quantity	2
Item Code	Custom Color
Price Each	5.00
To Be Printed	Yes
Tax Code	Non

Receive Payments

When a credit sale is recorded, QuickBooks records an account receivable at the time the invoice is created. The account receivable is the amount that Fearless Paint Store expects to receive from the customer later.

To record a payment received from a customer:

Step 1: Click the **Receive Payments** icon on the Customer Navigator.

Step 2: Record the following payments received by Fearless Paint Store from customers.

Date Received	01/30/2003
Customer	Diane Flowers
Amount Received	100.21
Payment Method	Check
Check No.	1001

Date Received	01/31/2003
Customer	Custom Interiors
Amount Received	171.50
Payment Method	Check
Check No.	4567

Make Deposits

When the customer's payment is deposited in Fearless Painting's checking account, record the bank deposit in QuickBooks.

To record a bank deposit:

Step 1: Click the **Deposits** icon on the Customer Navigator.

Step 2: On January 31, 2003, record the deposit of customer payments received from **Diane Flowers** and **Custom Interiors**.

Step 3: Print the deposit summary.

Make Adjusting Entries

Before preparing financial statements for Fearless Paint Store for January, print a trial balance and make adjusting entries to bring the accounts up to date.

Step 1: Print the trial balance for Fearless Paint Store at January 31, 2003.

Step 2: Make adjusting entries for Fearless Paint Store at January 31, 2003, using the following information:

- The store fixtures cost of $5,000 will be depreciated over a 10-year useful life with no salvage value. Depreciation expense is $42 per month.

- The paint mixing equipment cost of $4,000 will be depreciated over a 5-year useful life with no salvage value. Depreciation expense is $67 per month.

- The computer paint color match equipment cost $1,000 and has a useful life of four years with no salvage value. Depreciation expense is $21 per month.

> Supplies on hand have future benefit and are recorded in an asset account (No. 1300). Supplies that have been used and the benefits expired are recorded in the Supplies Expense account (No. 6770)

- A count of supplies on hand at the end of January totaled $400. The Supplies on Hand account balance before adjustment is $600. Therefore, reduce (credit) the Supplies on Hand account by $200 and increase (debit) Account No. 6770 Supplies Expense by $200.

Step 3: Print the Journal (including adjusting entries) for Fearless Paint Store for January 2003.

Step 4: Print the adjusted trial balance for Fearless Paint Store at January 31, 2003.

Step 5: ✎ On the adjusted trial balance, circle the account balances affected by the adjusting entries.

✓ **Total debits equal $13,656.71.**

> To eliminate the 0.00 for accounts with zero balances, from the *General Ledger* report window, click the **Customize** button, then click **In Use**.

Print Reports

Print the following reports for Fearless Paint Store for the month of January 2003. Remember to insert your name and Chapter 10 and in the report footer.

- ◆ General Ledger
- ◆ Profit and Loss, Standard
- ◆ Balance Sheet, Standard
- ◆ Statement of Cash Flows

After reviewing the financial statements for Fearless Paint Store, what are your recommendations to improve financial performance?

Back Up Chapter 10

Back up your Chapter 10 file to your floppy disk. Use the file name: [your name] Chapter 10.

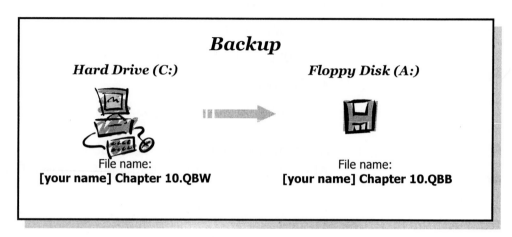

Backup

| Hard Drive (C:) | Floppy Disk (A:) |

File name:
[your name] Chapter 10.QBW

File name:
[your name] Chapter 10.QBB

Step 1:   Insert the **Chapter 10** backup disk in drive A.

Step 2:   Click **File, Back Up**.

Step 3:   Enter the file name: **[your name] Chapter 10.QBB**. Enter Location: **A:**.

Step 4:   Click **Back Up**.

Step 5:   Click **OK** after the backup is complete.

You have now backed up the Chapter 10 file to your Chapter 10 floppy disk.

If you are continuing your computer session, close the company file and then proceed to Project 10.1.

If you are quitting your computer session now, (1) close the company file and (2) exit QuickBooks.

Assignments

Activity 10.1: About Your Industry

If you were an entrepreneur, what small business would you like to own? Select an industry and then find out more about how to optimize QuickBooks for that industry.

Step 1: In QuickBooks, click **Help** (menu).

Step 2: Select: **Using QuickBooks for Your Type of Business**.

Step 3: Select the type of business of your choice.

Step 4: Print two items that you find most interesting or useful about how to use QuickBooks for your selected type of business.

Activity 10.2: WebQuest

The Business Resource Center is a web site containing useful information for small businesses.

Step 1: Go to the www.morebusiness.com web site.

Step 2: Print two items that you think might be useful to a small business.

Activity 10.3: WebQuest

Yahoo can be used to find information on the World Wide Web, including small business information. Yahoo Small Business contains articles and links to other small business sites.

Step 1: Go to smallbusiness.yahoo.com.

Step 2: Explore and print two items (articles or links) on the web site that you find the most useful for the small business owner.

Computer Accounting with QuickBooks 2002
Chapter 10 Printout Checklist
Name:_____ Date:_____

☑	***Printout Checklist – Chapter 10***
☐	Chart of Accounts
☐	Customer List
☐	Vendor List
☐	Item List
☐	Check
☐	Purchase Orders
☐	Item List: Quantity on Hand
☐	Checks
☐	Invoices
☐	Deposit Summary
☐	Trial Balance
☐	Journal
☐	Adjusted Trial Balance
☐	General Ledger
☐	Profit & Loss
☐	Balance Sheet
☐	Statement of Cash Flows
☑	***Printout Checklist – Activity 10.1***
☐	Using QuickBooks for Your Type of Business

☑	***Printout Checklist – Activity 10.2***
◻	Business Resource Center
☑	***Printout Checklist – Activity 10.3***
◻	Yahoo Small Business

Virtual Company Project 10.1

Project 10.1: Max's Mowers and More

Scenario

On March 1, 2003, your friend Max approaches you with another investment opportunity. He asks if you would like to buy stock in a business that sells lawn mowers and equipment. Max would like to buy the business but needs additional investors.

Max plans to invest $10,000 and you agree to invest $5,000 in the business. You also enter into an arrangement with Max whereby you agree to help Max with the accounting records for his new business in exchange for free lawn service for your paint store.

Task 1: Set Up a New Company

Create a new company in QuickBooks for Max's Mowers and More using the following information.

Company name	[your initials] Max's Mowers and More
Legal name	[your initials] Max's Mowers and More
Address	2300 Olive Boulevard
City	Bayshore
State	CA
Zip	94326
Federal tax ID	37-7879146
First month of income tax year	January
First month of fiscal year	March
Income tax form	Form 1120 (Corporation)
Type of business	Retail
Save in	QuickBooks Premier folder
File name	[your name] Project10.1
Sales tax	Yes
Single or multiple sales tax rates	Single tax rate paid to a single tax agency
Short name for sales tax	San Tomas
Sales tax description	CA sales tax, San Tomas County
Sales tax rate	7.75%
Government agency to which sales tax is paid	State Board of Equalization
Invoice format	Product
Use payroll feature?	No
Estimates	No
Time tracking	No
Classes	No
Handle bills and payments	Enter bills first and payments later
Reminders list	At start up
Accrual or cash-based reporting	Accrual
Company start date	03/01/2003

Customer balances (Accounts Receivable) entered in the EasyStep Interview are listed as uncategorized income on the financial statements.
To avoid this, you can:
1. Enter the customer balance in the Customer List, or
2. Enter the opening balance using the *Create Invoices* window (select Item: **Opening Balance**).

Other customer information will be added later.

This loan will not be paid in one year; therefore, it is a long-term liability.

Receipt of payment at time of service	Sometimes
Statement charges	No
Set up service item	No
Set up non-inventory item	No
Set up other charges	No
Inventory	I want to set up inventory items
Enter inventory part items now	No
Do any customers owe you money on your start date?	Yes
Do you want to track jobs for customers?	No
Customer name	Fowler, Gerry
Balance due on start date	200.00
Add another customer now?	No
Do you owe any vendors money on your start date?	No
Would you like to set up a credit card account?	Yes
Name of credit card	Bank Visa
Statement ending balance	0.00 on 01/01/2003
Add another credit card account	No
Any lines of credit	No
Loans and notes payable	Yes
Name of loan	Notes Payable
Unpaid balance	2,000.00
Long-term liability	Yes
Add another loan?	No
Would you like to set up a bank account?	Yes
Name of bank	Checking [your initials] National Bank
Statement ending balance	0.00
Add another bank account?	No

Click **Leave** to exit the EasyStep Interview.

To display account numbers:
1. Click **Company** in the *Navigators* window.
2. **Preferences**
3. **Accounting**
4. **Company Preferences**

Task 2: Customize the Chart of Accounts

Customize the Chart of Accounts for Max's Mowers and More as follows:

Step 1: Display account numbers in the Chart of Accounts.

Step 2: Add the following accounts to the Chart of Accounts. Abbreviate account titles as necessary.

Account No.	1300
Account Type	Other Current Asset
Account Name	Supplies on Hand
Account Description	Supplies on Hand
Tax Line	Unassigned
Opening Balance	500.00 as of 03/01/2003

Account No.	1600
Account Type	Fixed Asset
Account Name	Store Fixtures
Account Description	Store Fixtures
Tax Line	Unassigned
Opening Balance	0 as of 03/01/2003

Account No.	1610
Account Type	Fixed Asset
Account Name	Store Fixtures Cost
Subaccount of	Store Fixtures
Account Description	Store Fixtures Cost
Tax Line	Unassigned
Opening Balance	2500.00 as of 03/01/2003

Account No.	1620
Account Type	Fixed Asset
Account Name	Accumulated Depreciation - Store Fixtures
Subaccount of	Store Fixtures
Account Description	Accumulated Depreciation - Store Fixtures
Tax Line	Unassigned
Opening Balance	0 as of 03/01/2003

Notice that Accounts Receivable and Accounts Payable have balances. These balances were entered during the EasyStep Interview.

Step 3: Print the Chart of Accounts with opening balances for Max's Mowers and More. (Click the **Reports** button in the *Chart of Accounts* window, then select **Account Listing**. Insert **your name** and **Project 10.1** in the report footer.)

Task 3: Customer List

Create and print a Customer List for Max's Mowers and More.

Customer	Fowler, Gerry
Address Info:	
First Name	Gerry
Last Name	Fowler
Contact	Gerry
Phone	415-555-9797
Alt. Ph.	415-555-0599
Address	500 Lindell Blvd Bayshore, CA 94326
Additional Info:	
Type	Residential
Terms	Net 30
Tax Code	Tax
Payment Info:	
Account	3001

Select **Add New**.

Customer	Stanton, Mike
Address Info:	
First Name	Mike
Last Name	Stanton
Contact	Mike
Phone	415-555-7979
Alt. Ph.	415-555-0596
Alt. Contact	Work phone
Address	1000 Grand Avenue Bayshore, CA 94326
Additional Info:	
Type	Residential
Terms	Net 30
Tax Code	Tax
Payment Info:	
Account	3002

Customer	Grady's Bindery
Address Info:	
Company Name	Grady's Bindery
First Name	Mike
Last Name	Grady
Contact	Mike
Phone	415-555-7777
Address	700 Laclede Avenue Bayshore, CA 94326
Additional Info:	
Type	Commercial
Terms	Net 30
Tax Code	Tax
Payment Info:	
Account	3003

Task 4: Vendor List

Create and print a Vendor List for Max's Mowers and More.

Vendor	Lee's Mowers
Address Info:	
Company Name	Lee's Mowers
Address	100 Collinsville Road Bayshore, CA 94326
Contact	Bill
Phone	415-555-0500
Print on Check as	Lee's Mowers

Additional Info:	
Account	4001
Type	Mowers
Terms	Net 30
Credit Limit	20,000.00
Tax ID	37-4327651
Vendor Eligible for 1099	No
Opening Balance	0 as of 03/01/2003

Vendor	Mower Sales & Repair
Address Info:	
Company Name	Mower Sales & Repair
Address	650 Manchester Road Bayshore, CA 94326
Contact	Carol
Phone	415-555-8222
Print on Check as	Mower Sales & Repair

Additional Info:	
Account	4002
Type	Mowers
Terms	Net 30
Credit Limit	10,000.00
Tax ID	37-6510541
Vendor Eligible for 1099	No
Opening Balance	0 as of 03/01/2003

Vendor	Hartz Leasing
Address Info:	
Company Name	Hartz Leasing
Address	13 Appleton Drive Bayshore, CA 94326
Contact	Joe
Phone	415-555-0412
Print on Check as	Hartz Leasing

Additional Info:	
Account	4003
Type	Leasing
Terms	Net 30
Tax ID	37-1726354
Vendor Eligible for 1099	No
Opening Balance	0 as of 03/01/2003

To print the Item List, click the **Reports** button, then select **Item Listing**.

Task 5: Item List

Create and print an Item List for Max's Mowers and More.

Item Type	Inventory Part
Item Name	Mowers
Description	Lawn Mowers
COGS Account	5000 – Cost of Goods Sold
Tax Code	Tax
Income Account	4010 – Sales
Asset Account	1120 – Inventory Asset
Quantity on Hand	0 as of 03/01/2003

Item Type	Inventory Part
Item Name	Riding Mower
Subitem of	Mowers
Description	48" Riding Mower
Cost	2,000.00
COGS Account	5000 – Cost of Goods Sold
Tax Code	Tax
Sales Price	3,800.00
Income Account	4010 – Sales
Asset Account	1120 – Inventory Asset
Quantity on Hand	0 as of 03/01/2003

Item Type	Inventory Part
Item Name	Push Mower
Subitem of	Mowers
Description	Push Mower
Cost	400.00
COGS Account	5000 – Cost of Goods Sold
Tax Code	Tax
Sales Price	780.00
Income Account	4010 – Sales
Asset Account	1120 – Inventory Asset
Quantity on Hand	0 as of 03/01/2003

Item Type	Inventory Part
Item Name	Propel Mower
Subitem of	Mowers
Description	Self-Propelled Mower
Cost	600.00
COGS Account	5000 – Cost of Goods Sold
Tax Code	Tax
Sales Price	1150.00
Income Account	4010 – Sales
Asset Account	1120 – Inventory Asset
Quantity on Hand	0 as of 03/01/2003

Item Type	Inventory Part
Item Name	Trimmer
Description	Lawn Trimmer
COGS Account	5000 – Cost of Goods Sold
Tax Code	Tax
Income Account	4010 – Sales
Asset Account	1120 – Inventory Asset
Quantity on Hand	0 as of 03/01/2003

Item Type	Inventory Part
Item Name	Gas Trimmer
Subitem of	Trimmer
Description	Gas-Powered Trimmer
Cost	300.00
COGS Account	5000 – Cost of Goods Sold
Tax Code	Tax
Sales Price	570.00
Income Account	4010 - Sales
Asset Account	1120 – Inventory Asset
Quantity on Hand	0 as of 03/01/2003

Item Type	Inventory Part
Item Name	Batt Trimmer
Subitem of	Trimmer
Description	Rechargeable Battery-Powered Trimmer
Cost	200.00
COGS Account	5000 – Cost of Goods Sold
Tax Code	Tax
Sales Price	390.00
Income Account	4010 - Sales
Asset Account	1120 – Inventory Asset
Quantity on Hand	0 as of 03/01/2003

Task 6: Record Transactions

Max's Mowers and More entered into the following transactions during March 2003.

Step 1: Record the following transactions for Max's Mowers and More. Customers are billed monthly. Print invoices, checks, and deposit summaries as appropriate. Use memorized transactions for recurring transactions.

Date	Transaction
03/01/2003	Max Milan invested $10,000 cash in stock of Max's Mowers and More. You invested $5,000 cash in the stock of the business.
03/01/2003	Paid $800 store rent to Hartz Leasing (Check No. 601).
03/02/2003	Purchased $300 in supplies on account from Mowers Sales and Repair.
03/02/2003	Ordered (2) 48" riding mowers, 2 gas-powered trimmers, and 3 battery-powered trimmers from Lee's Mowers.
03/04/2003	Received items ordered from Lee's Mowers on 03/02/2003.
03/05/2003	Sold a 48" riding mower and a gas-powered trimmer to Grady's Bindery on account.
03/07/2003	Received bill from Lee's Mowers.
03/09/2003	Ordered 2 self-propelled mowers and one push mower from Lee's Mowers.

Use *Make Deposits* window.

Use *Write Checks* window, then create a memorized transaction.

Use *Enter Bills* or *Receive Bill* window. Record as Supplies Expense.

03/12/2003	Received the self-propelled mowers ordered on 03/09/2003 from Lee's Mowers.
03/13/2003	Received the bill from Lee's Mowers for the self-propelled mowers.
03/15/2003	Sold 1 self-propelled mower and 1 battery-powered trimmer to Mike Stanton on account.
03/16/2003	Sold a 48" riding mower to Gerry Fowler on account.
03/16/2003	Ordered (2) 48" riding mowers from Lee's Mowers to restock inventory.
03/20/2003	Received and deposited the customer payment from Grady's Bindery (Check No. 401).
03/29/2003	Paid bill from Lee's Mowers received on 03/07/2003 and due 04/06/2003. Paid $300 bill from Mowers Sales & Repairs.
03/31/2003	Received and deposited payment from Mike Stanton (Check No. 3001).
03/31/2003	Paid bill for self-propelled mowers due 04/12/2003.
03/31/2003	Paid $800 store rent to Hartz Leasing.

Step 2:   Print the Check Register for March 2003.

Task 7: Adjusting Entries

Step 1: Print the trial balance for Max's Mowers and More at March 31, 2003.

Step 2: Make adjusting entries for Max's Mowers and More at March 31, 2003 using the following information.

- A count of supplies revealed $350 of supplies on hand.

- March depreciation expense for store fixtures was $35.

Step 3: Print the Journal for March 2003, including the adjusting journal entries.

Step 4: Print the adjusted trial balance for Max's Mowers and More at March 31, 2003.

Step 5: ✐ On the adjusted trial balance, circle the accounts affected by the adjusting entries.

Task 8: Financial Reports

Step 1: Print the following reports for Max's Mowers and More. Remember to insert Project 10.1 and your name in the report footer.

> *Note:* The accounts receivable balance entered during the EasyStep Interview appears on the profit and loss statement as unrealized income of $200.

- 🗐 General Ledger
- 🗐 Profit & Loss, Standard
- 🗐 Balance Sheet, Standard
- 🗐 Statement of Cash Flows
- 🗐 Accounts Receivable Aging Summary

Step 2: Using the financial statements, determine the balance of the Supplies Expense account and explain how the account balance was calculated. $_____

Step 3: Using the balance sheet, determine the amount of sales tax that Max's Mowers and More collected and owes to the State Board of Equalization. $_____

Step 4: Discuss how the aging summary for accounts receivable might be used by a small business.

Task 10: Back Up Project 10.1

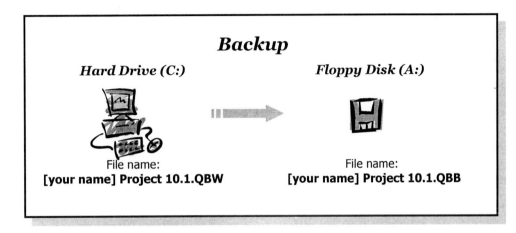

Step 1: ▢ Insert the **Project 10.1** backup disk in drive A.

Step 2: Click **File**, **Back Up**.

Step 3: Enter the filename: **[your name] Project 10.1.QBB**. Enter Location: **A:**.

Step 4: Click **OK** after the backup is complete. Close the company file.

Task 11: Analysis and Recommendations

Step 1: Analyze the financial performance of Max's Mowers and More.

Step 2: What are your recommendations to improve the company's financial performance in the future?

Computer Accounting with QuickBooks 2002
Chapter 10 Printout Checklist
Name:_____ **Date:**_____

☑	***Printout Checklist – Project 10.1***
☐	Chart of Accounts
☐	Customer List
☐	Vendor List
☐	Item List
☐	Invoices
☐	Purchase Orders
☐	Checks
☐	Deposit Summaries
☐	Check Register
☐	Trial Balance
☐	General Journal
☐	Adjusted Trial Balance
☐	General Ledger
☐	Profit & Loss
☐	Balance Sheet
☐	Statement of Cash Flows
☐	Accounts Receivable Aging Summary

Notes:

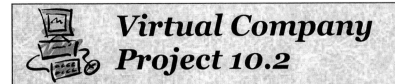

Virtual Company
Project 10.2

Project 10.2: Your Choice

Scenario

In this project, you will create a merchandising corporation. You will make decisions regarding the business, including creating transactions.

Additional information:

◆ To reduce costs, your new company will have no employees initially. The owners will perform all services provided to customers.

◆ Start date: 01/01/2003.

Task 1: Option 1

You can complete this project individually (Option 1A) or in teams (Option 1B). Ask your instructor whether you should use Option 1A or 1B to complete this project.

✐ Circle the option below that you are using for the project.

Option 1A: Complete Project 10.2 individually.

TEAMS *Option 1B:* Complete Project 10.2 in teams.

Ask your instructor for the student password to access the remaining instructions for Virtual Company Project 10.2 at the following website:

www.mhhe.com/ulmer2002

Notes:

11 Merchandising Corporation: Payroll

Scenario

After returning from his vacation, Richard Batt drops by the paint store to visit you and his former business. While the two of you are talking, customers in the store begin asking him for assistance. In cheerful good humor, he offers to tend the store for you while you go to lunch.

When you return after lunch, Richard tells you that Diane Flowers called, asking when you will have time to finish a paint job for her. Always ready to help, Richard suggests that you finish the Flowers job while he watches the store.

When you return later that afternoon, Richard appears to be thoroughly enjoying himself as he restocks the shelves and waits on customers. By closing time, you and Richard have reached an agreement: you will hire him to manage the store full-time, freeing you to return to your painting. Richard has only one condition—he wants one month of vacation every year.

11 Learning Objectives

In Chapter 11, you will complete the following QuickBooks activities:

Chapter 10 must be completed before starting Chapter 11.

Introduction

In Chapter 11, you will account for payroll for Fearless Paint Store. In Chapter 10, you set up a new merchandising company, Fearless Paint Store, in QuickBooks. In this chapter, you will record a bank loan. Then you will set up payroll and record payroll transactions for Fearless Paint Store.

To begin Chapter 11, first start QuickBooks software and then restore your backup file for Fearless Paint Store, the company file you created in Chapter 10.

Start QuickBooks software by clicking on the **QuickBooks** desktop icon or click **Start**, **Programs**, **QuickBooks Premier**, **QuickBooks Premier**.

Restore Back Up

Restore your Chapter 10 backup for Fearless Paint Store to the C: drive, renaming the file Chapter 11.

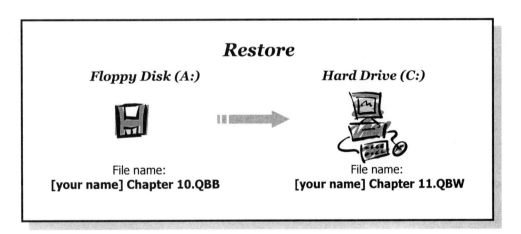

Restore

| *Floppy Disk (A:)* | | *Hard Drive (C:)* |

File name: **[your name] Chapter 10.QBB**

File name: **[your name] Chapter 11.QBW**

Step 1: ⊞ Insert the **Chapter 10** backup disk into drive A.

Step 2: Click **Restore a backup file** (or click **File, Restore**).

Step 3: Identify the backup file:

- Filename: **[your name] Fearless Paint Store Chapter 10.QBB**.

- Location: **A:**.

Step 4: Identify the restored file:

- Filename: **[your name] Fearless Paint Store Chapter 11.QBW**.

- Location: **C:\Program Files\Intuit\QuickBooks Premier**.

Step 5: Click **Restore.** If prompted, enter your User ID and Password.

Step 6: Change the company name to:
[your name] Fearless Paint Store Chapter 11.
(To change the company name, select Company (menu), Company Information.)

Bank Loan

Although Fearless Paint Store sales appear to be improving, business has been slower than you anticipated. As a result, you need an operating loan in order to pay your bills and Richard's salary.

Fearless Paint Store takes out a $4,000 operating loan from National Bank. You intend to repay the loan within one year.

Step 1: Create a new loan account: Notes Payable: National Bank.

> A loan to be repaid within 1 year is classified as Other Current Liability.

- ◆ Display the **Chart of Accounts**.
- ◆ Click the **Account** button, then click **New**.
- ◆ Select Account Type: **Other Current Liability**.
- ◆ Enter Account Number: **2050**.
- ◆ Enter Account Name: **Note Payable-National Bank**.
- ◆ Enter Description: **Note Payable – National Bank**.
- ◆ Enter Tax Line: **Unassigned**.
- ◆ Click **OK** to save.

Step 2: When the bank deposits the $4,000 loan amount in your checking account, record the loan as follows:

- ◆ From the Banking Navigator, select **Deposit**.
- ◆ Select Date: **02/01/2003**.
- ◆ Select From Account: **Note Payable-National Bank**.
- ◆ Enter Amount: **4,000.00**.
- ◆ Click **Save & Close**.

> You can also enable payroll using the EasyStep Interview.

Enable Payroll

To enable QuickBooks payroll for Fearless Paint Store, complete the following steps:

Step 1: Click **Company** in the *Navigators* window.

Step 2: Click **Preferences** icon on the Tools Navigator.

Step 3: Click **Payroll & Employees** in the left scrollbar of the *Preferences* window.

Step 4: Click the **Company Preferences** tab.

> Set employee defaults for information common to all employees, such as deductions for health insurance.

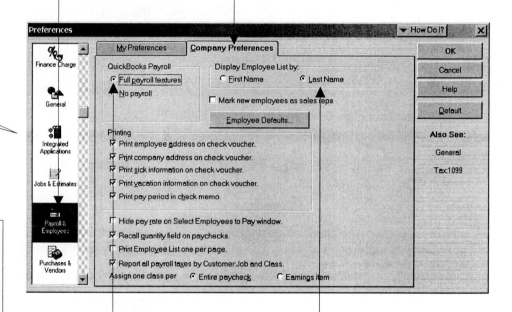

> During company setup, QuickBooks automatically creates the Chart of Accounts including the necessary payroll liability and payroll expense accounts. To track the supporting detail needed for payroll, QuickBooks uses Payroll Items (just as QuickBooks uses Items to track detail for the Inventory account).

Step 5: Select **Full payroll features** to enable QuickBooks Payroll.

Step 6: Select Display Employee List by: **Last Name**.

Step 7: Click **OK** to close the *Preferences* window.

Set Up Payroll

QuickBooks Pro and QuickBooks Premier provides three different ways to process payroll:

1. Use a QuickBooks Payroll Service: Basic, Deluxe, or Premier.
2. Manually calculate payroll taxes.

Information about each option appears below.

1. **Use QuickBooks Payroll Service:** When you subscribe to a payroll service, QuickBooks automatically calculates tax deductions and prepares payroll tax forms. In addition, you can obtain payroll tax updates online. See the following table for a comparison of the Basic, Deluxe, and Premier Payroll Services.

	Integrates with QuickBooks		
	Basic	Deluxe	Premier
Payroll Services Comparison			
Integrates with QuickBooks	x	x	
Earnings and deductions calculations	x	x	x
Federal and state tax table updates	x	x	x
Federal payroll tax forms[1]	x	x	x
Electronic direct deposit of paychecks[2]	optional	x	x
Automatic federal and state payroll tax deposits		x	x
Electronic payroll tax filings		x	x
W-2 printing and mailing		x	x
"No Penalties" Guarantee[3]		x	x
Submit payroll by phone or PC, or set up to process payroll automatically			x
Paycheck delivery to your office			x
Preparation of 1099-MISC forms for contractors and vendors			x
Preparation of state new hire reporting forms			x

[1]Federal forms included are 940, 941, 941 Schedule B and printing formats for W-2 and W-3 forms.

[2]Nominal additional fees apply for Direct Deposit.

[3]We assume complete responsibility for federal and state payroll filings and payments directly from your account(s) based on the data you supply. As long as the information you send us is correct and on time, and you have sufficient funds in your account, we'll file your forms and payments accurately and on time... or we'll pay the resulting payroll tax penalties.

For more information about QuickBooks Payroll Services, see *Learn About Payroll Options* on the Employee Navigator.

Intuit provided tax tables with QuickBooks 6.0 and 99; however to receive updated tax tables with QuickBooks 2000, 2001 and 2002, you must subscribe to one of Intuit's payroll services.

QuickBooks 2002 provides a free trial of the Payroll Tax Service. You can continue to use the latest update to calculate payroll without subscribing to the service until February 15 of the following year. After February 15, the tax tables will not function. If you continue to use the trial version, you will not receive online tax table updates after the 60-day trial period and your tax tables could be incorrect.

2. **Manually calculate payroll taxes.** If you do not use one of the payroll tax services, you can calculate tax withholdings and payroll taxes manually using IRS Circular E. Then enter the amounts in QuickBooks to process payroll.

In Chapter 6, you processed payroll with tax deductions calculated automatically by QuickBooks. In this chapter, you will learn how to enter payroll tax amounts manually instead of using a payroll tax service.

To set up payroll in QuickBooks:

Step 1: Click **Employees** in the *Navigators* window to display the the Employee Navigator.

Step 2: Click the **Set Up Payroll** icon to display the following *Payroll Setup* window.

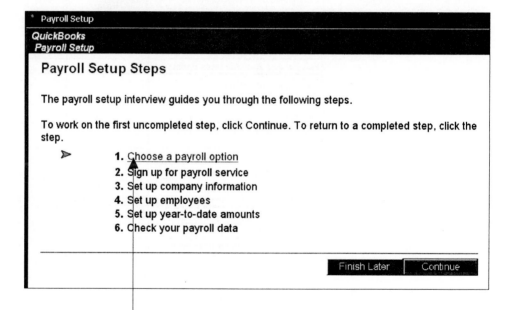

Step 3: Click **Choose a payroll option**.

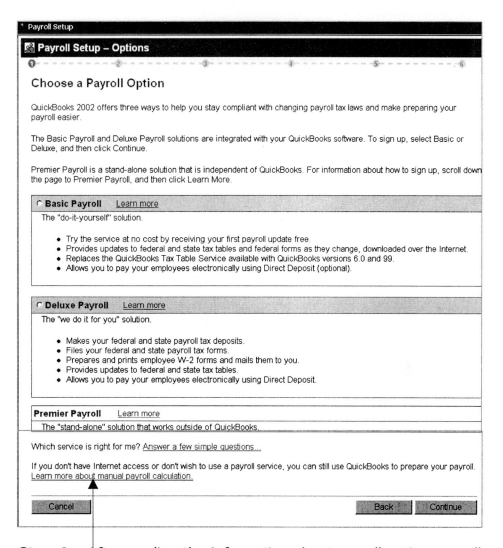

Step 4: After reading the information about payroll options, scroll to the bottom of the *Payroll Setup* window, click **Learn more about manual payroll calculation.**

Step 5: Read the information about manual payroll, then click **I choose to manually calculate payroll taxes.**

Payroll Setup

Doing payroll with QuickBooks 2002 without an Internet connection.

If you don't have Internet access you can use QuickBooks to prepare your payroll manually.

If you don't have Internet access, you can prepare payroll by manually calculating and entering payroll withholdings for each paycheck in QuickBooks 2002. Print this page for reference.

Calculating payroll taxes manually

First click the button to indicate that you don't want to sign up for a payroll service at this time.

➤ [I choose to manually calculate payroll taxes]

Then follow these steps to prepare your payroll:

1. Get the most recent payroll tax information from the IRS, your state tax agency and your accountant, including:
    *   Tax tables, including mid-year tax changes that can affect your payroll
    *   Wage limits on taxes such as FUTA
    *   The frequency in which you pay your payroll taxes (The frequency can change from year to year, depending on certain conditions in your company.)
2. Each pay period, use the information you gather in Step 1 to calculate the current and year-to-date federal and state tax information for each employee. Without a subscription to one of the QuickBooks Payroll Services, QuickBooks inserts a zero-tax amount for each payroll item associated with a tax. You must replace the zero-tax amounts with the appropriate tax for each employee paycheck.
3. Pay your payroll taxes using the tax schedules provided in the reference material. Payroll tax information for federal, state and local agencies can change throughout the tax year. To avoid penalties, be sure to consult your tax agencies often for any changes.

If you have Internet access from your QuickBooks computer but do not want to pay for the QuickBooks Basic Payroll or Deluxe Payroll services, you can calculate your payroll manually or request one free payroll update to receive the latest tax table.

*   To calculate payroll taxes manually
*   **To receive one free payroll update**
    Select Basic Payroll and complete the sign-up process without entering your credit card number. You will receive one free payroll update. (If you are a Tax Table Service subscriber, you may also apply the remainder of your subscription period toward Basic Payroll when you sign up). You may use this year 2002 tax table until February 15, 2003. At that time, tax tables from the previous year will not function in QuickBooks 2002 and you must subscribe to Basic Payroll to continue receiving automatic tax withholding calculations. Note: On February 15th of each year, tax tables from the previous year will no longer function in QuickBooks. This safeguard helps to ensure that, at the beginning of each year, QuickBooks payroll customers are not using outdated tax tables and forms. Because payroll regulations can change at any time, we strongly recommend that you maintain a Basic Payroll subscription to help ensure compliance.

Step 6: This will return you to the *Payroll Setup Steps* window. Select: **Set up company information**.

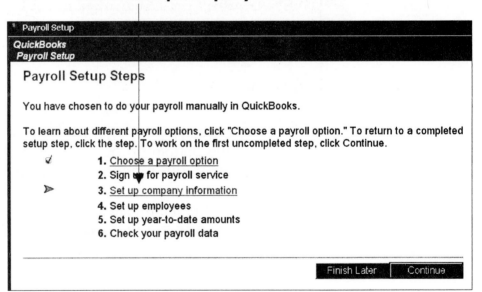

Step 7:   Select: **Set up payroll taxes**.

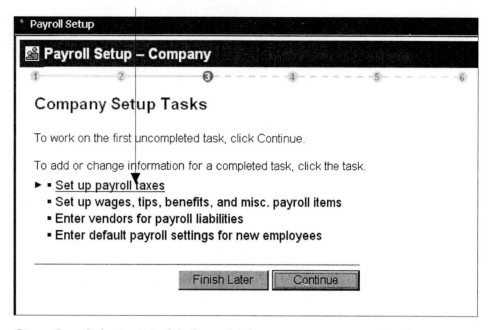

Step 8:   Select state(s) for which your company collects or pays payroll taxes: **California**. Then click **Continue**.

Payroll Setup

Payroll Setup – Company

Company Payroll States

Select all states for which your company collects or pays payroll taxes.

☐ Alabama	☐ Indiana	☐ Nebraska	☐ Rhode Island
☐ Alaska	☐ Iowa	☐ Nevada	☐ South Carolina
☐ Arizona	☐ Kansas	☐ New Hampshire	☐ South Dakota
☐ Arkansas	☐ Kentucky	☐ New Jersey	☐ Tennessee
☑ California	☐ Louisiana	☐ New Mexico	☐ Texas
☐ Colorado	☐ Maine	☐ New York	☐ Utah
☐ Connecticut	☐ Maryland	☐ North Carolina	☐ Vermont
☐ Delaware	☐ Massachusetts	☐ North Dakota	☐ Virginia
☐ Florida	☐ Michigan	☐ Ohio	☐ Washington
☐ Georgia	☐ Minnesota	☐ Oklahoma	☐ Washington DC
☐ Hawaii	☐ Mississippi	☐ Oregon	☐ West Virginia
☐ Idaho	☐ Missouri	☐ Pennsylvania	☐ Wisconsin
☐ Illinois	☐ Montana	☐ Puerto Rico	☐ Wyoming

Cancel   Back   Continue

Step 9: Review the information in the *Federal Payroll Taxes* window, then click **Continue**.

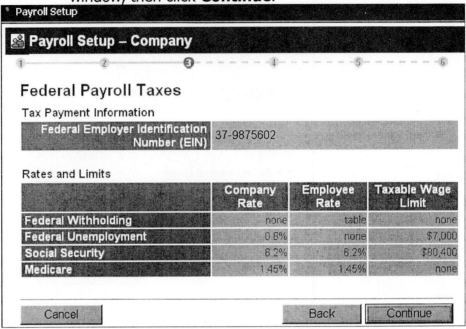

Step 10: Enter California EDD Employer Account Number: **999-9999-9**. After entering the California Unemployment Company Rate as shown below, click **Continue**.

Payroll Setup

Payroll Setup – Company

1 ——— 2 ——— **3** - - - - 4 - - - - 5 - - - - 6

California Payroll Taxes

Tax Payment Information

California EDD Employer Account Number	999-9999-9
	999-9999-9 or 999 9999 9
	Located on Forms DE88, DE6 (see This is your Account Number). Employment Development Department, (916) 464-3502

Rates and Limits

	Company Rate		Employee Rate	Taxable Wage Limit
CA - Withholding	none		table	none
CA - Unemployment Company *	Jan-Mar .7	%		
	Apr-Jun .7	%	none	$7,000
	Jul-Sep .7	%		
	Oct-Dec .7	%		
CA - Disability Employee		none	0.9%	$46,327
CA - Employment Training Tax	0.1%		none	$7,000

Step 11: From the *Payroll Setup* window, select: **Set up wages, tips, benefits, and misc. payroll items**.

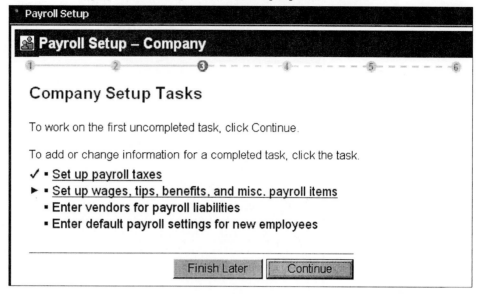

Step 12: Select types of wages, tips, and fringe benefits that you will use in processing payroll for your company as shown below, then click **Create**. Click **Continue**.

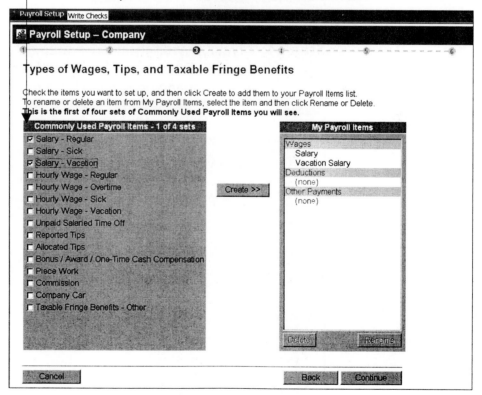

Step 13: If you needed to set up insurance benefits, you would select the appropriate items on this screen. Since you are not providing insurance benefits to your employee, simply click **Continue**.

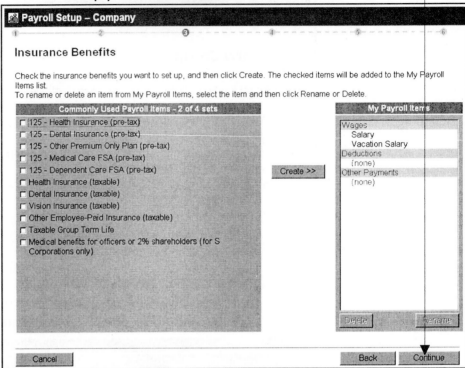

Step 14: If your payroll included retirement plan deductions, you would indicate those items on the following screen. Since your company does not, click **Continue**.

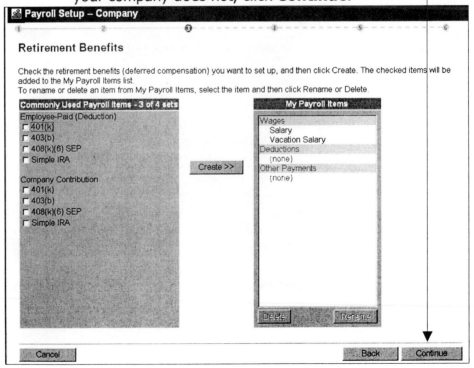

Step 15: Other payroll payments and deductions are indicated on the screen shown below. In this instance, simply click **Continue**.

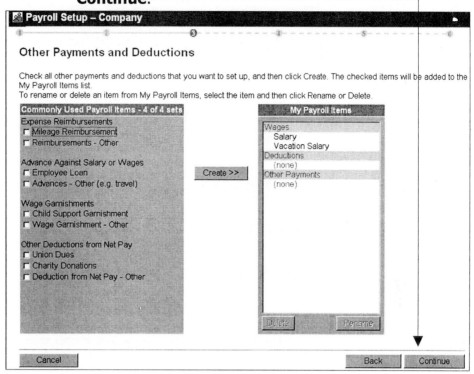

Step 16: Click **Enter vendors for payroll liabilities**.

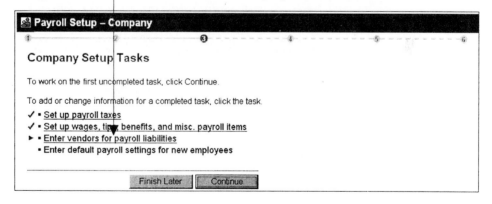

Step 17: Select the following tax agencies to which you pay federal and state payroll taxes, then click **Continue**.

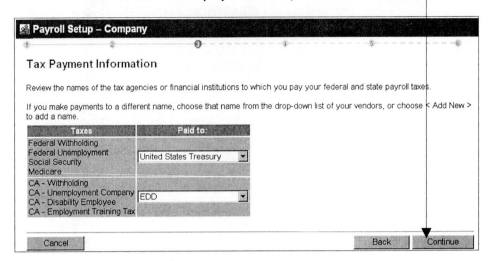

Step 18: Click **Continue** to advance to the *Company Setup Tasks* window. Then click **Enter default payroll settings for new employees**.

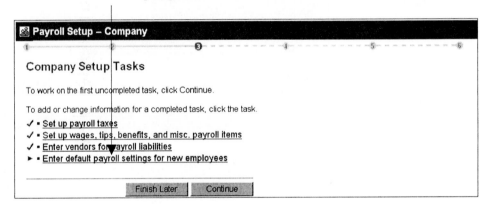

Step 19: Click **Edit** to enter default payroll settings that are common to most employees.

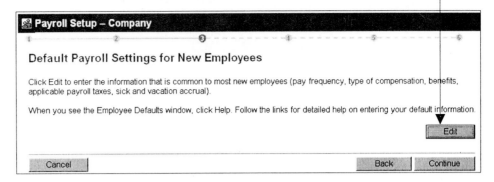

Step 20: Click the **Taxes** button. When the following *Taxes Defaults* window appears, on the Federal tab select Filing Status: **Married**.

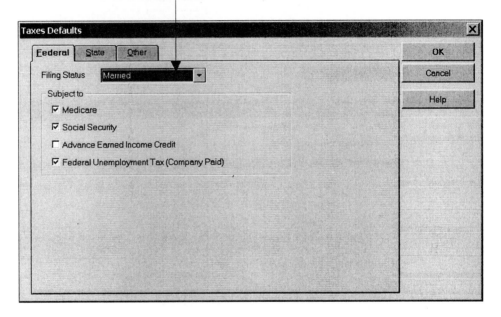

Step 21: Click the **State** tab, then select State Worked: **CA**. Select State Lived: **CA**. Click **OK**.

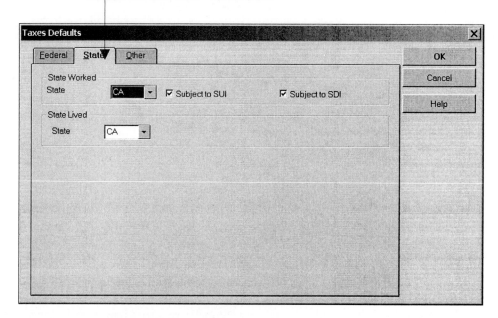

Step 22: When asked if the default employee is subject to California Employment Training Tax, select: **No**.

Step 23: Click **OK** to close the *Employee Defaults* window, then click **Continue** on the *Default Payroll Settings* window.

Step 24: Click **Done** to complete Company Payroll Setup Tasks.

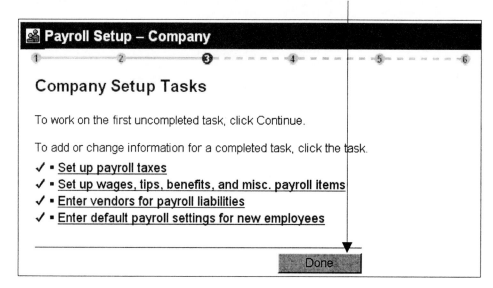

Step 25: When the *Payroll Setup Steps* window reappears, click **Set up employees**.

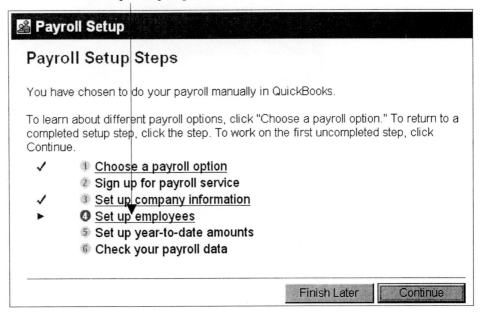

Step 26: To set up a new employee, click **Add Employee**.

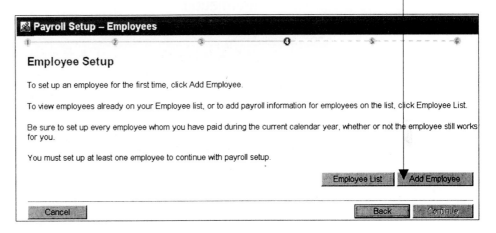

Step 27: When the *New Employee* window appears, click the **Address Info** tab and enter the following information for Richard Batt.

You can also add new employees from the *Employee List* window accessed from the Employees Navigator.

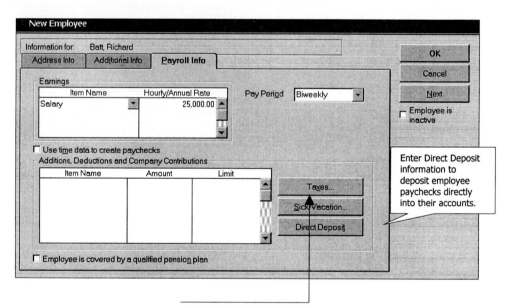

Step 28: Click the **Payroll Info** tab, then enter the following information.

Enter Direct Deposit information to deposit employee paychecks directly into their accounts.

Step 29: Click the **Taxes** button to display the *Taxes for Richard Batt* window.

Step 30: Click the **Federal** tab and enter Filing Status: **Married**, Allowances: **2**.

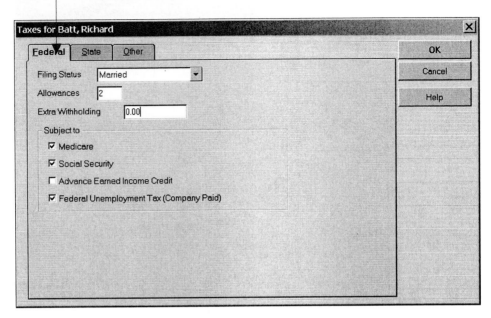

Step 31: Click the **State** tab and enter the following state tax information. Click **OK**.

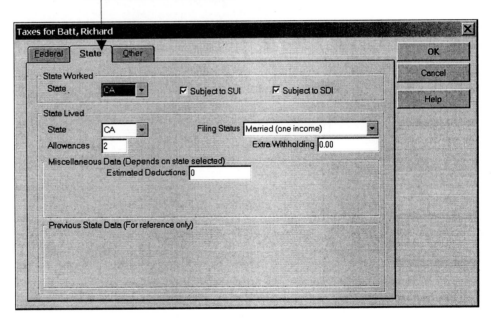

Step 32: If the following window appears, click **OK**.

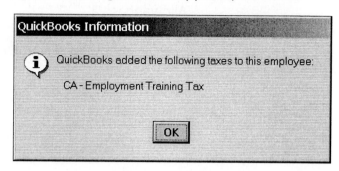

Step 33: Click **OK** to close the *Taxes for Richard Batt* window.

Step 34: Click **OK** to close the *New Employee* window. If asked if you wish to set up payroll information for sick/vacation, select **Leave As Is**.

Step 35: When the *Payroll Setup* window appears, click **Continue**. If necessary, click **Continue** again to return to the Payroll Setup Steps checklist.

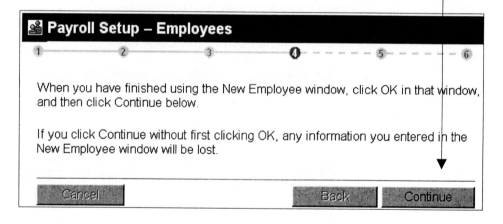

Step 36: In the *Payroll Setup Steps* window, click **Set up year-to-date amounts** to display the following window.

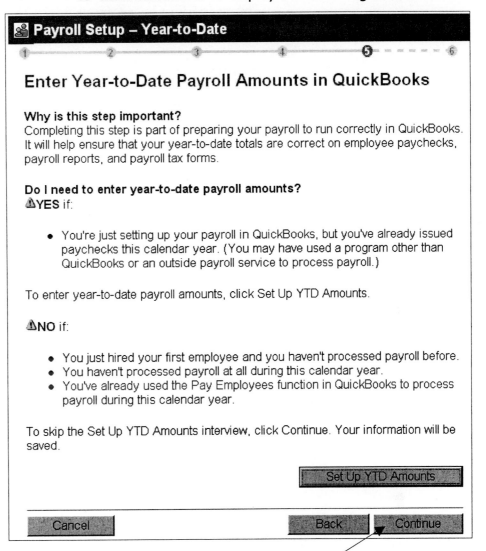

Step 37: If you started to use QuickBooks for payroll in midyear after previously writing some paychecks in the year, you would need to enter year-to-date amounts for payroll. In this instance, since you have just hired your first employee and you haven't processed payroll before, click **Continue** to skip the Set Up YTD Amounts interview.

Step 38: The following *Payroll Setup Steps* checklist should appear as follows. Click **Done** to complete the payroll setup process.

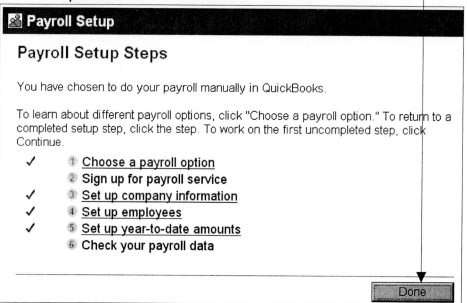

Print Employee List

Print the Employee List as follows:

Step 1: Click **Employees** in the *Navigators* window to display the Employees Navigator.

Step 2: Click the **Employees** icon to display the *Employee List* window.

Step 3: Click the **Reports** button in the *Employee List* window.

Step 4: Select: **Contact List**.

Step 5: The *Employee Contact List* window will display information about the employee, Richard Batt. Print the **Employee Contact List**.

Step 6: Close the *Employee Contact List* window and the *Employee List* window.

Print Paychecks

As you may recall from Chapter 6, processing payroll using QuickBooks involves the following steps:

1. Create paychecks for the employees.

2. Print the paychecks.

3. Pay payroll liabilities, such as federal and state income tax withheld.

4. Print payroll reports.

When you create paychecks using QuickBooks, you must deduct (withhold) from employees' pay for the following items:

• Federal income taxes.

• State income taxes.

• Social security (employee portion).

• Medicare (employee portion).

The amounts withheld for taxes are determined by tax tables that change periodically. Intuit offers two ways for a company to perform payroll calculations:

> QuickBooks 2002 provides a free trial of the Payroll Tax Service. You can continue to use the latest update to calculate payroll without subscribing to the service until February 15 of the following year. After February 15, the tax tables will not function. If you continue to use the trial version, you will not receive online tax table updates after the 60-day trial period and your tax tables could be incorrect.

1. **Use a QuickBooks Payroll Service**. For more information about QuickBooks Payroll Services, see *Learn About Payroll Services* on the Employee Navigator.

2. **Manually calculate payroll taxes**. You can manually calculate tax withholdings and payroll taxes using IRS Circular E. Then enter the amounts in QuickBooks to process payroll.

In this chapter, you will learn how to enter payroll tax amounts manually.

> The Check Date (payday) is the day the check is prepared; the Pay Period Ends date is the last day the employee works during the pay period.

Richard Batt was hired by Fearless Paint Store on February 1, 2003. He is paid an annual salary of $25,000. Richard will be paid biweekly, receiving a paycheck every two weeks. Therefore, the first pay period ends on February 14th and Richard is paid February 15th.

To create a paycheck for Richard Batt:

Step 1: From the Employees Navigator, click the **Pay Employees** icon.

Step 2: If the following window appears, click **No**.

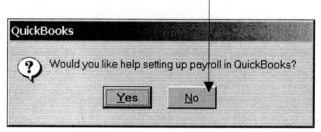

Step 3: If the following window appears, since you do not need to enter year-to-date payroll amounts, click **OK**.

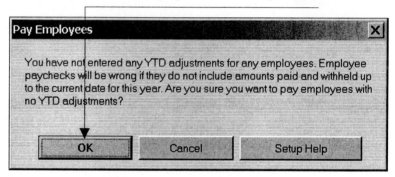

Step 4: When the following *Select Employees to Pay* window appears:

- Select Bank Account: **Checking**.
- Select: **To be printed**.
- Select: **Enter hours and tax amounts before creating paychecks**.
- Enter Check Date: **02/15/2003**.

        ◆ Enter Pay Period Ends: **02/14/2003**.

        ◆ Select Employee: **Richard Batt**.

        ◆ Click **Create**.

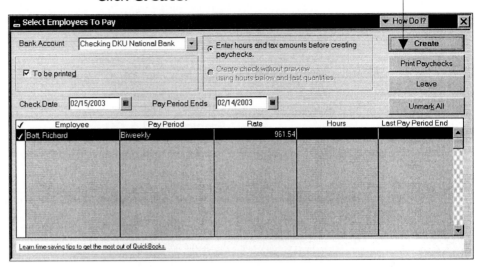

Step 5: If the following window appears, click **Continue** to enter payroll manually.

If you were using a payroll service, you would click **Payroll Options**. Payroll deductions would then be calculated automatically using payroll tax tables.

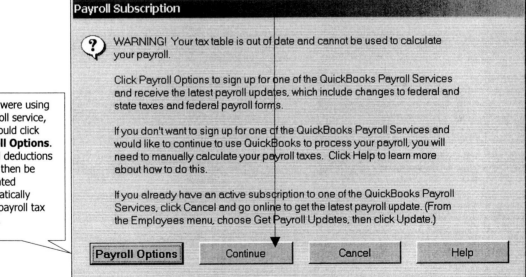

Step 6: When the following *Preview Paycheck* window appears:

- In the *Employee Summary* section, the Salary amount of $961.54 will automatically appear.

- In the *Employee Summary* section, enter Federal Withholding: **75.00**.

- In the *Employee Summary* section, enter Social Security Employee: **60.00**.

- In the *Employee Summary* section, enter Medicare Employee: **14.00**.

- In the *Company Summary* section, enter Social Security Company: **60.00**.

- In the *Company Summary* section, enter Medicare Company: **14.00**.

- Leave all other amounts at $0.00.

- Click the **Create** button to create Richard's paycheck.

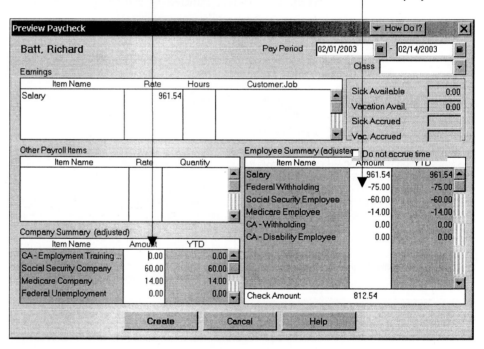

Step 7: When the *Select Employees to Pay* window reappears, click **Print Paychecks**.

Step 8: When the *Select Paychecks to Print* window appears, select **Richard Batt**, then click **OK**.

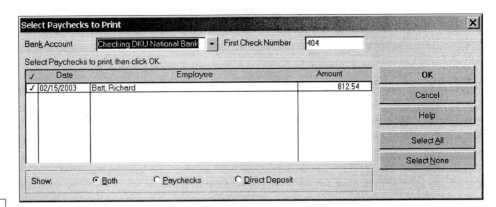

> When voucher checks are used, paystub information is printed on the voucher. If standard checks are used, print paystubs by clicking **File**, **Print Forms, Paystubs**.

Step 9: Select the following print settings:

- ◆ Select **Voucher Checks**.
- ◆ Select **Print company name and address**.
- ◆ Click **Print**.

Step 10: Create and print paychecks to pay Richard Batt through the end of March 2003.

Check Date	Pay Period
03/01/2003	02/15/2003 – 02/28/2003
03/15/2003	03/01/2003 – 03/14/2003
03/29/2003	03/15/2003 – 03/28/2003

Step 11: Click **Leave** to close the *Select Employee to Pay* window.

QuickBooks records gross pay (the total amount the employee earned) as salaries expense and records the amounts due tax agencies as payroll tax liabilities.

Print Payroll Entries in the Journal

When QuickBooks records paychecks and payroll tax liabilities, it converts the transaction to a journal entry with debits and credits.

To view the payroll entry in the Journal:

Step 1: Click **Reports** In the *Navigators* window to display the *Report Finder* window.

Step 2: Select Type of Report: **Accountant & Taxes**.

Step 3: Select Report: **Journal**.

Step 4: Select Dates From: **02/01/2003** To: **02/15/2003**.

Step 5: Click the **Display** button to display the Journal.

Step 6: To view only payroll entries, use a filter:

> Notice that Richard Batt's wages are recorded as payroll expense. Withholdings from his paycheck are recorded as payroll liabilities, amounts owed tax agencies. Payroll taxes that the company must pay, such as the employer share of social security and Medicare, are recorded as payroll expense.

- Click the **Modify Report** button in the upper left corner of the *Reports* window.

- Click the **Filters** tab.

- Choose filter: **Transaction Type**.

- Select Transaction Type: **Paycheck**.

- Click **OK**.

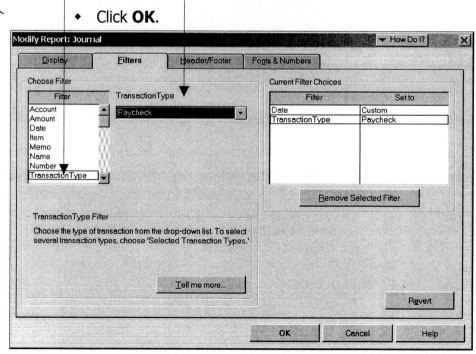

Step 7: Print the Journal report.

Step 8: Close the *Journal* window, then close the *Report Finder* window.

Pay Payroll Liabilities

Payroll liabilities include amounts Fearless Paint Store owes to outside agencies including:

- Federal income taxes withheld from employee paychecks.

- State income taxes withheld from employee paychecks.

- FICA (Social Security and Medicare), both the employee and the employer portions.

- Unemployment taxes.

Fearless Paint Store will pay federal income tax withheld and the employee and employer portions of Social Security and Medicare. Fearless Paint Store will make monthly deposits of these federal taxes by the 10th of the following month.

> Typically, a company deposits payroll withholdings and payroll taxes with a local bank. The local bank then remits the amount to the Internal Revenue Service on behalf of the company.

To pay payroll taxes:

Step 1: Click the **Pay Liabilities** icon on the Employee Navigator.

Step 2: When the *Select Date Range for Liabilities* window appears, enter dates from **02/01/2003** through **02/28/2003**. Click **OK**.

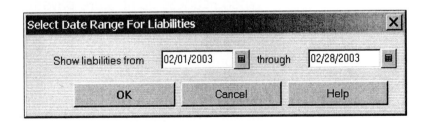

Step 3: When the *Pay Liabilities* window appears:

- Select Checking Account: **Checking**.
- Select Payment Date: **03/10/2003**.
- Check: **To be printed**.
- Select the following amounts to pay:
  ✓ Federal Withholding
  ✓ Medicare Company
  ✓ Medicare Employee
  ✓ Social Security Company
  ✓ Social Security Employee
- Select: **Review liability check to enter expenses/penalties**.

Step 4: Click **Create** to view the check to pay the payroll liabilities selected.

Step 5: To print the check:

- Click the **Print** button at the top of the *Liability Check* window.
- Enter the check number: **408**, then click **OK**.
- Select **Voucher** checks.
- Select **Print company name and address**.
- Click **Print**.

Step 6: Record and print the check to pay payroll liabilities for the month of March 2003 to be paid on April 10, 2003.

When Fearless Paint Store pays federal payroll taxes, it must file a Form 941 to report the amount of federal income tax, social security, and Medicare for the quarter. QuickBooks tracks the amounts to report on the Form 941.

To print Form 941 (Employer's Quarterly Federal Tax Return) for Fearless Paint Store for the first quarter of 2003 (January through March 2003):

Step 1: Click the **Process Payroll Forms** icon on the Employees Navigator.

Step 2: Select Payroll Form: **941 Form**.

Step 3: When the *Form 941* window appears:
- Select Date Quarter Ended: **03/31/2003**.
- Select State Code: **CA**.
- Click **Next** twice.

Step 4: Enter number of employees: **1**.

Step 5: Click **Next** until Overpayment appears in the window. Select: **Apply overpayment to next return**. Complete whether monthly or semiweekly depositor.

Step 6: Click **Next** until Print Form 941 appears on the screen. Print **Form 941**.

Step 7: Close the *Form 941* window.

Form 941 is filed with the IRS to report the amount of federal income tax, Medicare and social security associated with the company's payroll for the first quarter of the year. Form 941 for the first quarter of the year must be filed by April 30.

Print Payroll Reports

QuickBooks provides payroll reports that summarize amounts paid to employees and amounts paid in payroll taxes. Payroll reports can be accessed using the Report Finder.

To print the Payroll Summary report:

Step 1: Click **Reports** in the *Navigators* window to display the *Report Finder* window.

Step 2: Select Type of Report: **Employees & Payroll**.

Step 3: Select Report: **Payroll Summary**.

Step 4: Select Dates From: **02/01/2003** To: **02/28/2003**.

Step 5: Print the Payroll Summary report using **Portrait** orientation. Insert **your name** and **Chapter 11** in the report footer.

Back Up Chapter 11

Back up your Chapter 11 file to your floppy disk. Use the file name: [your name] Chapter 11.

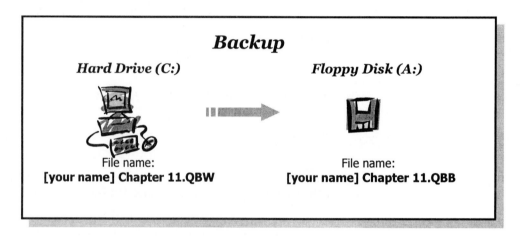

Step 1: 🖫 Insert the **Chapter 11** backup disk in drive A.

Step 2: Click **File, Back Up**.

Step 3: Enter the filename: **[your name] Chapter 11.QBB**. Enter location: **A:**.

Step 4: Click **Back Up**.

Step 5: Click **OK** after the backup is complete.

If you are continuing your computer session, close the company file and then proceed to Project 11.1.

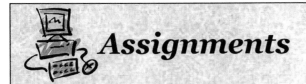

Assignments

Activity 11.1: Web Quest

Learn more about filing Forms 940 and 941 by visiting the IRS web site.

Step 1: Go to the www.irs.gov web site.

Step 2: Print instructions for preparing and filing Form 940.

Step 3: Print instructions for preparing and filing Form 941.

Activity 11.2: Web Quest

Employers must give employees Form W-2 each year summarizing wages and withholdings for tax purposes. In addition, employers must file Form W-3 with the IRS. Form W-3 summarizes the payroll information provided on the W-2 forms.

To learn more about filing Forms W-2 and W-3, visit the IRS web site.

Step 1: Go to www.irs.gov web site.

Step 2: Print instructions for preparing and filing Form W-2.

Step 3: Print instructions for preparing and filing Form W-3.

Computer Accounting with QuickBooks 2002
Chapter 11 Printout Checklist
Name:_____ **Date:**_____

☑	***Printout Checklist – Chapter 11***
☐	Employee Contact List
☐	Voucher Paychecks
☐	Journal
☐	Payroll Liability Check
☐	Form 941
☐	Payroll Summary Report
☑	***Printout Checklist – Activity 11.1***
☐	Form 940 and Form 941 Instructions
☑	***Printout Checklist – Activity 11.2***
☐	Form W-2 and Form W-3 Instructions

Virtual Company Project 11.1

Project 11.1: Max's Mowers and More: Payroll

Scenario

Max's Mowers and More hired Ryan Brothers as a sales clerk for evenings and weekends. You will keep the payroll records for Max's Mowers and More and print Ryan's payroll checks.

> Project 10.1 must be completed before starting Project 11.1.

Task 1: Restore Company File

Restore Project 10.1 backup to the C: drive, renaming the file Project 11.1.

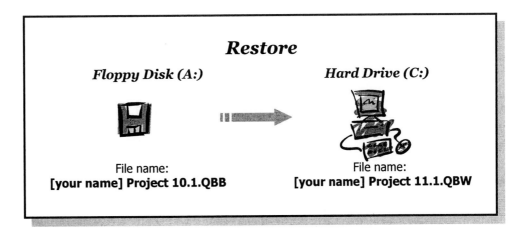

Restore

| *Floppy Disk (A:)* | | *Hard Drive (C:)* |

File name:
[your name] Project 10.1.QBB

File name:
[your name] Project 11.1.QBW

Step 1: ⊟ Insert the **Project 10.1** backup disk into drive A.

Step 2: Click **Restore a backup file** (or click **File, Restore**).

Step 3: Identify the backup file:

- Filename: **[your name] Project 10.1.QBB**.
- Location: **A:**.

Step 4: Identify the restored file:

- Filename: **[your name] Project 11.1.QBW**.
- Location: **C:\Program Files\Intuit\QuickBooks Premier**.

Step 5: Click **Restore.** If prompted, enter your User ID and Password.

Step 6: Change the company name to:
[your name] Project 11.1 Max's Mowers and More.
(To change the company name, select Company (menu), Company Information.)

Your Project 10.1 backup file has now been restored to the C: drive as Project 11.1.QBW

Task 2: Set Up Payroll

Set up QuickBooks Payroll for Max's Mowers and More by completing the following steps.

Step 1: Enable QuickBooks Payroll for Max's Mowers and More. (Click Preferences on the Company Navigator, click Payroll & Employees, Company Preferences, Full Payroll Features.)

Step 2: Set up payroll for Max's Mowers and More using the employee information on the following page.

First Name	Ryan
Last Name	Brothers
Address Info:	
Address	220 Mercy Drive
City	Bayshore
State	CA
ZIP	94326
Phone	415-555-9876
SS No.	343-21-6767
Type	Regular
Hired	03/01/2003
Payroll Info:	
Hourly Regular Rate	$8.00
Pay Period	Weekly
Federal and State Filing Status	Single
Allowances	1
State Tax	CA
Federal ID Number	37-7879146
State ID Number	888-8888-8
State Allowances	1
Subject to CA Training Tax?	No

Task 3: Print Employee List

Print the Employee Contact List.

Task 4: Print Paychecks

Using the information on the following page, create and print paychecks for Max's Mowers and More employee, Ryan Brothers. Use standard checks and print payroll stubs (File, Print Forms, Paystubs).

Check Date	Payroll Period	Hours Worked*
March 5	March 1-3	12
March 12	March 4-10	30
March 19	March 11-17	32
March 26	March 18-24	28
April 2	March 25-31	31

*Enter hours worked in the *Preview Paycheck* window.

To display the QuickMath Calculator:
1. Place your cursor in the federal withholding field, then press the **=** key.
2. Enter calculations. Use the ***** key to multiply.
3. Press **Enter** to enter the amount into the field.

Assume the following rates for withholdings:

Federal income tax	20.00%
Social security (employee)	6.20%
Social security (company)	6.20%
Medicare (employee)	1.45%
Medicare (company)	1.45%
State (CA) income tax	5.00%

Note that the wage base limit will not be exceeded for social security.

✓ **Ryan Brothers' March 12th paycheck is $161.64.**

Task 5: Pay Payroll Liability

On April 10, pay the payroll tax liability for federal income tax, Social Security, Medicare, and state income tax as of 03/31/2003.

Task 6: Print Form 941

Print Form 941 for the first quarter of 2003 for Max's Mowers and More. Using Form 941, determine the following:

1. Net taxes owed as listed on Form 941: $_____

2. Total deposits for taxes for the quarter: $_____

3. The overpayment for the quarter: $_____

Task 7: Back Up Project 11.1

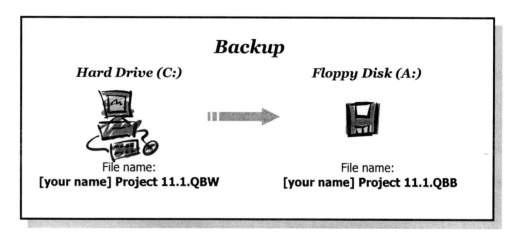

Backup

Hard Drive (C:)   Floppy Disk (A:)

File name: File name:
[your name] Project 11.1.QBW   **[your name] Project 11.1.QBB**

Step 1: 🖫 Insert the **Chapter 11** backup disk in drive A.

Step 2: Click **File, Back Up**.

Step 3: Enter the filename: **[your name] Project 11.1.QBB**. Enter location: **A:**.

Step 4: Click **Back Up**.

Step 5: Click **OK** after the backup is complete. Close the company file.

Computer Accounting with QuickBooks 2002
Project 11.1 Printout Checklist

Name:_____ Date:_____

☑	*Printout Checklist – Project 11.1*
☐	Employee Contact List
☐	Paychecks
☐	Paystubs
☐	Payroll Liability Check
☐	Form 941

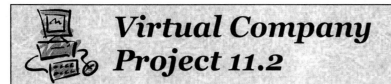

Virtual Company Project 11.2

> This project is a continuation of Project 10.2. Project 10.2 must be completed before you can start Project 11.2.

Project 11.2: Your Choice

Scenario

In Project 10.2 you created a new merchandising corporation. Initial decisions were made regarding the new business.

In this assignment, you will create payroll information and transactions for the new business. Assume the start date for your new employee(s) is 01/01/2003 or later.

Task 1: Option 1

You can complete this project individually (Option 1A) or in teams (Option 1B). Ask your instructor whether you should use Option 1A or 1B to complete this project.

✐ Circle the option below that you are using for the project.

Option 1A: Complete Project 11.2 individually.

TEAMS **Option 1B:** Complete Project 11.2 in teams.

Ask your instructor for the student password to access the remaining instructions for Virtual Company Project 11.2 at the following website:

www.mhhe.com/ulmer2002

Notes:

12   *Advanced Topics*

Scenario

During the month of January 2003 you continue to operate your painting service while still managing Fearless Paint Store. You know that you need to budget for the coming year, providing you an opportunity to develop a business plan for the company. In addition, you must prepare a tax return for Fearless Painting Service (Schedule C) to attach to your personal 1040 tax return.

In the new year, several commercial customers have approached you about custom painting for their offices and restaurants. Moreover, you continue to get referrals from your satisfied customers. The new customers want bids and estimates before they award contracts. Also, since some of these new jobs would require months to complete, you want to use progress billing (bill customers as the job progresses) in order to bring in a steady cash flow for your business.

12 *Learning Objectives*

In Chapter 12, you will learn the following QuickBooks activities:

Introduction

This chapter covers some of the more advanced features of QuickBooks software using Fearless Painting Service company files.

To begin Chapter 12, first start QuickBooks software and then restore your backup file for Fearless Painting Service, the company you created in Chapters 8 and 9.

Start QuickBooks software by clicking on the **QuickBooks** desktop icon or click **Start**, **Programs**, **QuickBooks Premier**, **QuickBooks Premier**.

Restore Back Up

Activity 9 must be completed before starting Chapter 12.

Restore your Activity 9 backup for Fearless Painting Service to the C drive, renaming the file Chapter 12.QBW.

Restore

Floppy Disk (A:)		*Hard Drive (C:)*
File name: **[your name] Activity 9.QBB**		File name: **[your name] Chapter 12.QBW**

Step 1: Insert the **Chapter 9** backup disk into drive A.

Step 2: Click **Restore a backup file** (or click **File, Restore**).

Step 3: Identify the backup file:

   ◆ Filename: **[your name] Activity 9.QBB**.

   ◆ Location: **A:**.

Step 4: Identify the restored file:

- Filename: **[your name] Chapter 12.QBW**.

- Location: **C:\Program Files\Intuit\QuickBooks Premier**.

Step 5: Click **Restore.** If prompted, enter your User ID and Password.

You have now restored the Activity 9.QBB backup file to the hard drive and renamed the file on the hard drive: Chapter 12.QBW.

Step 6: Change the company name to:
[your name] Fearless Painting Service Chapter 12.
(To change the company name, select Company (menu), Company Information.)

Income Tax Reports

QuickBooks provides you with the ability to print out an income tax summary, a summary of income and expenses to use when preparing a business tax return.

Corporations file Form 1120 and Subchapter S corporations file Form 1120S.

Fearless Painting Service is a sole proprietorship that files tax form Schedule C. Schedule C is attached to the owner's personal tax return (Form 1040), and income from the business is included on the owner's tax return.

To review taxable income and tax deductions for the business, print an Income Tax Summary report and an Income Tax Detail report. The Income Tax Summary report summarizes amounts for each tax line on the return. The Income Tax Detail report provides the supporting transaction detail for each tax line.

Income Tax Preparation Report

First, print an Income Tax Preparation report that lists the Tax Line for each account. Review this report to confirm that the correct Tax Line is shown for each account.

To print an Income Tax Preparation report for Fearless Painting Service:

Step 1: Click **Reports** in the *Navigators* window to display the *Report Finder* window.

Step 2: Select Type of Report: **Accountant & Taxes**.

Step 3: Select Report: **Income Tax Preparation**.

Step 4: Select Dates From: **01/01/2002** to **12/31/2002**.

Step 5: Print the Income Tax Preparation report. Insert **your name** and **Chapter 12** in the report footer. Select **Portrait** orientation.

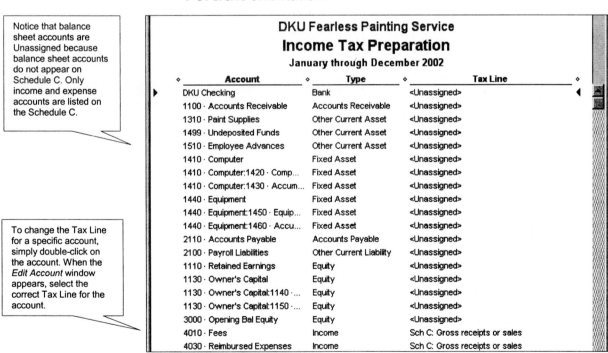

Notice that balance sheet accounts are Unassigned because balance sheet accounts do not appear on Schedule C. Only income and expense accounts are listed on the Schedule C.

To change the Tax Line for a specific account, simply double-click on the account. When the *Edit Account* window appears, select the correct Tax Line for the account.

DKU Fearless Painting Service
Income Tax Preparation
January through December 2002

Account	Type	Tax Line
DKU Checking	Bank	<Unassigned>
1100 · Accounts Receivable	Accounts Receivable	<Unassigned>
1310 · Paint Supplies	Other Current Asset	<Unassigned>
1499 · Undeposited Funds	Other Current Asset	<Unassigned>
1510 · Employee Advances	Other Current Asset	<Unassigned>
1410 · Computer	Fixed Asset	<Unassigned>
1410 · Computer:1420 · Comp...	Fixed Asset	<Unassigned>
1410 · Computer:1430 · Accum...	Fixed Asset	<Unassigned>
1440 · Equipment	Fixed Asset	<Unassigned>
1440 · Equipment:1450 · Equip...	Fixed Asset	<Unassigned>
1440 · Equipment:1460 · Accu...	Fixed Asset	<Unassigned>
2110 · Accounts Payable	Accounts Payable	<Unassigned>
2100 · Payroll Liabilities	Other Current Liability	<Unassigned>
1110 · Retained Earnings	Equity	<Unassigned>
1130 · Owner's Capital	Equity	<Unassigned>
1130 · Owner's Capital:1140 ·...	Equity	<Unassigned>
1130 · Owner's Capital:1150 ·...	Equity	<Unassigned>
3000 · Opening Bal Equity	Equity	<Unassigned>
4010 · Fees	Income	Sch C: Gross receipts or sales
4030 · Reimbursed Expenses	Income	Sch C: Gross receipts or sales

Step 6:   Close the *Income Tax Preparation* window.

Review the Tax Line for each account to verify that the correct Tax Line is listed. If necessary, correct the Tax Line.

Income Tax Summary Report

To print an Income Tax Summary for Fearless Painting Service:

Step 1:   From the *Report Finder* window, select Type of Report: **Accountant & Taxes**.

Step 2:   Select Report: **Income Tax Summary**.

Step 3:   Select Dates From: **01/01/2002** to **12/31/2002**.

Step 4:   Print the Income Tax Summary report.

> ✓   **On Schedule C, Fearless Painting Service should report Gross Receipts or Sales of $34,560.00.**

The Tax Summary contains information for Schedule C, the tax schedule used by Fearless Painting Service (a sole proprietorship). Schedule C is attached to the owner's 1040 tax return.

How accounts are listed depends upon the Tax Line selected for the specific account. If your accounts do not appear as shown here, edit the Tax Line for the account (Chart of Accounts, Edit). For more information, see Income Tax Preparation Report in this Chapter.

Many small businesses use the Cash Basis for income tax purposes. Tax Line Unassigned (balance sheet) of $31,285 consists of balance sheet account balances. Only income and expenses appear on Schedule C; balance sheet amounts are not listed on Schedule C.

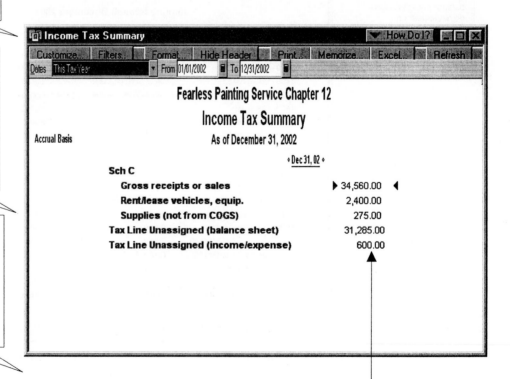

Step 5: To view more detail for Tax Line Unassigned (income/expense) on the Income Tax Summary report shown on the previous page, double-click on the amount shown for that item: **600.00**.

Step 6: The following *Tax Line by Account* window will appear, displaying additional detail about the tax line. Print the Tax Line by Account report.

> Depreciation expense is a tax deduction on Schedule C. In this case, straight-line depreciation is used. Current tax law also permits using MACRS (Modified Accelerated Cost Recovery System) to calculate depreciation. Seek the assistance of a tax professional when calculating depreciation deductions for a tax return.

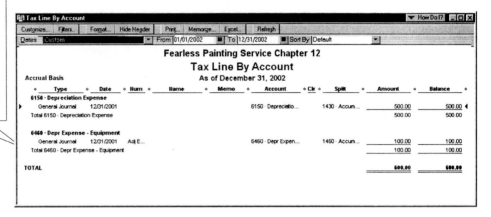

Step 7: Close the *Tax Line by Account* window and the *Income Tax Summary* window.

Income Tax Detail Report

The Income Tax Detail report provides supporting detail for the Income Tax Summary report. The Income Tax Detail report lists the detailed transactions summarized for each tax line of the Income Tax Summary report.

To print the Income Tax Detail report:

Step 1: From the *Report Finder* window, select Type of Report: **Accountant & Taxes**.

Step 2: Select Report: **Income Tax Detail**.

Step 3: Select Dates From: **01/01/2002** to **12/31/2002**.

Step 4: Print the Income Tax Detail report.

Step 5: Close the *Income Tax Detail* window.

Review the Income Tax Summary report and the Income Tax Detail report to verify that each of the items listed are appropriate tax deductions and taxable income.

Income Tax Return

After reviewing the QuickBooks tax reports, the next step is to prepare a tax return for the business. QuickBooks offers two ways to facilitate tax return preparation:

1. Manually copy information from the Income Tax Summary report to your business tax return.

2. Import your QuickBooks tax data into Intuit's TurboTax® software and then use TurboTax to complete your tax return. To import your QuickBooks tax data into TurboTax software, just start the TurboTax software and then import your QuickBooks company file into TurboTax.

Budgets

As Fearless Painting Service enters its second year of operation, planning for future expansion is important to its continued success. You develop the following budget for 2003.

- ◆ January sales are expected to be $3,000. Sales are expected to increase by 5% each month thereafter.

- ◆ Paint supplies expense is budgeted at $60 per month.

- ◆ The van lease will increase to $300 per month. (Use Account No. 6290.)

To prepare budgets for Fearless Painting Service using QuickBooks:

Step 1: Select the **Company** menu, then select **Set Up Budgets**.

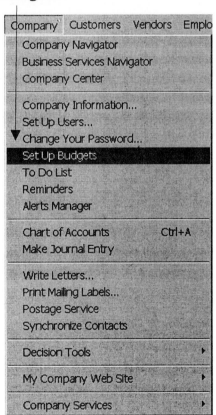

Step 2: When the following *Set Up Budgets* window appears:

♦ Select Budget for Fiscal Year: **2003**.

♦ Select Account: **4050 Sales**.

♦ Enter Budget Amount for January 2003: **3000.00**.

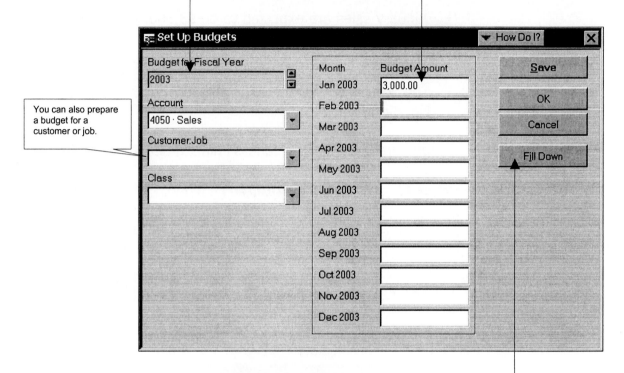

You can also prepare a budget for a customer or job.

♦ Click **Fill Down**.

♦ When the *Fill Down* window appears, enter the percentage increase that you would like to achieve: **5.0%**. Click **OK**.

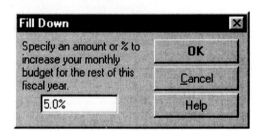

♦ The *Set Up Budgets* window should now appear with budget amounts increasing by 5% each month. Click **Save.**

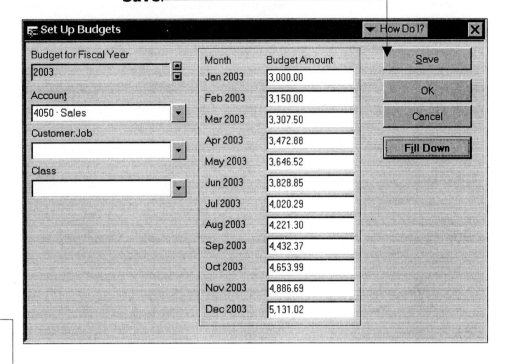

Tip: Enter the January amount and then enter 0.0% increase in the *Fill Down* window.

Step 3: Enter budget amounts for paint supplies expense and then equipment rental expense for the van.

Step 4: Click **OK** to close the *Set Up Budgets* window.

To print the budgets you have created for Fearless Painting Service:

Step 1: From the *Report Finder* window, select Type of Report: **Budget**.

Step 2: Select Report: **Profit & Loss Budget Overview**.

Step 3: Select Dates From: **01/01/2003** To: **12/31/2003**.

Step 4: Print the Profit & Loss Budget Overview using **Landscape** orientation.

Step 5: Close the *Profit & Loss Budget Overview* window.

Estimates

Note: If the Estimates icon does not appear on your screen, turn on the Estimates preference by clicking **Company**, **Preferences** icon, **Jobs and Estimates** icon, and **Company Preference** tab. Select **Yes** to indicate you create estimates.

Often customers ask for a bid or estimate of job cost before awarding a contract. Fearless Painting Service needs to estimate job costs that are accurate in order not to *overbid* and lose the job or *underbid* and lose money on the job.

To prepare a job cost estimate for Fearless Painting Service:

Step 1: Click the **Estimates** icon on the Customer Navigator.

Step 2: When the *Create Estimates* window appears, add a new customer as follows:

- From the drop-down customer list, select: **<Add New>**.

- Enter Customer Name: **Liz's Cafe**.

- Enter Address: **10 Broadway Blvd., Bayshore, CA 94326**.

- Click the *Job Info* tab, then enter Job Status: **Pending**.

- Click **OK** to close the *New Customer* window.

Step 3: Next, enter estimate information in the *Create Estimates* window:

- Select Template: **Custom Estimate**.

- Select Date: **01/05/2003**.

- Enter Item: **Labor: Exterior Painting**.

- Enter Quantity **40**.

- Enter a second item: **Labor: Interior Painting**.

- Enter Quantity: **65**.

The estimate can be given to a customer when bidding on a job.

Step 4: Print the estimate, then click **Save & Close** to close the *Create Estimates* window.

Progress Billing

When undertaking a job that lasts a long period of time, a business often does not want to wait until the job is completed to receive payment for its work. The business often incurs expenses in performing the job that must be paid before the business receives payment from customers. This can create a cash flow problem. One solution to this problem is progress billing.

Progress billing permits a business to bill customers as the job progresses. Thus, the business receives partial payments from the customer before the project is completed.

After you give Liz's Cafe your estimate of the paint job cost, Liz awards you the contract. The job will last about three weeks. However, instead of waiting three weeks to bill Liz, you bill Liz every week so that you will have cash to pay your bills.

To use progress billing in QuickBooks, first you must turn on the preference for progress invoicing.

To select the preference for progress invoicing:

Step 1: Click **Company** on the *Navigators* window to display the Company Navigator.

Step 2: Click the **Preferences** icon in the Company Navigator.

Step 3: When the following *Preferences* window appears, click the **Jobs & Estimates** icon on the left scrollbar.

Step 4: Click the **Company Preferences** tab.

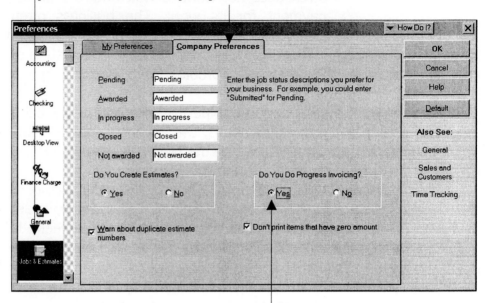

Step 5: Select **Yes** to indicate you want to use Progress Invoicing.

Step 6: Check: **Don't print items that have zero amount**.

Step 7: Click **OK** to save the Progress Invoicing preference and close the *Preferences* window.

After selecting the Progress Invoicing preference, the Progress Invoice template is now available on the *Create Invoices* window.

To create a Progress Invoice:

Step 1:   Click the **Invoices** icon on the Customer Navigator.

Step 2:   When the *Create Invoices* window appears, select Customer: **Liz's Cafe**.

Step 3:   Select the **Liz's Cafe** estimate to invoice, then click **OK**.

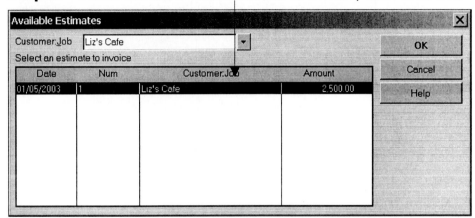

Step 4:   When the *Create Progress Invoice Based on Estimate* window appears:

   ◆ Select: **Create invoice for the entire estimate (100%)**.

   ◆ Click **OK**.

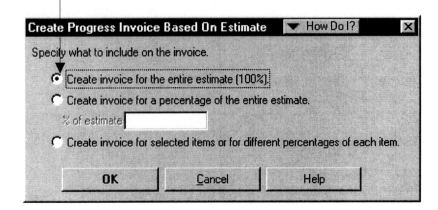

Step 5: When the following *Create Invoices* window appears, the Form Template should now be: **Progress Invoice**.

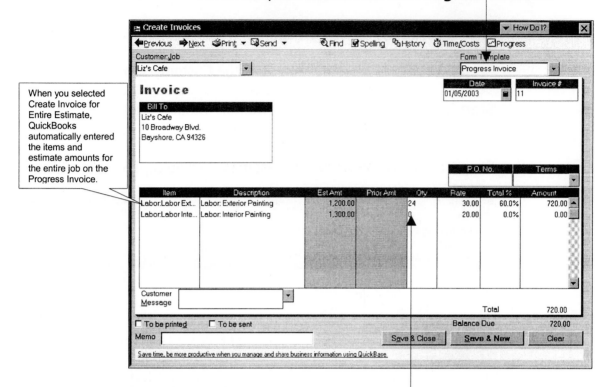

When you selected Create Invoice for Entire Estimate, QuickBooks automatically entered the items and estimate amounts for the entire job on the Progress Invoice.

Step 6: Enter the number of hours actually worked on the Liz's Cafe job.

Notice the Total % column now shows 60% for Exterior Painting Labor, indicating 60% of estimated hours have been worked.

+ Enter Exterior Painting Labor Quantity: **24**.

+ Enter Interior Painting Labor Quantity: **0**.

Step 7: Print the Progress Invoice.

Step 8: Click **Save & Close** to close the *Create Invoices* window.

The following week you complete the exterior painting for Liz's Cafe and work 6.5 hours on interior painting.

Create another progress invoice for Liz's Cafe by completing the following steps.

Step 1: Display the *Create Invoices* window.

Step 2: Select Customer: **Liz's Cafe**.

Step 3: Select the **Liz's Cafe** estimate to invoice, then click OK.

Step 4: When the following *Create Progress Invoice Based on Estimate* window appears:

◆ Select **Create invoice for selected items or for different percentages of each item**.

◆ Click **OK**.

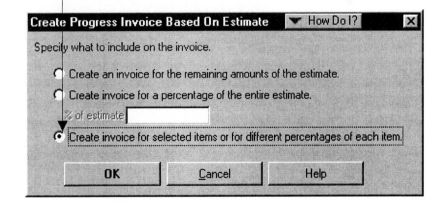

Step 5: When the following *Specify Invoice Amounts for Items on Estimate* window appears:

- ◆ ✓ Check: **Show Quantity and Rate**.
- ◆ ✓ Check: **Show Percentage**.
- ◆ Enter Exterior Painting Quantity: **16**.
- ◆ Enter Interior Painting Quantity: **6.5**.
- ◆ Click **OK** to record these amounts on the progress invoice.

Notice that the 24 hours you entered earlier appears under Prior Qty.

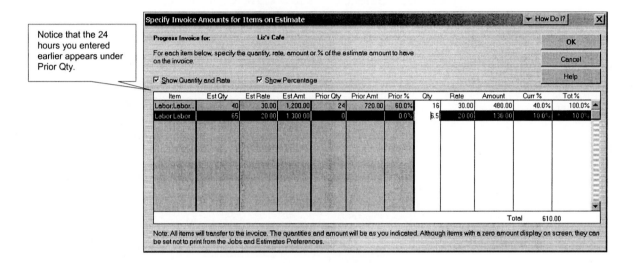

Step 6: When the *Create Invoices* window appears, change the date of the Progress Invoice to: **01/12/2003**.

Step 7: Print the invoice.

✓   ***The invoice total is $610.00.***

Step 8: Click **Save & Close** to record the Progress Invoice and close the *Create Invoices* window.

Customer payments received on Progress Invoices are recorded in the same manner as customer payments for standard invoices (See Chapter 4).

Credit Card Sales

As a convenience to your customers, you agree to accept credit cards as payment for services you provide. Liz's Cafe would like to make its first payment using a VISA credit card.

In QuickBooks, you record credit card payments in the same manner that you record a payment by check; however, instead of selecting Check as the payment method, you select the type of credit card used.

To record a credit card sale using QuickBooks:

Step 1: Click **Receive Payments** on the Customers Navigator to display the *Receive Payments* window.

Step 2: When the *Receive Payments* window appears, select Received From: **Liz's Cafe**. QuickBooks will automatically display any unpaid invoices for Liz's Cafe.

> If the specific credit card is not listed on the Payment Method list, select **Add New**, then enter the name of the credit card.

Step 3: Enter the Date: **01/30/2003**.

Step 4: Enter Amount: **720.00**.

Step 5: Select Payment Method: **VISA**.

Step 6: Enter Card No.: **13575757578013**. Enter Exp. Date: **12/2003**.

Step 7: Select outstanding Invoice No. 11, dated **01/05/2003**.

Step 8: Your *Receive Payments* window should appear as shown below.

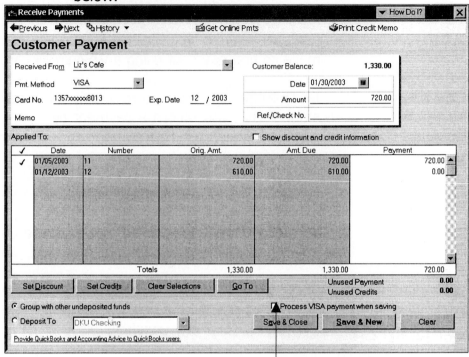

Step 9: Check **Process VISA payment when saving** to learn more about using QuickBooks Merchant Account Service that permits you to process and authorize customer credit card payments from QuickBooks. In addition, payments are automatically processed. Read the following *Tell Me More* window to learn more about credit card processing in QuickBooks.

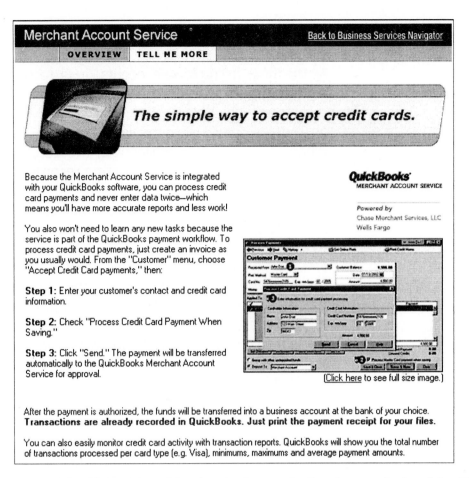

Step 10: Close the Merchant Account Services window(s). To record the customer payment and close the *Receive Payments* window, click **Save & Close**.

> Banks will accept bank credit card payments, such as Visa or MasterCard, the same as a cash or check deposit. You can record the credit card payment as a deposit to your checking account.

Step 11: Since you are not using the Merchant Account Services, when the credit card payment is deposited at the bank on 01/30/2003, record the deposit just as you would a check or cash deposit.

   ◆ Click the **Deposit** icon on the Customers Navigator.

   ◆ Select Liz's Cafe credit card payment for deposit. Click **OK**.

   ◆ Print the deposit summary.

Bad Debts

At the time a credit sale occurs, it is recorded as an increase to sales and an increase to accounts receivable. Occasionally a company is unable to collect a customer payment and must write off the customer's account as a bad debt or uncollectible account. When an account is uncollectible, the account receivable is written off or removed from the accounting records.

There are two different methods that can be used to account for bad debts:

1. Direct write-off method. This method records bad debt expense when it becomes apparent that the customer is not going to pay the amount due. If the direct write-off method is used, the customer's uncollectible account receivable is removed and bad debt expense is recorded whenever a specific customer's account becomes uncollectible. The direct write-off method is used for tax purposes.

2. Allowance method. The allowance method *estimates* bad debt expense and establishes an allowance or reserve for uncollectible accounts. When using the allowance method, uncollectible accounts expense is estimated in advance of the write-off. The estimate can be calculated as a percentage of sales or as a percentage of accounts receivable. (For example, 2% of credit sales might be estimated to be uncollectible.) This method should be used if uncollectible accounts have a material effect on the company's financial statements used by investors and creditors and the company must comply with Generally Accepted Accounting Principles (GAAP).

Fearless Painting Service will use the direct write-off method and record the uncollectible accounts expense when an account actually becomes uncollectible.

When Liz paid the bill for $720 for Liz's Cafe, she tells you that her business has plummeted since a new restaurant opened next door. To your dismay, she tells you her cafe is closing and she will not be able to pay you the remainder that she owes. You decide to write off Liz's remaining $610 account balance as uncollectible.

First, create an account for tracking uncollectible accounts expense, and then write off the customer's uncollectible account receivable.

To add a Bad Debt Expense account to the Chart of Accounts for Fearless Painting Service, complete the following steps:

Step 1: Click the **Chart of Accounts** on the Company Navigator to display the *Chart of Accounts* window.

Step 2: Add the following account to the chart of accounts.

Account Type	Expense
Account Number	6700
Account Name	Bad Debt Expense
Description	Bad Debt Expense
Tax Line	Sch C: Bad debts from sales/services

Next, record the write-off of the uncollectible account receivable. There are three different methods to record a bad debt using QuickBooks:

1. Make a journal entry to remove the customer's account receivable (credit Accounts Receivable) and debit either Bad Debt Expense or the Allowance for Uncollectible Accounts.

2. Use the *Receive Payments* window (Discount Info button) to record the write-off of the customer's uncollectible account.

> If you charged sales tax on the transaction, use this method.

3. Use the *Credit Memo* window to record uncollectible accounts.

To record the write-off of an uncollectible accounts receivable using the *Receive Payments* window, complete the following steps:

Step 1: Click the **Receive Payments** icon on the Customer Navigator to display the *Receive Payments* window.

Step 2: When the *Receive Payment* window appears, select Received From: **Liz's Cafe**.

Step 3: Enter Date: **01/30/2003**.

This memo will appear in the customer's account to provide a payment history for the customer.

Step 4: Leave the Amount as **$0.00**.

Step 5: Enter Memo: **Write off Uncollectible Account**.

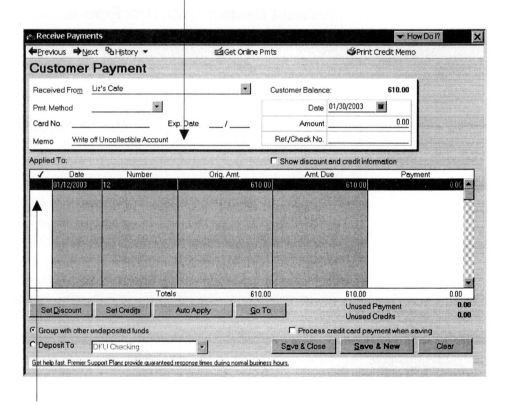

Step 6: Select the outstanding invoice dated: **01/12/2003**.

Step 7: Because the Amount field is $0.00, the following warning will appear. Click **OK**.

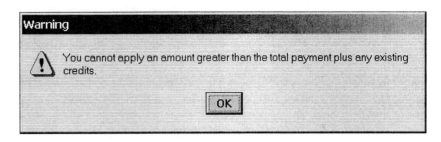

Step 8: Click the **Set Discount** button in the *Receive Payments* window.

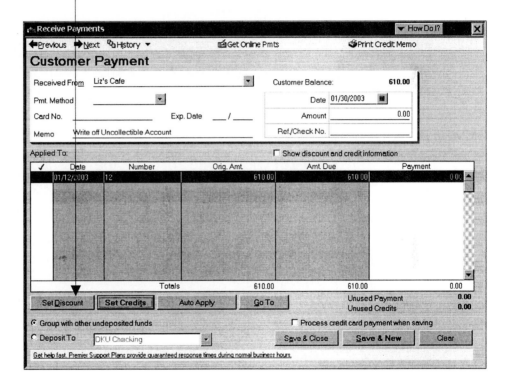

Step 9: When the following *Discount and Credits* window appears:

- Enter Amount of Discount: **610.00**.
- Select Discount Account: **6700 Bad Debt Expense**.

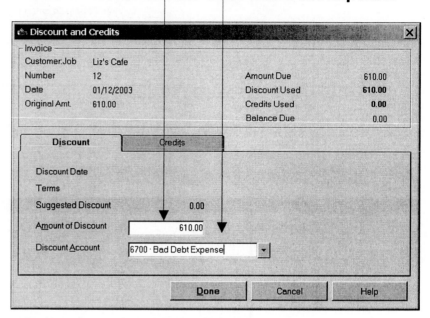

Step 10: Click **Done** to close the *Discount and Credits* window. Click **Save & Close** again to close the *Receive Payments* window.

To view Liz's Cafe account:

Step 1: Click **Reports** in the *Navigators* window to display the *Report Finder* window.

Step 2: Select Type of Report: **Customers & Receivables**.

Step 3: Select Report: **Customer Balance Detail**.

Step 4: Select Date: **All**.

Step 5: Click **Display** to display the *Customer Balance Detail* report.

Step 6: Customize the Customer Balance Detail report so the Memo field appears on the report:

- ◆ Click the **Modify Report** button to display the *Modify Report* window.

- ◆ Click the **Display** tab.

- ◆ Select Columns: **Memo**.

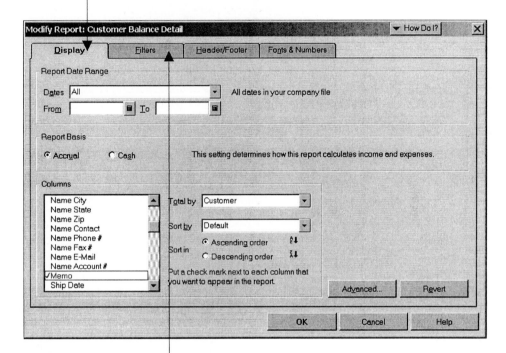

Step 7: Next, create a filter to display only Liz's Cafe account information.

- ◆ Click the **Filters** tab in the *Modify Reports* window.

♦ Select Filter: **Name**.

♦ Select Name: **Liz's Cafe**.

♦ Click **OK** to close the *Modify Report* window.

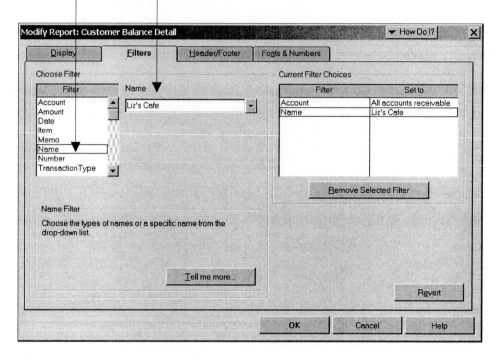

Step 8: The *Customer Balance Detail* window should now appear as shown below. Double-click on the entry for 01/30/2003 to drill down to the *Receive Payments* window that displays the entry to write-off $610 of Liz's account. Close the *Receive Payments* window.

The write-off on 01/30/2003 reduced the account receivable balance by $610.

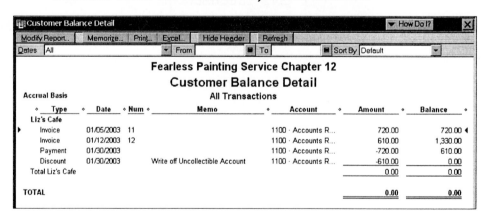

Step 9: Print the *Customer Balance Detail* report for Liz's Cafe from **01/01/2003** to **01/30/2003**.

The aging report for accounts receivable (discussed in Chapter 4) provides information about the age of customers' accounts receivable which can be useful for tracking and managing collections.

To reduce uncollectible customer accounts, some companies adopt a policy that requires customers to make a deposit or advance payment before beginning work on a project. In addition, companies often evaluate the creditworthiness of customers before extending credit.

Memorized Reports

On March 1, 2003, a potential buyer contacts you, expressing an interest in purchasing your painting service business. The potential buyer offers to purchase your business for a price equal to five times the operating income of the business.

The buyer asks for a copy of the prior year financial statements for his accountant to review.

▣ Profit & Loss (P&L)

▣ Balance sheet

▣ Statement of cash flows

When you prepare the reports, you create memorized reports for future use. To memorize a report, first create the report and then use the memorize feature of QuickBooks.

To create a memorized Profit and Loss report for Fearless Painting Service:

Step 1: Click **Reports** in the *Navigators* window to display the *Report Finder* window.

Step 2: Select Type of Report: **Company & Financial**.

Step 3: Select Report: **Profit & Loss Standard**.

Step 4: Select Date: From: **01/01/2002** to: **12/31/2002**.

Step 5: Click **Display** to display the Profit and Loss report.

✓ ***Income for Fearless Painting Service was $31,285. Therefore, the purchase price of the business would be $156,425 (five times income of $31,285).***

Step 6: To memorize the report:

* Click the **Memorize** button at the top of *the Profit and Loss* window.

* When the following *Memorize Report* window appears, enter Memorized Report Name: **Profit and Loss**. Click **OK**.

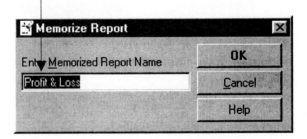

Step 7: Close the *Profit and Loss* window.

Step 8: To use a memorized report:

- Click **Reports** (menu).
- Click **Memorized Reports**.
- Click **Memorized Report List**.
- When the following *Memorized Report List* window appears, double-click on **Profit and Loss** to display the Profit and Loss report.

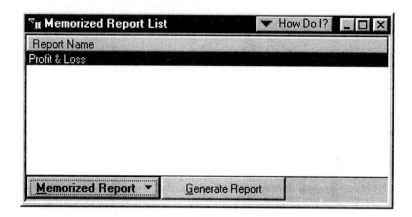

Step 9: Print the Profit and Loss statement.

Step 10: Leave the *Profit and Loss* window open to export the report.

Export Reports

In Chapter 7, you learned how to export reports to Excel spreadsheet software. Now, you will export to Excel the Profit and Loss statement you just created.

To export the Profit and Loss statement to Excel:

Step 1: Click the **Excel** button at the top of the *Profit and Loss* report window.

Step 2: When the *Export Report to Excel* window appears, select: **Send report to a new Excel spreadsheet**.

Step 3: Click **OK** to export the profit and loss statement to an Excel spreadsheet.

Step 4: Save the Excel spreadsheet as follows:

- In Excel, click **File** on the menu bar.
- Select **Save As**.
- Select drive **A**.
- Enter the file name: **Profit and Loss**.
- Click **Save** to save the Profit and Loss Report to your floppy disk as an Excel spreadsheet file.

Step 5: Close the Excel software by clicking the ☒ in the upper right corner of the window.

Step 6: Close the QuickBooks *Profit and Loss Report* window.

In addition to exporting reports to Excel from the *Reports* window, QuickBooks can save reports as a file to a disk. QuickBooks permits you to select from the following file formats:

- **ASCII text file**. After saving as a text file, the file can be used with word processing software.
- **Spreadsheet file.** After saving as a spreadsheet file, the file can be used with spreadsheet software, such as Excel.
- **Tab delimited file.** Tab delimited files can be used with word processing or database software, such as Microsoft® Access®.

Next, you will create a balance sheet for Fearless Painting Service and then save the balance sheet as an ASCII text file.

Step 1: Create and memorize a balance sheet for Fearless Painting Service at December 31, 2002.

Step 2: Save the balance sheet as an ASCII text file to a disk.

- Click the **Print** button near the top of *the Balance Sheet* window.

◆ When the *Print Reports* window appears, select Print to: **File**.

◆ Select File Format: **ASCII text file**.

◆ Click **Print** to save the text file on your floppy disk, specifying the file name: **Balance Sheet**.

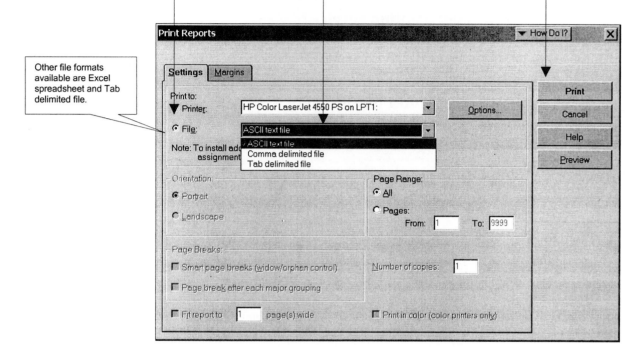

Other file formats available are Excel spreadsheet and Tab delimited file.

Step 3: Create and memorize a statement of cash flows for Fearless Painting Service for the year 2002. Export the report to Excel as follows:

◆ With the *Statement of Cash Flows* window still open, click the **Excel** button at the top of the report window.

◆ Select **Send report to a new Excel spreadsheet**, then click **OK** to export the report to Excel software.

◆ Close the Excel software without saving the your changes, then close the *Statement of Cash Flows* window.

Based on the financial statement results for Fearless Painting Service, decide whether to sell the painting service business.

Sell painting service?	Yes	No
If you sell, the selling price you will accept:	$_____	
Reason(s) for decision:		

Audit Trail

The Audit Trail feature of QuickBooks permits you to track all changes made to your QuickBooks records. This feature is especially important in tracking unauthorized changes to accounting records.

Using QuickBooks audit trail involves two steps:

1. Turn on the audit trail. After the audit trail is turned on, any changes that are made to transactions are tracked by QuickBooks.

2. Print an audit trail report that lists transactions and all changes made to your accounting records.

To turn on the audit trail:

Step 1: Click **Company** in the *Navigators* window to display the Company Navigator.

Step 2: Click the **Preferences** icon on the Company Navigator.

Step 3: Click the **Accounting** icon in the left scrollbar of the *Preferences* window.

Step 4: Click the **Company Preferences** tab.

Step 5: ✓ Check: **Use audit trail**.

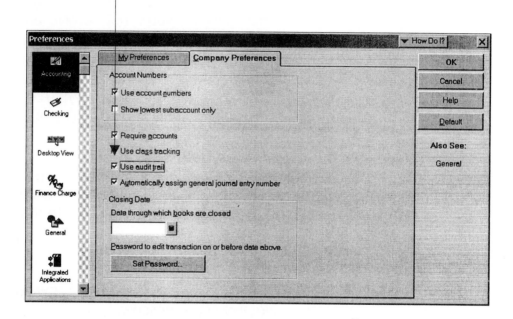

Step 6: Click **OK** to record the preference and close the *Preferences* window.

After the audit trail is turned on, QuickBooks will maintain a record of all changes made to your accounting records.

> The employee might also try to write off the customer's account as uncollectible in order to ensure the customer does not receive another bill.

To illustrate how an accounting clerk, Ima M. Bezler, might attempt to embezzle funds, assume Ima pockets a customer's cash payment and deletes any record of the customer's bill from QuickBooks.

To test the audit trail, first record a customer invoice to Diane Flowers for $80.

Step 1:   Using the *Create Invoices* window, on 02/01/2003 record 2 hours of mural painting on the Diane Flowers Kitchen job. Print the invoice.

Step 2:   On 02/02/2003, Diane Flowers pays her bill in cash. If Ima decides to keep the cash and delete the invoice (so that Flowers would not receive another bill), when the audit trail is turned on, there is a record of the deleted invoice.

   To delete the invoice on 02/02/2003, open the Flowers invoice for $80, click **Edit** (menu), then select **Delete Invoice**.

The audit trail report lists the original transaction and all changes made after the audit trail is turned on. The audit trail report will list the above change that was made to delete the customer's invoice.

To print an audit trail report:

Step 1:   Click **Reports** in the *Navigators* window to display the *Report Finder* window.

Step 2:   Select Type of Report: **Accountant & Taxes**.

Step 3:   Select Report: **Audit Trail**.

Step 4:   Select Date: From: **01/01/2003** To: **02/02/2003**.

Step 5:   Print the Audit Trail Report.

Step 6:   ✎ Circle the record of the deleted invoice dated 02/01/2003.

The audit trail report is especially useful if you have more than one user for QuickBooks. This report permits you to determine which user made which changes. The audit trail should usually be turned on if someone other than the owner of the business has access to the QuickBooks company accounting data.

> *Important!* Access to the audit trail should be restricted to only the QuickBooks Administrator.

The audit trail feature improves internal control by tracking unauthorized changes to accounting records. The owner (or manager) should periodically review the audit trail for discrepancies or unauthorized changes.

The audit trail feature requires more storage for larger files because both original transactions and changed transactions are saved. In addition, the audit trail feature may slow processing time.

To facilitate tracking of changes made by users, export the audit trail report to Excel using the Autofilter feature:

Step 1: With the *Audit Trail* window open, click the **Excel** button at the top of the report window.

Step 2: Select: **Send report to a new Excel spreadsheet**.

Step 3: Click the **Advanced** button on the *Export Report to Excel* window.

Step 4: ✓ Check **Auto Filtering**, then click **OK** to close the *Export Report to Excel – Advanced Options* window.

Step 5: Click **OK** on the *Export Report to Excel* window to export the report to Excel.

> Use the Auto Filter to show all items recorded by a specific user.

Step 6: The Audit Trail report is exported to Excel with the Auto Filter feature. Each column heading is a drop-down list to use for filtering. Select a filter of your choice from one of the drop-down lists.

Step 7: Close Excel software without saving your changes.

Step 8: Close the *Audit Trail* window.

Accountant's Review Copy

If you use an accountant to make adjustments for you, QuickBooks can create a copy of your company data files for your accountant to use (Accountant's Review Copy). The accountant can make adjustments and changes to the Accountant's Review Copy. Then you can merge the Accountant's Review Copy with your original company data. This permits you to continue using QuickBooks to record transactions at the same time your accountant reviews and makes changes to your records.

To create an accountant's review copy of Fearless Painting Service:

Step 1:   🖫 Insert a 3.5 floppy disk in drive A.

Step 2:   Click **File** on the Menu Bar.

Step 3:   Select **Accountant's Review**, then select **Create Accountant's Copy**....

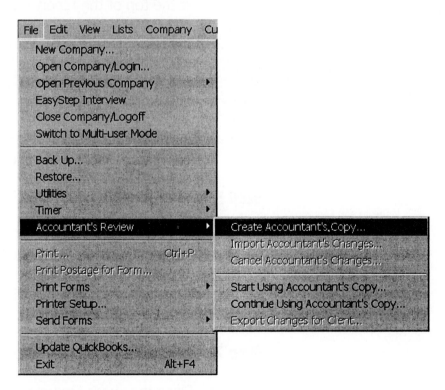

Step 4: When the message appears that QuickBooks must close all windows to prepare an accountant's copy, click **OK**.

Step 5: When the following window appears:

- ◆ Select Save in: **3 1/2 Floppy (A:)**.
- ◆ Enter File name: **AcctCopy2002**.
- ◆ Select Save as Type: **Accountant Transfer File (*.QBX)**.
- ◆ Click **Save**.

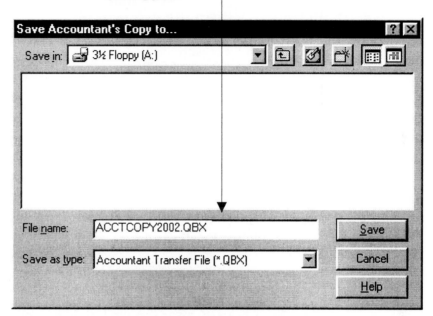

QuickBooks will create a copy of your QuickBooks company file for your accountant's temporary use. After the accountant has made necessary adjustments to the accountant's review copy, the accountant's copy is then merged with your QuickBooks company data file, incorporating the accountant's changes into your company's records.

Back Up Chapter 12

Back up Chapter 12 file to your floppy disk. Use the file name: [your name] Chapter 12.

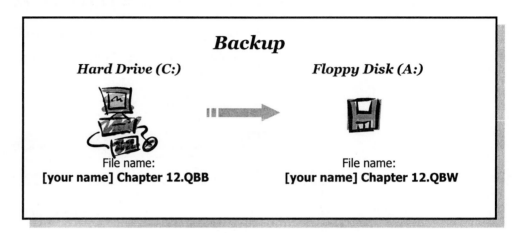

Step 1:   Insert the **Chapter 12** backup disk in drive A.

Step 2:   Click **File**, **Back Up**.

Step 3:   Save the filename:**[your name] Chapter 12.QBB**. Enter location: **A:**.

Step 4:   Click **Back Up**.

Step 5:   Click **OK** after the backup is complete.

If you are continuing your computer session, close the company file and then proceed to Project 12.1.

If you are quitting your computer session now, (1) close the company file and (2) exit QuickBooks.

Assignments

Activity 12.1: QuickBooks Remote Access

QuickBooks Remote Access permits you to access your QuickBooks company data from remote locations. To learn more about remote access:

Step 1: Click **Company** in the *Navigators* window.

Step 2: Click the **Remote Access** icon in the Company Navigator.

Step 3: Read about remote access.

Step 4: Summarize how remote access might be useful to a small business.

Activity 12.2: Web Quest Assignment

Not ready to file your tax return by April 15? File for a tax extension and postpone filing your tax return until mid August. File Form 4868 by April 15 and send a check for an estimate of the tax you owe to avoid penalties.

To learn more about filing for a tax extension:

Step 1: Learn more about filing for a tax extension at the IRS web site: www.irs.gov.

Step 2: Print Form 4868 and instructions for filing a tax extension for a personal 1040 return and Schedule C.

Computer Accounting with QuickBooks 2002
Chapter 12 Printout Checklist
Name:_____ Date:_____

☑	*Printout Checklist – Chapter 12*
☐	Income Tax Preparation Report
☐	Income Tax Summary
☐	Tax Line by Account report
☐	Income Tax Detail report
☐	Profit and Loss Budget Overview
☐	Estimate
☐	Invoice Nos. 11 and 12
☐	Deposit Summary
☐	Customer Balance Detail
☐	Invoice No. 13
☐	Audit Trail Report
☑	*Printout Checklist – Activity 12.1*
☐	QuickBooks Remote Access
☑	*Printout Checklist – Activity 12.2*
☐	IRS Form 4868 and Instructions

Virtual Company Project 12.1

Project 12.1: Max's Lawn Service: Payroll

Scenario

Project 12.1 is a continuation of Project 9.1. Project 9.1 must be completed before starting Project 12.1.

Max's Lawn Service needs to prepare an income tax return for 2002 and a budget for 2003.

Task 1: Restore Company File

Restore Project 9.1 backup to the C: drive, renaming the file Project 12.1.

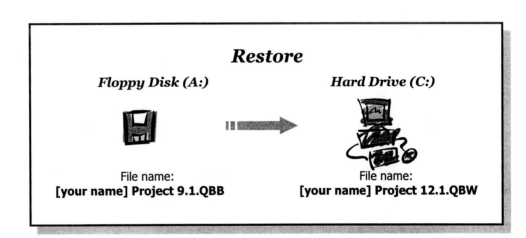

Restore

Floppy Disk (A:)   **Hard Drive (C:)**

File name:
[your name] Project 9.1.QBB

File name:
[your name] Project 12.1.QBW

Step 1: 🖫 Insert the **Project 9.1** backup disk into drive A.

Step 2: Click **Restore a backup file** (or click **File**, **Restore**).

Step 1: Identify the backup file:

- Filename: **[your name] Project 9.1.QBB**.
- Location: **A:**.

Step 2: Identify the restored file:

- Filename: **[your name] Project 12.1.QBW**.
- Location: **C:\Program Files\Intuit\QuickBooks Premier**.

Step 3: Click **Restore.** If prompted, enter your User ID and Password.

Step 4: Change the company name to:
[your name] Project 12.1 Max's Lawn Service.
(To change the company name, select Company (menu), Company Information.)

Your Project 9.1 backup file has now been restored to the C: drive as Project 12.1.QBW.

Task 2: Income Tax Summary, Memorize Report

Prepare an Income Tax Summary report for Max's Lawn Service by completing the following steps.

Step 1: Prepare an Income Tax Summary for Max's Lawn Service for the year 2002. Display the report on your screen.

Step 2: Memorize the Income Tax Summary report.

Step 3: Print the Income Tax Summary report. Insert **your name** and **Project 12.1** in the report footer.

Task 3: Budget, Save as Excel File

Prepare a budget for Max's Lawn Service for the year 2003.

Step 1: Prepare a Profit & Loss Budget Overview for Max's Lawn Service for the year 2003 using the following information:

- January sales are expected to be $800. Sales are expected to increase by 2 percent each month.

- Gasoline and supplies for January are budgeted at $60. These costs are expected to increase by 1 percent each month.

Step 2: Memorize the P&L Budget Overview for Max's Lawn Service for the year 2003.

Step 3: Print the P&L Budget Overview for Max's Lawn Service for the year 2003. Insert **your name** and **Project 12.1** in the report footer.

Step 4: Export the P&L Budget Overview to Excel software.

Task 4: Memorize Reports, Export to Excel

Prepare the following reports for Max's Lawn Service for the year 2002. Insert **your name** and **Project 12.1** in the report footers.

- Profit and Loss, Standard
- Balance Sheet, Standard
- Statement of Cash Flows

Step 1: Memorize each report.

Step 2: Print the reports.

Step 3: Export the reports to Excel software.

Task 5: Back Up Project 12.1

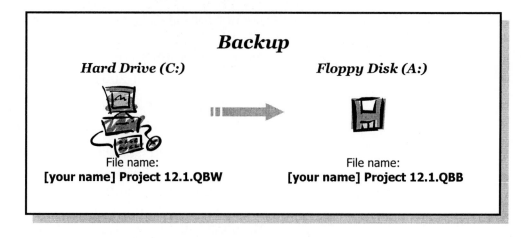

Backup

Hard Drive (C:)

Floppy Disk (A:)

File name:
[your name] Project 12.1.QBW

File name:
[your name] Project 12.1.QBB

Step 1: 💾 Insert the **Chapter 12** backup disk in drive A.

Step 2: Click **File**, **Back Up**.

Step 3: Enter the filename: **[your name] Project 12.1.QBB**. Enter location: **A:**.

Step 4: Click **Back Up**.

Step 5: Click **OK** after the backup is complete. Close the company file.

Computer Accounting with QuickBooks 2002
Virtual Project 12.1 Printout Checklist
Name:_____ Date:_____

☑	***Printout Checklist – Project 12.1***
☐	Income Tax Summary
☐	Budget
☐	Profit and Loss, Standard
☐	Balance Sheet, Standard
☐	Statement of Cash Flows

Virtual Company Project 12.2

This project is a continuation of Project 9.2. Project 9.2 must be completed before Project 12.2 can be started.

Project 12.2: Your Choice

Scenario

In Project 9.2 you created a new service company that was a partnership. You made initial decisions for the new business and created transactions for the first year.

In this assignment, you will create a budget and an Income Tax Summary report for the business.

Task 1: Option 1

You can complete this project individually (Option 1A) or in teams (Option 1B). Ask your instructor whether you should use Option 1A or 1B to complete this project.

✐ Circle the option below that you are using for the project.

Option 1A: Complete Project 12.2 individually.

TEAMS *Option 1B:* Complete Project 12.2 in teams.

Ask your instructor for the student password to access the remaining instructions for Virtual Company Project 12.2 at the following website:

www.mhhe.com/ulmer2002

Notes:

A *Real World QuickBooks Project*

Appendix A provides an opportunity to use experiential learning with QuickBooks. This appendix contains a framework for developing a QuickBooks project for a real small business or nonprofit organization. The milestones for project development are similar whether for a small business or not-for-profit organization; however, the specifics of the project, such as the accounts used, may differ.

The Real World QuickBooks Project consists of the following seven milestones:

Milestone 1: Develop a proposal. In this milestone, you will identify a real world user (either a small business or a nonprofit organization) that needs assistance in establishing an accounting system using QuickBooks. After identifying the user, gather information from the user and develop a plan for a QuickBooks accounting system that will meet the user's needs.

Milestone 2: Develop a prototype or sample QuickBooks accounting system for the user. Set up a company in QuickBooks with a sample chart of accounts for the user to review. After obtaining approval of the chart of accounts from the user and your instructor, enter beginning balances for the accounts.

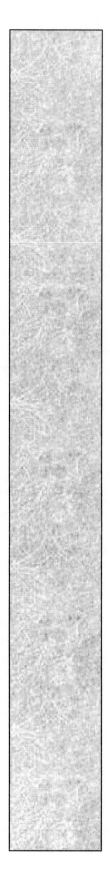

Milestone 3: Develop sample QuickBooks lists for customers, vendors, items, and employees. Obtain user and instructor approval for the lists and enter the list information.

Milestone 4: Enter sample transactions to test the prototype.

Milestone 5: Identify the reports that the user needs and then create memorized reports using QuickBooks.

Milestone 6: Develop documentation for the project including instructions for future use.

Milestone 7: Present the final project first to your class and then to the user.

Learning Objectives

Appendix A contains guidelines and tips to complete the following seven milestones for a Real World QuickBooks Project:

Introduction

The Real World QuickBooks Project is divided into 7 milestones. Each milestone should be reviewed by your instructor before you proceed to the next milestone. In addition, the QuickBooks Project Approval form should be signed by the project user as each step is completed and approved.

Milestone 1: Proposal

For Milestone 1, complete the following steps to develop a project proposal:

Step 1: Identify a real world QuickBooks project.

Step 2: Gather project information.

Step 3: Write the project proposal.

Identify Project

The first step is to identify an actual user who needs a QuickBooks accounting system. The user can be either a small business or a not-for-profit organization. For example, the user can be a friend or relative who operates a small business and needs a computerized accounting system. Some colleges have Service Learning Coordinators who assist in matching student volunteers with charitable organizations needing assistance.

Gather Project Information

After identifying the user, the next step is to interview the user to determine specific accounting needs. Communication is extremely important to the process of designing and developing a successful accounting system. Listening to the user's needs and then communicating to the user the possible solutions are part of the ongoing development process. If users are not familiar with accounting or QuickBooks, they may not be able to communicate all of their needs. This requires you to gather enough information from the user to identify both the need and the solution.

Create a checklist to use when gathering information from the user.

A sample checklist follows:

❑	Organization Name
❑	Type of Business (Industry)
❑	Chart of Accounts Information
❑	Customer List Information
❑	Vendor List Information
❑	Employee List Information
❑	Item List Information
❑	Types of Transactions to Be Recorded
❑	Types of Reports Needed
❑	Users of the QuickBooks System

Before the interview, review all seven milestones of the project to identify the types of information you need. For example, when gathering information for the customer list, what customer fields does the user need?

Write Proposal

After gathering information from the user, write a proposal that describes your plan for designing and developing your project. The proposal is a plan of what you intend to accomplish and how you will accomplish it.

Your proposal should include:

1. Cover page. Include the project name, your name, course name and number, and the date.

2. Overview. Describe the user organization and its operations. Identify the user's requirements for a computerized accounting system. For example, the user needs accounting records for tax purposes. Evaluate the feasibility of meeting the organization's needs with QuickBooks.

3. Identify and list the major tasks involved in completing the project. Include a timeline with completion dates for each task. See the sample format below.

Task	Projected Completion Date
1._____	_____
2._____	_____
3._____	_____
4._____	_____
5._____	_____
6._____	_____
7._____	_____

4. Identify and list any obstacles or difficulties that you foresee and discuss how you plan to overcome the obstacles should they occur.

Submit the proposal to both the user and your instructor. The proposal should have a professional appearance. Obtain approval from both the user and your instructor. Ask the user to sign off on the proposal using the approval form that appears on a following page.

> *Tip:* When creating the Chart of Accounts, refer to the tax form the organization will use. Obtain copies of tax forms at www.irs.gov.

Milestone 2:
Company Setup and Chart of Accounts

In this milestone, you will set up a prototype or sample company for the user to review and revise.

Step 1: Based on the information collected from the user, prepare a chart of accounts for the company.

Step 2: Submit the chart of accounts to your instructor for review and recommendations.

> *Tip:* Nonprofits use fund accounting. Use subaccounts or the class tracking preference for fund accounting.

Step 3: Have the user review the chart of accounts and make recommendations. Ask the user to sign off on the chart of accounts using the approval form.

Step 4: After obtaining approval from both the user and instructor, enter beginning balances for the accounts.

Milestone 3:
Customer, Vendor, Employee, and Item Lists

After the chart of accounts has been approved, proceed to developing lists for the user.

Step 1: After consulting with the user, list the customer information (fields) needed for each customer. If necessary, create user-defined fields in QuickBooks to accommodate the user's needs.

Step 2: List the information needed by the organization for each vendor. Create any user-defined fields that are needed for vendors.

Step 3: List the employee information needed by the organization for each employee. Determine any payroll items needed to accurately record payroll.

Step 4: Determine the items (inventory, non-inventory, and service items) required to meet the organization's needs. List the information needed for each item.

Step 5: After obtaining approval for the lists from the user and your instructor, enter information into the customer, vendor, employee, and item lists. Enter year-to-date information for employee payroll if applicable.

Tip: For ideas on how to customize QuickBooks for your specific company, click **Help**, **Using QuickBooks for Your Type of Business.**

Milestone 4: Transactions

Complete the following steps for Milestone 4.

Step 1: Determine the types of transactions the user will enter in QuickBooks (for example: cash sales, credit card sales, purchase orders).

Step 2: Enter sample transactions in QuickBooks. Obtain the user and instructor's approval of the results.

Step 3: Modify forms as needed to meet the user's needs. For example, if the user needs a Date column on the invoice, customize the invoice by following the instructions in Project 9.1.

Step 4: After obtaining the user's approval for transactions, create memorized transactions for the transactions that will be repeated periodically.

It is important that you and the user reach an agreement regarding what you will complete before you turn the project over to the user. Discuss with the user whether you will be entering only a few sample transactions or entering all transactions for the year to date. For example, if entering all transactions is too time consuming, you may agree that you will enter only sample transactions and the user will enter the real transactions after you submit the final project.

Milestone 5: Memorized Reports

Complete the following steps for Milestone 5:

Step 1: Determine which reports the user needs. Review Chapters 4, 5, 6, and 7 to obtain information about the different reports that QuickBooks can generate. You may need to make the user aware of the reports that are available in QuickBooks and then let the user select the reports they would find useful.

Step 2: Obtain user and instructor approval for the reports.

Step 3: After obtaining approval concerning the reports, create and memorize the reports using QuickBooks.

Milestone 6: Documentation and User Instructions

Create documentation for the user. Include a history of the project development as well as instructions that the user will need. For example, instructions regarding how and when to back up and restore company files are essential. Providing instructions on how to use memorized transactions and memorized reports is also advisable.

Tip: Provide the user with instructions for using QuickBooks Help feature.

An easy way to provide the user with adequate instructions is to recommend existing training materials to the user and then simply reference pages in the training materials. For example, if the user obtains a copy of this book, you may wish to reference pages of the text for each task the user will be performing.

Milestone 7: Presentation

There are three parts to this milestone:

Step 1: Make any final changes to your project.

Step 2: Make the project presentation to your class.

Step 3: Make a project presentation to the user.

The presentation to your instructor and classmates is practice for the final presentation to the user. You may want to ask your classmates for suggestions you can incorporate into your final presentation for the user.

A suggested outline for the project presentation follows:

1. History and overview of the project. Provide background about the user and the user's needs.

2. Demonstrate your QuickBooks project. If the classroom has projection equipment, display memorized transactions and memorized reports and list information for the class to view. *Remember to use test/sample data for the class presentation instead of actual user data that is confidential.*

> *Tip:* Be prepared for users to ask if they may call you if they need assistance in the future. Adequate user instructions (Milestone 6) are essential in minimizing the user's future dependence on you.

3. Present examples of the documentation and user instructions you are providing (see Milestone 6).

4. Briefly present advantages and disadvantages of using QuickBooks for this particular project.

5. Summary.

6. Question and answer. Provide classmates or the user an opportunity to ask questions about the project.

QuickBooks® Project Approval

Milestone	Approved by:	Date
1. Proposal	_____	_____
2. Company Setup and Chart of Accounts	_____	_____
3. Lists: Customers, Vendor, Employee, and Item	_____	_____
4. Transactions	_____	_____
5. Memorized Reports	_____	_____
6. Documentation	_____	_____
7. Final Presentation	_____	_____

Comments
1. Proposal:
2. Company Setup and Chart of Accounts:
3. Lists: Customers, Vendor, Employee, and Item:
4. Transactions:
5. Memorized Reports:
6. Documentation:
7. Final Presentation:

Correcting Errors

In Appendix B, you will learn to correct errors in the following ways:

Introduction

QuickBooks provides a number of ways to correct errors. Often how you correct an error in QuickBooks depends upon *when* you discover the error.

For example, if you make an error when you are entering information into an onscreen check form, you can correct the error using the Backspace key. However, if you do not discover the error until after the check is saved, to correct the error, you should void the check and prepare a new check.

Correcting Errors before Document Is Saved

In general, errors detected before the document is saved can be corrected in one of the following ways:

1. **Backspace key:** Deletes characters to the left of the cursor in the current field you are entering.

2. **Delete key:** Deletes characters to the right of the cursor.

3. **Undo command:** Before you press the *Enter* key, you can undo typing on the current line.

4. **Clear button:** On some onscreen forms, a Clear button appears in the lower right corner of the window. Clicking this button clears all fields on the screen.

5. **Revert command (Edit menu):** Reverts the entire screen back to its original appearance.

Backspace

The Backspace key erases the character to the *left* of the cursor. The Delete key erases the letter to the right of the cursor.

The Backspace key is used to correct errors that occur when you are entering data. For example, if you mistype a company name on a check, you can use the Backspace key to delete the incorrect letters. Then enter the correct spelling.

Assume you need to write a check to Davis Business Associates for professional services performed for your company.

Use the company data file for any of the Chapter 1 through 7 company files.

To use the Backspace key to correct an error on a check:

Step 1: With Rock Castle Construction Company file open, click **Write Checks** on the Navigation Bar to display the *Write Checks* window.

Step 2: When the *Write Checks* window appears:

Davis Business Associates should automatically appear in the Address field.

- ◆ Select **To be printed**.

- ◆ Select from the *Pay to the Order of* drop-down list: **Davis Business Associates**.

- ◆ Type the street address: **1234 Brentwodo**.

Step 3: The correct address is 1234 Brentwood. Press the **backspace** key **twice** to erase "**do.**"

Step 4: Type "**od**" to finish entering Brentwood.

Undo

The Undo command can be used to undo typing before you press the Enter key.

To use the Undo command:

Step 1: With the same *Write Checks* window still open and the check for Davis Business Associates displayed, type the city and state for the Davis address: **Bayshore, CA**. Do not press Enter.

Step 2: After you type the address, Mr. Castle tells you the address is San Diego, CA, not Bayshore. To use the undo command, click **Edit** on the menu bar. Then click **Undo Typing**. Bayshore, CA, will be deleted.

Step 3: Next, enter the correct city and state: **San Diego, CA**.

The Undo command is useful if you want to delete an entire line of typing.

Clear

The Revert button permits you to revert the onscreen form back to its appearance when you opened the saved onscreen form. This feature can be used before the onscreen form has been resaved.

The Clear button is usually located in the lower right corner of an unsaved onscreen form. If you started entering data and want to clear all the fields in the onscreen form, click the **Clear** button.

After an onscreen form has been saved, the Clear button changes to a Revert button.

The Revert command appears on the Edit menu while the Revert button appears on the onscreen form.

Revert Command

The Revert command (Edit menu) is used to revert the screen back to its original appearance. This command can be used before a document, such as a check, has been saved.

To illustrate, assume that you decide to wait to pay Davis Business Associates until they complete all the work they are performing for you. Therefore, you want to erase everything that you have entered on the check.

To use the Revert command:

Step 1: With the *Write Checks* window still open and the check for Davis Business Associates displayed, click **Edit** on the menu bar.

Step 2: Click **Revert**. The *Write Checks* window reverts to its original appearance with blank fields. The information you entered about Davis Business Associates has been erased.

The Revert command on the Edit menu and the Clear button perform the same function: both clear the contents of an onscreen form that has not yet been saved.

Correcting Errors on Saved Documents

Once a document has been saved, you can use one of three approaches to correct the error:

1. Display the document, correct the error, then save the document again.

2. Void the erroneous document, then create a new document.

3. Delete the erroneous document, then create a new document.

Tip: If the correction involves a check (Write Checks, Pay Bills, or Create Paychecks), display the check in the *Write Checks* window by clicking **Previous** or use the **Find** command on the **Edit** menu.

Enter Corrections in Saved Onscreen Form

To enter corrections in a saved onscreen form, complete three steps:

Step 1: Display the erroneous onscreen form. For example, display an incorrect invoice in the *Create Invoices* window.

Step 2: Correct the error by entering changes directly in the onscreen form.

Step 3: Save the onscreen form.

Note: You cannot correct deposits using this approach. If you attempt to make changes to a saved deposit, you will receive a warning that you must delete the deposit and then reenter the appropriate information.

Void

The Void command will void a document and remove its effect from your accounting records. For example, if you void a check, the check amount is no longer deducted from your checking account. However, the check will still appear in your QuickBooks records, but is labeled Void.

To void a document in QuickBooks, first display the document on your screen. Then select **Edit** from the menu bar. The Edit menu will change depending upon the document that has been opened. For example, if you open a check, the Edit menu will display "Void Check." If you open an invoice, then the Edit menu will display "Void Invoice."

To void a check in QuickBooks:

Step 1: With the *Write Checks* window open, enter the following information for Davis Business Associates:

Date	12/15/2002
Check Amount	$200.00
Account	Professional Fees

Step 2: Click **Save & Close** to save the check.

Step 3: Next, you decide to void the check and pay Davis Business Associates at a later time. Display the check for Davis Business Associates on 12/15/2002 for $200.

Notice that VOID now appears in the Memo field of the check and the amount of the check has been changed to $0.00.

Step 4: Click **Edit** on the menu bar.

Step 5: Click **Void Check**.

The voided check will remain in your QuickBooks records but the amount of the check will not be deducted from your checking account.

If you wanted to void an invoice:

Step 1: Open any invoice.

Step 2: Click **Edit** (menu).

Step 3: If you wanted to void the invoice, you would click Void Invoice. For this activity, close the Edit menu by clicking anywhere outside the Edit drop-down menu.

Delete

The difference between the Delete command and the Void command is that when the Delete command is used, the document is deleted and completely removed from your QuickBooks records. The document is no longer displayed in the QuickBooks records.

When the Void command is used, the document's effect upon your accounts is removed from your accounting records, but the voided document still appears in the QuickBooks records marked "VOID".

Only if the audit trail is turned on will a record of a deleted document exist. If the audit trail is on, then a record is maintained of all changes made to your QuickBooks records, including deleted documents. If someone other than the business owner has access to the QuickBooks accounting records, the audit trail should be turned on to maintain a record of all changes.

To delete the Davis Business Associates' check:

Step 1: Display the voided check to Davis Business Associates.

Step 2: With the check displayed on your screen, click **Edit** (menu).

Step 3: Click **Delete Check** to delete the check. Now this check will no longer appear in your QuickBooks accounting records.

Step 4: Close the *Write Checks* window.

The Delete command removes the document from your records. If you want to maintain a record of the document but simply remove its effect from your records, use the Void command. The Void command provides a better trail of changes made to your accounting records.

C

Using Microsoft Word & Excel with QuickBooks

In Appendix C, you will learn the following activities:

Introduction

QuickBooks software offers the ability to exchange data with other software, including Microsoft Word and Excel. The three different ways to import and export data covered in this appendix are:

1. Using Microsoft Word with QuickBooks
2. Using Microsoft Excel with QuickBooks
3. Using Information Interchange Files (IIF File Format)

Using Microsoft Word with QuickBooks

QuickBooks provides you with the ability to use Microsoft Word to create letters with information contained in QuickBooks. For example, this feature can be used to create collection letters as well as other letters.

To create a collection letter in QuickBooks:

Step 1: From the Customer Navigator, click the **Write Letters** icon.

Step 2: Select **Prepare a Collection Letter**, then click **Next**.

Step 3: Select the settings shown below, then click **Next**.

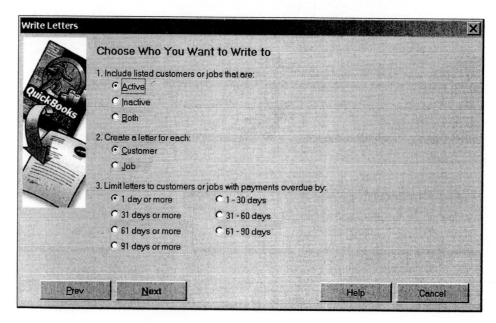

Step 4: Complete the onscreen steps to prepare a collection letter.

Using Microsoft Excel with QuickBooks

There are two ways to export data from QuickBooks into Microsoft Excel:

1. With a report displayed on your screen, click the Excel button at the top of the window. This will export the report data to an Excel worksheet.
2. Instead of printing a report to the printer, you can print the report to an Excel spreadsheet.

See Chapter 7 and Chapter 12 for additional information on exporting QuickBooks data to Excel spreadsheets.

Information Interchange Files (IIF files)

Information Interchange Files (IIF files) can be used to import or export data with QuickBooks. For example, IIF files can be used to import data into a QuickBooks Customer List.

For more information about how to import and export IIF files:

1. Click **Help** on the menu bar.
2. Select **Help Index**.
3. Enter **IIF File Format**.
4. Read the instructions for using IIF Files with QuickBooks.

QuickBooks ⚡ Online

In Appendix D, you will learn the following online features of QuickBooks:

Introduction

Online features available in QuickBooks 2002 include:

1. Company Website
2. Online Banking
3. Online Billing
4. Online Resources

Company Website

You can create a company website using QuickBooks Web Site Solutions. Select **Company Web Site** from the Company menu. Then simply follow the onscreen directions to create your company web site.

Online Banking

QuickBooks permits you to use online banking. First, you must set up online banking with a participating financial institution and then you can bank online using an Internet connection. See Chapter 3 for more information about setup and use of online banking.

Online Billing

In QuickBooks Pro and Premier 2002, you can E-mail or efax invoices to customers. See Chapter 4 for instructions about how to E-mail invoices to use online billing.

If you sign up for QuickBooks Online Billing and send E-mail invoices, your customers can pay you electronically. Use the QuickBooks Help Index (Online Billing), to learn more about how to use QuickBooks to accept online customer payments.

Online Resources

See the textbook website (listed on the back cover of the textbook) for links to useful online resources and websites.

E

Updating QuickBooks

In Appendix E, you will learn the following:

Introduction

QuickBooks software has both a Version number and a Release number. For example, QuickBooks Pro 2001 and QuickBooks Pro 2002 are different versions. If you use QuickBooks Pro 2001, you could *upgrade* to the new version, QuickBooks Pro 2002.

Intuit provides maintenance releases to correct problems found in a specific version of QuickBooks. For example, if you have QuickBooks Pro 2001, you could *update* from Release 1.0 to Release 3.0.

This appendix provides instructions on how to update QuickBooks by downloading new maintenance releases. First, determine the version and release number for your current QuickBooks software as follows.

To view the serial and registration number, select **About QuickBooks Pro** on the Help menu.

Display QuickBooks Product Information

To view the version and release number of your QuickBooks software, display the *Product Information* window.

Step 1: Hold down the **Ctrl** key and the **1** key at the same time to display the following *Product Information* window.

Step 2: For example, the version (QuickBooks Pro Version 2000) and maintenance release (R4P) are listed at the top of the window.

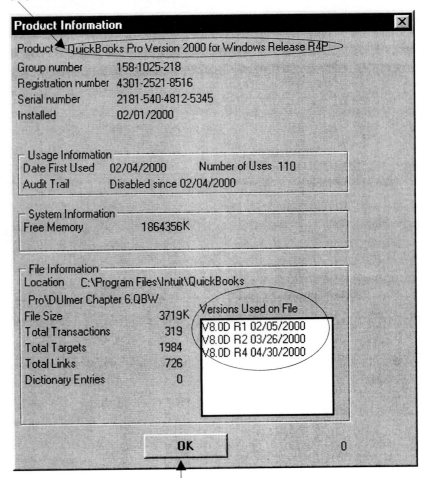

Product Information

Product	QuickBooks Pro Version 2000 for Windows Release R4P
Group number	158-1025-218
Registration number	4301-2521-8516
Serial number	2181-540-4812-5345
Installed	02/01/2000

Usage Information
Date First Used 02/04/2000   Number of Uses 110
Audit Trail   Disabled since 02/04/2000

System Information
Free Memory   1864356K

File Information
Location   C:\Program Files\Intuit\QuickBooks
Pro\DUlmer Chapter 6.QBW
File Size   3719K
Total Transactions   319
Total Targets   1984
Total Links   726
Dictionary Entries   0

Versions Used on File
V8.0D R1 02/05/2000
V8.0D R2 03/26/2000
V8.0D R4 04/30/2000

OK   0

Step 3: Click **OK** to close the *Product Information* window.

> Update QuickBooks on a regular basis, such as the first of each month.

> You can also download an update file from Intuit's web site to a disk and then use the file to update QuickBooks.

✗ *Update QuickBooks*

After determining the version and maintenance release, the next step is to update QuickBooks by downloading the latest maintenance release.

If you have an Internet connection, you can update QuickBooks using the QuickBooks Update Service as follows:

Step 1: Backup up your company file (see Chapter 1 for backup instructions).

Step 2: Establish your Internet connection.

Step 3: From the **File** menu, select **Update QuickBooks** to display the following *Update QuickBooks* window.

Step 4: Click the **Options** button.

> If the Automatic Update is turned on, QuickBooks is automatically updated each time you connect to the Internet.

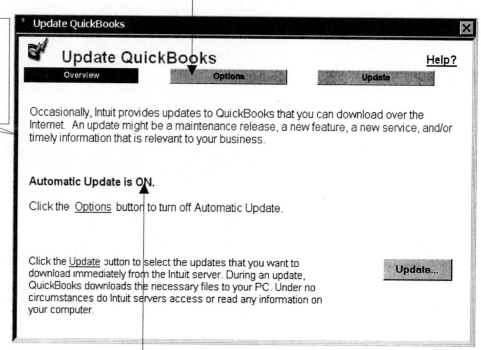

Step 5: If you want to have QuickBooks automatically update each time you connect to the Internet, select **ON** for Automatic Update.

Step 6: To download an update, click the **Update** button, then click the **Get Updates** button.

Step 7: When asked if you want to update QuickBooks, click **Yes**.

Appendix

F Single-User & Multi-User Modes

In Appendix F, you will learn the following activities:

Introduction

QuickBooks Pro and Premier 2002 has a single-user and a multi-user mode. The multi-user mode is used when QuickBooks is networked and more than one user accesses the QuickBooks company data file.

Switch Modes

You can switch from one mode to the other as follows:

1. Select **File** (menu).

2. If you are in the multi-user mode, select **Switch to Single-User Mode**. Click **OK**.

3. If you are in the single-user mode, select **Switch to Multi-User Mode**. Click **OK**.

Set Default User Mode

Select a default user mode for a specific company data file as follows:

1. Select **File** (menu).

2. Select **Open Company**.

3. When the *Open A Company* window appears, in the lower left corner of the window, check **Open file in multi-user mode**.

4. Click **Open**.

G

QuickBooks Premier: Accountant Edition

In Appendix G, you will learn the following activities:

Introduction

Intuit now offers 4 different software options for a small business accounting system:

1. **QuickBooks Basic 2002** provides a basic accounting system for a small business.
2. **QuickBooks Pro 2002** offers the features of QuickBooks Basic plus advanced features including:
   ♦ Estimates.
   ♦ Time tracking for paychecks, invoicing, and profitability analysis.
   ♦ Integrate with Microsoft Excel, Word, Outlook, ACT! And other industry-specific software applications.
   ♦ Remote access.
3. **QuickBooks Premier 2002** offers the same features as QuickBooks Pro 2002 plus:
   ♦ Customized reports and analyses.
   ♦ Reconciliation discrepancy report.
   ♦ Password protected closing date.
   ♦ Closing date exception report.
   ♦ Remote access.
4. **QuickBooks Premier 2002: Accountant Edition** is designed for accounting professionals with multiple clients using QuickBooks. It offers the following features, including some of the same features as QuickBooks Premier.
   ♦ Auto-reversing and auto-numbering of general journal entries.
   ♦ Reconciliation discrepancy report.
   ♦ Closing date exception report.
   ♦ Password-protected closing date.
   ♦ Remote access.
   ♦ Accountant Navigator

If you have installed QuickBooks Premier 2002: Accountant Edition, start the software and then open the sample_product-based company.qbw.

Two changes that you will notice in the QuickBooks Premier: Accountant Edition are the addition of an Accountant Navigator and an Accountant menu on the menu bar.

Accountant Navigator

To use the Accountant Navigator:

1. Click **Accountant** in the *Navigators* window to display the following Accountant Navigator.

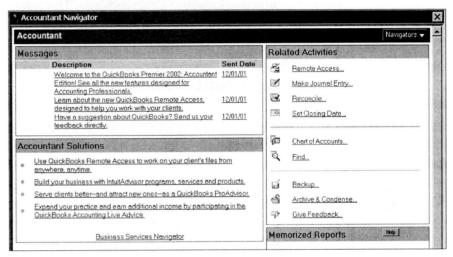

2. To learn more about the features of the Accountant Edition, click **Welcome to the QuickBooks Premier 2002: Accountant Edition! See all the new features designed for Accounting Professionals.**

3. To set the closing date, click **Set Closing Date** in the *Related Activities* section. Enter the closing date and the password.

4. To use the General Journal, click **Make Journal Entry**. Read the following message about auto-numbering of journal entries, then click **OK**. Close the *General Journal Entry* window.

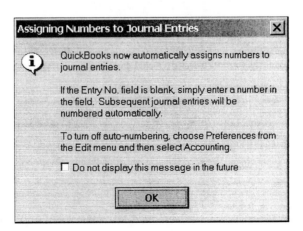

5. To learn more about using QuickBooks Remote Access, click **Remote Access** in the Related Activities section and read about how to use remote access.

6. The Archive and Condense feature in the Related Activities section permits you to archive closed transaction before a specified date. This reduces the size of the company file in order to speed up processing time.

Accountant Menu

Another difference in QuickBooks Premier 2002: Accountant Edition is the addition of the Accountant menu to the Menu Bar.

1. Click **Accountant** on the menu bar, to display the following Accountant menu.

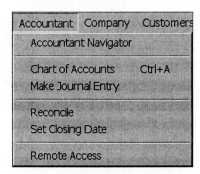

2. Notice that the Accountant menu contains the same features as the Accountant Navigator.

Close the Accountant Navigator and close the sample company file.

Index